THE POLITICS OF THE CROSS

The Politics of the Cross

A Christian Alternative to Partisanship

Daniel K. Williams

WILLIAM B. EERDMANS PUBLISHING COMPANY
GRAND RAPIDS, MICHIGAN

Wm. B. Eerdmans Publishing Co.
4035 Park East Court SE, Grand Rapids, Michigan 49546
www.eerdmans.com

Hardcover edition 2021
Paperback edition 2024

Printed in the United States of America

30 29 28 27 26 25 24   1 2 3 4 5 6 7

ISBN 978-0-8028-8468-8

Library of Congress Cataloging-in-Publication Data

Names: Williams, Daniel K., author.
Title: The politics of the cross : a Christian alternative to partisanship /
    Daniel K. Williams.
Description: Grand Rapids, Michigan : William B. Eerdmans Publishing
    Company, 2021. | Includes bibliographical references and index. | Summary:
    "A theologically and historically informed treatise on a Christian approach
    to politics that foregrounds the priorities of God's kingdom instead of blind
    partisan loyalty"—Provided by publisher.
Identifiers: LCCN 2020033822 | ISBN 9780802884688 (pbk.)
Subjects: LCSH: Christianity and politics.
Classification: LCC BR115.P7 W55 2021 | DDC 261.70973—dc23
LC record available at https://lccn.loc.gov/2020033822

Biblical quotations are from the New International Version (NIV) unless otherwise noted.

Contents

Acknowledgments

This book would not have been possible without the encouragement of my wife, Nadya, and the assistance of many friends and colleagues in the Christian academic world who reviewed early drafts of this manuscript and offered helpful feedback. I am especially grateful to Jonathan den Hartog, Karen Johnson, Kelly Kapic, Andy Lewis, Bruce Lowe, Ethan Schrum, and John Wilsey for taking the time to read part or all of the manuscript and sending me their comments. The discussions that I had with these readers helped me avoid numerous pitfalls and prompted me to sharpen or nuance some of my arguments. Three pastors from King's Chapel Presbyterian Church—Andrew Hendley, Andy Woznicki, and Ben Weber—also read the manuscript and offered their encouragement and suggestions. I am grateful to my editor at Eerdmans, David Bratt, for his support of the project from the beginning. Needless to say, my colleagues and friends who read early drafts of the manuscript cannot be held responsible for the political views and historical and biblical interpretations that I offer—let alone any errors that remain in the text—but their thoughtful suggestions made this book much stronger.

I'm thankful to Nadya for encouraging me to write this book and then sacrificing some of her own activities so that I could have the time to write in the midst of our busy teaching schedule and family life.

The opportunity to write this book was a door that God opened for me, and I pray that God will be glorified in this endeavor. Writing about God's will is always a dangerous undertaking because of the magnitude and seriousness of the matter and because of our own fallibility. I pray that my efforts to apply scriptural principles to contemporary politics will lead other Christians to become more effective witnesses of the gospel, but if I have erred in my scriptural exegesis or analysis of our current political situation, I pray that the Lord will keep this book from leading others astray. In any case, I am thankful to the Lord for giving me the time, resources, and opportunity to complete this project. I have enjoyed the work, and I pray that God will use the end result for good.

Introduction

A Different Kind of Politics

Do not conform to the pattern of this world, but be transformed by the renewing of your mind. Then you will be able to test and approve what God's will is—his good, pleasing and perfect will.

—Romans 12:2

One of them, an expert in the law, tested him with this question: "Teacher, which is the greatest commandment in the Law?" Jesus replied: "'Love the Lord your God with all your heart and with all your soul and with all your mind.' This is the first and greatest commandment. And the second is like it: 'Love your neighbor as yourself.' All the Law and the Prophets hang on these two commandments."

—Matthew 22:35–40

Then he called the crowd to him along with his disciples and said: "Whoever wants to be my disciple must deny themselves and take up their cross and follow me."

—Mark 8:34

In September 2018, bestselling evangelical author and New York City Presbyterian pastor Timothy Keller wrote an op-ed for the *New York Times* on the question of how Christians should think about politics. Eighty-one percent of white evangelical voters had cast their ballots for the Republican presidential candidate in the previous election, and white evangelicals were viewed as perhaps the only firewall that could stop a Democratic blue wave in the upcoming congressional midterms. Several nationally known evangelical leaders, such as Franklin Graham and Robert Jeffress, had given President Donald Trump their full-throated endorsement. But Keller was sharply critical of attempts to identify the gospel or the kingdom of God with a partisan agenda. "While believers can register under a party affiliation and be active in politics, they should not identify the Christian church or faith with a political party as the only Christian one," he wrote. The headline for the article phrased the sentiment more starkly: "How Do Christians Fit into the Two-Party System? They Don't."[1]

Keller's gospel-centered denunciation of Christian partisanship was hardly new, even if it might have seemed novel to a few secular readers who thought of evangelical Christianity and the Republican Party as almost synonymous. Evangelical leaders, along with Christian academics and political activists, have been issuing warnings about the dangers of the Christian Right's alliance with the GOP for years. In the last decade or so, evangelical critiques of Christian Right partisanship have included Charles D. Drew's *Surprised by Community: Republicans and Democrats in the Same Pew* (2019), John Fea's *Believe Me: The Evangelical Road to Donald Trump* (2018), Philip Yancey's *Christians and Politics: Uneasy Partners* (2012), Amy E. Black's *Honoring God in Red or Blue* (2012), Benjamin P. Dixon's *God Is Not a Republican* (2012), and Lisa Sharon Harper's *Evangelical Does Not Equal Republican . . . or Democrat* (2008). And these are only the latest contributions to a long-standing genre. In previous decades, Jim Wallis, Ron Sider, Tony Campolo, and other progressive evangelicals critiqued Christian Right partisanship from the left, while politically conservative defectors from the Christian Right, such as Ed Dobson, Cal Thomas, and David Kuo, cautioned evangelicals, in books such as *Blinded by Might: Why the Religious Right Can't Save America* (1999) and *Tempting Faith: An Inside Story of Political Seduction* (2006), against trusting the Republican Party to carry out God's agenda. As early as the 1980s, Charles Colson—himself an experienced political operative and a sympathizer with much of the Christian Right's agenda—warned in *Kingdoms in Conflict* that God's kingdom and the state were fundamentally different entities that often pursued opposing goals.[2]

But despite all the warnings, white evangelical loyalty to the Republican Party has steadily *increased* during the past twenty years, and the Christian Right, despite numerous predictions of its demise, is still alive and well. At the same time, a small but vocal contingent of politically progressive evangelicals have attempted to identify the cause of Jesus with the politics of the left, questioning how any Christian can faithfully support the Republican Party and especially (after 2016) Donald Trump. These political divisions are now rending evangelicalism, alienating groups of believers from one another. Even more alarmingly, the identification of evangelical Christianity with a conservative political agenda has prompted a sizeable number of millennials to leave evangelicalism—and sometimes, Christianity itself—because they consider it incompatible with their ethical values.[3]

"After an election in which 81 percent of my white coreligionists supported Trump, the faith that has been my home for 20 years seems foreign, even hostile," former *Christianity Today* managing editor Katelyn Beaty wrote in the *Washington Post*. Trump's election—especially because it occurred only because of strong support from her fellow white evangelicals—brought her "waves of grief" and felt "something like soul abandonment." She wondered whether it was now time for her to "leave the table."[4]

If Beaty was sure that Trump did not represent her values—values that she held as a follower of Jesus—other Christians were certain that Trump was the man of God's choosing. "It seemed evident to us on election night that the Lord gave us victory," *Focus on the Family* founder James Dobson declared. The accusations of scandal in Trump's administration and even the evidence of Trump's own sexually crude language and behavior did not diminish Dobson's support for the president, because "what was at stake" in Trump's election was nothing less than the entire agenda that Dobson and other politically conservative Christians had devoted their lives to achieve: "the makeup of the Supreme Court of the United States, the sanctity of marriage, the preservation of religious liberty, the sanctity of human life, and so many other pro-life, pro-family, and pro-moral issues that we have prayed for for generations." But even with Trump's election, Dobson feared that these values were under attack by the "mainstream media," the "entertainment industry," and a host of other influences. "This generation of children," he said, "have been subjected to such wickedness as has probably never occurred in the history of this country." If Beaty was fearful for the future, Dobson was equally anxious, even with his preferred candidate in the White House. Conservative Christians were not winning in the culture, and their political gains could be taken away at any moment. He called on

Christians across the nation in January 2018 to pray that Trump would not be impeached.[5]

While these divisions have grown worse in the past few years, they have roots in trends that long predated Trump's election, because they reflect a long-standing (and growing) tendency to associate a particular political party with the cause of morality, while demonizing the other. For many Americans today, both inside the church and out, their political party has become a more important moral guide than their religious tradition. As a result, they view members of the opposing party not simply as people with whom they might disagree but as potentially evil people who are on the wrong side of moral truth. In the fall of 2018, 61 percent of Democrats said they viewed Republicans as "racist," "sexist," or "bigoted," according to an Axios poll. Twenty-one percent considered Republicans "evil"—a view that was reciprocated by 23 percent of Republicans who thought the same of Democrats. Fifty-four percent of Republicans considered Democrats "spiteful," and 49 percent called them "ignorant." Forty-one percent of Democrats (and 26 percent of Republicans) said that they would be "extremely" or "somewhat" disappointed if a "close family member" married someone from the opposing party. One 2016 Pew Research Center survey found that Americans are now more likely to marry someone of a different religion than someone who does not share their political partisan identification.[6] Christians are certainly not immune from the temptation to make political ideology or partisan loyalty a litmus test in our fellowship, but when we do, it is probably a sign that we have fallen into the trap of identifying one particular party with morality and righteousness and the other with evil.

What is the answer to this intense political partisanship in the body of Christ? What is the solution to the polarization between two groups of believers, both of whom are fearful and both of whom believe they are losing the political fight? It is not merely to trade one set of political commitments for another, as though the remedy for white evangelicals' history of Republican partisanship is loyalty to the Democratic Party. Nor is it to abandon the evangelical church as a sell-out to the GOP or to throw up our hands in frustration and withdraw from politics. And the solution is not even a simple reminder that Jesus was not a Republican or a Democrat—even though this is true. Such simplistic statements fail to engage with the reasons why Christians have made particular political choices—and thus, have little effect on Christian partisans who see their own theology reflected in the platform of a particular political party. The political differences between Beaty and Dobson, or between other politically progressive and politically conservative evangelicals, reflect different moral priorities, as well as deeply rooted differences in fundamental values and understandings of the purpose of the American government.

Dobson was passionate about ensuring that a Republican president remained in office because he believed that unborn babies' lives and the freedom of Christians to practice their faith depended on it. Beaty was passionately opposed to Trump because she believed that his actions, rhetoric, and policies were racist and harmful to millions of marginalized people who were created in God's image. Many Christians who identify themselves as pro-life wonder how any Christian could vote for a party that endorses abortion rights, while many who are engaged in protecting the civil rights of minorities and immigrants and who understand racism to be a sin wonder how any Christian could support building a wall on the border or breaking up families in order to enforce restrictive immigration laws. The comments from *New York Times* readers who encountered Keller's op-ed online reveal the deep political chasm that divides Christians on issues of policy and partisanship. Christian bipartisanship "works for me until I think of abortion," Mandy from Texas wrote. "Abortion is clearly divided according to party. It's a life and death situation, so there should be no excuse for supporting the party that advocates for abortion, over the party that wants to end it. . . . What's more important than life? Christians should be on the side of life first. Then, if the ONLY party on the side of life has problems in other areas—work to change those. But—don't support the anti-life party." Bruce from southern coastal England disagreed. "Jesus healed the sick, fed the hungry, and welcomed the lowest tiers of society into his flock," he wrote. "His teaching on the eye-of-the-needle passage suggests that the rich might not be getting it right. He told us to welcome immigrants. . . . I am always dismayed when the so-called Christians allow one issue—abortion—to dominate their political party and fail on all of the other teachings of Christ." And Debbie from New Jersey wrote, "As a Christian I cannot understand how anyone claiming to be a follower of Christ can align themselves with the Republican Party. The foundation of Christianity is forgiveness, acceptance, generosity, justice, compassion, love. . . . Jesus said it was easier for a camel to go through the eye of a needle than for a rich man to enter the kingdom of heaven. Does this sound like the prosperity gospel? I can't think of one parable that is consistent with the platform of the right wing Republican Party that is in power at the moment."[7] The themes are consistent: One side raises the issue of abortion and wonders how anyone could support policies that allow ending the lives of the unborn. The other side raises a host of humanitarian and human rights issues and wonders how people who follow a Savior who cared for the poor and marginalized could support a party that they believe stands for the exact opposite. Both groups are talking past each other.

Perhaps the remedy for this political divide among Christians is closer than we might think. Perhaps the answer is to combine the biblically based defenses of marriage and unborn human life that are high priorities for Christian conservatives with the equally biblical concerns about poverty and racial justice that drive politically progressive Christians. This is not a new idea, of course, because biblically minded Christians share all these concerns. For years, Minneapolis Baptist pastor John Piper made it a practice to preach two social justice sermons every January: one on racial reconciliation and the other on protecting unborn human life. "This has the unsettling effect of making me sound like a Democrat one week and a Republican the next," he wrote. "Which is just the way I want it, because I am neither."[8]

But putting this nonpartisan ethic into practice in a polarized political environment may prove more challenging. Can we find a political platform that will allow us to simultaneously protect unborn children, promote God's plan for the family, pursue racial reconciliation, and help the poor? I think we can. The solution, I believe, is to recognize both the limits of government regulation to curb sin in a fallen world and the power of personal economic self-sacrifice on behalf of the poor to achieve some of the goals that conservative Christians share—including the goals of promoting godly marriage and saving the unborn from abortion. When we start caring for the poor by addressing the structural problems of poverty, we will achieve more for the cause of kingdom-minded social justice than any amount of moral regulation might accomplish. But to do that, we will need to make some difficult choices if we are white, middle-class Christians. We will need to give up our decades-long quest for political power and our traditional political strategies and exchange them for the politics of the cross—a political approach that will require us to follow Jesus in sacrificing our own interests for those of others and identify with the marginalized rather than merely try to regulate their behavior (Phil. 2:4–8).

The Politics of the Cross

This book is not for everyone. It probably will be of very limited value to non-Christians, Christians outside the United States, or Christians who are not concerned about contemporary American political debates. If you have picked up this book and have made it to this point, I will assume that, most likely:

1. You are a Christian who allows the cross-centered gospel and the Bible to shape your thinking in all areas of life.
2. You care about policy issues that affect Americans, and you participate in American political elections.
3. You want your political choices to honor Christ.
4. And finally, you are probably disappointed or frustrated with contemporary American politics and are looking for an alternative model to contemporary American Christian political activism, but you are not sure what that model might be.

If all four of these statements are true about you, keep reading, because this book will address your concerns.

Most of this book will focus on specific policy debates, but before delving into issues of abortion, sexuality, and other political issues, I want to ask a broader question that will frame how we might approach any specific issue: What is the purpose of Christian engagement in the political system? Is it to save the nation from immorality? Is it to protect the rights of Christians? Is it to bring civil law into closer conformity with the laws of God?

While these goals—which have commonly guided American white evangelical political participation for the past few decades—may have their place, they fall short of the fundamental purpose of all of life, which is to glorify God. As the opening line of the Westminster Shorter Catechism declares, our "chief end" is to "glorify God and enjoy him forever." Everything that we do is to be done for God's glory, according to 1 Corinthians 10:31. So, the first question a Christian should ask about politics is this: What type of political stance would most glorify God?

The Bible is quite clear that God has already established a political order, and it is called the "kingdom of God." From Genesis through Revelation, we read about how God's authority has clashed with—and will ultimately overcome—human kingdoms. While human empires crumble, God's kingdom will endure forever (Dan. 2). The kingdom of God brings healing to the sick, a restoration of creation, and an end to suffering and injustice (Isa. 11:1-5; Luke 10:9). It brings an end to sinful rebellion against God and a sanctification of the people who are part of this kingdom (1 Cor. 6:9-10). But it is a kingdom that God brought about not through conquest or majority vote but through the weakness of the cross, and it is a kingdom that Jesus's followers enter by dying to themselves and suffering for the sake of the kingdom (2 Thess. 1:5). Just as Jesus was glorified through the shame of the cross, so, too, will his followers glorify God and reveal God's kingdom to others when they die to themselves (John 12:23-26).

The cross gives a radically different rationale for Christian political participation, because it demonstrates that we do not win through displays of power. It also shows that we have already won the ultimate victory, and our sovereign king is already on the throne. We therefore do not need to vote out of fear or an anxious desire for self-protection, because we know that Jesus is already reigning. When we vote, we are not trying to force others to comply with the mandate of our king—a move that might indicate that we lack faith in the Holy Spirit's power to convict and regenerate. Our task is simply to reveal God's kingdom to others, something that we do in our daily work, in our conversations with others, and even in the voting booth. We can do this by showing in some small measure what God's righteous order might look like—a demonstration that is probably best accomplished by a demonstration of love for our neighbor. If the sovereign king of God's kingdom declared that the second greatest commandment—a commandment that summarized all of God's law governing interpersonal relations in the political sphere—was to love our neighbor as ourselves (Matt. 22:39-40), then we can safely assume that one of the central ways that we can reveal God's kingdom to others through politics is to vote in such a way that shows the maximum amount of love for our neighbors even if (and maybe *especially* if) this means voting against our own self-interest.

In a system of representative democracy, one of the ways to "seek the welfare of the city" in which we live (Jer. 29:7) is to vote. If we did not vote, it would be a sign of a lack of concern about the community and country in which we live—and that would not be a Christlike disposition. But how we vote also matters. If we seek our own interests rather than the interests of others in our ballot choices, we are not acting in accordance with the mandate of God's kingdom (Phil. 2:4).

This will require giving up blind partisan loyalties. Cross-centered politics of the type I am advocating will sometimes entail supporting Republican policies and sometimes Democratic ones, but most often, it may require adopting some of the biblically informed *values* of Republican-voting Christian conservatives (such as the value of all human beings, including the unborn) while simultaneously supporting the *policies* of progressive Democrats as the best way to put those values into action. A pro-life Christian, for instance, might sometimes find that the best way to fight abortion is not to pass an abortion ban but to vote for a candidate whose economic and healthcare policies will reduce abortion rates by empowering pregnant women to care for their babies. A central argument of this book is that Christians can be biblically and consistently pro-life, pro-family, and anti-racist not by supporting the candidates whom conservative white evangelicals have usually supported but by pursuing policy goals that result in the greatest amount of love shown to the most vulnerable people in our society—especially the poor, the very people whom Jesus said would possess the kingdom of God (Luke 6:20).

But regardless of which political party's policy position we select, our attitude will usually be radically different from either party's mindset, because our thinking will be cross-centered rather than rights-based. Instead of thinking about how best to protect our own rights and interests or how to seize and preserve power for ourselves (concerns that too often have been central to the agenda of both political parties), we will be guided by the question: How can I best love my neighbors, especially when it will require taking the time to listen to their concerns, understand the struggles they face that may be different from my own, and sacrifice my own interests in order to promote theirs? When we do that, voting will become an act of cross-centered love, because it will involve dying to our own interests in order to be a blessing to other people in reflection of our gratitude for the much greater sacrifice that Jesus made for us. We will go to the voting booth not out of fear for our own self-preservation and not out of a sense of grudging obligation to vote for the lesser of two evils, but rather out of a loving and prayerful desire to show love to our neighbor in a fallen world by supporting policies that reflect, however dimly, the justice of God's kingdom. And when some of our brothers and sisters in Christ make different political choices, we will not be particularly perturbed, because we will realize that both the Democratic and Republican parties (along with all third-party options) represent imperfect choices and cannot be equated with the kingdom of God. What matters is not primarily *how* we vote but *why* we vote. If our votes are shaped by a biblically guided, politically informed love for our neighbor, we will be doing the work of the kingdom, regardless of which party we might support in any given election.

Why This Book?

This is not the way that most white evangelical Christians have usually thought about politics. For the past few decades, most white evangelicals who attend Bible-believing churches have tended to vote for candidates who affirmed Christian values on abortion and sexuality, regardless of the results of their policies or their stances on other issues. But when we adopt a larger theology of sin, we will realize that sin includes anything that violates God's standard of righteousness—which means that the systemic injustice that pervades our culture goes far beyond a few hot-button issues. Furthermore, pursuing God's justice in the area of abortion and sexuality will likely involve far more than regulation. We cannot settle merely for political slogans such as "pro-life" or "family values" or even for a law that restricts abortion or gay rights; instead, we need to know which policies really promote marriage, stop abortion, help the poor, and promote the values of the kingdom of God. For that reason, this book focuses far more on detailed policy analysis than most other books on Christian politics do, because I want to know not merely which policies *promise* to promote the values of God's kingdom but which policies *actually* do so.

But before embarking on this policy analysis, I need to confront one common idol for Christians and answer one question that a lot of thoughtful Christians ask. The idol is political partisan loyalty, and the question is why neither party fully reflects biblical values. Christians who succumb to the idolatry of partisanship fail to sufficiently criticize their party when it deviates from God-centered morality. Politically conservative Christians who are partisan Republicans might loudly denounce abortion but fail to critique their party for the harm that its policies often do to the poor. Politically progressive Christians who are partisan Democrats might issue a clarion call for racial justice and a humane immigration policy but remain silent on abortion or even defend a pro-choice position. Both groups are blinded by partisan loyalty and risk mistaking a partisan distortion of the gospel message for the gospel itself.

Because of the widespread partisan loyalty among white evangelical Christians, I begin this book with two chapters that trace the complicated relationship that both parties have had to Christianity. Both of America's major political parties are deeply rooted in Christian principles, but both have also distorted Christian teaching and have mixed it with assumptions that are antithetical to the message of the Bible. Christian voters need to exercise discernment in recognizing when each party is echoing gospel truth and when it is presenting a distorted form of the gospel that amounts to heresy.

After presenting evidence that neither party is a Christian party—because both parties mix biblical truth with heretical distortions of Christian principles in ways that reflect the parties' particular histories—I then take on the challenge of answering the question that millions of Christians who recognize the pitfalls of both the Democratic and Republican parties may be wondering: As nonpartisan Christians, how do we work within a two-party American political system to further the cause of the kingdom of God? By delving into specific policy debates and examining the merits of proposals from each party, I suggest ways that both Republican and Democratic Christians can look beyond political slogans and partisan rhetoric to find specific policies that might accomplish kingdom objectives more effectively than most Christian political programs have in the recent past.

Rather than comprehensively surveying every issue of political debate in contemporary America, I have selected two issues (abortion and marriage) that are usually the highest-priority political issues for socially conservative evangelicals and two other issues (poverty and race) that have long been central concerns for progressive evangelicals. Other issues, of course, could have been selected. If this book had been significantly longer, perhaps it could have covered issues of war and peace or environmental stewardship, among other matters. But I selected the four issues that I did not only because these are the leading areas of concern for evangelical political activists on either side of the partisan divide but also because they offer excellent case studies of the way that cross-centered politics can offer a promising alternative to our contemporary culture of partisanship. If I can show that there are policy solutions that will allow us to simultaneously care for the unborn, protect the family, and bring justice to the poor and oppressed, I think that I will have provided a compelling political blueprint that can then be applied to other issues beyond the ones discussed in this book.

The Difference between Cross-Centered Politics and Power-Centered Politics

White evangelical Christians have traditionally had several priorities in voting, including preserving the Christian identity of the nation, legislating against immorality, and protecting their own religious liberty. Unfortunately, each of these goals is based on a false assumption. The United States was never a "covenant" nation chosen by God in the sense that ancient Israel was, and at the time of the framing of the Constitution, it was not founded on an explicit religious identity. This does not mean that our Christian principles should not influence us when we vote. But it does mean that attempting to Christianize the nation through politics reflects a poor understanding of both politics and the Bible.[9]

The goal of legislating against immorality is perhaps a wiser goal, but even this aim needs to be approached with extreme caution. Governments have been instituted by God as "God's servants, agents of wrath to bring punishment on the wrongdoer" (Rom. 13:4). But not every immoral activity can be the subject of legislation. Even in the divinely instituted law code that God established in ancient Israel, God did not legislate against every sinful action but instead made allowance for people's "hardness of heart" (Matt. 19:8 ESV). And if God made allowance for people's "hardness of heart" even in a law code designed for a covenant people, how much more is this true for a noncovenant nation such as the United States? A Christian should be disturbed by immoral actions, because every violation of God's moral standards disturbs the created order and results in harm both to the perpetrators of such actions and to their victims. Immorality is socially harmful. A Christian who recognizes that God's law is a reflection of God's character will delight in every aspect of this law and grieve over any violation of it (Ps. 119, especially vv. 47, 53, and 136). But at the same time, Christians who read their Bibles should be well aware of the limited potential of law in changing behavior. If Christians need the indwelling work of the Holy Spirit to follow God's moral standards, perhaps it is not surprising that when we attempt to legislate morality through civil law, it sometimes has only a very limited influence on people's actions.

A law is most effective when it reflects widely shared views in a society. When a societal consensus no longer supports a particular law, it usually becomes a dead letter. When the nation's sexual mores changed in the late twentieth century, anti-sodomy laws became ineffective and were eventually overturned. In this case, the cultural change in values started long before the Supreme Court overturned the nation's last state anti-sodomy laws in 2003. The same has been true of numerous other moral laws that have been repealed. The no-fault divorce laws of the 1970s were not the primary reason for the increased prevalence of divorce in the late twentieth century. Instead, a rapid rise in the divorce rate in the late 1960s created the political pressure to liberalize divorce laws. Similarly, the repeal of Prohibition was not the catalyst for a national increase in alcohol consumption. Instead, drinking rates began increasing in the mid-1920s, while Prohibition was still the law of the land, and this, along with concerns about organized crime and state revenues, led to Prohibition's repeal.[10] White evangelical Christians who entered politics in the late 1970s for the purpose of changing the law in order to create cultural renewal had their priorities reversed; they should have attempted to change the culture, and if they had, changes in the law would have followed suit.

Christians who enter the voting booth intent on ending social injustice or fighting sin by legislating against it need to ask whether a legislative prohibition is the most effective way to fight a particular evil. Sometimes it is. Laws against racially segregated public accommodations were remarkably effective in ending the old system of separate water fountains and unequal, segregated restrooms. But these legislative changes would likely have been ineffective if they had not been preceded by a shift in cultural mores. When advocates of African American freedom passed the Civil Rights Act of 1875, it was quickly overturned by the Supreme Court, and it had almost no lasting effect on the nation, even when its principles were supported by the

Fourteenth Amendment. It was only during the next century, after decades of African American activism and cultural shifts in northern white understandings of race, that the groundwork was laid for the more lasting civil rights legislation of the 1960s. There are limits to what a law can do if it is out of step with prevailing cultural norms, and Christians need to be aware of this. One of our goals in the voting booth should be to reduce immorality—but that may or may not take place through a legal prohibition.

The goal of protecting our own religious liberty through politics would make sense if Christians were a secular political interest group seeking to protect our own rights through the force of law. But surely Christians who believe in a sovereign Lord do not need to vote primarily out of fear. There are biblical precedents for Christians using the power of law to protect their own rights (see Acts 16:37; 22:25; and 25:11, for instance). But there are far more instances of divine injunctions for Christ-followers to voluntarily surrender their rights and welcome the hatred of authorities (Matt. 5:10-12, 38-42; 1 Cor. 6:1-8; 1 Pet. 3:14-17). Even in the instances when the Christians of the New Testament era defended their rights—as Paul did on a few occasions when he exercised his rights as a Roman citizen—it appears that their main motivation was not to gain comfort or security for themselves but rather to win a hearing for the gospel. If our political choices are motivated primarily by a desire to protect our own interests, are we acting as Christians?

The most Christlike goal in voting is to seek the good of our neighbor. We should want to create a society that reflects God's goals for humanity. This means seeking justice and alleviating the effects of sin. If God's prophets rebuked even pagan nations for their injustices (see Amos 1 and Mic. 1, for instance), surely God expects noncovenant nations such as the United States to behave in a manner that reflects divinely instituted standards of justice. If God cares about widows, orphans, and the poor (James 1:27; 2:5-8; 5:1-6), surely God would want Christians to vote in a way that reflects a concern for those groups—whether it means voting for a candidate whose economic policies will address poverty or whether it means seeking improvements in the foster-care system. If God holds all people, whether Christian or non-Christian, accountable for the murder of people who have been created in the image of God (Gen. 9:6), surely God wants us to pursue policies that protect human life and honor the dignity of every person.

But isn't seeking justice—such as justice for the unborn—the same as legislating against immorality? No. Christians have made two major errors when attempting to codify God's moral standards in civil law: They have overestimated the power of civil law to change behavior, and they have neglected to consider the entirety of God's moral standards when selectively appropriating particular biblical moral principles for legal application. Too often, Christians who become upset about violations of God's sexual standards have failed to become similarly outraged about laws that hurt the poor. Christians who are upset about structural racism and discrimination against immigrants sometimes downplay the injustice of abortion. And Christians on both sides of the aisle are often guilty of overlooking injustices that are not a matter of political controversy at the moment. Over the last thirty years, politically active evangelical Christians have generally talked about same-sex marriage more often than divorce, abortion more than child abuse, and racism more than gender discrimination, rape, and sexual harassment. Certainly marriage, abortion, and racism are vitally important issues of justice. But sometimes partisan-minded Christians can forget that the hot-button political issues of the moment do not exhaust the sum total of justice concerns that should occupy our thinking. Nor does pursuing one particular issue of justice—such as abortion, for instance—justify ignoring some of God's other moral principles for the sake of achieving a political victory in this one area. When we meditate on the holiness of God and think about Isaiah's vision of the Almighty God sitting on his throne as angels continually proclaim his holiness without ceasing (Isa. 6), we will soon recognize that legislating morality in a few areas will do nothing to turn a nation back to the standards of an absolutely holy God. America's problem is not abortion; America's problem (and the world's problem) is sin, and the sin of our nation is far more pervasive than a Christian political program might indicate.

Seeking justice, then, does not merely mean signing on to a campaign for a particular type of moral regulation. It instead means that we take all of God's moral law when making political choices. This does not mean that all of God's moral laws should be codified in civil law. In fact, only a small fraction can be. But even when a legal prohibition would be ineffective, we can often still find ways to use the power of government to encourage good behavior and deter sin. And we should do that, because we believe that all social sin damages the community. Part of doing good to our neighbors (Gal. 6:10) involves seeking justice for our community. As Christians, we will seek to enact policies that will lead to greater social justice by encouraging behavior that aligns with God's standards and discouraging behavior that does not.

Most of the time, the justice that aligns with the standards of God's kingdom will be focused heavily on the treatment of the poor and oppressed. "The Lord is a refuge for the oppressed, a stronghold in the day of trouble," Psalm 9 declares. "God will never forget the needy; the hope of the afflicted will never perish" (Ps. 9:9, 18). "A father to the fatherless, a defender of widows, is God in his holy dwelling," Psalm 68:5 states. The people of Israel under the Mosaic covenant were supposed to have this same priority of helping the afflicted, because they were God's delegates tasked with pursuing the social justice that characterized God's priorities. "Cursed is anyone who withholds justice from the foreigner, the fatherless or the widow," God instructed Moses to tell the people who entered into a national covenant with the Lord (Deut. 27:19). The leaders of the people had a special responsibility to carry out this mandate. "Defend the weak and the fatherless; uphold the cause of the poor and oppressed," God told judges who were supposed to help the defenseless but who were instead arrogantly acting as "gods." "Rescue the weak and the needy; deliver them from the hand of the wicked" (Ps. 82:3–4). And when the people violated God's covenant, God pointed to their treatment of the poor as one of the main areas where they needed to repent. "Woe to those who make unjust laws, to those who issue oppressive decrees, to deprive the poor of their rights and withhold justice from the oppressed of my people, making widows their prey and robbing the fatherless," God told the people of Israel through his prophet Isaiah (Isa. 10:1–2). When Jesus came, he inaugurated his ministry by quoting a passage from Isaiah, highlighting the deliverance that he would offer to the poor (Luke 4:18). Although the ultimate application of Jesus's promise is deliverance from the oppression and poverty of sin, this should not blind us to the application that would have been most obvious to Jesus's original hearers: deliverance from injustice for people who are facing economic, political, and social oppression. Anytime we seek to bring justice to those who are oppressed, we are doing the work of God's kingdom, just as the ancient Israelite kings were when they "defend[ed] the afflicted among the people and save[d] the children of the needy" (Ps. 72:1–4).

The pursuit of kingdom-oriented justice will require creative thinking, because when we seek justice for the oppressed along the lines that God intends, we will not go to the voting booth merely to pass laws against immorality every time we have the option. Instead, we will ask questions such as these: What set of policies will produce the most good for my neighbor, if "good" is defined by the set of standards and outcomes that God has given in the Bible (Gal. 6:10)? What set of policies might promote peace for all people and facilitate godly living (1 Tim. 2:2)? What set of policies will allow the gospel to go forth unimpeded and will potentially facilitate the positive reception of the gospel by equating Christianity in the public's minds with the principles of Jesus rather than with a flawed political ideology (1 Tim. 2:3–4)? What policies will protect the poor, the needy, and the defenseless from economic exploitation and will result in the protection of human life? If we ask these questions, our highest priority will not be aligning national law with Christian standards (a goal that can never be fully realized) but rather producing divinely ordained good outcomes for the people around us—people of all races, all socioeconomic levels, all genders, all immigration statuses, all ages (including the unborn), and all manners of sin. We will not go to the voting booth motivated by power, partisan loyalty, or fear. Instead, we will go to the voting booth motivated by the desire to do kingdom work by loving our neighbor and seeking to promote the behaviors and relationships in our community that reflect God's ideal for humanity.[11] True social justice will not fully arrive until the return of Jesus. But as we wait for Jesus, we can exercise love for our neighbors by seeking justice on a small scale in our communities, and we can thank God for the privilege that we have of voting in a democratic system—even if, as citizens of another kingdom, we know that the imperfect options we have at the voting booth cannot compare with the government we will one day have when "every knee" bows to Jesus as king.

In my examination of social problems that cry out for justice, I begin with the two issues that have received the greatest attention from most white conservative Christians for the past few decades: abortion and marriage. I then examine an issue that is of great concern to progressive evangelicals and that has begun to attract the attention of conservative Christians as well: race. Yet in the end, I suggest that the best approach to all of these issues may be to pursue justice in an area to which the Bible devotes extensive attention: our treatment of the poor. Once we learn how to give justice to the poor, we will go a long way toward addressing the other social justice issues that often receive more attention from Christians. And we will likely see that genuine justice-seeking in the area of economics will require us to renounce our partisan thinking and embrace a very different set of political assumptions.

A Note on My Own Perspective

When my pastor invited me a couple of years ago to lead a discussion for the young-professionals class in our church about how Christians should make political choices, I encountered a lot more skepticism from this group of twenty-somethings than I had expected. The group was politically divided, but neither the Democrats nor the Republicans in the room seemed entirely sure they could trust me. Finally, one asked, "What news channel do you watch?" He wanted to know which side of the line I was on. Was I a FOX viewer whom the conservatives in the room could trust? Or was I a loyal MSNBC watcher whose opinions the conservatives could safely discount but whom the progressives should pay attention to?

Perhaps you're wondering the same thing. Which side of the partisan line am I on?

The answer is that I have been on both sides of the line at different points in my life, and I'm currently on neither. I write as a Reformed evangelical Christian who believes that my political choices, like all my other actions, should be conducted under God's authority for his glory and the cause of Christ's kingdom. I believe that the Scriptures should be the final authority for all my actions, including my political choices. I believe in the necessity of personal salvation by grace through faith in Christ, and the work of the Holy Spirit in conversion. Because I know that sin affects all people in every area of their being, and that only the grace of God and the regenerating and sanctifying work of the Holy Spirit can overcome the effects of sin, I am skeptical about any proposals that suggest a social salvation or societal transformation through politics, whether those proposals come from the left or the right.

I am also wary of any political agendas that represent radical breaks with the way that Christians have traditionally understood Scripture. As a Reformed Protestant, I am impressed with the wisdom of the two-thousand-year Christian tradition, which is why I think that evangelical Protestants can learn a lot from the ancient church and from centuries of Catholic, as well as Protestant, political thought. I do not equate this tradition with

Scripture, and I realize that there might even be times when the tradition is incorrect, but in most cases, I think it is much more likely that the wisdom of Christians from earlier centuries, or from other cultures, might correct some of our own erroneous ideas. This is one reason why a study of history can be valuable for a Christian seeking a better understanding of God's word.

In addition to being a Christian, I am also an American historian, and much of my thinking about politics has been shaped by my reading of American history, as well as the many opportunities that my job as a history professor has given me to listen to the political perspectives of other people, whether those people are students, colleagues, or fellow believers whom I meet at church. My historical studies have given me a much greater awareness of the reality of structural inequities in American society than I had before, as well as the historical reasons why conservative white evangelicals have not been sufficiently concerned about these inequities. I have spent the past eighteen years studying Christian political choices in the United States and have written three books on the subject: *God's Own Party: The Making of the Christian Right*; *Defenders of the Unborn: The Pro-Life Movement before Roe v. Wade*; and *The Election of the Evangelical: Jimmy Carter, Gerald Ford, and the Presidential Contest of 1976*. But in my previous books, which were historical accounts (not works of theology or messages specifically aimed at Christians), I did not feel free to speak from a distinctively Christian theological perspective. In this book, I do. In keeping with the commitments of my Christian faith, I discuss Scripture and Christian theology frequently in this book, with the goal not only of understanding it academically but of applying it to our political decision-making.

I have struggled with these issues ever since reaching adulthood, and my political choices—and accompanying theology—have changed at least two or three times over the years. I grew up in a family that was culturally and politically conservative, and as a young adult, I believed that the Republican Party lined up much more closely with Christian values than the Democratic Party did. My opinion changed in graduate school, when I began doing extensive reading about the history of African American Christians who embraced the opposite political perspective even while holding to a theologically conservative view of the Bible and the necessity of trusting Jesus for salvation. As I examined a host of issues, including wars in the Middle East, health care, tax policy, and civil rights, I changed my view about which party best represented Christian values. I also realized the degree to which my own behavior and political choices in the past had reflected an indifference to injustice. This new conviction of my complicity in sinful structures of injustice was good and probably Spirit-driven, but like many young evangelicals who become disillusioned with the Christian Right and who then swing to the opposite side of the political spectrum, I overreacted. If the Republican Party has distorted Christian principles, the Democratic Party also has a long list of its own sins in this regard. Christians who wholeheartedly embrace the Democratic Party's agenda will probably end up with something much closer to a secularized version of liberal Protestantism than to an authentically Christian political ethic. But after briefly drinking from this political fountain, I then discovered Catholic social theology, which I still believe offers a much better alternative to either the secularized liberal Protestant values of the Democratic Party or the civil religious nationalism of the Republicans. Combining a deep commitment to poverty relief and concern for minority rights with a strongly pro-life opposition to abortion and commitment to the protection of the family, Catholic political theology challenges the assumptions of both Republicans and Democrats. There is a lot that evangelicals can learn from theologically attuned, politically thoughtful Catholics. But I am also a Reformed Protestant, which means that my political thinking has also been shaped by the ideas that are central to Calvinist theology, such as the sovereignty of God over human kingdoms, the pervasiveness of original sin both in individuals and in social institutions, the conviction that salvation comes from Christ alone and not through any amount of human effort, and the need to guard against all forms of idolatry. I draw a lot from the insights of Catholic political theology in this book, but I read these insights through a Reformed Protestant lens.

As a Reformed Protestant Christian, I believe in the central authority of Scripture in every area of life, which is why this book is filled with biblical references. In keeping with the Reformed Protestant tradition, I read the Bible as a unified, interconnected whole, whose moral principles are consistent because they emanate from the same God. This means that no biblical passage is irrelevant for the Christian.[12] Biblical passages—especially those from the Old Testament that contain specific regulations for a pre-Christian covenant—have to be interpreted in light of their specific historical context, and every section of Scripture has to be read through the lens of the gospel-centered message of redemption and correlated with the entire message of God's word. But no part of Scripture (not even the legal code of Leviticus!) can be ignored or dismissed. This is why, throughout this book, I frequently reference Old Testament passages (including those from the Mosaic law) along with New Testament verses, because both the Old and New Testament present a consistent message about God's character and ethical concerns.

I recognize, of course, that the Mosaic law code was given to a people who lived in a different time and place, and many of the details of the Mosaic legislation do not fully apply to Christians today, both because the secular government of the United States is not (and should not be) analogous to the theocratic order and divinely created covenant community that existed in Israel and because regulations that were appropriate reflections of God's moral character in an agrarian society of three thousand years ago might be anachronistic in twenty-first-century America, at least in their literal form. No one should imagine, for instance, that an Old Testament command to give day laborers their wages before nightfall on the day of their field work (Deut. 24:14–15) should be used to condemn modern American employers who pay on a biweekly or monthly schedule. However, a Christian should not hesitate to use these verses to rebuke an employer who withholds wages indefinitely or who violates a pay contract, as a similar injunction in the New Testament epistle of James suggests (James 5:4). In other words, the specific application of a biblical principle may change over time, and a Christian has to use discernment in determining both what the principle in any specific Bible passage might be and how it might be applied today. But the fact that all Scripture consists of "God-breathed" principles for instruction and application and that individual Christians have a divinely given responsibility to study all of it and interpret it properly (2 Tim. 3:15–17) is a fundamental conviction that guides my use of Scripture in this book. Any genuinely cross-centered approach to politics will be an approach guided by the word of God.

In applying the principles of the word of God to contemporary political questions, I am also shaped by the knowledge that I have gleaned from my academic study of American political history—a study that has led me to see the importance of public policy for addressing the concerns about justice that many Christians have. Most other evangelical books on Christian political behavior present general scriptural principles without engaging in any systematic analysis of the demonstrable *effects* of specific policies that they claim the Scripture might lead Christians to support. This book is different: it engages in a level of detailed policy analysis that most other popular evangelical prescriptions for Christian politics do not. After studying American politics and evangelical political behavior for nearly two decades, I have realized that many Christian voters have given little thought to how the policies they claim to support will actually work in practice. I have written this book partly because I am equipped to provide some policy analysis that goes beyond typical news headlines and that may lead to a helpful alternative to the Christian partisan political approaches that have damaged the cause of the gospel.

Given my own conviction that the issues are more complex than many assume, I am not going to try to feed you a partisan line; in fact, I am going to do the opposite by encouraging you to rise above partisanship, even while thoughtfully engaging with the perspective from various ideologies and Christian perspectives on politics. For those of you who are anxiously wondering, let me assure you that I am not going to end this book by telling you exactly how to vote. But if you reach the end of the book with a deeper understanding of your own political choices and the advantages and disadvantages of each potential Christian political commitment, this book will have accomplished its purpose. Even better, if you reach the end of the book with a better understanding of how you can best love your neighbor through your ballot choices and a deeper empathy toward Christians in your own congregation with whom you disagree politically, this book will have been worth the effort.

Regardless of your political allegiances, I think, in the end, that you will decide that Tim Keller was right to tell Christians that cross-centered politics do not neatly align with American partisan political choices. In a short op-ed, he did not have the space to fully explain why. This book is for those who might be curious about Keller's suggestion and who want to know more about the history, theology, and political analysis that will help us make more informed political choices in light of the gospel.

1

The Protestant Moralism of the Republican Party

For rulers hold no terror for those who do right, but for those who do wrong. Do you want to be free from fear of the one in authority? Then do what is right and you will be commended. For the one in authority is God's servant for your good. But if you do wrong, be afraid, for rulers do not bear the sword for no reason. They are God's servants, agents of wrath to bring punishment on the wrongdoer.

—Romans 13:3–4

A ruler with discernment and knowledge maintains order.

—Proverbs 28:2b

If ever there was a political party devoted to social justice, the Republican Party should have been it. Founded by Protestant Christians (many of whom were evangelical) who opposed slavery and were devoted to Protestant moralism, the party began with a call for both racial and economic justice. But over the course of its 150-year history, the GOP has generally not been a champion of the interests of the poor, and for the past century or more, many of its policies have arguably made the lives of the poor more difficult.

What might account for this? How did a party of moral fervor and social-justice advocacy become a party of the privileged? The answer is that the Protestant moralism that gave rise to the Republican Party was an insufficient foundation for the holistic, gospel-centered justice that might have resulted in a greater degree of economic uplift for the impoverished. Driven by righteous indignation—but devoid of a biblical theology of sin—its message quickly degenerated into the gospel of self-help rather than the gospel of Jesus or a commitment to helping others. Within a generation of the party's founding, the evangelical antislavery ethos largely gave way to a moralistic championship of middle-class standards that the party has advocated ever since.

White evangelicals have long been attracted to the Republican Party's Christian-inspired moralism, and in recent decades their loyalty to the party has only increased. But evangelicals' devotion to the moral agenda of the Republican Party has often blinded them to the devastating effects that this agenda has often had on people outside of the white middle and upper classes.

Protestant Moralism in the GOP's Early Years

The Republican Party of Abraham Lincoln was founded on the principle of a moral cause. In the wake of the early nineteenth-century Second Great Awakening, a religiously diverse coalition of black Christians and northern white Unitarians, Quakers, and a growing number of evangelicals such as revivalist Charles G. Finney and Congregationalist Harriet Beecher Stowe mobilized against slavery and campaigned to make it a political issue. Their efforts prompted the formation of several short-lived antislavery parties in the 1840s and early 1850s. In 1854, these antislavery coalitions formed a longer-lasting political party: the Republican Party, which was devoted to one central objective—stopping the expansion of slavery.[1]

In 1860, the party won its first presidential election with Abraham Lincoln on the ticket. Though Lincoln spent much of his adult life as a religious skeptic and was never an evangelical Christian in the traditional sense, he was deeply influenced by the Calvinism of his Baptist mother, and he filled his speeches with the cadences and phrases of the King James Bible. His Second Inaugural Address's speculation on the divine purposes for the mass slaughter in the Civil War was an exercise in theology that few other political speeches have equaled.

But Lincoln was far from the only Civil War–era Republican who saw the cause of the Union—and, by extension, the Republican Party—as fundamentally theological. Northern Republicans who joined together to sing "The

Battle Hymn of the Republic," which linked the Union and antislavery cause with Christ's atoning death, or who imbibed the messages of numerous other Union songs that linked God and country, such as "A Nation's Trust in God," "God and Liberty," and "God for Our Native Land," knew in their hearts that the war they were fighting was fundamentally righteous, and they rarely tempered their religiously inspired enthusiasm with Lincoln's pensive reflections on the inscrutable nature of a sovereign God's mysterious purposes. Though the Republican Party platform of 1864 did not explicitly claim the endorsement of God, it hardly needed to, because it was steeped in the moralistic language of righteousness that most Americans at the time associated with religion. Slavery, it declared, was a "gigantic evil," and the party was pledged to "terminate and forever prohibit" it. The Confederates were "rebels and traitors" who had committed crimes; the Union soldiers and civilians, by contrast, had demonstrated "self-sacrificing patriotism," "heroic valor," and "undying devotion." For many Republicans, the cause of Lincoln's reelection was quite literally a holy cause for the redemption of the nation through the emancipation of slavery and the victory of the Union. "Never was grander cause or sublimer conflict," Massachusetts Senator Charles Sumner declared at one campaign rally in the fall of 1864. "Never holier sacrifice. Who is not saddened at the thought of the precious lives that have been given to Liberty's defence? The soil of the rebellion is soaked with patriot blood. . . . Surely they have not died in vain. The flag which they upheld will continue to advance. But this," he warned, "depends upon your votes. . . . Let us so conduct this contest that we shall not shock mankind or sin against liberty. Let us so conduct it that we shall have Providence on our side."[2]

The Republican Party remained a party of righteousness long after the Civil War. Although business interests and economic concerns quickly began to eclipse the cause of African American civil rights for most Republicans within a decade of the surrender at Appomattox, the GOP retained the loyalty of the northern Protestants who saw the party as a bulwark against the corruption of the Irish Catholic Democrats, the traitorous southerners, and the hated liquor interests. In 1884, one Republican Presbyterian minister in New York famously charged only a few days before the presidential election that the Democrats were the party of "rum, Romanism, and rebellion." The attack backfired that year—indeed, it probably helped mobilize critical Irish Catholic votes for Democratic candidate Grover Cleveland, who eked out a narrow election victory—but for decades the Republican Party continued to be a home for northern temperance advocates, as well as the majority of northern Protestants, many of whom feared the political influence of "papist" immigrants. The platform statements of the party reflected this widespread Protestant suspicion of threats to the nation's Protestant identity and moral order. In 1880, the party adopted a platform plank against the use of "public funds" to support "sectarian" (by which they meant "Catholic") schools. In 1884, the party called on Congress to "suppress the system of polygamy within our territories" and "divorce the political from the ecclesiastical power of the so-called Mormon church." Four years later, the party reiterated its intention to use the power of the federal government to "stamp out the attendant wickedness of polygamy." The party platform of 1888 closed with an amendment directly affirming the Republican Party's Protestant moral leanings: "The first concern of all good government is the virtue and sobriety of the people and the purity of their homes. The Republican party cordially sympathizes with all wise and well-directed efforts for the promotion of temperance and morality."[3]

All of these efforts at moral reform focused entirely on regulation of individual vice, not alleviation of poverty. The way to escape poverty was to be industrious and avoid poverty, many late nineteenth-century Americans believed. Virtuous citizens, they thought, would be productive citizens—which is why many Republicans believed that moral reform was perfectly compatible with business interests. Some evangelicals (especially those who were wealthy) thought the same.

Several of the Republican presidents of the late nineteenth century were influenced by the Second Great Awakening version of evangelicalism that had given birth to their party. Rutherford B. Hayes's wife was a teetotaling Methodist who earned the sobriquet "Lemonade Lucy" because of her refusal to serve alcohol in the White House. James Garfield was a former lay revivalist minister in the Disciples of Christ—which, in the nineteenth century, was still a thoroughly evangelical denomination. Benjamin Harrison was a Presbyterian elder who taught Sunday school. And William McKinley was such a devout Methodist that he hosted hymn sings in the White House on Sunday evenings. When he agreed to the American annexation of the Philippines, he did so, he said, only because he viewed the Catholic island region as a field for American Protestant mission work. "There was nothing left for us to do but to take them all, and to educate the Filipinos, and uplift and civilize and Christianize them, and by God's grace do the very best we could by them, as our fellow-men for whom Christ also died," he said.[4]

Throughout much of the twentieth century, the Republican Party remained heavily Protestant, but it also became less evangelical and more mainline—a shift that closely paralleled the theological evolution of Protestant denominational traditions such as Congregationalism and northern Methodism, both of which had a close relationship with the GOP. While evangelicals emphasized the importance of a personal conversion to Christ, mainline Protestants deemphasized individual salvation and focused more on civil religion and societal reform.[5] From 1920 through 2008, every Republican presidential nominee was affiliated with a mainline Protestant denomination—usually Episcopalian or Methodist, but with a handful of Quakers, Presbyterians (that is, PCUSA or its equivalent), Congregationalists, Northern Baptists, and Disciples of Christ members also thrown into the mix. Middle-class, mainline Protestants were so closely associated with the GOP that the Episcopal Church was merely "the Republican Party at prayer," some quipped.

The Republican Party of the mid-twentieth century adopted positions that reflected the priorities of northern mainline Protestants, who were increasingly concentrated among the upper-middle class and who strongly believed in the capitalist system. More liberal than many of the Democrats on issues of race and women's rights, the GOP of the 1940s was also more supportive of both business interests and public expressions of a vaguely Christian civil religion. For years, the GOP also championed moral regulation, at least in certain areas that reflected middle-class white Protestant values. In the early twentieth century, the GOP gave Prohibition much stronger support than the Democratic Party did—partly because many middle-class Protestants saw alcohol regulation as a way to control the alleged intemperance of Catholic immigrants and the working class—and in the late twentieth century, the GOP led the way in implementing harsher antidrug laws. Above all else, the Republican Party supported the traditionally American Protestant ethic of hard work, individualism, and "self-reliance"—a virtue that the Republican Party platform of 1928 explicitly endorsed as an antidote to the "feeling of dependence" on the federal government, which the party "deplored."[6]

The beginning of the Cold War in the late 1940s prompted the Republican Party to become more overtly religious and moralistic as it rallied Americans around the cause of both God and country in opposition to "atheistic" Communism. Though Democrats during the early years of the Cold War also endorsed public expressions of the national faith, Republicans, in keeping with their party's long tradition of championing both morality and religion, were even more enthusiastic in their public piety. The party platform became explicitly religious. "America's trust is in the merciful providence of God, in whose image every man is created," the 1956 GOP platform declared in its opening sentence. The "Founding Fathers," the Republican platform declared, "proclaimed that the freedom and rights of men came from the Creator and not from the State," and the Republicans of the 1950s echoed this belief by declaring that the divinely created image was the basis for "every man's dignity and freedom." At a time when governments now had the power to wipe out the human population with the atomic bomb and when the threat of "godless Communism" seemed more acute than ever before, the Republican Party of Eisenhower loudly proclaimed the belief that only faith in a sovereign Creator grounded the democratic principles and human rights that would preserve the American people from totalitarianism and nuclear destruction.[7]

Dwight Eisenhower, who joined a mainline Presbyterian church within weeks of becoming president, became the only president to personally lead a prayer at his own inauguration ceremony. He then signed into law legislation adding the words "under God" to the pledge of allegiance and making "In God we trust" the national motto. A few years later, President Richard Nixon continued this civic religious tradition by holding White House worship services and recruiting Billy Graham to mobilize the conservative Protestant vote for the GOP. In the 1960s and 1970s, Republican leaders in Congress led the (unsuccessful) fight to rescind the Supreme Court's school prayer rulings and restore classroom prayer in public schools through a constitutional amendment.[8]

In the mid-twentieth century, this generic religious moralism united a broad spectrum of Protestants, ranging from evangelical Methodists to high-church Episcopalians. And it also deeply influenced the white Protestant Christians who created the evangelical movement of the mid-twentieth century. Nearly all the major evangelical institutions of the 1940s and 1950s—

including the National Association of Evangelicals (NAE), *Christianity Today* magazine, Fuller Theological Seminary, Billy Graham's ministry, and a host of conservative Christian colleges—were steeped in the moderately conservative Republican civil religion of the time.

The Evangelical Alliance with the Republican Party of Eisenhower and Nixon

The white conservative Protestants who created modern American evangelicalism in the mid-twentieth century continued a long-standing tradition of northern evangelical Republican voting. The leading northern conservative Protestant pastors of their parents' generation—whether people associated with Billy Sunday's evangelical revivals or those who were associated with the dispensationalist theology of Moody Bible Institute and magazines such as *The King's Business*—had voted Republican much of the time, because they were strongly opposed to a party that nominated the anti-Prohibitionist Catholic Al Smith in 1928 and that led the charge in repealing Prohibition in 1933. But beyond that, northern conservative Protestants were also heirs to a decades-long tradition of Republican voting that united the causes of Protestant moralism, opposition to socialism, and support for business interests and balanced federal budgets. In the 1930s, the most widely circulated northern fundamentalist periodicals, such as *Moody Monthly*, lined up against President Franklin D. Roosevelt's New Deal, despite its widespread popularity. Wheaton College, located in an Illinois town that was a longtime bastion of Republican voting, declared in the 1930s that its professors would hold firmly to "conservative social and economic views," and that in their classes, communism would be "conclusively disproven."[9]

The conservative Protestants who founded the NAE in the 1940s continued and expanded this tradition, especially after they started to consider the policies of the Republican Party the best antidote to Communism and the most reliable defense of the nation's Christian heritage. Most of the northern evangelicals who founded *Christianity Today* magazine and Fuller Theological Seminary were Republicans. Though Billy Graham remained a registered Democrat for decades (which was common for southerners of his generation), he was such a fervent Eisenhower supporter that he wrote a letter a year before the 1952 election urging the general to run for president, and then repeatedly lauded him during his time in office, promising him during his reelection campaign of 1956 that he would do "all in my power during the coming campaign to gain friends and supporters for your cause." Eisenhower, he announced hopefully, had demonstrated "spiritual leadership" by putting a "spiritual emphasis in the White House."[10]

This confidence in Eisenhower's faith was not entirely misplaced, because Eisenhower himself claimed on at least one occasion to be leading "America in a religious revival." Though not a church member before he entered the White House, he made weekly attendance at a Presbyterian church a priority as soon as he became president, and he also made it a practice to open all Cabinet meetings with prayer. But although evangelicals lauded the president's piety, his religious devotion was not a sign of evangelical faith but rather an indication of a more generic mainline Protestant support for religion as a bulwark of democracy in opposition to international Communism during the early years of the Cold War. Americans of all theological and political persuasions were becoming increasingly religious in the 1950s, and many of them had trouble separating their faith from their patriotism. By the end of the decade, 69 percent of Americans were church members—a higher percentage than at any other point in the twentieth century.[11]

Though the national fusion of democracy, anticommunism, and religion was a product of mainline Protestantism more than evangelicalism, evangelicals of the 1950s enthusiastically signed on to it. Graham's sermons regularly warned of the Communist threat, as did the messages of other popular evangelists of the era. Though they had good reason to label the Soviet version of Communism "atheistic" and to oppose it, their anticommunism sometimes led them to equate the cause of God with a defense of the free market and to view all government poverty relief programs as a slippery slope toward socialist totalitarianism. The NAE passed resolutions against Communism and organized anticommunist conferences, but the pages of its magazine also complained about "New Dealism and its neo-socialism." While numerous evangelicals, especially in the South, had voted Democratic in the 1940s, they became increasingly Republican in the 1950s, especially if they were affiliated with the NAE or subscribed to Graham's *Christianity Today* magazine. A *Christianity Today* poll showed that 85 percent of Protestant ministers planned to vote for Eisenhower in 1956, while only 11 percent supported his Democratic opponent, Adlai Stevenson. Four years later, another *Christianity Today* survey showed that among its subscribers, Republicans outnumbered Democrats by approximately four-to-one. And in the election of 1960, which pitted Eisenhower's vice president, Richard Nixon, against the Catholic Democrat John F. Kennedy, even some evangelicals who were registered Democrats crossed party lines to vote against a Catholic whose election, Dallas Baptist pastor W. A. Criswell declared, would "spell the death of a free church in a free state and our hopes of continuance of full religious liberty in America."[12]

The close alliance between conservative Protestants and the Republican Party's brand of civil religion during the mid-twentieth century came at a theological cost. Evangelicals who allied themselves with the Eisenhower administration in the name of anticommunism and civil religion lost their ability to critically question government policies that targeted African American leaders for surveillance or resulted in the deaths of hundreds of thousands of poor, nonwhite civilians in Vietnam. *Christianity Today* regularly published articles from FBI director J. Edgar Hoover that linked anticommunism with Christianity. Billy Graham repeatedly endorsed the righteousness of America's cause in the Cold War and continued to support the American government's policy in Vietnam long after many liberal Protestant and Catholic clergy turned against it. Before the 1940s, many conservative Protestants, especially Pentecostals, had been opposed to Christian involvement in war, but by the 1960s, white evangelicals (including members of denominations that had been opposed to war only a few decades earlier) became the nation's most enthusiastic supporters of the military campaign against international Communism. In 1968, at a time when only 21 percent of American college students favored increasing America's military involvement in Vietnam, 54 percent of students at Moody Bible Institute supported the idea. Among liberal Protestants, opposition to the Vietnam War became almost an article of faith; the pages of *Christian Century*, the flagship magazine of liberal Protestantism, were filled with denunciations of the war during the late 1960s. But evangelicals did not follow suit. Their strong commitment to anticommunism and the civil religious vision that they had acquired in the 1950s made it almost impossible to decide that America's military commitment to South Vietnam was a mistake. When the World Council of Churches passed a resolution in the spring of 1966 demanding an end to the American bombing of North Vietnam, *Christianity Today* denounced the resolution and declared that America's military engagement in Vietnam was a fight to "bring peace and freedom to enslaved people."[13]

White evangelicals' moderately conservative political vision also shaped their view of the civil rights cause—a view that, like that of the Republican Party, shifted from moderate endorsement in the 1950s to opposition in the 1960s. In the early 1950s, when the Republican Party was slightly more progressive than the Democratic Party on civil rights, the Republican-leaning northern evangelicals who led the NAE found it easy to endorse a moderately progressive vision of civil rights. In 1951, the organization endorsed "equal rights" for the "American negro" in education, wages, and housing, a resolution that closely accorded with the 1948 Republican Party platform statement that "the right of equal opportunity to work and to advance in life should never be limited in any individual because of race, religion, color, or country of origin." As long as white evangelicals and Republicans saw the civil rights cause as a matter merely of legislating against discriminatory practices and enforcing the principles of free enterprise, they supported it, in opposition to southern whites who wanted to continue the practice of legal segregation. Billy Graham's insistence on holding only racially integrated crusades after 1953 was a product of his egalitarian reading of the gospel and a break with the norms of his southern upbringing—but it was also a reading that accorded well with the views of the northern evangelicals with whom he had been associating since attending Wheaton College in the early 1940s, and it was a view that aligned with the official statements of the Republican Party at a time when northern Republicans still held onto a vestige of their party's Civil War-era human rights heritage and thought of themselves as heirs to Lincoln's legacy. As President Eisenhower stated—and as the Republican Party platform of 1956 reiterated—Republicans were fiscal conservatives and social moderates; they believed that "in all those things which deal with people, be liberal, be human. In all those things which deal with people's money, or their economy, or their form of government, be conservative."[14]

As long as racial justice did not require the expansion of government or the creation of new social welfare programs, Republicans supported it. And as long as racial justice was merely a matter of regulating and correcting individual behavior or repealing unjust segregationist laws, northern evangelicals supported it, too. In 1956, the NAE passed another racially progressive resolution declaring that because "the teachings of Christ are violated by discriminatory practices against racial minorities," Christians should "use every legitimate means to eliminate unfair discriminatory practices." Graham reflected these sentiments in his public appearance with Martin Luther King Jr. a year later.[15]

But evangelicals such as Graham and the editors of *Christianity Today* opposed any violation of local, state, or national laws, so when King and other civil rights activists embraced the strategy of nonviolent civil disobedience and shifted the civil rights cause from the courts to the streets, many evangelicals who had been moderately supportive of civil rights legislation denounced the movement for violating the apostle Paul's command in Romans 13 to "be subject to the governing authorities" (RSV). Civil disobedience, *Christianity Today* and other conservative evangelical publications argued, was not only a sin against God but also an incitement to violence that would destabilize the American republic and aid the Communists. And King, who had been a hero of sorts to some evangelicals in the late 1950s, became a target for denunciation in the evangelical press. In 1964, the year King received the Nobel Peace Prize, *Christianity Today*, which cautiously endorsed the landmark Civil Rights Act passed that year, spared no punches in attacking King. The magazine repeated J. Edgar Hoover's charge that the civil rights leader was "the most notorious liar in the country." When three civil rights activists were murdered in Neshoba, Mississippi, that summer, *Christianity Today* used the occasion not to denounce the Ku Klux Klan and white racism but rather to once again lambaste civil rights activists' strategy of nonviolent civil disobedience. "The tragic murders in Mississippi may possibly have stemmed in part from the shift of the Church's mission from persuasion to compulsion," the *Christianity Today* editorial declared, adding, "For preachers to argue that 'civil disobedience' is justified helps to encourage those who would resort to violence."[16]

In all of this, white evangelicals merely followed the lead of the conservative Republicans with whom they had allied themselves. Because they read the Bible through the lens of anticommunism and American civil religion, the injunction in Romans 13 to "be subject to the governing authorities" seemed a more urgent command than any of the Scriptures that liberal Protestants sometimes cited (such as the exhortation in Amos to "let justice roll down like waters" or the command in Micah to "do justly, and to love mercy") as justification for their campaign for fair treatment for people of all races. King's distinction between "just" and "unjust" laws that he outlined in his "Letter from a Birmingham Jail" did not make much difference to Graham or the editors of *Christianity Today*; what mattered instead was maintaining "law and order." This reflected the view of other conservatives at the time. The Republican Party platform of 1964 devoted several pages to a discussion of Communism, socialism, and the importance of preserving the freedom of the individual against the growth of government bureaucracy and social programs that conservatives believed the country did not need. But it spent only a few sentences on the need for justice in race relations, saying merely that the party wanted to "open avenues of peaceful progress in solving racial controversies while discouraging lawlessness and violence." This was almost exactly what *Christianity Today* and Billy Graham said at the time as well—though they went further than the Republican Party in claiming the support of Scripture for their stance.[17]

Half a century later, in 2018, the editors of *Christianity Today* issued an apology for their magazine's role in opposing the civil rights movement.[18] In retrospect, they could see that their magazine had been on the wrong side of the gospel in its denunciation of civil rights campaigns and its relative lack of concern for racial justice. But what they may not have realized, even in 2018, was that the magazine's mid-twentieth-century stance toward the civil rights movement—both its endorsement of civil rights legislation and its strong denunciations of King's strategy of nonviolent civil disobedience— was a direct outgrowth of white evangelicals' larger political views. Even Christians who read their Bibles daily and lived under the leading of the Holy Spirit found it very difficult to escape the prejudices and blind spots of the political culture in which they lived or to oppose the political party with which they had allied themselves.

White evangelicals' mid-twentieth-century alliance with the Republican Party also blinded them to the issue of wealth inequality in their nation and the structures that perpetuated poverty. At their worst, Republican evangelicals sometimes scornfully dismissed the notion that government programs could alleviate poverty. "We do not think it possible to abolish poverty, nor are we sure that its abolition would be better for society as a whole," *Moody Monthly* declared in July 1933, immediately after Roosevelt implemented his First New Deal. Fifty years later, Christian Right leaders expressed similar sentiments when supporting conservative Republican politicians who wanted to roll back some of the social welfare programs of the Great Society. The federal government's social welfare provisions were "giveaway programs, supported by those people who work hard for a living," Jerry Falwell declared in 1980. To be fair, contemporary evangelicals—especially those who live in conservative, Republican-voting regions—give away a higher percentage of their income than most other Americans do, which suggests that they are in fact concerned about poverty.[19] Conservative evangelicals of the 1970s and early 1980s were also probably correct in some of their critiques of federal welfare programs, which were based on flawed premises and which were not nearly as focused as they later became on providing a means for job training and a path to self-sufficiency. But conservative evangelicals' deeply rooted suspicion of government antipoverty programs obscures the effectiveness of some of these programs—especially Medicaid, Medicare, and Social Security—in alleviating poverty among the most vulnerable populations, especially children and the elderly, and it also underestimates the degree to which structural inequities perpetuate poverty in ways that churches, individuals, and private charities are not always well equipped to address.[20]

Like many political partisans, white evangelical Republicans of the 1970s sometimes excused or denied the sins of their party leaders long after they became glaringly obvious to members of the opposition party. This was especially evident in the case of President Richard Nixon. Eighty-four percent of white evangelical voters supported Nixon's reelection in 1972, and many viewed him as a moral leader. Nixon knew that the nation's "greatest problem" was "moral permissiveness and decadence," Graham told his fellow evangelicals, and he promised that Nixon would put "a lot more emphasis on moral and spiritual affairs" in his second term. Other evangelical leaders also rallied to Nixon's side. "I believe in Mr. Nixon because of his high moral integrity," Harold J. Ockenga, the president of Gordon-Conwell Theological Seminary and president emeritus of the NAE, said. "Mr. Nixon understands the Communist movement. . . . He knows the conflict in Vietnam is not a civil war but an effort of Communism to infiltrate a nation. . . . Mr. Nixon will not be taken in by this strategy. We may trust him!" Immediately after the election, *Eternity* magazine celebrated the result by saying that Nixon would be remembered as "one who by precept and example guided the nation out of its ethical morass." After giving Nixon their trust, many evangelicals—especially Graham—found it difficult to believe that he could be guilty of the dishonest behavior that he was alleged to have engaged in during the coverup of the Watergate scandal. Nixon's "moral and ethical principles wouldn't allow him to do anything like that," Graham insisted in February 1973. Years later, as Graham recalled his feelings of betrayal after finding out how naive he had been, he said that he "felt like a sheep led to the slaughter."[21]

Why did evangelicals think they could trust Nixon? Why did Graham give him stronger support than he gave to any other president? Why did Nixon win a higher percentage of the white evangelical vote than any presidential candidate before or since? White evangelical Christians felt that the nation was experiencing a rapid moral deterioration amidst the sexual revolution, the race riots, the antiwar movement, and the rising crime rate of the late 1960s, and they were looking for a political figure who could stop these forces of cultural decay. Having served as Eisenhower's vice president, Nixon was well positioned, they thought, not only to win the war in Vietnam but to return the nation to the civil religion of the 1950s. Nixon's White House church services, his calls for "law and order," his policies against illicit drugs, and his escalation of the bombing in Vietnam were confirmations for conservative evangelicals that he was on the right side of the nation's moral divide. They found it almost impossible to believe that he was actually a cynical, profane, devious politician.

After Watergate, the nation's evangelical leaders temporarily resolved to make personal character, rather than party affiliation or policy positions, their litmus test in deciding whom to support for president. "What is uppermost is that whoever our national leader may be, that he first of all must manifest not protection of image, self or party-interest, and surrender to expedience, but rather political competence coupled with devotion to truth and right and justice," Carl Henry wrote in January 1976.[22] Throughout the campaign season, evangelical journalists who interviewed the presidential candidates for Christian periodicals focused their questions almost entirely on issues of personal faith and moral character rather than policy positions. For those who cared about personal character, the election of 1976 could hardly have offered better candidates: both the Republican incumbent Gerald Ford and the Democratic challenger Jimmy Carter were men of integrity, piety, and personal decency. In the end, white evangelicals split their votes almost evenly between the born-again Southern Baptist Sunday school teacher Carter and the quietly devout, moderately conservative Episcopalian Gerald Ford. Southern Baptists tended, at least before Carter's *Playboy* interview, to be far more enthusiastic about the Democratic candidate, while both southern self-identified fundamentalists and northern evangelicals (especially those in the Midwest) were more supportive of the Republican incumbent. But nearly all the evangelicals who issued their own commentary in the election insisted that evangelical Christians would not necessarily vote as a bloc for a particular candidate or party, and that that was okay.[23] They were determined not to make the same mistake they had with Nixon. It was a short-lived resolution. In 1980, conservative evangelicals forged a new relationship with the Republican Party that was far stronger than any partisan alliance they had made before.

The Christian Right: Evangelical Control of the Republican Party

By the late 1970s, millions of evangelicals had been voting Republican for decades, and their thinking about politics had been shaped by moderately conservative Republican values, but there was one thing they felt they had never done: use their electoral muscle to seize political power and take over both the Republican Party and the national government. The Christian Right emerged not when evangelicals first began talking about politics in their churches or voting Republican (they had been doing both of those things for years) but when prominent pastors and television evangelists decided to mobilize evangelical voters as a bloc in order to act as a political interest group within the Republican Party. They did so because they thought that political power offered the only hope of achieving a cultural renewal that they believed was necessary to save the country from moral licentiousness and destruction. Most of the founders of the Christian Right—men such as Jerry Falwell, Pat Robertson, and James Dobson, and women such as the conservative Catholic Phyllis Schlafly and the Baptist antifeminist Beverly LaHaye—had come of political age in the 1950s, when America's Cold War fusion of civil religion, anticommunism, and public morality was at its height. They were therefore shocked by the rapid cultural changes of the late 1960s, which challenged all the civil religious tenets that they considered sacrosanct. In 1965, the divorce rate was only 26 percent, only 9 percent of all children (and only 3 percent of white babies) were born to unmarried mothers, abortion was illegal in every state, and a movie production code still sharply restricted the content that could be shown on screen. By the end of the 1970s, the divorce rate had doubled and was now 50 percent, the out-of-wedlock birthrate had also doubled to reach 18 percent, there were eight hundred adult movie theaters showing X-rated films, and abortion was legal everywhere, with one abortion occurring for every two live births—a total of 1.5 million abortions per year. Some conservative evangelicals blamed these cultural changes partly on a liberal Supreme Court, which they accused of forcing legal abortion on unwilling state legislatures and blocking efforts to restrict pornography. While politics could not save souls, it could save the country from moral disintegration, they thought. And for the first time, they realized, born-again Christians—a group *Newsweek* magazine said accounted for one-third of all Americans—might have the voting power to force a change in the nation's moral direction. A rapid growth in the Southern Baptist Convention and other conservative denominations at a time when liberal Protestant churches had started to shrink gave evangelicals a confidence in their own strength that they had lacked only a decade before. Evangelical pastors led the nation's largest megachurches, the biggest religious television programs, and some of the most financially successful ministries. Now they could become political players as well. "We have together, with the Protestants and the Catholics, enough votes to run the country," Pat Robertson declared in 1979. "And when the people say, 'We've had enough,' we are going to take over."[24]

Some of the evangelicals' desire to take political power was largely self-interested: they feared that the government would take away their right to run their religious broadcasting ministries and Christian schools in the way they chose. In the mid-1970s, a rumor that the Federal Communications Commission (FCC) might issue a temporary freeze on broadcasting licenses to "sectarian" religious broadcasters led evangelicals to send the FCC 700,000 letters of protest. And in 1978, Christian school administrators, including Jerry Falwell, mobilized against an IRS directive to deny tax exemptions to private schools that had low minority enrollments and that did not demonstrate a good-faith effort to increase the number of minority students in compliance with federal civil rights law.[25]

But the main reason that evangelicals launched new political organizations was not to defend their own interests but rather to change the moral direction of the nation. They blamed the nation's moral slide on "secular humanism," arguing that when prayer was taken out of public schools, God was replaced with a secular philosophy that offered no foundation for morality. Christian Right organizations such as the Moral Majority advocated a comprehensive political program to restore the civil religious vision of the 1950s. National faith in God would be reaffirmed through a constitutional amendment to restore classroom prayer in public schools. Legislation to prevent "homosexuals" from teaching in the nation's public schools would curb the spread of sexual immorality. A constitutional amendment to ban abortion and protect human life from the moment of conception would correct the evils of *Roe v. Wade*. A national promise to defend Israel, along with a strong military commitment to stop the spread of Communism, would reaffirm the Cold War foreign policy that evangelicals in the 1950s had endorsed.[26]

Some political pundits at the time assumed that the conservative evangelical alliance with the Wall Street wing of the GOP would be short-lived. But conservative evangelicals such as Falwell had more in common with fiscal conservatives than many people assumed. Like other fiscal conservatives, Falwell was strongly committed to free enterprise, just as most white evangelicals had been for decades. He was suspicious of government social programs, federal regulation of business, and higher taxes. He believed that churches and private organizations, not the federal government, should spearhead social welfare provision and societal reform. Like many other conservative Republicans, he supported nuclear arms buildup and a stronger military in order to defend against Communism. Even the moral regulation that he proposed was not as incompatible with mainstream Republican Party policy as some observers assumed. Though a few libertarian-leaning conservatives in the GOP resisted the Christian Right's moral agenda, it actually accorded well with the party's antidrug policies of the 1970s, its resistance to the counterculture in the 1960s, and its affirmation of civil religion in the 1950s. In Falwell's view, his proposed constitutional amendments were merely an attempt to reverse liberal Supreme Court decisions on school prayer and abortion during the previous twenty years, and protect the right of families and local communities to follow their own moral standards—a principle of local control that conservatives had long supported.[27]

In 1976, evangelicals had prioritized the personal character of candidates over their policy stances, but in 1980, those who joined the Christian Right made policy positions a political litmus test. Following the lead of New Right organizations associated with Paul Weyrich and Richard Viguerie, Christian Voice issued "morality ratings" for all members of Congress that were based solely on their voting records, not their personal character. When the organization gave a few members of Congress who were convicted in a financial scandal high morality ratings solely because of their votes on abortion and other social issues, some journalists questioned the accuracy of the "morality" label, but in the Christian Right's new political calculus, the rubric made sense.[28] The Christian Right, like other political interest groups, expected specific policy results, and the only thing that therefore mattered was a candidate's issue positions. Carl Henry had argued in 1976 that the key to restoring the country's moral direction was to elect leaders of integrity, but after the disappointment of the Carter administration—which Christian Right leaders believed had exacerbated the nation's moral slide, even with a born-again Southern Baptist deacon in the White House—the Christian Right looked solely at candidates' positions on issues, not at their personal faith.

The candidate they most wanted to see elected to office was Republican presidential nominee Ronald Reagan. The divorced former Hollywood actor was less personally religiously observant than Carter, but his vision of a Christian America with a strong military defense against Communism accorded much more closely with the Christian Right's civil religious vision than Carter's moderate liberalism did. He also shared evangelicals' belief that the country had lost its moral anchor, and he was just as angry with the liberal Supreme Court as they were. Somewhat surprisingly for a California governor who had signed into law a liberal abortion bill a decade earlier, he even endorsed their call for an antiabortion constitutional amendment. Some evangelicals considered electing him to the White House almost a Christian imperative. Christian Voice's enthusiasm for the Republican presidential candidate was so great that it launched the subsidiary "Christians for Reagan" to provide direct support to the Reagan campaign. When Reagan won, Falwell declared that it was "the greatest day for the cause of conservatism and morality in my adult life."[29]

The Republican Party officially endorsed the Christian Right's proposed constitutional amendments on school prayer and abortion, but enough northern moderate Republicans and Western libertarian-leaning conservatives opposed these measures to prevent their passage in a Republican-controlled Senate. In response, the Christian Right abandoned its quest for a school prayer amendment and changed its strategy on abortion. From 1973 until 1983, the pro-life movement placed all its emphasis on a Human Life Amendment (HLA)—that is, a constitutional amendment that would not merely reverse *Roe v. Wade* but would ban abortion nationwide and protect all human life from the moment of conception. Evangelicals did not come up with the idea for this amendment; they borrowed the concept from the Catholics who had launched the pro-life movement years before they became concerned about abortion. But, following the lead of the pro-life movement, Christian Right organizations such as the Moral Majority endorsed the HLA in the late 1970s, and the Republican Party pledged to support it. By the mid-1980s, though, pro-lifers and some of their conservative Republican allies realized that there was a much shorter path to rescind *Roe*—shifting the Supreme Court to the right through new conservative judicial appointments. This strategy accorded much better with the goals of the Republican Party, since a conservative judicial strategy could serve a much broader conservative agenda than merely restricting abortion. Even though the Republican Party had officially endorsed the HLA in its party platform, the idea had never received very much support from party leaders at a time when several of the most prominent members of the party, including senate majority leader Howard Baker, were pro-choice—a stance that accorded well with the mainline Protestant denominations that for decades had been the party's strongest source of support. But the conservative judicial strategy appealed to a much larger group of Republicans, because even those who were ambivalent about overturning *Roe v. Wade* could be persuaded to support conservative judicial nominees for other reasons—especially when those judicial nominees made it a practice (as they did after 1987) of refusing to state exactly how they might vote on abortion cases. Nearly all Democrats, by contrast, were firmly opposed to the conservative judicial strategy; even some of the few Democratic senators who opposed abortion and supported a Human Life Amendment voted against conservative judicial nominees in the late 1980s and early 1990s. By embracing a conservative judicial strategy as one of their highest priorities, both the pro-life movement and the Christian Right strengthened their alliance with the Republican Party and ended whatever hope they had of finding common ground with Democrats.[30]

Abortion had not been a stand-alone issue for the Christian Right when Reagan ran for president in 1980, but by the time he ran for reelection in 1984 it was. During Reagan's first campaign, most conservative evangelicals treated abortion mainly as a product of secularism, which they viewed as the nation's primary problem. The best way to combat feminism, the sexual revolution, pornography, homosexuality, Communism, and abortion, they thought, was to restore God to a place of prominence in the nation's public life. That might entail passing an antiabortion amendment as part of this agenda, but the agenda could also be accomplished by a school prayer amendment—which some Christian Right organizations, such as the Religious Roundtable, treated for a while as an even more urgent priority. By 1984, though, most of the Christian Right had united around abortion as their highest priority and an urgent matter of social justice. When Moral Majority vice president Cal Thomas urged Christian radio listeners to go to the polls, he portrayed the presidential election as a contest for Supreme Court nominations that would determine the fate of unborn human lives. "There is no doubt that the future of our nation for the rest of this century and into the beginning of the 21st century rides on the outcome of this election," he said. "Supreme Court judges will probably be chosen by the next President. Will they keep the abortion floodgates open or start to close them? It's up to you."[31]

The abortion issue especially appealed to younger baby boomers and Gen-Xers who had come of age at a time of rights consciousness and social justice. The leading national evangelical champions of a school prayer constitutional amendment in the early 1980s, including Bill Bright, Ed McAteer, and Adrian Rogers, were old enough to remember World War II and to have voted for Dwight Eisenhower, so their vision of Christian politics was shaped by a dream to return the nation to the unified civil religious vision of the early Cold War years. By contrast, some of the leading evangelical champions of the pro-life agenda in the late 1980s—especially Operation Rescue founder Randall Terry—were too young to remember the Eisenhower presidency, let alone World War II, the beginning of the Cold War, or the era of classroom prayers in public schools. Their vision of politics had been shaped by the direct action and social justice priorities of the civil rights and antiwar movements—which they had, for the most part, not participated in themselves, but which they often admired in retrospect. Conservative Christian politics became for this generation both a campaign for human rights and a matter of spiritual warfare. Evangelical college students read the works of theologian and apologist Francis Schaeffer, which framed legalized abortion not only as a human tragedy of Holocaust-like proportions but also as the frightening product of a secular legal system that no longer had a basis for considering any human rights absolute. Younger teens imbibed a militantly antiabortion message from the lyrics of Christian rock songs, which, during the 1980s, frequently combined biblical imagery of spiritual battle with denunciations of secular liberalism and exhortations to save the unborn. Evangelical churches began celebrating annual Human Life Sundays in the mid-1980s, and more evangelicals began participating in pro-life marches or, if they favored more direct action, clinic sit-ins. Inundated with these messages from the pulpit, their youth groups, and the Christian music playing on their Walkman radios, evangelical Christian teens in the 1980s enlisted in the fight against abortion. Forty thousand people—mostly evangelical, and many of them in their teens and twenties—faced arrest for illegally blocking abortion clinics in the late 1980s. Even Jerry Falwell, a longtime critic of the civil rights movement's strategy of nonviolent civil disobedience, followed the lead of younger evangelicals by declaring in 1988 that civil disobedience was a justified strategy to stop abortion. Martin Luther King Jr. was now "everybody's American hero," he said, and it was time for evangelicals to emulate his actions on behalf of a civil rights cause for America's unborn.[32]

The human rights message, the call to follow the lead of the civil rights movement in embracing nonviolent civil disobedience, and the strong denunciation of "killers of the unborn" (which was the title of one Christian metal song of 1988) sounded like a far cry from the quiet mainline Protestant conservatism of the Republican Party—some of whose most prominent members, including Barry Goldwater and the family of George H. W. Bush, had been longtime supporters of Planned Parenthood. But the vast majority of young evangelicals who embraced the message of pro-life activism in the late 1980s became loyal conservative Republicans, despite the party's previous lack of interest in the pro-life cause. Randall Terry even ran for Congress as a Republican and, after he left Operation Rescue, became a conservative talk-show host.[33] Evangelicals felt comfortable in the Republican Party partly because they were remaking the party into their chief offensive brigade in the culture wars.

In the 1980s, evangelicals were a minority interest group in a party whose leaders were mostly mainline Protestants and who did not share their concerns about abortion. While conservative evangelicals found many areas of common ground with nonevangelical Republicans in the 1980s (just as they had previously united around shared areas of concern in the 1950s), abortion remained an area of division. Evangelicals during the 1980s did not make nearly as much progress in overturning *Roe v. Wade* as they had hoped—largely because two of the three justices that President Reagan appointed to the Supreme Court voted to uphold most of the key provisions of *Roe* in *Planned Parenthood v. Casey* (1992). Nor were evangelicals able to get the school-prayer amendment they wanted or restrictions on gay rights. Only when their concerns overlapped with those of mainstream Republicans—as they did, for instance, on increasing military funding, protecting Israel, and securing expanded child tax credits—were they able to secure more than token concessions from the Republican Party.

But after a wave of conservative Christians from the Sunbelt were elected to Congress in the 1990s, there were signs by the end of the century that the Christian Right might finally be in control of the party. In the early 1980s, one-third of Senate Democrats (many of whom represented northern states with low numbers of evangelicals) were consistently pro-choice, but by the mid-1990s, after the Republican congressional delegation became both more southern and more evangelical, more than 90 percent were willing to vote for abortion bans at least some of the time. One researcher estimated that 74 percent of Republican gubernatorial and senatorial candidates in the mid-1990s could be described as social conservatives, whereas in the early 1980s, fewer than half had been. As northeastern socially liberal Republicans moved into the Democratic Party, and as southern Democrats switched to the Republican Party, the Republican Party finally became sufficiently evangelical for Christian Right activists to dictate their agenda to the party. A 2017 Public Religion Research Institute survey indicated that 35 percent of Republicans are white evangelicals, and 16 percent are white Catholics—which means that religiously conservative voters who embrace the Christian Right positions on abortion and marriage might comprise a majority of the Republican Party. Evangelical dominance in the GOP kept the Republican Party from moderating its abortion position in 1996—despite Republican presidential nominee Bob Dole's desire to do so—and it also prompted John

McCain to select evangelical Alaska governor Sarah Palin as his running mate in 2008 despite his desire to select the pro-choice former Democrat Joe Lieberman.[34]

By the twenty-first century, it was obvious that no pro-choice Republican could win the party's presidential nomination—nor could any candidates who distanced themselves too far from the Christian Right. The party also loudly proclaimed its allegiance to religious values. Its 2016 platform mentioned God fifteen times and "faith" more than two dozen times. It also alluded to the country's "Judeo-Christian heritage" and endorsed "the public display of the Ten Commandments," "the rights of religious students to engage in voluntary prayer at public school events," and other principles of "religious liberty." "As George Washington taught, 'religion and morality are indispensable supports' to a free society," the 2016 Republican platform proclaimed.[35] The GOP changed in many respects between the late nineteenth century and 2016, but on this point, nineteenth-century Republicans who championed a Protestant moral order and their twenty-first-century Christian Right descendants would probably have been in agreement.

In the early twenty-first century, evangelicals also gained support from the Republican Party for a constitutional amendment to define marriage as a union between a man and a woman, although this campaign was unsuccessful and remarkably short-lived. When evangelicals embarked on this campaign in 2003, public opinion polls showed that a majority of Americans opposed same-sex marriage, and evangelicals thought they had a chance of winning. But support for conservative Christians' view of marriage rapidly declined over the course of the Obama administration.[36] When the Supreme Court invalidated all legislation against same-sex marriage in *Obergefell v. Hodges* in 2015, many conservative Catholics and evangelicals were outraged, but they recognized that they did not have sufficient support to overturn the decision through a constitutional amendment, so—in contrast to their initial response to *Roe*—they did not even try. Instead, they renewed their efforts to change the court, but their purpose in doing so was no longer to return the nation to a Christian moral standard. Instead, they were primarily concerned about protecting their own freedom. No longer did they think they had a chance of upholding biblical standards on marriage, sexuality, or abortion in national law, as many members of the Moral Majority envisioned in the early 1980s. They were now willing to settle for the lesser goal of protecting their own rights to practice their faith without governmental interference—which was a sign of how much ground they thought they had lost in the thirty-five years since Reagan's election.

Many liberals were surprised that Christian Right activists felt beleaguered, because in their view, religious conservatives were winning. Pro-life Republican presidents controlled the White House for twenty-three of the thirty-nine years between 1981 and 2020. Republicans controlled at least one House of Congress for all but twelve of those years. Republican-appointed justices also comprised a majority on the Supreme Court for the entire period. By the time Justice Brett Kavanaugh joined the Supreme Court in 2018, the court was arguably the most conservative that it had been in more than half a century. Conservative state legislatures adopted dozens of new abortion restrictions between 2013 and 2019, and the nation's abortion rate fell to the lowest it had been since *Roe v. Wade*. Why then were Christian conservatives issuing such pessimistic assessments of their political activity as the one Rod Dreher presented in *The Benedict Option* in early 2017, immediately after an evangelical-dominated Republican Party took control of all branches of government for the first time in more than a decade?[37]

In fact, Dreher's pessimistic assessment was nothing new. Numerous conservative evangelicals who had been active in politics had decided in the end that their conservative lobbying had accomplished little. In 1999, nearly twenty years before Dreher's book, former Moral Majority vice-presidents Cal Thomas and Ed Dobson declared in *Blinded by Might* that they had expected too much from the Christian Right's efforts, and they wondered whether their alliance with political conservatism had hurt the cause of the gospel.[38] It certainly had not changed the culture.

The evangelicals who launched the Christian Right in the late 1970s believed that if they could pass the right legislation, they could change the country's morals. But that didn't happen. They won the fight against the Equal Rights Amendment (ERA), only to discover that a series of Supreme Court decisions resulted in the same changes in state and federal laws that they thought they had blocked by stopping the ERA. They rejoiced in the closing of many adult movie theaters and gay bathhouses in the 1980s, only to discover that the rise of video rental stores, followed in the next decade by the internet, made these victories meaningless. Their fight against gay rights ultimately ended in complete failure, even though they won a few state ballot initiatives or local ordinances along the way. But the shifting targets for the movement should have been a sign that Christian conservatives were losing ground. In 1978, their goal was to keep "homosexuals" from teaching in public schools. In the 1980s, Jerry Falwell advocated quarantining "homosexuals" to stop the spread of AIDS. In the 1990s, Christian Right activists settled for the more modest goal of preventing sexual orientation from being listed as a protected category in nondiscrimination ordinances. At the beginning of the twenty-first century, they largely abandoned these other battles and focused all their efforts on preventing the legal recognition of same-sex marriage. They lost every one of these fights. Now the main concern for the movement is no longer preventing same-sex marriage but rather protecting the rights of people who choose, on religious grounds, not to support it. In other words, after losing nearly all the battles they fought in the culture wars, conservative Christians are now no longer attempting to make America Christian; their only concern is protecting the right to exercise their own beliefs and dissent from what has become the new secular norm.[39]

Conservative evangelicals are right to sense a sea change in cultural attitudes during the last half century and to recognize that their political activity has done nothing to stop this shift. In particular, the United States has experienced four major secular shifts:

1. A culture of civil religion and religiously based moral norms reflecting mainline Protestant values and a generic expression of "Judeo-Christian" faith has been replaced with a secularized culture of religious pluralism in which public moral norms are no longer viewed as in any way tied to religion.

2. A vaguely Christian endorsement of heterosexual marriage as the most proper location for sex and childrearing has been replaced by an individualistic view of sex and gender that no longer privileges or endorses heterosexual marriage.

3. An individualistic rights-consciousness, grounded above all in personal identity, now supersedes all other moral claims.

4. Christian institutions, including churches, are no longer seen as bulwarks of social morality but rather as private interest groups that are tolerated only to the extent that they conform to the new societal rights consciousness.

Collectively, these four shifts have put conservative evangelicals on the defensive. While evangelicals never enjoyed majority-status in the United States during the twentieth century, they were comfortable enough in the mainline Protestant-dominated world of the 1950s to feel that their moral codes and religious projects had the support of the nation's leaders. By the 1970s, they sensed that they no longer had this support, but they thought they could regain it through an exercise of political power. Now they realize that the cultural changes that they had long opposed are more permanent and far-reaching than they had ever imagined, and they want protection from a society that is likely to be hostile to their values. Their alliance with the Republican Party was not enough to prevent these cultural shifts, but ironically, the more cultural battles they lost even under Republican administrations, the more committed to the GOP they became, because they perceived that the Democratic Party was on the wrong side of all these issues, and they were terrified of what a liberal Supreme Court and a Democratic-controlled government might do. After losing their campaign against same-sex marriage, their fears of the future became far more apocalyptic, and it determined how they approached the election of 2016. "[Hillary] Clinton has said she will seek to overturn religious liberty and bring the power of government against people of faith," Focus on the Family founder James Dobson told *Christianity Today* in the fall of 2016, in a statement typical of many Trump-supporting conservative evangelicals. "I'm convinced that with the wrong president, we will soon see a massive assault on religious liberty. . . . I believe this great country is hanging by a thread. If we make another tragic mistake after putting Barack Obama in office for eight years, we will never recover from it."[40]

Donald Trump's personal behavior concerned Dobson, who had devoted his entire career to defending "family values." But putting conservatives on the Supreme Court was a matter of survival for conservative Christians, he believed. A majority of conservative evangelical voters apparently agreed with Dobson. They gave Trump a higher percentage of their vote than any presidential candidate had received since Richard Nixon.

Is Christian Conservatism Really Christian?

The Republican Party, in all its many political incarnations, has always been the party of God and morality, and white evangelicals have been attracted to it. But is the morality of the GOP the same as the moral standards of the Bible? The GOP's selection of moral issues has always been selective and much more reflective of middle-class white Protestant moral norms than a comprehensive biblical worldview. The party's eagerness to prosecute Mormon polygamy in the 1880s or to keep alcohol out of the hands of working-class Catholic immigrants in the early twentieth century could be supported, perhaps, with Bible verses on marriage or drunkenness, but the effect of such legislation inevitably directed the power of the state against more marginal members of society, while leaving most members of the middle class untouched. Sometimes selective enforcement involved outright hypocrisy. In the early 1920s, for instance, Republican president Warren Harding, a Baptist from the Protestant moral heartland of central Ohio, kept both a mistress and a well-stocked liquor cabinet, even in the midst of Prohibition.[41]

But even when the guardians of morality were not so blatantly hypocritical as Harding, they turned a blind eye to the sins of their middle-class Protestant supporters. While championing "self-reliance" and celebrating the prosperity of the 1920s, they said nothing about the black sharecroppers who were trapped in debt peonage or the child laborers who were working in southern textile mills and Appalachian coal mines. Their public invocations of God in the 1950s usually endorsed, rather than questioned, American values. Rather than seek to apply God's standards as a corrective to American sin, they instead sought God's blessing for the pursuit of the "American way of life." Most of this was the work of mainline Protestants, but when evangelicals gained control of the party at the end of the twentieth century, their choice of moral issues was just as selective. The Christian Right showed little concern for the issues that energized liberal Christians—that is, issues of structural racism, poverty, lack of access to health care, unjust wars, and a growing divide between the rich and the poor. Even on "family values" issues, the movement largely ignored divorce, which arguably had a more direct effect than homosexuality on most American families, and demonstrated little ability to counteract the effects of the sexual revolution. The out-of-wedlock birthrate continued to rise during Reagan's time in office, increasing from 19 percent of all births in 1981 to 27 percent in 1989. Today it is 40 percent.[42]

The Christian Right's selection of moral issues probably reflected the values of the early Cold War years more than the values of Jesus. It was based on the assumption that the fusion of militaristic, anticommunist patriotism, civil religion, and intact heterosexual families that had been the public face of America during the Eisenhower administration of the 1950s could be restored through the election of the right political leaders. While there were a few parts of this agenda that could be traced to the Bible—after all, warnings about sexual immorality are pervasive in Scripture—the general assumptions behind the Christian Right's program are difficult to square with the gospel. In particular, its fusion of social morality, military might, and public expressions of Christian piety is a uniquely American distortion of Christianity that reflects the state of American politics in the early years of the Cold War. This distortion was based in part on a confusion between God's covenant promises to ancient Israel and God's relationship with the United States. The most popular verse for the Christian Right was 2 Chronicles 7:14: "If my people, which are called by my name, shall humble themselves, and pray, and seek my face, and turn from their wicked ways, then will I hear from heaven, and will forgive their sin, and will heal their land" (KJV). When President Reagan took the oath of office, he had his Bible open to this verse, because it was popular with his Christian Right supporters.[43] But if read in context, it is clear that this verse pertains specifically to God's covenant people in the Old Testament; it is not a blanket promise to bless the United States if the nation seeks the Lord. In assuming that the United States was a Christian nation that could repent through political change and therefore receive God's blessing, the Christian Right confused theological, national, and political categories and demonstrated a distorted understanding of the nature of God's covenants.

The project of Christian moral regulation has overestimated the power of law to redeem society. Jerry Falwell, like many other conservative evangelicals of his generation, believed that God would judge the United States as a nation if it failed to repent of its sins, and he assumed that conservative Christians could save the nation from this judgment by passing laws enforcing morality. But was this a theologically valid assumption? Both the Old Testament prophets and the book of Revelation describe judgments on pagan nations, as well as individuals, who rebelled against God's standards of justice, so it might be reasonable to assume that the United States could experience God's judgment as a nation. Indeed, conservative Protestants in North America have been warning about the possibility of collective judgment since the seventeenth-century New England Puritans. And perhaps the United States has already experienced many divine judgments. Abraham

Lincoln thought that the bloodshed of the Civil War might have been God's judgment for the sin of slavery. Others have interpreted national catastrophes, financial collapses, and foreign wars as judgments of God.[44] It is impossible to know for certain whether they are, but the idea that God might mitigate the effects of sin by curbing evils through violent or catastrophic means certainly accords well with the biblical record.

But Christian Right activists are mistaken to think that the passage of legislation can be a primary means of averting national judgment, since there is no indication that righteous laws alone can protect a nation of people whose hearts are wicked. In fact, the opposite is the case. Under the covenant that God made with Israel, God called the prophet Jeremiah to issue a message of judgment during the reign of one of the most righteous legal reformers ever to occupy the throne of David (Jer. 1:2). If Josiah's top-down reforms were not enough to save the people of Judah from captivity, it is unlikely that whatever judgment God might have in store for the United States can be averted with laws that are not supported by a majority of the population. In the late 1970s, some conservative evangelicals erroneously believed that a majority of Americans supported their moral views, but that a small number of men on the Supreme Court or in Congress had stopped the majority from enforcing their moral code. They realized they were mistaken when they saw how little support they had for their agenda among both voters and governing officials, even in their own party. Though they eventually gave up most of their campaigns to impose morality through law, they still believed that on the issue of abortion, they could use a narrow majority to enforce an important moral precept. Protecting human life was a matter of such supreme importance, they thought, that even if they were able to get only a five-to-four majority on the Supreme Court and a narrow majority among voters, they could save unborn lives and end a great evil by legislating against abortion. But this view probably greatly overstates the ability of a law to change behavior. Some legislation undoubtedly does affect people's personal choices, but only when it is accompanied by cultural changes that reinforce such legislation. Laws that do not reflect prevailing cultural norms are usually ineffective. The Christian Right has focused far too much on changing laws and far too little on changing cultural values—and as a result, it has often experienced frustration at a lack of results. It is ironic, perhaps, that it has been "evangelicals"—a group whose name suggests the power of the gospel, rather than the law, to change behavior—who have been most blind to the dangers of trusting too much in the power of moral regulations.

Conservative Christians' current trust in a conservative Supreme Court to protect their own religious liberty is perhaps one of the most tragic chapters in their long relationship with political conservatism. Evangelicals' paranoia about what they might experience from a liberal Democratic administration is a deep sign of the distrust that pervades American politics today. It is an indication that evangelicals see little hope for their future in the normal democratic process; their only hope is to fill the nation's courts with as many conservatives as possible in hopes that their rights might be protected even when a majority moves against them. As John Fea argues in *Believe Me*, evangelicals who voted for Trump because of deep concern about what a liberal Democratic administration might do to them chose fear over faith.[45] This does not necessarily mean that no evangelical should have voted for Trump. But it does mean that the grounds on which many evangelicals made that decision represented a self-interested calculation or an anxiety about protecting their own interests that does not accord well with gospel injunctions to love our neighbor and to not be anxious about the future. If the early Christians had devoted as much effort to protecting themselves against the possibility of religious persecution as American conservative Christians are doing today, the book of Acts would have unfolded very differently.

The heresy of the Christian Right and evangelicals' long-standing alliance with political conservatism has manifested itself during the past seventy years in an uncritical patriotism, an unthinking acceptance of foreign wars, a lack of concern about structural racism and poverty, and a confusion about the power of law to change behavior. Perhaps most tragically, the Christian Right has confused the public about the meaning of evangelical Christianity and has caused people to mistake a political program for the gospel.

The Christian Nationalism of the Trump Era

Evangelical opponents of the Christian Right have warned for decades about the dangers of confusing middle-class values with the gospel. What they did not foresee was the possibility that the Republican Party would change and become the party not of the suburban middle class but the rural disillusioned white working class. As recently as 2012, the rural white areas of the northern and eastern Midwest were still largely Democratic, and the Republican Party was still the party of white suburbanites and wealthier whites. But the 2016 presidential election and 2018 midterms suggest that this is changing. For the first time in the Republican Party's history, the GOP's strongest base of electoral support may come from white rural low-income areas. While white voters with college degrees supported Trump by a four-point margin in 2016, this level of support for Trump increased to a thirty-nine-point margin among whites without college degrees. Whites without college degrees, especially in the rural South, had been trending Republican for several years, but never by such large margins. The 2016 election saw the largest gap between college-educated and non-college-educated voters in more than three decades, and this time, the non-college-educated were voting Republican—a reversal of historic patterns.[46] It may still be too early to say definitively whether this phenomenon was a temporary aberration or, as is more likely, the beginning of a long-term shift in the Republican Party's identity, but if it does last, it may change how we as Christians should think about the GOP. If historically, Christians who have allied with the Republican Party have made the mistake of ignoring the needs of the poor and conflating middle-class values with the gospel, will the rebranding of the GOP as the party of the white working class solve this problem?

No, it will not. Most of the white Republican working-class voters are at least culturally or nominally Christian. And they are sensitive to the needs of those with lower-than-average incomes, since they themselves largely fit this category. But their concept of the meaning of Christianity may be even further removed from the gospel than the Christian Right's version of religion was.

For all its faults, the Christian Right's moral campaigns were at least rooted in a concern for justice and for others' well-being, because they reflected the long-standing evangelical desire to see a moral transformation in society based on an application of the Christian message. Just as some of the early nineteenth-century evangelicals of the Second Great Awakening wanted to make society more holy by eradicating slavery, drunkenness, and dueling, so the evangelicals who launched the Christian Right in the late twentieth century wanted to save lives and fight sin by banning abortion and same-sex marriage. And just as some of the northern evangelicals of the mid-nineteenth century wanted to "die to make men free" as Christ "died to make men holy," so the evangelicals of the mid- to late twentieth century supported wars against international Communism (and, in the early twenty-first century, wars against international Islamic terrorism) in the name of Christianity in order to protect religious liberty and democracy around the globe. But the populist Christian nationalists of the early twenty-first century lack this transformative vision for society. They are very interested in reestablishing a culturally Christian national identity— as evidenced, for example, by protests against the replacement of "Merry Christmas" with "Happy holidays"—but there is no vision for national moral transformation or international freedom.

The Christian nationalism of the Trump era bears a close resemblance not to traditional American evangelical political campaigns but rather to the Christian nationalism of the European populist far right, as conservative Catholic columnist Ross Douthat noted in 2015.[47] The European right is not rooted in evangelicalism (because evangelicalism has virtually no political influence in Europe), but it is nominally Christian. Yet its "Christian" identity has less to do with any specific moral platform than with a strong opposition to Muslim immigration and a vague support for keeping Europe white and nonalien. The same has been true of President Trump's approach to immigration and other related cultural issues. And just as the "Christian" identity movements of Europe's far right are rapidly gaining ground in a society that has been post-Christian for at least half a century, so the populist "Christian" nationalism of the Republican Party has rapidly gained ground in white rural areas where church attendance rates might have fallen, but where a residual cultural Christianity still thrives. The result has been a party that champions the causes most appealing to its white rural constituency, with a libertarian stance on Second Amendment rights combined with a strongly nonlibertarian stance on support for the police. It is a party that has now largely abandoned a neoconservative desire to defend freedom around the world and has exchanged this for a neo-isolationism of "America first." Above all, the new rural conservative populism is strongly suspicious of immigration, just as Europe's right-wing parties are. In the 1980s, the Republican Party of Ronald Reagan was arguably more pro-immigrant than many Democrats were—since business interests have long championed more open borders—and as late as the first decade of the twenty-first century, Republican candidates George W. Bush and John McCain favored immigration reform that would offer a path to citizenship for the millions of undocumented immigrants currently in the United States. But this is no longer true of the Republican Party today.

There have been a few cases in American history when at least some evangelicals have embraced a populist, rural Christian nationalism that might look vaguely similar to the populist, rural Christian nationalism of the contemporary Republican Party. In the 1930s, Christian newspaper editor Gerald Winrod of Kansas and Christian broadcaster Gerald L. K. Smith promoted a strongly anti-Semitic, isolationist brand of Christian nationalism that Smith, a Disciples of Christ minister, called "America First."[48] In the late 1960s, a number of white southern Protestants supported Alabama governor George Wallace's presidential campaign platform that combined opposition to civil rights for African Americans with a call for a return of classroom prayer in public schools and a restoration of traditional values in opposition to the liberal "pointy-headed bureaucrats."[49] But thankfully, evangelical support for these rural populist movements was low, and neither of the nation's political parties embraced these movements at the time. Most of the nation's evangelical leaders tried to distance themselves from the openly racist or xenophobic Christian nationalist movements of the early to mid-twentieth century. At first, the same was true with Trump. Wallace's voters in the presidential election of 1968 bore a distinct resemblance to Trump's supporters in the Republican presidential primaries of 2016: they were likely to hold "fundamentalist" beliefs, but they were less likely than others to attend church.[50] There was probably a good reason for this. The Christian nationalism of Winrod, Smith, and Wallace was grounded not in a hope for gospel transformation or even for the success of moral regulation but rather in a rural white anxiety about forces that they believed were threatening their way of life. And the same is probably true of the rural white Christian nationalism of many of Trump's supporters, just as it is true of much of the European anti-immigrant right today.

Yet even though Trump's candidacy initially appealed most strongly to unchurched "evangelicals" rather than to faithful church attenders, after Trump won the Republican presidential nomination, many white evangelicals who had not supported him in the primaries rallied to his side, and since then, white evangelicals have been his strongest base of support. For some, this is a matter merely of political expediency, while others have genuinely come to believe in the need for a strong "warrior" protecting Christian interests, as Trump supporter and Baptist pastor Robert Jeffress phrased it.[51] And just as some evangelical supporters of Republican conservatism in the 1970s and 1980s conflated white middle-class suburban fears about rising crime rates and social welfare costs with Christian principles, so some evangelical supporters of the contemporary Republican Party have conflated white working-class rural fears about immigration, gun control, and cultural change with Christianity. The result may be even more catastrophic for the gospel than the Christian conservatism of the late twentieth century was, because the Christian nationalism of the contemporary Republican Party is even further removed from historic evangelicalism—and certainly further removed from historic Christian principles, at least in its attitude toward immigrants and marginalized racial minorities.

What Can Christians Do?

Like most Christian heresies, the political conservatism of the Republican Party is a distortion of the truth, not a complete negation of it. The moral regulation that the GOP has long championed was based on a justified abhorrence of social evils. Alcohol abuse was a genuine social problem in the late nineteenth and early twentieth centuries, and the supporters of Prohibition were right to be alarmed by it. Soviet Communism was diametrically opposed to many of the principles of God. The sexual revolution of the 1960s promoted sinful thinking. Abortion is an assault on human life that the church has rightly considered evil, whether in the second century or the twentieth. Marriage is a divinely created institution that is an essential foundation for a healthy society, and it deserves to be protected. Negative social consequences really do result from separating sex from marriage or individual rights from social responsibility. Though they might sometimes overestimate the power of law to effectively regulate individual vice, conservatives are certainly right to believe that in a world of sin, prohibitions on sin are needed—a point that too many liberals have completely ignored.

Political conservatism has also preserved an important biblical truth about the best way to fight social evils such as poverty: a belief that churches and families, rather than the state, should be the primary agents of social change. Christians who believe in original sin and who heed the warnings about sinful empires that pervade much of the Bible (especially the books of Daniel and Revelation) should be suspicious about any attempt to transfer large amounts of responsibility from families and churches to a secular state. It is no accident that many of the leading conservative intellectuals of the twentieth century—such as William F. Buckley Jr., a lifelong Catholic, and Russell Kirk, a Catholic convert—were strong believers in God and the role of the church. Both in their skepticism about the possibility of substantially improving society in a world of sin and in their insistence that social reform should be directed by the church and the family rather than by the state, conservatives both in the mid-twentieth century and today are much closer than liberals to historic Christian theology. To a large extent, the Republican Party's current faults are a result not of being too conservative but rather of embracing a free-market individualism that has departed from the cautionary pessimism about unregulated human nature that pervaded the writings of conservative intellectuals, from the eighteenth-century Edmund Burke to the twentieth-century Kirk and Buckley.

Christians' answer to the heresies of the Republican Party, then, is not necessarily the liberalism of the Democratic Party. For many Christians, it might instead be a thoughtful conservatism that preserves the tradition's healthy suspicion of federal bureaucracy and that honors the Bible's injunctions to care for the poor and protect the sojourner, while insisting that churches and families, rather than the federal government, should take the lead in doing this. This thoughtful conservatism might retain the Republican Party's historic interest in moral regulation, but it would look at the likely effect, and not merely the language, of each legislative proposal to determine whether it would promote moral behavior. And it would not be satisfied with merely ratifying the morality of middle-class white America in public law. In keeping with the Christian vision of a gospel for all races and nations, it would be sensitive to the concerns of racial minorities, immigrants, and other groups that the Republican Party has too often ignored. But to do this, Christians who are thoughtful conservatives will need to avoid a partisan loyalty to the GOP.

The moral regulation that the Republican Party has championed has largely been a failure. It has not been very effective in eradicating the vices that it targeted, and it has too often hurt the poor. But there is a way that Christians can reduce abortion rates and promote biblical marriage while also providing substantive help for the poor and racial minorities. The policies of the Republican Party will not accomplish this. But when coupled with a holistic biblical worldview and an ethic of love for one's neighbors, the long-standing conservative commitment to defending Christian-based morality can achieve these aims. The solution, though, might look very different from what conservative evangelical Republicans have envisioned.

2

The Secularized Liberal Protestantism of the Democratic Party

I know that the LORD secures justice for the poor and upholds the cause of the needy.

—Psalm 140:12

The righteous care about justice for the poor, but the wicked have no such concern.

—Proverbs 29:7

"The humblest citizen in all the land when clad in the armor of a righteous cause is stronger than all the whole hosts of error that they can bring," the speaker at the 1896 Democratic national convention declared at the beginning of what would become one of the famous political speeches in American history. "I come to speak to you in defense of a cause as holy as the cause of liberty—the cause of humanity." During the next few minutes, he outlined the evils of a gold-based monetary system that exacerbated the wealth divide between the wealthy capitalists and their struggling workers, never hesitating to use the moral language of what he said were "eternal" principles. But what brought the audience to their feet in loud cheers and prompted some to throw their coats in the air in exultation was his closing invocation of Christian imagery on behalf of the principle of economic justice. "You shall not press down upon the brow of labor this crown of thorns," he thundered. "You shall not crucify mankind upon a cross of gold." The next day, the excited Democratic delegates nominated the speaker, thirty-six-year-old evangelical Presbyterian William Jennings Bryan, as their party's candidate for president. Over the course of his campaign, he received thousands of adulatory letters from evangelical Christians across the Midwest, Great Plains, and rural South who shared his view that the Republican Party's monetary policy was morally wrong and opposed to the principles of Jesus. And though he never won the presidency, Bryan was the Democratic presidential nominee in three different elections—a record for any presidential candidate.[1]

Bryan's brand of evangelical Democratic populism reflected the values of numerous evangelicals, especially in the South and rural Midwest. Until at least the 1950s, a majority of the nation's Baptists and southern evangelicals consistently voted Democratic in presidential elections and lauded the party's championship of the white working class. If the evangelicals of the northern Midwest were loyal Republicans, the evangelicals of the South and, for a while, parts of the Great Plains voted Democratic, and they were no less convinced than Republican Christians that their party reflected the principles of Jesus. While the Republican Party was the party of Protestant moral regulation and piety, the Democratic Party was the party that claimed to emulate Jesus's injunction to care for the poor. Over the course of the twentieth century, the Democratic Party's message of Christian-inspired social justice attracted the support of the vast majority of Catholics, black Christians, and liberal Protestant clergy. Even today, the group of people who, according to public opinion surveys, are the most consistent churchgoers, dedicated Bible readers, and committed prayer warriors in the United States are also the most strongly committed Democrats, because black women are, in general, simultaneously the most dedicated Christians and the most loyal Democratic voters in the nation.[2] The Democratic Party has been filled with religious believers for decades—which is why its recent secular turn has perhaps been surprising. Contemporary Democratic secular liberalism is a Christian heresy, but like most heresies, it contains under its layer of falsehoods a certain measure of Christian truth.

The Democratic Party's Origins

The Democratic Party of the nineteenth century would be almost unrecognizable to most Democrats today. Closer to modern libertarianism than to the social welfare liberalism that most Democrats have favored for the past eighty years, the Democratic Party of Andrew Jackson and his political heirs favored states' rights and limits on moral regulation, especially when the issue was civil rights for African Americans. Proudly proclaiming itself the party of white men and eschewing the moralistic rhetoric of their northern evangelical opponents, the Democrats of the antebellum era became a majority party by creating a coalition of ambitious southern slaveholders, poorer southern whites, and northern urban workers. The antebellum Democrats took a dim view of the rights of Native Americans (which some Whigs occasionally championed on humanitarian grounds), and they eagerly supported the nation's expansion in the Mexican War and the hardnosed negotiations with Britain over Oregon. All of this was justified, they believed, for the sake of expanding democracy.

But behind this support for numerous racist measures that modern liberal Democrats now oppose was one constant: a concern for the rights of people who did not have much wealth or privilege. Though initially the party's interest in the poor did not extend much beyond the number of lower-income people who happened to be both white and male, the party was strongly devoted to their cause in their battles against the wealthy. Favoring universal white manhood suffrage, regardless of wealth or property ownership, Democrats were the champions of the idea of one man, one vote. The president who is often credited as a founder of the party, Andrew Jackson, gloried in his lack of formal education and rough ways, which included frequent swearing, dueling, and threats to use physical violence against his opponents—an image that endeared him to commoners that the upper class considered the unruly "rabble."[3]

It might have seemed like an odd party for evangelicals. Jackson was a Presbyterian (though his level of theological awareness or piety could be questioned), but he found himself at odds with Presbyterian ministers over governmental Sabbath observances. Many Presbyterian ministers opposed Sunday mail delivery as a violation of the fourth commandment, but Jackson and other Democrats argued that Sabbath observances were beyond the purview of Congress to legislate. Maintaining a stronger separation of church and state than some of the Whigs wanted, Democrats argued that it was not the government's place to legislate either religious observances or moral precepts. Even dueling should be free from federal legislation, some argued; if men wanted to shoot at each other to settle a matter of honor, they should have that right, regardless of the New England Whig Congregationalist preacher Lyman Beecher's campaign against the practice. And certainly slavery should not be the federal government's concern, they said. Many northern Congregationalist and Presbyterian evangelicals were aghast, but in the southern states and on the frontiers, and among some of the low-church, working-class evangelicals in the North, a large number of Bible believers championed the Jacksonian Democrats as true egalitarians who would protect Christians against the tyranny of a moral or religious establishment. A number of southern white evangelicals were alarmed at the propensity of northern Christians to impose their own moral opinions that went far beyond the Bible. The Bible explicitly sanctioned slavery, they argued, yet liberal northern antislavery advocates were abandoning biblical orthodoxy in order to impose their unbiblical moral opinions on southern Christians.[4]

But in spite of their unapologetic racism, Jacksonian Democrats, in their best moments, were their era's leading defenders of the God-given human dignity that belonged to every person regardless of income or social status (even if they did not recognize that it belonged to every person regardless of race). "The rights of man belong to him as man . . . an immediate gift from him that is over all," the *Democratic Review* declared in 1840. "They belong to man as an individual, and are higher than human constitutions or human laws."[5]

This enthusiastic endorsement of the right of the common people gave the Democrats a string of political victories between the 1830s and the 1850s, but the Civil War ended the Democratic Party's dominance of national politics for more than half a century. Although most southern whites, along with many Catholic (especially Irish) immigrants, remained loyal to the Democratic Party in the late nineteenth and early twentieth centuries, the strong support that the Republican Party enjoyed among Union veterans and their families was sufficient to deprive the Democrats of national victories most of the time. The Democrats held the White House for only sixteen of the sixty-four years between 1869 and 1933. And during many of those years, the Democrats struggled to forge a cohesive political philosophy. In the early twentieth century, the party was badly divided between two groups who had almost nothing in common except poverty and a hatred of Republicans: urban Catholic workers in the North who opposed Prohibition, and rural Protestants in the South who supported Prohibition and were suspicious of both Catholics and blacks. Even on the issue of monetary policy or the level of appropriate federal regulatory control, Democrats could not agree.[6] But during the course of the early twentieth century, a shift in Christian theology occurred that laid the groundwork for a sea change in the Democratic Party's ideological orientation.

Liberal Protestantism, Catholic Social Teaching, and American Political Liberalism

In the 1880s and 1890s, several northern Protestant ministers, including Ohio Congregationalist Washington Gladden and New York Baptist Walter Rauschenbusch, began proclaiming that the pursuit of the kingdom of God required the reform of social structures that perpetuated wealth inequality. In the absence of a minimum wage, unemployment insurance, or other government social welfare programs, unskilled urban laborers were often only a paycheck away from starvation. In times of economic prosperity, immigrants poured into New York harbor at the rate of several thousand per day, and they crowded into cheap, decrepit tenement apartment buildings, where twenty people shared a single toilet and where sometimes as many as a dozen men shared a bedroom. The women worked in garment factories, where they sewed clothes for more than seventy hours per week, at the rate of only pennies per hour. The men worked on the docks or in factories. The children sold newspapers on the streets if they were lucky or cobbled together less reliable sources of income if they were not. And in times of economic downturn, workers could be turned out into the streets. So could orphans. When journalist Jacob Riis took his camera to the streets of New York to document the city's poverty at the end of the 1880s, one of the shocking pictures he captured was of two young boys, neither one of whom was yet an adolescent, huddled together on top of a steam grate as they tried to sleep outdoors in the middle of a New York winter. Neither boy was wearing shoes. Another image showed two equally young boys staring at the camera with sunken eyes while wearing ragged clothes that they had outgrown. One of the barefoot boys in the picture had toes that were blackened and eaten away by frostbite.[7]

Rauschenbusch could have avoided looking at these scenes of poverty if he had chosen. He grew up in upstate New York in a relatively privileged family and earned a seminary degree from a school in Rochester that could have set him on the path toward a comfortable pastoral position at an up-standing middle-class northern Baptist church. But Rauschenbusch instead accepted a pastorate in one of the poorest areas of New York City—an area around West 42nd Street nicknamed "Hell's Kitchen," where Irish gangs had once roamed and where poverty was still rampant. As he reflected on how the church could address the needs of the community, he began proclaiming that Christians could usher in the kingdom of God by helping their neigh-bors, a path that often required political action.[8]

Protestant advocates of this "social gospel," as Rauschenbusch called it, distanced themselves from more conservative forms of evangelicalism by abandoning evangelicalism's traditional emphasis on personal conversion and instead giving primacy to societal reform. They also, in many cases, abandoned conservative Protestantism's emphasis on the atoning death of Christ, the doctrine of original sin, and the belief in the Bible's infallibility. Combining a deep admiration for the personal example and moral teach-ings of Jesus with an interest in the new social science and evolutionary theory of their day, they proclaimed a scientifically minded Christianity that emphasized social progress through humanitarian efforts and the pro-motion of democracy. Politics became a holy calling for a new generation of college-educated liberal Protestants. In the early twentieth century, some left-leaning secular critics of capitalism, such as Eugene V. Debs and Upton Sinclair, embraced socialism, and some evangelical revivalists, such as Billy Sunday, uncritically endorsed the capitalist system, but the liberal Christian advocates of the social gospel proclaimed a third way: regulated capitalism, with an emphasis on the protection of workers. Unlike many of the more conservative evangelicals of the era, they were enamored with the idea of creating large democratic institutions to combat social evils. The idea of creating a unified Protestant front for social action especially appealed to them. In 1908, representatives from most of the nation's mainline Protes-tant denominations, including Congregationalists, Methodists, Presbyteri-ans, and Northern Baptists (but not Southern Baptists), formed the Federal Council of Churches, whose name would later be changed to the National Council of Churches.[9]

The Federal Council made it clear from the outset that the reform of society through politics would be one of their major goals. The "Social Creed of the Churches" that the Federal Council adopted in 1908 proclaimed, "We deem it the duty of all Christian people to concern themselves directly with certain practical industrial problems." "The Churches," the Federal Council stated, "must stand for equal rights and complete justice for men in all stations of life." This included the "abolition of child labor," "the protection of the worker from dangerous machinery, occupational disease, injuries and mortality," "a living wage," "suitable provision for the old age of workers and for those incapacitated by injury," and "the abatement of poverty."[10]

This was not the first time that American Protestants had taken the lead in spearheading a progressive reform cause. Fifty years earlier, the pastors of some of the same northern Protestant churches that supported the Federal Council had joined in the campaign against slavery. But most previous evangelical political campaigns (especially the temperance movement, nineteenth-century American evangelicalism's signature political cause) focused on the regulation of vice; they had rarely seen sin in structural, rather than strictly individual, terms. The Federal Council and the liberal Protestants who supported it did not abandon these efforts; indeed, they may have equaled evangelicals in their zeal for the campaign against alcohol. But they also believed that social evil was rooted not only in individual moral choices but in the social economic structure. The pursuit of social justice, they believed, would involve not only the regulation of vice but the promotion of human rights—and not only the prohibition of individual actions but the legal mandate for better working conditions.

The social gospel was an important impetus for the Progressive movement in the late nineteenth and early twentieth centuries. Not all Progressives were liberal Protestants, but a large number were, and many viewed their campaigns for the regulation of working hours, wages, monopolies, and child labor as a product of their Christian faith. One of the most widely distributed Christian books in America, Kansas Congregationalist minister Charles Sheldon's *In His Steps* (1897), answered the question, "What would Jesus do?" with a vision for social reform. When President Theodore Roosevelt launched his Progressive Party in order to promote a social vision that the Republican Party under William Howard Taft's leadership refused to accept, he attracted many liberal Protestant supporters. His Progressive Party convention of 1912 had the feel of a religious revival. "We stand at Armageddon, and we battle for the Lord," Roosevelt proclaimed. His delegates showed their enthusiasm for his campaign by singing "Onward, Christian Soldiers."[11]

Even though Roosevelt did not win the 1912 presidential election, the candidate who did—Woodrow Wilson—was perhaps even more committed to a liberal Protestant vision of social justice. The son of a southern Presbyterian minister, Woodrow Wilson was reared in the Calvinist tenets of an evangelical faith, but as a college student, he exchanged his Calvinism for a liberal Protestant faith that accepted higher criticism of the Bible, evolutionary theory, a more optimistic vision for individual and social betterment, and, above all, a vision of Christianity that centered on the promotion of democracy and societal reform. Politics for him became a Christian calling that would "make the world safe for democracy." As president, he signed into law legislation abolishing child labor, regulating monopolies, restricting workdays to eight hours in some industries, and creating the Federal Reserve Board to regulate banking and the nation's monetary system. But his greatest effort for justice and the promotion of democracy came in international relations. After contributing to the Allied victory over Germany in the First World War, he convinced the peace conference that followed the conflict to agree to the creation of a League of Nations, the forerunner to the United Nations. The idea of a global democratizing effort to guard against future wars appealed to liberal Protestants, who emphasized the equality of all humanity under the universal fatherhood of God. Wilson's commitment to universal equality never entirely transcended his own prejudices. Despite being elected with the support of several prominent African American leaders, including W. E. B. DuBois, he acted against African American rights as president by segregating the post office. He also agreed to the greatest restriction on civil liberties, including especially the right of free speech, that the United States has ever had during wartime. The expanded state power that Wilson favored could be used for anti-egalitarian ends, even when pursued in the name of equality. Wilson's own party members were not always entirely sure what to make of it, and a substantial number of Democrats remained committed to the vision of limited federal power and defense of states' rights that had characterized the party for nearly a century. But Wilson did take an important initial step in infusing the party with a liberal Protestant vision of expanded state power on behalf of democracy and social justice.[12] It would be up to Franklin D. Roosevelt to complete the implementation of that vision.

As a president who took office in a landslide during the depths of the Great Depression, Roosevelt was given a mandate to completely restructure the nation's economy and government, and he used that mandate not only to create the New Deal but also to change the Democratic Party and even the meaning of the word *liberal*. Before the twentieth century, the word *liberal* had meant an advocate of free trade and civil liberties, but Roosevelt used the term to describe the social welfare vision that was similar in some ways to early twentieth-century Progressivism. Under his administration, the Democratic Party became thoroughly committed to liberalism. No longer would it be the states' rights party of the past. Instead, it would adopt the social welfare vision of many liberal Protestants.[13]

As a Harvard-educated Episcopalian, Franklin Roosevelt shared the generic liberal Protestant belief of many people of his social class and background that the essence of Christianity was the Golden Rule and a concern for equal treatment for all. Though he did not invoke religious imagery nearly as often as Woodrow Wilson had, he indicated on occasion that he saw the New Deal as a fundamentally Christian project, if Christianity was defined in terms of the liberal Protestantism of his day. "We call what we have been doing 'human security' and 'social justice,'" he told a group of Protestant ministers in 1938. "In the last analysis all of these terms can be described by one word, and that is 'Christianity.'"[14]

For Roosevelt, one central question he faced was how to persuade the wealthy that they had a moral duty to sacrifice their own self-interest by voting to pay higher taxes on their own income for the sake of helping others. This was the essence of the egalitarian democracy he favored, and for him, it was a moral imperative. But it required a change of vision from a narrow self-interest to a realization that all people were part of a universal human community—a principle that early twentieth-century liberal Christianity, with its emphasis on universal human "brotherhood," considered a cardinal principle, just as Roosevelt did. "The test of our progress is not whether we add more to the abundance of those who have too much," he declared in his Second Inaugural Address in 1937. "It is whether we provide enough for those who have too little. . . . In our seeking for economic and political progress as a nation, we all go up, or else we all go down, as one people." Those who, in his view, violated this egalitarian tenet for the sake of their own greed were worthy of the same excoriation that Jesus gave to his opponents, because they were acting contrary to the principles of both Christianity and morality. "The money changers have fled from their high seats in the temple of our civilization," he exulted when he took office in 1933. "We may now restore that temple to the ancient truths. The measure of the restoration lies in the extent to which we apply social values more noble than mere monetary profit."[15]

This moral framework depended directly on Christian ideals, in the view of Franklin and Eleanor Roosevelt. Because American democracy was "a method of government conceived for the development of human beings as a whole," "the citizens of a Democracy must model themselves on the best and most unselfish life we have known in history," Eleanor Roosevelt wrote in 1940. To secure the "vital gain in Democracy for the future," it was important to "base it on the Christian way of life as lived by Christ."[16] Eleanor's husband expressed the same sentiments. "It is my deep conviction that democracy cannot live without that true religion which gives a nation a sense of justice and moral purpose," he declared in 1936. "We have need of that devotion today. It is that which makes it possible for government to persuade those who are mentally prepared to fight each other to go on instead, to work for and to sacrifice for each other. That is why we need to say with the Prophet: 'What doth the Lord require of thee—but to do justly, to love mercy and to walk humbly with thy God.'"[17]

The Roosevelts acquired their understanding of Christianity's political vision from liberal Protestantism, but in some respects, it also closely accorded with the vision that many American Catholics held. The American Catholic Church of the early twentieth century was an immigrant church and a church for the poor. Built largely by Irish immigrants who had fled their country to escape the Potato Famine of the 1840s, the church had then welcomed successive waves of working-class Italian, Polish, and central European immigrants who depended on low-wage factory jobs for their survival. Accordingly, Catholics started talking about social justice for workers long before most American Protestants did. In the 1880s, Cardinal James Gibbons of Baltimore endorsed the rights of labor unions at a time when several state governors were using their state militias to break up strikes. When Pope Leo XIII issued the social justice encyclical *Rerum Novarum* in 1892, calling for industrialists to recognize their social obligations to those they employed, some American Catholic priests seized the opportunity to call for the government's commitment to protect the rights of workers. Father John A. Ryan wrote a book in defense of the "living wage" in 1906. The National Catholic Welfare Conference, the political arm of the nation's bishops, included a "living wage" in its list of social commitments in 1919, along with other proposals for an expanded social welfare state.[18]

After World War II, many American Catholic theologians and clergy argued for an international human rights ethic based on natural law. In accordance with the thinking of theologian Jacques Maritain, they argued that all human rights were derived from God (an idea they believed was enshrined in the Declaration of Independence's reference to the rights that were "endowed by their Creator"), and that these rights could be known by a reflection on the natural-law principles of Thomas Aquinas. The most foundational right was the right to life, followed closely by the principle of human dignity. All human relationships should be based on the principle of treating people with the dignity that they deserve as persons, Catholics argued, and the rights that the state recognized should be especially focused on the protection and preservation of the two-parent family. That meant, the nation's Catholic bishops argued in 1947, that people had a "right to economic security sufficient for the stability and independence of the family," along with "the right to housing adapted to the needs and functions of family life." Families had a right to receive financial assistance for their children, if needed, just as they had a right to governmental assistance in their children's education.[19]

Much of the liberal Catholic social vision—especially its advocacy of equitable wages, legal recognition of labor unions, and the need for governmental social assistance—closely paralleled New Deal liberalism and the views of liberal Protestants at the time. But Catholic social liberalism was more communal than Protestant liberalism was; it often gave more attention to the rights of families than the rights of individuals. For American civil libertarians, free speech was a nonnegotiable individual right, but for Catholic bishops of the 1940s, the right of families to receive "protection against immoral conditions in the community" could sometimes legitimate "decency laws" and other restrictions on pornographic literature.

The clash between Catholic and liberal Protestant versions of liberalism was especially evident in birth control policy. Many liberal Protestants of the 1930s and 1940s considered birth control a positive social good, and they advocated federal programs to make it available to the poor. Catholic bishops of that era viewed contraception as a devaluation of human life and a distortion of the purpose of sex, and they lobbied to keep birth control illegal in predominantly Catholic states, such as Connecticut and Massachusetts, where they still exercised strong political influence. But despite these occasional clashes between liberal Protestants and Catholics in the New Deal coalition, tension between the two groups rarely prevented either one from supporting the Democratic Party. Liberal Protestants, along with a few Jewish and secular allies, dominated New Deal policymaking, but Catholics were strongly supportive of the New Deal, and some, including Father John A. Ryan, held administrative posts in New Deal agencies.[20]

Evangelical Protestants, by contrast, were much less supportive of the New Deal, partly because many held to a strongly individualistic theology that made them suspicious of the large institutions that both liberal Protestants and Catholics favored. Many, especially in the North, held a dim view of the ability of the federal government to solve social and economic problems. In the South, many Baptists and other evangelicals who faced severe poverty welcomed the New Deal, at least initially. Although the Alabama Baptist Convention chided Roosevelt for repealing Prohibition, it enthusiastically endorsed his administration's attempts "to spread wealth; secure higher wages and shorter hours for labor; abolish child labor; to promote a planned industry to prevent unemployment; insurance and old age security; and other measures of social justice." But over the course of the 1950s, many white southern evangelicals distanced themselves from the support of poverty relief measures that they might have supported during the Great Depression. Particularly among the most fundamentalist of southern evangelicals, skepticism about the United Nations, a centerpiece of the postwar liberal agenda, remained strong. And when President Harry Truman proposed a system of government-administered national health insurance, Bob Jones College hosted a forum on its alleged dangers.[21]

But with or without evangelical support, both the Democratic Party and American liberals of the early postwar era connected their agenda of global democracy and social welfare provisions at home to a religious mandate. "Slowly but surely we are weaving a world fabric of international security and growing prosperity," President Truman declared in his inaugural address of 1949, in a typical liberal conflation of democracy, economic uplift, and a generic civil religion that was loosely based on a liberal Protestant interpretation of the social ethics of Jesus. "We are aided by all who long for economic security—for the security and abundance that men in free societies can enjoy. We are aided by all who desire freedom of speech, freedom of religion, and freedom to live their own lives for useful ends. Our allies are the millions who hunger and thirst after righteousness. . . . Steadfast in our faith in the Almighty, we will advance toward a world where man's freedom is secure. . . . With God's help, the future of mankind will be assured in a world of justice, harmony, and peace."[22] This liberal Protestant vision of international democracy remained the faith of postwar liberals until the 1960s. But at that point, the political ideology that had united liberals since the New Deal fragmented. So did the liberal Protestantism and Catholic political theology that had undergirded it.

The Fragmentation and Secularization of American Liberalism

The mid-twentieth-century liberal Protestant political vision rested on the assumption that democracy and human rights required a religious foundation—and possibly Christianity in particular, although most liberal Protestants of the early postwar era also accepted Jews as equal partners in the democratic enterprise.[23] But the social changes of the 1960s caused a younger generation of liberal Protestants to question this. Perhaps somewhat paradoxically, the initial cause of their doubts was a grassroots human rights movement that was so steeped in biblical language that one historian has called it a "religious revival."[24]

Many white liberal Protestant ministers and seminarians of the early to mid-1960s viewed the civil rights movement for African American equality as the primary moral cause of their own time, because it was a quest for equality and the full promise of American democracy—the values on which they had been raised. But they were shocked to discover that white Protestant churches gave the movement, at best, tepid support. Some white congregations in the South directly opposed the movement. Many others were silent about civil rights and acted as though the movement did not exist. The most theologically and politically liberal denominations gave the movement rhetorical support, but some of the younger progressives in those churches felt that they did little in the way of direct action. But on marches in the South, surrounded by other activists—most of whom were Christian, but a few of whom were Jews, Muslims, and nonbelievers—they experienced a more emotionally moving spiritual awakening than they had ever felt in seminary, even though many of their opponents were white Christians. If a significant section of the white church did not support the most important democratic and human rights cause of their own time, how could one believe that religion was necessary for democracy or human rights?

Much of the white church was also on the wrong side of the debate over the Vietnam War, progressives believed—as were many older liberals. While many Christians supported the Vietnam War as an anticommunist cause, a large number of young ministers on the left denounced it as evil, because of its use of napalm, Agent Orange, and a draft they believed was unjust. And if the Vietnam War was wrong, perhaps the entire Cold War and the American effort to spread democracy across the globe were based on wrong assumptions. Liberal Protestants who concluded this found that they had lost faith not only in their own Christian tradition but in Cold War liberalism itself.[25]

What was left of their shattered faith was a strong commitment to human rights and pluralism. Both of these were core values of mid-twentieth-century liberal Protestantism, but after the 1960s a growing number of liberal Protestants stripped these of their religious foundation—which now seemed superfluous or even misguided—and pursued these values for their own sake. And if some of the most politically progressive ministers of the late 1960s were pursuing this course, the liberal Protestants in the pews were doing so at an even greater rate. The Democratic Party increasingly became populated with a younger generation of white liberal Protestants who sometimes distanced themselves from religious observance but who remained more committed than ever to the liberal human rights, pluralistic vision that their religious heritage had produced.[26]

All the Democratic nominees for president after the 1960s shared this vision, and many were influenced in some way by liberal Protestantism—even as they often sought, in the name of pluralism, to avoid linking themselves too closely with a single religious tradition. George McGovern, the Democratic presidential nominee of 1972, was the son of a Methodist minister and was deeply shaped by the social gospel. Although he had largely abandoned church by the time he ran for president, he still quoted from the Sermon on the Mount on the campaign trail, and he denounced the Vietnam War with a moral fervor worthy of a revivalist. Jimmy Carter, the Democratic Party's presidential candidate of 1976, was a churchgoing Southern Baptist whose commitment to the church remained intact but whose theology moved to the left after reading Reinhold Niebuhr and Paul Tillich and embracing the cause of African American civil rights and international human rights. Walter Mondale, the party's nominee in 1984, was another Methodist minister's son, and Bill Clinton was another Baptist. Al Gore was a Southern Baptist who had attended Vanderbilt Divinity School. Barack Obama wrote at length about his spiritual home in a black congregation that was affiliated with the liberal Protestant denomination United Church of Christ. Hillary Clinton was a lifelong Methodist whose political ideology was shaped by the progressive commitments of some members of her denomination in the midst of the civil rights and antiwar movements. Although she was somewhat reticent to say very much about religion on the campaign trail, when she did, she spoke the theological language of the liberal Protestantism that she had imbibed as a child and that remained her moral guide as an adult. "I have always cherished the Methodist church because it gave us the great gift of personal salvation but also the great obligation of the social gospel," she told a gathering of Methodist women in 2014. "And I took that very seriously and have tried, *tried* to be guided in my own life ever since as an advocate for children and families, for women and men around the world who are oppressed and persecuted, denied their human rights and human dignity. . . . Like the disciples of Jesus, we cannot look away, we cannot let those in need fend for themselves and live with ourselves. We are all in this together."[27]

Regardless of their own personal religious backgrounds, all recent Democratic Party presidential candidates have shared the liberal Protestant commitment to pluralism and social betterment, along with the faith of Martin Luther King Jr. that "the moral arc of the universe is long, but it bends toward justice." As a result, even the most evangelically Christian (such as Jimmy Carter) have honored the value of pluralism by insisting that their moral commitments transcend their religious faith and that even non-Christians can share them, and even the most secular (such as Bernie Sanders) have proclaimed a message of social justice that seems indistinguishable from the exhortations preached from many liberal Protestant pulpits. Sanders, a Jew who characterized himself as "not actively involved with organized religion," sometimes sounded like a liberal Protestant on the campaign trail in 2016, as he cited Jesus's Sermon on the Mount in support of his calls for policies that would help the poor.[28]

In recent years, the Democratic Party has acquired a reputation among both secular people and Christians as the secular party, but this is not entirely accurate. It is true that religious "nones" are now much more likely to be Democrats than Republicans, and that at least among white evangelicals, higher church attendance rates are usually closely correlated with opposition to the Democratic Party.[29] And it is also true that Democratic Party platforms mention God less often than Republican Party platforms do. But the Democratic Party still receives some of its support from liberal Protestants, and its values, even when expressed in secular language, closely correlate with the values of liberal Protestantism. In addition, the Democratic Party receives strong support from at least four other groups of Christians: black Protestants, Hispanic Catholics, liberal white Catholics, and a relatively small contingent of progressive evangelicals.

African American Christians (most of whom are Protestant, but a few of whom are Catholic) are the most committed Bible readers and faithful church attenders in the United States today, and they share a strong commitment to social justice that leads them to support the Democratic Party. Approximately 90 percent of African American voters support the Democratic Party in presidential elections, with those who attend church every week nearly as likely as all other African Americans to favor the Democrats.[30] Although for decades they were significantly less likely than white liberals to support the Democratic Party's position on LGBT issues and abortion policy, black Christians became the nation's most loyal Democratic voters, because they shared the Democratic Party's commitment to poverty relief and concern for minority rights. For more than two centuries, African American Christians have read the Bible through the lens of the Exodus story and God's promise of deliverance for a community of the poor and enslaved, and as a result, the black church's theology has been much more communal than individualistic. And because they are much less likely than whites to see a sharp distinction between church and state, they believe that the policies of the government should reflect the social justice message of the Bible. Politics for many black churches is a holy and moral cause—which is why black congregations have for decades not hesitated to invite Democratic politicians to deliver campaign messages from their pulpits on Sunday mornings, and why black pastors have often been much less reticent than many white ministers to openly endorse candidates during church.[31]

White conservative evangelicals have often wondered how the black church can endorse a party that supports abortion rights, but black Christians have wondered how white Christians can support a party that, in their view, tramples on the rights of the poor. When North Carolina black Protestant pastor William Barber organized a "Moral Monday" movement to hold weekly demonstrations to bring attention to social injustice, his list of moral issues centered on health care, poverty relief, and voting rights, because the Bible said far more about caring for the poor than it did about abortion or homosexuality. "When you attack voting rights and then use that power gained by that, to attack living wages, then you attack health care and hurt millions of people," he said. "It's probably one of the most immoral things I've ever seen." Lives were literally at stake in the debate over health care, he thought—which meant that Republican politicians who tried to repeal Obamacare were about to "commit the sin of taking health care from the sick so that they can give tax cuts to the greedy, knowing that thousands will die unnecessarily." "The Bible talks about it in Ezekiel 22," he declared, "when politicians become like wolves devouring the people and do not care for the needy."[32]

If African American Christians have supported the Democratic Party because of their strong desire for economic and racial justice, Hispanic Catholics likewise vote Democratic (usually by a margin of more than two to one) because of their support for the party's immigration and economic policies.[33] More than half of Hispanic Catholics believe that abortion should be illegal—which means that Hispanic Catholics are more likely than non-Hispanic white Catholics to favor restrictive abortion policies. But for most of them, other issues are more important, and on those other issues, they overwhelmingly favor the Democrats. One 2016 Pew Research Center poll found that 87 percent of Latino Catholic voters listed immigration as an issue that would be important to their presidential choice. Health care and economic issues were also important determinants of how they would vote, they said.[34]

Perhaps it is not surprising that both black Protestants and Hispanic Catholics see poverty as a moral issue, because both of those groups are some of the most likely groups in America to be impoverished. In 2017, at a time when fewer than 9 percent of non-Hispanic whites were in poverty, 21 percent of blacks and 18 percent of Hispanics lived below the poverty line. For blacks, the experience of poverty remains especially acute. While non-Hispanic white households had a median annual income of $68,000, the median black household income was only $40,000. In 2017, nearly 20 percent of black households earned less than $15,000 a year, and an additional 24 percent earned between $15,000 and $35,000 a year. Black unemployment rates have consistently been twice as high as white unemployment rates for decades. When whites are experiencing record-low unemployment levels, blacks are experiencing recession-level downturns. And when whites are experiencing a recession, blacks are experiencing a Great Depression. Most of the African Americans fortunate enough to remain employed are only a missed paycheck or two away from a financial crisis, because they lack the wealth reserves that many whites take for granted. Only 38 percent of blacks have any retirement savings (compared to 66 percent of whites), and only 41 percent own their own homes (compared to 72 percent of whites). A few African Americans have, of course, earned comparatively high salaries; nearly 7 percent of black households in 2017 had an annual income of more than $150,000 per year. But even among wealthier blacks, Democratic voting and concerns about poverty predominate, perhaps because of the communal emphasis of black theology and the racism and economic insecurity that even high-income-earning African Americans experience. Even prosperous African Americans are far more likely to fall into poverty than whites earning similar incomes.[35] Given this experience, it's not surprising that blacks have noticed the two thousand verses in the Bible that discuss God's concern for the poor and less fortunate, even as those verses have been less central to the theology of many white evangelicals.[36]

The verses on poverty have also been central to the theology of many white Catholics, just as they have for Hispanic Catholics. "A basic moral test for any society is how it treats those who are most vulnerable," the United States Conference of Catholic Bishops declared in 2015. "In a society marred by deepening disparities between rich and poor, Sacred Scripture gives us the story of the Last Judgment (see Matt. 25:31–46) and reminds us that we will be judged by our response to the 'least among us.'" Just as the American Catholic Church supported the principles behind the New Deal in the 1930s, so today the American Catholic clergy are advocating for a social safety net to protect the most economically vulnerable members of society. "Afford-able and accessible health care is an essential safeguard of human life and a fundamental human right," the bishops declared in 2015.[37]

Similarly, immigrants' human dignity needed to be respected, regard-less of whether they entered the United States legally. Immigration reform should "include a broad and fair legalization program with a path to citizen-ship" for undocumented immigrants in the United States, the bishops stated. It should include a "work program with worker protections and just wages," along with "family reunification policies," "access to legal protections," and "refuge for those fleeing persecution and violence." All of this was a prac-tical application of Christian theology, the bishops believed. "The Gospel mandate to 'welcome the stranger' requires Catholics to care for and stand with newcomers, authorized and unauthorized, including unaccompanied immigrant children, refugees and asylum-seekers, those unnecessarily de-tained, and victims of human trafficking," they asserted.[38]

In keeping with the church's teaching, dozens of nuns, priests, and Cath-olic lay people subjected themselves to arrest in 2018 for engaging in civil disobedience in protest against what they considered inhumane immigra-tion policies by the Trump administration. And in 2019, the Catholic Legal Immigration Network, an agency founded by the United States Conference of Catholic Bishops, brought a lawsuit against the Trump administration to stop its policy of separating undocumented immigrant children from their families and detaining them in holding facilities at the border—a policy that may have contributed to the deaths of six children while in detention and the long-term involuntary separation of thousands of others.[39]

Progressive evangelicals joined in this call as well, as did liberal Prot-estants. But while liberal Protestants, most of whom were pro-choice and supportive of LGBT rights, generally had no reservations about support-ing the Democratic Party, Catholics and progressive evangelicals often felt more conflicted in their partisan allegiance. Although the Catholic bishops strongly opposed the Trump administration's immigration policies and its opposition to the Affordable Care Act, they also said that respect for all hu-man life, including the unborn, was their highest political priority, just as it had been for more than half a century. Abortion is such a deep concern for the Catholic Church that some Catholic bishops have denied communion to pro-choice Catholic politicians and have suggested that no Catholic can vote for a pro-choice politician in good conscience. While most bishops have not gone this far, nearly all of them hold to the Church's stance that abortion is a grave moral evil that may supersede other political issues. Similarly, the bishops have argued that because marriage and the family are the most important societal institutions, the Democratic Party's endorsement of same-sex marriage is a serious problem. Some evangelicals otherwise inclined to support the Democratic Party have also hesitated to do so because of these issues. Indeed, the Democratic Party's support for abortion rights and LGBT rights is only likely to increase, making it extremely difficult for Christians who care about the unborn and who hold to a historically Christian understanding of marriage and sexuality to be loyal Democrats.

The Democratic Party and the Sexual Revolution: Abortion and LGBT Rights

In 1976, 48 percent of Democratic voters supported a constitutional amendment to protect human life from the moment of conception and ban most abortions in the United States. But an equal number of Democrats supported abortion rights. Faced with the dilemma of balancing the concerns of these two groups at the 1976 Democratic national convention, party leaders at first tried to keep abortion out of the platform altogether and then, when that led to vociferous complaints from pro-choice feminists, steered the party toward a moderately worded compromise that repudiated attempts to reverse *Roe* through a constitutional amendment, but stopped short of directly endorsing abortion rights.[40] But however tepid this initial commitment to the pro-choice side was, Democrats had set their party's course on the trajectory of support for abortion rights, and over the course of the 1980s and early 1990s, they strengthened their party's stance on this issue. At the same time, the pro-life movement strengthened its commitment to the Republican Party, a commitment that turned the abortion debate into a heated partisan battle.

In the mid-1970s, the debate over abortion did not fall along partisan lines. Some of the strongest pro-choice advocates were Republicans, and some leading Democrats were pro-life. Pro-life activists, most of whom were Catholic, were often Democrats themselves. The Catholic Church still exercised a strong influence over the Democratic Party, but not as strong an influence as liberal Protestants did. In the contest between two liberal human rights claims—the right to life versus the right for women to equality and control of their own bodies—the Democratic Party opted for the right that most liberal Protestant denominations, and most of the party's growing secular contingent, favored. The Democratic Party became a strongly pro-feminist party by the end of the 1970s, choosing to deny funding in 1980 to any Democratic candidate who did not endorse the Equal Rights Amendment. Support for abortion rights seemed to many Democrats a necessary part of that feminist agenda, even if some Democrats held dissenting views. Also, in 1980, the party for the first time endorsed legislation to protect Americans from discrimination on the basis of "sexual orientation," a move that presaged its growing commitment to gay rights. This, too, was a move that liberal Protestants supported. In fact, the United Church of Christ had already adopted a similar resolution of opposition to discrimination on the basis of "sexual preference" five years earlier.[41]

When the Democratic Party's proposals for large federal social programs had been based on a set of values that both Catholics and Protestants shared, it had been easy for the two groups to unite in their support. But the sexual revolution and the feminist movement ended that moral consensus. Liberal Protestants and their secular allies adopted an individualistic understanding of sexuality that included support for abortion rights and gay rights (and eventually, same-sex marriage), and they no longer favored privileging the two-parent, male-headed nuclear family in their policies, as they had during the New Deal. In their view, they were merely continuing their traditional quest for equality. But in the view of many Catholics and their socially conservative Protestant allies, the liberal endorsement of abortion rights and alternative definitions of marriage undermined the entire liberal project, which they had always believed rested on the principle of human dignity, the right to life for all people, and the primacy of the family. Once this split in the Democratic coalition occurred, it became nearly impossible to unite the two groups of erstwhile allies in support of any legislation.[42]

Even health care, which the Catholic Church had supported for decades as one of its highest priorities, became a sore point for many theologically conservative Catholics because of abortion. President Barack Obama thought that he could unite a coalition around a health-care measure that would not include funding for surgical abortion, but would include a mandate for health plans to cover emergency contraception, such as Plan B and Ella, which were designed to block implantation of a fertilized egg within three to five days after sexual intercourse. The Obama administration did not consider these a form of abortion, but many pro-life advocates, including conservative Catholics and some evangelicals, did. They were outraged by a federal requirement that violated their deepest values and might require them to subsidize what they considered the destruction of human life at its earliest stages. The battle—fought over whether employers who had a conscientious objection to the contraceptive coverage mandated by the Affordable Care Act could opt out of providing such coverage—ended up in the Supreme Court. Although social conservatives won the case, many considered it a close call. Had it been up to the Obama administration, their right of religious liberty (as they saw it) would not have been protected.[43]

As battles over abortion and gay rights moved through the courts, Democrats rallied around a platform that advocated more aggressive defenses of both of these principles. In 2016, the Democratic Party added a promise to its platform to repeal the Hyde Amendment, a forty-year-old measure that had prevented federal taxpayer dollars from being used to fund most abortions. Because Democrats believed that every woman who wanted an abortion should have access to one, "regardless of where she lives, how much money she makes, or how she is insured," requiring the use of taxpayer money for abortion services was a necessary action. Similarly, the party's commitment to LGBT rights meant that Democrats could not allow private businesses to deny services to gay couples on the basis of their religious opposition to same-sex marriage. Conservative Catholics and evangelicals argued that religious freedom was a fundamental right of greater importance than most other rights, but many Democrats believed that the right to equality limited the parameters of religious freedom. "We support a progressive vision of religious freedom that respects pluralism and rejects the misuse of religion to discriminate," the 2016 Democratic Party platform declared.[44]

Since 2016, the Democratic Party's defense of abortion rights has only become more strident, especially as pro-choice activists in the party fear that *Roe* is more endangered than ever. In 2019, progressives in Illinois called for the state Democratic party to stop fundraising for a pro-life Democratic member of Congress from a Chicago suburb. The head of the Democratic Congressional Campaign Committee (who was also from Illinois) said that she could not deviate from party policy directing her to support incumbent members of her party, but she did signal her opposition to the pro-life congressman by refusing to attend his fundraiser.[45] The message was clear: Any Democrat who did not support the party's position on abortion could expect a cold shoulder from party officials and could anticipate a primary challenge from an abortion rights supporter. And indeed, the Illinois pro-life Democratic congressman did lose his party primary to a pro-choice challenger in the spring of 2020. But there were very few of these pro-life Democrats left anyway. In 1992, more than one-third of the Democratic members of the House of Representatives were pro-life, but by 2020 only two were left. And in the Senate, only two Democrats had lifetime ratings from the Planned Parenthood Action Fund of less than 100 percent.[46]

This was a pronounced shift from the Democratic Party platform of 2000, a year when the presidential nominee was Al Gore (a centrist Southern Baptist who had voted to restrict abortion in the 1980s before shifting to a pro-choice position) and the vice presidential candidate was the Orthodox Jew Joe Lieberman, a senator who was so far to the right of many members of his party that he would leave the Democrats and become an Independent only six years later. Gore, like Bill Clinton, believed that he could find common ground with pro-lifers by pursuing policies that would reduce the abortion rate by increasing access to contraception. He was wrong about the widespread appeal of this strategy among pro-life activists, but it was nevertheless an attempt to shift the Democratic Party's strategy on abortion toward the center, where Gore and many other Democrats of the 1990s believed that most voters were. The 2000 Democratic Party platform therefore declared: "Our goal is to make abortion less necessary and more rare, not more difficult and more dangerous. We support contraceptive research, family planning, comprehensive family life education, and policies that support healthy childbearing. The abortion rate is dropping. Now we must continue to support efforts to reduce unintended pregnancies, and we call on all Americans to take personal responsibility to meet this important goal." This was an effort to find common ground across the abortion divide, but in an even more direct bid for the support of pro-lifers, the party platform declared:

> The Democratic Party is a party of inclusion. We respect the individual conscience of each American on this difficult issue, and we welcome all our members to participate at every level of our party. . . . While the party remains steadfast in its commitment to advancing its historic principles

and ideals, we also recognize that members of our party have deeply held and sometimes differing views on issues of personal conscience like abortion and capital punishment. We view this diversity of views as a source of strength, not as a sign of weakness, and we welcome into our ranks all Americans who may hold differing positions on these and other issues. Recognizing that tolerance is a virtue, we are committed to resolving our differences in a spirit of civility, hope and mutual respect.[47]

This "spirit of civility, hope and mutual respect" toward different attitudes on abortion did not last very long, because many members of the Democratic Party believed that access to abortion was a fundamental right without which gender equality and the treatment of women as full human beings would be impossible. At times when access to abortion was still reasonably secure—as might have been the case in 2000, when abortion rights supporters could be confident of a comfortable six-to-three majority on the Supreme Court—pro-choice Democrats were more willing to extend an olive branch to members of their party with differing views. But when *Roe* appeared in imminent danger, the olive branches were withdrawn. In 2008, Democrats added stronger language in support of *Roe* to the platform, saying that "the Democratic Party strongly and unequivocally supports *Roe v. Wade* and a woman's right to choose a safe and legal abortion, regardless of ability to pay, and we oppose any and all efforts to weaken or undermine that right."[48] The 2012 and 2016 platforms reiterated and even expanded that language, with the 2016 platform representing the strongest expression of pro-choice views of any Democratic Party platform adopted up to that point.

Given the fear that many Democratic voters and candidates have expressed about the future of abortion rights in the United States, the 2020 Democratic Party platform will likely be even more specific and unequivocal in its defense of abortion rights, if that is possible. Most likely, it will suggest even stronger measures to make abortion a matter of federal rather than state policy, and to preserve federal funding for abortion as a fundamental right. And there will certainly be no suggestion that the party return to its pre-2004 stance of tolerance toward fellow party members who oppose abortion. Even though 14 percent of Democratic voters would like to make abortion illegal altogether and 29 percent identify themselves as "pro-life," party leaders and convention delegates will ignore these voters—as they have for more than a decade—and will make an uncompromising defense of abortion rights a centerpiece of their party platform.[49] The same will be true of LGBT rights. The 2016 platform suggested no compromise with those who held dissenting views on this issue, and the 2020 platform will not either.

As the Democratic Party moved against conservative Christian values on the issue of abortion rights and gay rights, many Christians believed that the party represented a threat to their own right to follow their conscience. If the Democrats had their way, conservative Christians' tax dollars would be used to fund abortions. Conservative Christian business owners would have to pay for their employees to have access to the morning-after pill. As they see it, they would be compelled to tacitly endorse same-sex marriages through the services that they would be forced to provide. Their religious liberty would be restricted to their own churches and religious organizations, but beyond those walls, they would not be free to live out the dictates of their faith without facing penalties. And that might be just the beginning of the changes. A new Democratic national health-care plan might go even further in funding abortions or sex-change surgeries.

Such fears are understandable, because the contingent of vocal secular voices in the Democratic Party is growing. While the Democratic Party is still home to a large contingent of Christians, it has also become the preferred choice of young secular voters, many of whom have little patience for the demands of Christian conservatives. Even as black and Hispanic Democrats remain heavily religious, the party's white voters (especially those who are millennials or who have graduate degrees) have become overwhelmingly secular. While 47 percent of black Democrats attend church every week (and an additional 36 percent attend at least once a month), only 22 percent of white Democrats are weekly church attenders, and 44 percent attend religious services "seldom or never." For some secular whites, their antipathy to conservative Christianity motivates them to embrace the secular, rights-conscious, LGBT-affirming policies of the Democratic Party. Sixty-eight percent of religious "nones" cast their ballots for Hillary Clinton in 2016; they favored Clinton over Trump by a more than two-to-one margin.[50] With 81 percent of white evangelical voters supporting Trump, it was easy to caricature the race as a contest between atheist Democrats and conservative Christian Republicans. The reality, of course, was considerably more complicated. A majority of Democrats were still Christian, just as Hillary

Clinton and her running mate, Tim Kaine, were. But it is also true that the particular strands of Christianity that the Democratic Party represents are not particularly sympathetic to conservative evangelical and Catholic views on abortion and same-sex marriage. Evangelical and conservative Catholic Christians would undoubtedly lose ground in both of those areas if the government were under Democratic control.

For some conservative Christians, the Democratic Party's perceived threat to Christian religious liberty was sufficient reason to reject it. For others, an even greater evil was the Democratic Party's adamant refusal to consider any curb on abortion, which pro-lifers believed amounted to murder. The abortion issue especially troubled some progressive evangelicals who would otherwise have been inclined to support the Democratic Party. Even Ron Sider, president of Evangelicals for Social Action and author of the politically progressive *Rich Christians in an Age of Hunger*, acknowledged sometimes voting for Republican presidential candidates because of his concern about the Democrats' stance on abortion.[51]

But perhaps the Democratic Party's stances on abortion, same-sex marriage, transgender rights, and religious liberty are not even the party's greatest deviation from a biblically shaped Christian theology. Perhaps instead it is a distortion of Christian teaching about sin and humanity that goes back to the origins of the social gospel and twentieth-century liberal Protestantism.

Liberal Protestants of the twentieth century were strongly committed to religious pluralism, human equality, and human perfectibility, because they minimized the problem of individual sin. They also had enormous faith in human institutions—whether denominational, educational, or political—to improve the world through democratic action. They had no use for the doctrine of original sin, at least in any recognizable orthodox form. The Democratic Party absorbed all these heretical beliefs.

Thus, when Bill Clinton accepted the Democratic presidential nomination in 1992, he gave a convention acceptance speech that was infused with scriptural language distorted to advance human possibility. Calling his campaign theme the "New Covenant," he declared, "In the end, my fellow Americans, this New Covenant simply asks us all to be Americans again. . . . When we pull together, America will pull ahead. Throughout the whole history of this country, we have seen, time and time and time again, that when we are united we are unstoppable. We can seize this moment, make it exciting and energizing and heroic to be American again. We can renew our faith in each other and in ourselves. We can restore our sense of unity and community. As the Scripture says, 'our eyes have not yet seen, nor our ears heard, nor minds imagined' what we can build."[52]

What Scripture actually says is "Eye hath not seen, nor ear heard, neither have entered into the heart of man, the things which God hath prepared for them that love him" (1 Cor. 2:9 KJV). Clinton, like many other liberal Protestants, reinterpreted scriptural promises of God's kingdom as descriptions of an earthly, human-created kingdom. Because there was no room in this theology for original sin, there was no perceived need for divine rescue.

One central danger for Christians who become enamored with the Democratic Party and contemporary American progressivism is that as they begin to equate the values of their party with the Bible's prophetic injunctions against injustice, they will likely find it difficult to keep their focus on the atonement and the coming of Jesus's kingdom. They will find it much easier to talk about Amos than Isaiah 53. They will find it easier to talk about Luke's Sermon on the Plain rather than Paul's Epistle to the Romans. While a Christian might be able to keep a focus on the gospel while working in a party whose scriptural invocations are nearly always saturated with the human-centered message of liberal Protestantism, it will not be easy. It was not easy for Christians to do this even in the era of the New Deal, when the Democratic Party's understanding of human life, sexuality, and the family largely reflected the beliefs of conservative Christians. It will be even more difficult for Christians to do this today, when the Democratic Party's understanding of these issues, like that of many liberal Protestants, has veered so far from historic Christian norms.

The Democratic Party has also veered away from what Catholic theology calls the principle of "subsidiarity" and what evangelical Protestants might call a family-centered politics. This principle says that although the social justice that the Democratic Party has pursued is a worthy goal, the primary agents for its pursuit are the local institutions that God has created: first the family, then the church, and then finally, as a last resort, the state. When the state attempts to solve a social problem, its goal should be to empower families, not interfere with them or replace them.[53] There are certainly social justice tasks that are too large for the family or church to solve. The economic problems of the Great Depression in the 1930s were large enough to require the intervention of the federal government, just as the health-care crisis is probably too large for any private institution to solve without federal intervention today. But not every crisis is like that, and even when it is, the federal government needs to do as much as it can to empower families, churches, and local institutions. When it does not, Christians need to be cautious. Conservative evangelical fears of the New Deal and the overreach of the federal government were probably greatly overblown, but they were also based on a legitimate scriptural principle: an overgrown state that usurps the responsibility of families and communities is a dangerous entity.

Perhaps it would be easier for biblically minded Christians who are concerned about the poor to vote Democratic if the Democratic Party's version of liberalism were less individualistic and sexually permissive and more strongly committed, as the party was in the late 1930s, to the biblical principles of human dignity, social responsibility, and the value of lifelong, heterosexual marriage. For the last half century, the Democratic Party has been moving away from these values, and it now appears that each successive election will drive the party even further away from the Christian principles that shaped modern Democratic Party liberalism in the New Deal era.

A Christian who votes Democratic will have to embrace a very different set of values than some of the ones outlined in recent Democratic Party platforms, especially in the areas of sexuality and rights-consciousness. Instead of insisting on their rights, as contemporary secular liberals (along with too many Christians) often do, followers of Jesus will have to be willing to relinquish their own privileges for the sake of others. If they vote Democratic, it will be because they are cross-centered rather than rights-centered. A middle-class white Christian who votes Democratic because she cares about the poor and is willing to pay higher health-care premiums herself in order to make sure that those with fewer economic resources will have access to affordable medical care may be practicing a version of cross-centered politics. A white Christian who supports a higher minimum wage, a path to citizenship for undocumented immigrants, or a scholarship program for African Americans—even if he knows that each of these programs may incur economic costs that will increase the amount of money that he has to pay for food or college—may be practicing the self-sacrificial politics of following

Jesus. This does not mean, of course, that Jesus would necessarily want an American Christian to vote Democratic. Christians will no doubt differ on the question of whether a Christian can legitimately work for the cause of Christ within a Democratic Party whose values are clearly antithetical to Christian principles on at least a few questions. But regardless of the choices that individual Christians may make at the voting booth, one thing is clear: The principle of the cross will prompt Christians to vote out of love for their neighbor, not out of the identity politics or rights-consciousness that has shaped the latest iteration of secular liberalism in America. If Christians do vote Democratic, it will not be because of the party's celebration of sinful values but rather because Christians recognize that in a world of imperfect political choices, the party's policies offer the best opportunity to protect the human dignity of the poor and the marginalized and to show love for their neighbor. In fact, Christians may even conclude that the *policies* of the Democratic Party—if not its values and rhetoric—offer the best opportunity to protect the lives not only of the poor but also of the unborn. Even on the issue of abortion, pro-life Christians might find that the Democratic Party offers more hope than they have been led to believe.

3

Abortion

For you created my inmost being;
you knit me together in my mother's womb.
I praise you because I am fearfully and wonderfully made;
your works are wonderful,
I know that full well.
My frame was not hidden from you
when I was made in the secret place,
when I was woven together in the depths of the earth.
Your eyes saw my unformed body;
all the days ordained for me were written in your book
before one of them came to be.

—Psalm 139:13–16

So God created mankind in his own image, in the image of God
he created them; male and female he created them.

—Genesis 1:27

Whoever sheds human blood, by humans shall their blood be
shed; for in the image of God has God made mankind.

—Genesis 9:6

As I write this chapter, pro-lifers are more hopeful than they have been in a long time. In 2019, six states passed "heartbeat" bills banning abortion after the sixth week of pregnancy, and a seventh state (Alabama) adopted a bill banning all abortions, at any stage of pregnancy, except when necessary to save a woman's life. Those laws were immediately blocked by lower courts, but many pro-lifers are optimistic that the Supreme Court, which now has a five-to-four solidly conservative majority for the first time in decades, will listen favorably to their cause and use one of these test cases to overturn *Roe v. Wade*. The goal for which pro-lifers have been striving for decades is now tantalizingly within reach, and all the years of marches, lobbying, and Republican voting may finally pay off.

Or will it? In the spring of 1992, pro-lifers were certain that they were only months away from overturning *Roe*, and they were therefore shocked when the Supreme Court decided instead to reaffirm its central tenets in *Planned Parenthood v. Casey*.[1] There are good reasons to believe that the court may not be as ready to overturn *Roe* as many pro-life activists suspect. But beyond that, there is even more reason to think that regardless of what the Supreme Court does, legal abortion in this country will not go away, and neither will the abortion debate. For the past half century, pro-life Christians' strategy for fighting abortion has focused mainly on legislating against it and seeking to overturn *Roe*. But if this strategy is likely to lead only to failure or, at best, a pyrrhic victory, is there anything that pro-life Christians can do to protect the unborn? Indeed, there is. The strategy that pro-life Christians need to adopt is one that many pro-life activists at least partly employed in the years immediately before *Roe v. Wade*—but which a lot of conservative pro-life evangelicals never learned. It might even require rethinking our partisan strategy on abortion.

Should Christians Oppose Abortion?

For the past thirty-five or forty years, most conservative evangelicals in the United States have been surrounded with pro-life messages, which they hear at church, from their Christian friends, from Christian radio stations, and from Christian books. Not surprisingly, the majority of both white and black evangelicals (69 percent of white evangelicals and 64 percent of black Protestants, according to a 2011 survey) consider abortion a sin.[2] And evangelicals are by no means alone among Christians in thinking that abortion is wrong. The Catholic Church has long stated definitively that abortion is a grave moral evil, and theologically conservative Catholics have for decades advocated legislating against abortion. But a sizeable minority of evangelicals have always supported making abortion legal, and, especially among progressive evangelicals, a few younger voices in the evangelical coalition are now questioning whether abortion really is a moral evil, as they have been told. Republican party identification is now a stronger predictor of opposition to legal abortion than white evangelical identity is.[3] Given this, it's now more important than ever to begin any discussion of pro-life strategy with two foundational questions: Is abortion a sin, and should Christians oppose it?

My answer to these questions is an unequivocal yes, which I believe is supported by historic Christian theology, the biblical evidence, and the philosophical or scientific arguments of the modern pro-life movement. Christians have defended the value of fetal life almost since the origins of Christianity. The Didache, a second-century manual of Christian doctrine, prohibited abortion, along with infanticide. The Epistle of Barnabas in the early second century, Athenagoras of Athens in the late second century, and Tertullian at the beginning of the third century likewise denounced abortion. Several of the ante-Nicene church fathers suggested that fetuses were full human beings and that abortion was therefore murder, and none suggested that abortion was permissible. It is true, as some pro-choice Christians point out, that in the medieval and early modern period, many Catholic theologians (especially Thomas Aquinas) followed Aristotle's lead in speculating that human ensoulment did not occur until forty days after conception for males and eighty days for females, and as a result, the Catholic Church imposed lighter penalties for abortion before "quickening"—the point at which a pregnant woman could feel the fetus move within her—than for abortion at later stages. But the Church never countenanced abortion at any stage, and in the seventeenth century, some Catholic theologians began to suggest once again that human life began at conception—an idea that medical science seemed to support through studies of embryology that showed a continuous development of the embryo or fetus after conception, with no observable difference at forty-days gestation or at the point of quickening.[4]

The earliest Protestant theologians shared the Catholic Church's negative view of abortion. Martin Luther condemned those who "prevent conception and kill and expel tender fetuses," while John Calvin wrote in his commentary on Exodus that "the foetus, though enclosed in the womb of its mother, is already a human being, and it is almost a monstrous crime to rob it of the life which it has not yet begun to enjoy. If it seems more horrible to kill a man in his own house than in a field, because a man's house is his place of most secure refuge, it ought surely to be deemed more atrocious to destroy a foetus in the womb before it has come to light."[5]

Both in the ancient and in the early modern period, Christian theologians who condemned abortion connected the prohibition to the universal Christian proscription against contraception, as well as to biblical allusions to fetal life, such as Luke's description of the preborn John the Baptist being filled with the Spirit in his mother's womb. More broadly, they assumed that Christian married couples had a duty to procreate and welcome new life into their homes, in accordance with the original creation mandate and the value that the Bible placed on human beings who were made in the image of God.

Although the Bible never mentions abortion or clearly defines the moment when human personhood begins, it consistently affirms the value of procreation as an innate good and a participation in God's work, because humans are made in the image of God (Gen. 1:26-28; Ps. 127:3). Both the Old and New Testaments portray the womb as a place of God's creative activity, in which God knits together the bones of someone who already exists as a person and is capable of activity (Ps. 139:15; Luke 1:41). In the poetry of the Hebrew Bible, the terms "womb" and "birth" are sometimes interchanged in parallel lines, with both signaling the earliest stages of personal existence (Ps. 22:9-10; 51:5). And in the New Testament, the Gospel of Luke describes the fetus not merely as a potential person but as an actual person, capable in extraordinary cases of being filled with the Holy Spirit (Luke 1:15, 44). In fact, even before a child is conceived, God foreknows that individual and has plans for that person (Jer. 1:5). An interruption of the pregnancy at any time, therefore, would appear to be an interruption of God's creative work and a sin not only against an image-bearer of God but against God himself.

Christians have also had another theological reason for valuing prenatal life and considering the moment of conception as the most likely point at which human life begins: the attention that the Scriptures give to Jesus's conception, which occurred through the Holy Spirit. Throughout the Scriptures, the Holy Spirit is the divine agent of creation, commissioning, new birth, and regeneration (Gen. 1:2; Ezek. 37:14; John 3:5-8; Titus 3:5). While this alone does not prove that the incarnation of the Son of God began with the Spirit-produced conception, that is the way that many early Christians interpreted it. They honored Jesus's annunciation and conception with a feast that at one time rivaled the celebration of Christmas in importance and may even have predated it, because they believed that it marked the moment at which God took on human flesh.[6] Christians are thus on solid biblical and historic theological ground in upholding the value of prenatal life and expressing concern about any attacks on it.

Pro-life advocates also believe that they are on solid scientific ground. Although science cannot determine when human personhood begins, since the answer to this question depends on philosophical or theological presuppositions about what constitutes a person, it can demonstrate that from the moment of fertilization, the zygote has a genetic makeup that is distinct from either of its parents. It can show that there is a continuous, progressive development from zygote to newborn baby, suggesting that if one chooses to connect the beginning of personhood to any particular developmental stage along the way (such as the moment when the fetus develops a heartbeat, or the instant when brain waves first develop, or the moment when the fetus can begin to feel pain), that moment will be largely arbitrary.[7]

If the fetus is a unique creation of God with an identity that is dependent on its mother but separate from her, abortion is wrong for the same reason that murder of an adult is wrong—that is, not because it necessarily causes pain to the victim, interrupts the thoughts of a conscious being, or breaks social relationships, but because it destroys an image-bearer of God who has a part to play in God's eternal story of redemption. Regardless of whether the fetus has brain waves or can feel pain, its value or status as a person does not depend on those attributes. Its value comes from being a divine image bearer. And the idea that the *imago dei* attaches to the soul alone, which enters the body only at a later stage of fetal development, reflects a dualistic mind-body distinction that the Bible does not teach. Based on Scriptures such as Psalm 139:15, it appears that the unique value of a person begins even before the person acquires consciousness, and that the value comes from being created by God and known by God.

The value of prenatal life has been affirmed for centuries in the theology of all major branches of Christianity—Catholic, Orthodox, and Protestant—but nevertheless, in the 1960s and 1970s, Christians divided over abortion. A number of Catholics from both the clergy and the laity sharpened their opposition to abortion, but many liberal Protestants, along with some evangelicals and even a few Catholics who dissented from their church's official teachings, began to argue that abortion was morally justified in some cases. Some who adopted this position claimed that the idea that human life began at conception was a nineteenth-century innovation and not a historic part of Christian theology. After all, they said, didn't Thomas Aquinas believe that ensoulment did not occur until several weeks after conception?[8]

But while these pro-choice advocates were correct in noting that there was a centuries-long debate in the Catholic Church over the timing of ensoulment, this was not as relevant to the abortion debate as the pro-choice Christians of the late twentieth century suggested, both because Aquinas's arguments were not universally accepted among Christians (Luther and Calvin, for instance, did not find them compelling, and eventually even Catholic theologians repudiated them) and because the belief that ensoulment occurred several weeks after conception did not lead the Catholic Church or even Aquinas himself to condone abortion.

But furthermore, it is striking that the twentieth-century debate among Christians about the point at which Christian theology suggests that human life begins occurred *after* the debate about abortion was already underway. This was not the real issue in the early debates about abortion, and it is not necessarily the real issue even today. The earliest calls for abortion legalization came from people who believed that human life probably did begin long before birth, but they nevertheless argued on utilitarian grounds that abortion should be legalized anyway, since they thought that laws against abortion were ineffective and were creating greater harm than good. Only later, after they expanded their call for abortion rights, did they develop the idea that the fetus in its earliest stages was merely a cluster of cells, with no intrinsic value. And even this idea was not necessarily widespread in the abortion rights movement. More typically, even today, pro-choice advocates have adopted some variation of the liberal Protestant argument of the late 1960s and early 1970s that fetuses have value as potential human beings and that the decision to terminate them is a decision freighted with moral implications—but implications that each woman has to determine for herself, in consultation with her own spiritual advisors and community support.[9]

This emphasis on the freedom of individual choice in abortion decisions reflected a prevailing liberal Protestant view of the 1960s that, while some social evils (such as racial injustice) were absolutely wrong, many choices about individual morality were less clear-cut. In its most extreme form, "situation ethics," as the liberal Episcopal theologian Joseph Fletcher called it, produced the view that the only absolute moral principle was love. But even liberal Protestant ministers who did not go as far as Fletcher were often willing to question traditional Christian sexual ethics, especially the long-standing proscription against premarital sex. In the first half of the twentieth century, mainline Protestant denominations and their clergy reversed their views on contraception; what Protestants once considered a moral evil prohibited by law was now a positive good that they promoted through public campaigns and federal funding. Liberal Protestant denominations also changed their views on divorce and gender roles, with several mainline denominations opening pastoral positions to women for the first time in the early postwar years.[10]

Especially for younger liberal Protestant ministers, who were active in the civil rights movement and who were sympathetic to calls for women's rights, proscriptions against abortion seemed antiquated and harmful to women. Having rejected the traditional theological framework that undergirded the church's long-standing opposition to abortion, they found rejecting the proscription on abortion a relatively easy move. American Protestants had long believed that abortion could be justified in exceptional cases, such as saving a pregnant woman's life and perhaps even her health. And now that liberal Protestant ministers who were influenced by the population control movement no longer shared the traditional Christian view of procreation as a positive good, they found the arguments of pro-choice women's rights advocates far more persuasive than traditional Christian teaching on abortion—especially when that traditional Christian teaching came from Catholic clerics, whose views on contraception they considered badly outdated. Abortion legalization would reduce the number of unwanted children born into poverty and abuse, and it would give women control of their own bodies, health, and sexuality. Persuaded by these arguments, the American Baptist Convention, the United Church of Christ, the United Methodist Church, and the United Presbyterian Church (which is now the PCUSA) endorsed the legalization of abortion in the late 1960s or early 1970s. Though a sizeable minority of members of these denominations dissented from these endorsements and supported the pro-life movement, public opinion polls have consistently shown that the majority of mainline Protestants are pro-choice.[11]

In the battle between pro-life Catholics and pro-choice liberal Protestants, evangelicals at first tried to steer a middle course. Unlike many liberal Protestants, they opposed premarital sex and the sexual revolution, and they were not nearly as sympathetic toward the feminist movement. But unlike theologically conservative Catholics, they had recently come to accept contraception, and most lacked a firm conviction about when exactly human life began. Among evangelical clergy in the late 1960s and early 1970s, one could find every imaginable position on abortion, from the view that all abortion was "murder" (the position of the fundamentalist Baptist *Sword of the Lord* editor John R. Rice) to the view that unrestricted abortion was perfectly fine because human life did not begin until a baby took its first breath (the view that former Southern Baptist Convention president W. A. Criswell expressed in 1973). Some cited Exodus 21:22, an ambiguous legal discussion of the penalties applied in cases of prenatal injury or miscarriage, as proof that the Bible assigned a lesser value to a fetus than to a pregnant woman, which implied that a fetus was only a potential person, not an actual person. John Calvin had interpreted this text as an affirmation of the full personhood of the fetus, but in the late 1960s, the Calvinist theology professor and Old Testament scholar Bruce Waltke interpreted it to mean the exact opposite. But most commonly, evangelicals took the view that, even if one could not know for certain when human personhood began, abortion was a matter of serious moral concern and a procedure that should be used only in the most exceptional cases. Both Billy Graham and *Christianity Today* editor Carl Henry believed that abortion was morally justified only in cases of rape or incest or when a woman's life was in danger, which was the position that the National Association of Evangelicals adopted in 1973. Beyond that, abortion was "murder," Henry believed. Although some evangelical doctors (including Graham's conservative Presbyterian father-in-law, L. Nelson Bell) performed abortions in cases that they believed were medically necessary, they were generally opposed to legalizing elective abortion. Bell, who wrote editorials against abortion for *Christianity Today* in the early 1970s, certainly was, because he, like many other evangelicals, believed that legalizing unrestricted abortion would cheapen societal respect for human life.[12]

The nation's evangelical magazines, including *Christianity Today* and

Eternity, were thus cautiously supportive in the late 1960s of a very modest liberalization of state abortion laws to allow for abortion in cases of rape and incest and when a doctor determined that an abortion was necessary to protect a woman's health. As long as abortion was not used as a casual form of birth control, and as long as it did not contribute to an increase in pre- marital sex or a disrespect for fetal life, they thought that slightly expanding its legal availability to cover a few exceptional cases might not be a bad idea. Almost no evangelicals joined Catholics in speaking out against the liberal- ization of state abortion laws before 1970. But in the early 1970s, after four states, including New York, legalized elective abortion through the second trimester, *Christianity Today* and *Eternity* began publishing sharply worded denunciations of abortion that did not hesitate to use the term "murder" to describe the procedure. Their condemnations became even more pointed after *Roe v. Wade*.[13]

But for the most part, evangelicals of the 1970s had not yet decided how to translate their opposition to abortion into political action. Most evangel- icals were not yet ready to join pro-life organizations that were still over- whelmingly Catholic. And most, including Henry, were not ready to make a presidential candidate's position on abortion a political litmus test, even in 1976, three years after *Roe*. Most evangelicals who opposed abortion did not yet consider it a stand-alone political issue or even the most important issue of political concern; instead, they viewed abortion as only one symptom among many of a societal shift away from Christian values. Pornography, the sexual revolution, the increase in illicit drug use, and homosexuality often attracted more attention from evangelicals in the mid-1970s than abor- tion did. And some evangelicals of the time still believed that the best way to oppose the legalization of abortion on demand was to restrict abortion to a few specific allowable reasons but not to prohibit the procedure entirely. From 1971 through the mid-1970s, the Southern Baptist Convention's offi- cial position on abortion was a moderate endorsement of what were called "therapeutic" abortion laws, which would allow abortion for specific med- ical reasons but not permit elective abortion. The resolutions spoke of the "sanctity of human life, including fetal life," but at the same time rejected the idea of making all abortions illegal.[14]

Evangelicals' opposition to abortion hardened in the late 1970s and early 1980s, after they began to see legalized abortion as a symbol of the sexual revolution and a product of a liberal and secular Supreme Court that, in their view, had rejected both biblical and constitutional standards. They adopted many of the absolutist arguments against abortion that Catholic pro-life activists had already developed. In doing so, they brought their own views into closer congruity with historic Christian understandings of abortion as a moral evil. But they also connected their campaign against abortion to a political program that was very different from what the mid-twentieth-century Catholic pro-life activists had envisioned.

How Conservative Evangelicals Changed the Campaign against Abortion

Many of the Catholics and their liberal Protestant allies who mobilized against abortion in the late 1960s and early 1970s, when states across the nation were beginning to liberalize their abortion laws, were liberal Democrats who supported the antipoverty measures of the Great Society and opposed the Vietnam War. A few, including Jesse Jackson (who later reversed his position on abortion) and Minnesota social worker Erma Craven, were African American civil rights advocates who saw a connection between their work on behalf of the poor and the marginalized and their advocacy of the rights of the unborn. Many others were white Catholics or liberal Protestants who believed in their church's social justice teachings and the importance of protecting life at all stages through government action. "The anti-abortion forces are not instruments of political and social conservatism," Richard John Neuhaus declared at a youth march against abortion in 1972, at a time when the future Catholic priest was still an antiwar Lutheran minister and McGovern Democrat. "Rather they are related to the protest against the Indochina war, the militarization of American life, and the social crimes perpetrated against the poor."[15]

Legal protection for the unborn was always a primary goal of the pro-life movement, even before *Roe v. Wade*, because pro-lifers saw their campaign against abortion as a human rights issue, and they believed that human rights should be enshrined in law—especially when the right in question was the right to life, which they considered the most basic of all human rights. If the right to life for one class of human persons were arbitrarily taken away, no one's rights would be safe, they believed. But many of them also viewed legal protection of life before birth as only the first step in a larger project of protecting all human life from conception to natural death and providing governmental assistance to women facing crisis pregnancies, so that all women would be empowered to choose life. When a woman did choose abortion, it was often a sign that the community had not done enough to help the woman. "It's not so much that the woman rejects the child as that society rejects the pregnant woman," Edythe Thompson, a leader in the student organization Save Our Unwanted Life, declared in 1971. Several state pro-life organizations called for an expansion in governmental social services, as well as a commitment from individual pro-lifers to ameliorate the effects of crisis pregnancies by adopting children and providing assistance for pregnant women. Catholic medical student and pro-life activist Thomas Hilgers advocated "birth insurance," a state-run medical insurance program that would provide payments to families of children with disabilities that would go beyond existing social welfare programs. The North Dakota Right to Life Association's annual convention in January 1973 featured workshops on "health insurance for unwed mothers," "day care centers," and "subsidized adoption." All of this was closely in keeping with Minnesota Citizens Concerned for Life's pledge to "promote and encourage assistance to mother and child in difficult, unwanted and illegitimate pregnancies."[16]

The pro-life movement's interest in expanding social welfare programs for pregnant women largely ended after *Roe v. Wade*, because at that point most pro-lifers decided to make a constitutional amendment protecting the unborn from the moment of conception their top priority and their political litmus test for congressional and presidential candidates. When the Republican Party endorsed the proposed antiabortion constitutional amendment and the Democratic Party did not, even some of the movement's most loyal liberal Democrats decided to vote Republican.

A few liberal Democratic pro-life activists, such as Eunice Kennedy Shriver (the sister of John F. Kennedy and wife of Peace Corps founder Sargent Shriver), argued that reducing the number of abortions was more important than an antiabortion constitutional amendment. "No one—not even if the Lord came down himself—could get through a constitutional amendment to override the Supreme Court decision in favor of allowing abortion," Shriver declared in 1976. Why then should pro-lifers devote their resources to a quixotic quest for a politically impossible cause when they could instead secure bipartisan support for federally funded "life support centers" that would reduce the abortion rate by offering assistance to pregnant women?[17]

But most pro-life leaders were not persuaded by this argument, because their primary mission was not reducing the abortion rate but rather providing legal protection for the most fundamental human right. As they repeatedly said, they believed that *Roe* was a travesty of justice because it deprived a class of human beings of constitutional protection in the same way that *Dred Scott v. Sandford* (1857) had deprived African Americans of constitutional protection in the previous century.[18] The arbitrariness and injustice of this decision meant that no people's constitutional rights were safe. The only way to correct this, they thought, was to pass a constitutional amendment that would enshrine the protection for life that the Supreme Court had refused to recognize. Only then could they continue with the project of building a society that respected all human life and that offered assistance to women facing crisis pregnancies. But in the meantime, as the pro-life movement's focus narrowed to a constitutional amendment that the Democratic Party was not willing to support, the movement became increasingly identified with political conservatism, and a number of the most prominent liberal supporters of the pro-life cause left the movement. During the 1970s and 1980s, leading Democrats such as Ted Kennedy, Sargent Shriver, Al Gore, Dick Gephardt, and Jesse Jackson—all of whom had once considered themselves allies of the pro-life cause and some of whom had voted for abortion restrictions for years—cut their ties to the movement and became pro-choice. They continued to insist that they would support federal programs to reduce the abortion rate, but this was not what pro-lifers really wanted; they wanted a pledge to offer legal protection to the unborn, and the Democrats were not willing to give this.[19]

This was the state of the pro-life movement when evangelicals discovered it in the late 1970s. Until then, only a handful of evangelicals had joined a pro-life organization, even though many were becoming increasingly concerned about abortion. But Francis Schaeffer's books *How Should We Then Live?* (1976) and *Whatever Happened to the Human Race?* (1979), both of which became the basis for film documentaries that were shown in thousands of churches and Christian colleges, convinced a younger generation of evangelicals to make the campaign against abortion their central focus.

Abortion was not merely a symptom of the sexual revolution or one small component of a tapestry of evils, as evangelicals had often treated it. Instead, it was the central evil of modern times, because it was an attack on human life. But for Schaeffer, the evil of abortion in the United States was entirely a matter of law. He said nothing about abortion (whether legal or illegal) before *Roe v. Wade*, because in his view, *Roe* represented the arbitrary dictatorship of a Supreme Court that was poised to deny the right to life to any group that it deemed inconvenient. "In regard to the fetus, the courts have arbitrarily separated 'aliveness' from 'personhood,' and if this is so, why not arbitrarily do the same with the aged?" he wrote. "So the steps move along, and euthanasia may become increasingly acceptable. . . . Law has become a matter of averages, just as the culture's sexual mores have become only a matter of averages."[20]

Schaeffer's focus on the Supreme Court and constitutional law lined up with the pro-life movement's new priorities in the mid- to late 1970s. A movement that had just rejected Shriver's focus on positive programs that would reduce the abortion rate and that decided instead to make a constitutional amendment its highest priority was also ready to receive the Schaeffer-inspired young evangelicals who viewed abortion mainly as a legal problem to be solved through a constitutional prohibition. If many of the Catholic and liberal Protestant pro-life activists of the early 1970s had tried to connect their antiabortion activism to the larger cause of promoting a culture of life through antiwar and antipoverty campaigns, the evangelical pro-lifers of the late 1970s and early 1980s instead connected their campaign against abortion to the larger project of returning the nation's law to a system of absolutes that were grounded in Christian morality and conservative interpretations of the Constitution. Like Schaeffer, they said almost nothing about the hundreds of thousands of both legal and illegal abortions that occurred annually in the United States before 1973. Instead, their entire focus was on reversing *Roe*, first through a campaign for a constitutional amendment and then, when that effort failed, through an effort to change the Supreme Court by appointing conservative justices.

The pro-life movement's decision in the mid-1980s to focus its immediate efforts on changing the Supreme Court and defer a constitutional amendment until a later date was a significant concession, since it meant that there would be no immediate nationwide legal protection for the unborn. But what sold pro-lifers on the judicial strategy was the support they had from the Republican Party (which they thought made it a politically viable strategy) and the illusion that by changing the court, they could get *Roe* overturned in less than a decade. By 1992, pro-life activists were certain that they had the votes needed to overturn *Roe*, since Republican presidents Reagan and Bush had added five new (presumably conservative) justices to the court in addition to the two anti-*Roe* justices who were already on the court when Reagan took office.[21] But to their shock and dismay, two Reagan-appointed justices and one whom Bush had appointed joined two other Republican-appointed justices in upholding abortion rights in *Planned Parenthood v. Casey*. Instead of striking down *Roe*, as pro-lifers had expected, they reaffirmed its key tenets. Pro-lifers were in despair, but they doubled down on their strategy of appointing conservative justices who might overturn *Roe*. This has required a consistent commitment to Republican voting, since Republicans are the only ones who will appoint justices who might overturn *Roe v. Wade*. And though the strategy did not work in 1992, many pro-lifers are sure that it will work today, now that they once again believe that they have a majority on the Supreme Court.

Overturning *Roe* has for decades been the holy grail for pro-life activists, but their reasons for targeting *Roe* have changed. Originally, pro-lifers opposed *Roe* because it stripped the unborn of constitutional protection. Their fight to overturn *Roe* through a constitutional amendment was partly a fight to save unborn human lives, but perhaps even more significantly, it was a fight to enshrine an important human right in American law. But by the late 1980s, a significant number of pro-life evangelicals had lost interest in the legal movement and were focused almost entirely on saving the unborn. For the last few decades, they have imagined that overturning *Roe* will be their best chance to do this. And since Republican presidents and senators are the only ones who will ever put anti-*Roe* justices on the Supreme Court, they equate saving unborn lives with voting Republican.[22]

But if their goal is reducing the number of abortions, they have probably chosen the wrong strategy. Their long history of Republican voting may not even give them the end of *Roe*. There are good reasons to question whether the current Supreme Court is as willing to overturn *Roe* as some pro-life activists think that it is. Given Chief Justice John Roberts's caution, it is more likely that the court will attempt a more incremental chiseling away of the parameters of *Roe* while still leaving some degree of protection for abortion rights intact for the moment.[23] But even if the court overturns *Roe* entirely, few abortion opponents have given sufficient thought to what the end of *Roe* will really mean. It will not mean the end of legal abortion in the United States. At best, it may only marginally reduce the number of legal abortions. And at worst, it may lead to a pro-choice Democratic backlash that will expand the number of legal abortions by repealing the Hyde Amendment (which prohibits federal Medicaid funding for most abortions) and possibly even enshrining abortion rights in national law.

Abortion in the Twilight Years of *Roe*

If *Roe v. Wade* is overturned, both the states and the federal government will be free to restrict or expand access to abortion as they see fit. This will no doubt set off major political battles in state legislatures and in Washington. If the government is under Democratic control at the time, Democrats in Congress will almost certainly respond by repealing the Hyde Amendment, and they may even try to pass a federal law making abortion legal in every state. But even if they do not succeed in doing either of these things, and if states remain free to restrict abortion as much as they would like, the number of legal abortions will still not decrease nearly as much as many pro-lifers expect. When the dust of all the legislative debates settles, abortion will probably be illegal or severely restricted in much of the South and the Great Plains and parts of the Midwest, but abortion will undoubtedly continue to be legally available in the states with the highest number of abortions, including especially New York and California, both of which offer Medicaid funding for the procedure. By 2017, more than half of the nation's abortion clinics were located in just five states: California, New York, New Jersey, Florida, and Washington. As long as all or most of these states, along with a few other states that are solidly pro-choice, keep abortion legal, there will continue to be hundreds of thousands of legal abortions per year in the United States. In 1972, the year before *Roe*, the Centers for Disease Control and Prevention (CDC) reported that there were 586,760 legal abortions in the United States.[24] Even though thirty-three states still banned the procedure in almost all cases and only four had fully legalized elective abortion through the second trimester, New York and a handful of other states offered enough hospital abortion services to accommodate hundreds of thousands of women who crossed state lines to get an abortion. The same would no doubt happen again if *Roe v. Wade* were overturned.

But what most people involved in the abortion debate seem not to realize is that we have largely returned to a pre-*Roe* past even without a direct repeal of *Roe*. The number of abortions per year in the United States is now lower than in any year since 1973. The great disparities in the regional availability of abortion also mirrors the situation that the United States faced in 1972, immediately before *Roe*. While New York has ninety-five abortion clinics and California has 152, eight states have only one.[25] While New York and California offer Medicaid funding for abortion, women in much of the South, Great Plains, and Midwest have to pay $600 out of their pockets for the procedure and schedule time to go to the clinic for a mandated counseling session a day or two in advance of their scheduled abortion, thus necessitating multiple visits to a clinic that may be several hours away. Strict state regulations are resulting in a massive wave of clinic closures throughout the United States, and as a result, the number of abortion clinics has fallen by about two-thirds during the past twenty-five years. There are now more than three times as many pro-life crisis pregnancy centers as there are abortion clinics.[26] *Roe v. Wade* may technically still be in force, but few in 1973 would have envisioned *Roe* resulting in the wide variability of abortion policy that we see today.

Some of this reduction in the number of abortion clinics and in the abortion rate is undoubtedly due to pro-lifers' successful efforts to restrict abortion access, almost all of which has come about because of the support of the Republican Party. At the national level, the most successful abortion restriction by far has been the Hyde Amendment, which was first passed in 1976 and which prohibits federal Medicaid funding for most abortions. Before the Hyde Amendment, approximately one-quarter of all abortions were funded by Medicaid. If Medicaid funding for abortion were reinstated, the percentage would almost certainly be much higher today, because abortion is even more concentrated among low-income women than it was forty years ago. More than half of all women currently getting abortions qualify for Medicaid. Today many of them have to pay out of pocket, because unless they live in New York, California, or a handful of other states that offer state Medicaid funding for abortion, they cannot get government health insurance that covers the procedure.[27]

The Democratic Party is pledged to repeal the Hyde Amendment, and if that happens, it might reverse some of the recent declines in abortion rates—which is why pro-lifers probably need to be more concerned about protecting the Hyde Amendment than reversing *Roe*. Both sides in the abortion debate agree that the abortion rate would rise if federal Medicaid funding for abortion were reinstated. One pro-life research group estimated that the Hyde Amendment is responsible for reducing the number of abortions by 60,000 per year, but the pro-choice Guttmacher Institute estimates that the number might be even higher.[28] For decades, the national Democratic Party grudgingly acquiesced to the Hyde Amendment as an acceptable compromise, but today, in reaction to attempts by conservative states to limit abortion access, the party is pledged to its repeal. Democrats argue that the Hyde Amendment and state restrictions on abortion clinics hurt the poor. Pro-choice activists used to argue that abortion restrictions or the denial of state funding for abortion would drive women to seek out dangerous methods of terminating their pregnancies themselves, but now they are more likely to argue that low-income women who are forced to choose childbirth instead of abortion will probably remain much poorer than if they had had an abortion.[29]

This suggests that pro-lifers were right in at least one respect: restricting access to abortion, whether by shutting down abortion clinics or denying state funding for the procedure, does reduce abortion rates by prompting more women to choose childbirth over pregnancy termination. But pro-choice advocates are also right in saying that this method of reducing abortion rates is likely to keep more women in poverty. This suggests that if pro-lifers really care about protecting all human life, including the life of low-income pregnant women, they will not merely try to rescind *Roe v. Wade* but will instead couple their restrictions on abortion with expanded efforts to provide economic resources to the women whose poverty has been exacerbated by an additional pregnancy.

The Women Who Get Abortions

Who is most likely to get one of the 800,000 or more abortions that occur in the United States each year? The answer is: economically disadvantaged single mothers in their twenties who do not believe they can support another child. Fifty-nine percent of women who have abortions are already mothers, according to a 2014 Guttmacher Institute study. Forty-nine percent are below the poverty line and another 26 percent reported an income that was no more than twice as high as the poverty line—meaning that 75 percent of the women having abortions are impoverished or classified as "low income." Eighty-six percent are unmarried. Twenty-eight percent are black and another 25 percent are Hispanic. Nonwhites comprise a majority of the women who get abortions, although 39 percent of women who get abortions are white. And, despite their poverty, most paid for their own abortions without help from Medicaid or health insurance.[30]

When asked why they were having an abortion, 40 percent of the women surveyed in 2008–2010 said that they were "not financially prepared" to have the baby. Twelve percent said they wanted "a better life for the baby" than they could provide. Twenty-nine percent said they needed to "focus" on their other children. Thirty-one percent cited problems with their partner as a factor in their decision. Only 4 percent said they didn't want a baby.[31]

Many of these women are a lot like "Erin," a woman from Mississippi who described her reasons for having two abortions, in a testimony she sent to the pro-life organization Silent No More. Erin had a baby boy at the age of twenty-two, when she was unmarried. Caring for him on her own was a difficult experience, so when she got pregnant three years later, at the age of twenty-five, she decided she needed an abortion. "I saved up the little money I had, and my boyfriend took me to the clinic," she said. "He wasn't allowed inside, and I was completely alone. I wasn't allowed to have my cell phone and all I kept thinking as the lobby kept filling up was, 'Oh my God . . . all these innocent babies.' I started to think of their reasons, were they as selfish as mine? That I didn't want to be a mom with two kids? I couldn't see past all the women. I felt empty and humiliated. But I knew what I had to do for myself and for my son." "I still have nightmares about that day," she wrote. "I was in a dark place afterwards. I cheated on my boyfriend, and I acted out. I finally wrote a letter to my baby, and I told myself I had to let it go for my family. I did what I did for the reasons I thought were right, and I had to accept that."

A few months later, though, Erin was pregnant again. She had another abortion. "The second one was harder," she said. "I got fired from my job. I couldn't get off the floor, I stopped crying, I stopped answering people's texts. I completely pushed all my friends away. I was bitter and mad that I was about to have another innocent baby on my hands, and I wasn't sure how I was going to survive this one. Everything went dark in my life and I couldn't stop it." "My feelings have changed," she wrote. "Raising my 4-year-old is the hardest thing I have ever had to do. No one loved me growing up—hell, I'm not even sure if anyone has ever loved me, period. But I love him. I cry all the time, because I let my other babies fall through the cracks. . . . I'll forever think about them. I do at least once a day. But I forgave myself, or at least I'm trying to by loving my son correctly. I got my tubes tied. . . . I pray to a god that I'm not quite sure I believe in just to make sure they are okay and that, if He is real, that I'll be able to see their faces, and they will be able to forgive me for letting them go. I remember everything, and I always will. I never looked for help . . . my help was my 4-year-old that need [sic] his mom to be okay, so that's what I did."[32] There are, of course, many different abortion experiences. But in Erin's case, at least, it appears that Eastern Orthodox Christian writer Frederica Mathewes-Green was right: "No woman wants an abortion as she wants an ice-cream cone or a Porsche. She wants an abortion as an animal caught in a trap wants to gnaw off its own leg."[33]

Being Pro-Life in a Way That Will Help Women

The most common liberal pro-choice response to women like Erin is to encourage them to take charge of their lives by getting reliable birth control and a path to education and a career, but to keep abortion clinics open for them in case they need that option. The conservative pro-life response is to make abortion illegal and tell them to be more responsible. But what Erin likely needs is an investment in her life that neither strategy offers.

Erin and the hundreds of thousands of women like her who cite, as their main reason for abortion, the inability to financially support another child would clearly benefit from some economic resources. With a national minimum wage stuck at $7.25 an hour, women like Erin will remain below the poverty line even if they are working forty hours a week. If pro-lifers really want to lower the abortion rate and give women such as Erin the power to carry their pregnancies to term, they will support expanded economic assistance, beginning with health-care funding. Hospital births cost many parents hundreds of dollars even if they have health insurance, but the fees can be catastrophic if they do not. So can subsequent medical bills for pediatric appointments. As of 2014, 22 percent of working-age adults in Mississippi—and 37 percent of those whose income was at or below 138 percent of the poverty level—were uninsured. Mississippi could have insured all of its residents who were at 138 percent of the poverty line if it had accepted the Medicaid expansion that the Obama administration offered. Instead, like thirteen other conservative states, Mississippi continues to resist this federal offer, leaving tens of thousands of its residents—including 25 percent of the state's African Americans and 48 percent of its Hispanics—without health insurance coverage.[34] Perhaps not coincidentally, low-income members of those two groups account for half of all the nation's abortions.

Someone like Erin may also need more than health insurance to feel economically secure enough to welcome a second child into her home. Twenty-seven percent of children in Mississippi in 2018 were living in households below the poverty line. Twenty-two percent of working-age women were below the poverty line. This was not because most of these women were unemployed; it was because they were part of the growing number of working poor. A single mother with two children who works fifty-five hours a week at two or three minimum-wage jobs will still, at the end of the year, be living below the poverty line, because she will have earned less than $20,000 even before FICA taxes are deducted. At such low salaries, even providing children the basic necessities of food and clothing can be a challenge. Seventeen percent of Mississippi children in 2018 were "food insecure," which means that their families at some point during the year did not have enough money to buy food. Twelve percent of Mississippi households in 2015 resorted to payday loans, pawning, and other forms of high-interest credit outside of the banking and credit card system to pay their bills or buy necessities.[35] If economic concerns are the number-one reason why women have abortions in the United States, the battle against abortion must make the fight against poverty a central focus.

But if pro-life liberals are correct in saying that abortions are largely the result of poverty, pro-life conservatives are also right in arguing that abortions are a product of the collapse of the marital ideal and the abandonment of traditional Christian sexual ethics. Eighty-six percent of women who have abortions today are unmarried.[36] Why are unmarried women far more likely than married women to have abortions? In most cases, it is not because of a stigma about having children out of wedlock—a stigma that has rapidly disappeared in American society, especially among low-income and minority women. Today 40 percent of all children born in the United States are born to unmarried mothers, and the majority of children in black and Hispanic homes are now born to single parents.[37] Because the majority of women who have abortions have already given birth to at least one child, it seems clear that they are not going to abortion clinics because they do not want to be single mothers. Instead, the women who obtain abortions are the women who were once most confident that they could have children out of wedlock without interrupting any of their life plans. They did not consider terminating their first pregnancy. But by their second or third pregnancies, they realize that it will be nearly impossible to care for a child on their own, and the dream of marriage that they likely once had appears elusive. If we want these women not to choose abortion, we need to give them a path not only to economic security but toward marriage as well. In fact, the two may be related.

Forty years ago, in 1978, the sociologist William Julius Wilson argued that the reason blacks were less likely than whites to marry was that the higher poverty rates among blacks meant that fewer blacks had the economic resources to provide for a family and enter into marriage. If we want to encourage marriage, he argued, we need to provide more jobs for people in economically marginalized situations.[38] Wilson's argument is probably correct. Today there is an even greater socioeconomic class divide in marriage practices than there was when Wilson formulated his theory. While 56 percent of middle-class and upper-class adults between the ages of eighteen and fifty-five are currently married, only 39 percent of working-class adults (and only 26 percent of those who are poor) are. As marriage rates have declined among low-income groups, poor and minority women have increasingly expected to give birth out of wedlock. When Wilson wrote, the majority of black children were still born to married mothers, even though the black out-of-wedlock pregnancy rate was much higher than the rate for whites. But that is no longer the case. For the past twenty-five years, the percentage of African American children born out of wedlock has hovered at about 70 percent, and today, the rate is high among poor women of all races. Fifty-three percent of Hispanic children are born out of wedlock, as are 29 percent of white children. Sixty-four percent of children born to a poor mother are born out of wedlock, while only 13 percent of middle- and upper-class children are. Young women from upper-middle-class homes who are on a track to attend highly selective colleges and graduate schools usually have a firm conviction that they must avoid getting pregnant out of wedlock at all costs, but poorer women often do not. In a 2010 survey, only 48 percent of unmarried women without a high school diploma and 61 percent of those with a high school education or some college said that they would be "embarrassed" by a pregnancy—compared to 76 percent of those with a bachelor's degree or graduate education. Sexually active unmarried women who are poor use birth control much more inconsistently than sexually active middle-class women do.[39]

Many pro-choice advocates assume that this is because they cannot afford birth control, but more likely, it is because they don't view having a child out of wedlock as the life-ruining development that middle-class women often consider it to be. Several studies have shown that sexually active, unmarried blacks, Hispanics, and lower-income women of other races do use contraception but use it inconsistently—not because they don't know how to use birth control properly or cannot afford it but because they have a more positive view of unplanned pregnancy than unmarried upper-middle-class women do, while their views of hormonal-based contraception and the attempt to regulate pregnancy are more negative.[40] Whenever family planning advocates have tried to give the poor contraceptives without changing their attitudes toward the number of children they want, the effort to lower the population rate has not worked.[41] For that reason, efforts to distribute contraceptives to women whose attitudes toward family planning and childbearing differs from the middle-class people who are giving them contraception are probably not going to be nearly as effective in reducing the abortion rate as they imagine.

But there is another, more important reason for evangelicals who care about social justice to be skeptical about liberal efforts to reduce the abortion rate by distributing contraceptives to the poor: it is not primarily an anti-abortion effort but is instead an effort to prevent unplanned or unwanted pregnancy. For many pro-choice activists, the birth of an unplanned or unwanted child is a greater problem than abortion, and while they might want to reduce abortion rates, they are far more strongly committed to reducing unplanned pregnancy—by contraception if possible and by abortion if necessary. This is reflected in the academic studies of the effect of IUD distribution. When Texas discontinued state funding for Planned Parenthood's contraceptive distribution to low-income women, the number of abortions in the state did not increase (in fact, they actually decreased), but the number of Medicaid-funded childbirths increased. Some medical researchers cited this as evidence of the social problems that would result if states did not provide free IUDs to low-income people.[42] But this is not an example of Christian thinking. The goal of the Christian should not be to make every pregnancy a planned one, and it certainly should not be a Christian's goal to reduce birth rates among low-income women. The goal of the Christian should be to welcome new image-bearers of God into the world and to create a culture in which people respect all human persons, born and unborn—while also ensuring that people have the resources to care for new life.

What approach will be effective both in reducing abortion rates and in creating a society that honors families, values women, and honors God's principles for sexuality? It is an approach that centers on extending marriage access to the poor. Researchers who have studied poor women who have children out of wedlock have noted that they often strongly desire to get married—sometimes even more than middle-class women do.[43] If they had lived fifty years ago, at a time when there was only a marginal difference between the rich and poor in regard to marriage practices, many of these women probably would have gotten married before getting pregnant. But in the course of the last few decades of the twentieth century—particularly in the 1980s and 1990s—there developed in American culture a widespread idea that marriage was such a life-altering, serious commitment that young adults should not enter into it until they were economically and emotionally prepared to do so. Young people began postponing marriage until a much later stage of life than they had earlier. In 1970, the median marriage age for men was only twenty-three, and for women only twenty-one—only slightly higher than in 1950. Few adults, whether rich or poor, spent very many years saving up for marriage or postponing marriage until they had finished their graduate education or settled into a stable career. Marriage was a rite of passage that most people expected to experience immediately after high school or college, and for most, it was a prerequisite for having children. But by 1990, the median age for first marriage was twenty-six for men and twenty-four for women, and today it is thirty and twenty-eight. Young adults of a higher socioeconomic status are likely to wait until after college, graduate school, and the beginning of their professional career to get married, while an increasing number of those who are economically impoverished and unlikely to ever finish college are not getting married at all. [44]

Many of these poorer women choose life when it comes to their first child, and perhaps even their second. But at some point in their twenties, when faced with the prospect of raising yet another child without a father in the home, they realize the insurmountable difficulty of the task, and they reluctantly decide that abortion is the more responsible choice. If these women could get married, as many of them would like, they would be far more likely not to terminate any of their pregnancies. They would also likely be happier, because what they really want is not abortion or an IUD, but a way to care for their children and provide for them while experiencing the joy of a happy marriage and the promise of a path forward in their education and career.

Fighting abortion thus means finding a way to empower people to get married even in economically difficult circumstances. The cultural message that marriage requires an enormous financial investment or years of preparation has not been a helpful message for the pro-life cause—nor has it been helpful to the single mothers who would like to be married. The pro-choice movement, with its emphasis on pregnancy prevention as the path to women's empowerment, misunderstands this, but so do many pro-life evangelicals who think that they can solve the problem of abortion merely by taking that choice away from women. Instead, the only way to stop abortion is to create a vast cultural change that addresses many issues that go far beyond the matter of abortion itself.

Understanding the Complexity of the Abortion Issue through Two Stories

I have given a lot of statistical data to convey the complexity of the abortion issue today, but sometimes it is hard for people who are not social scientists to appreciate the story that the numbers convey. What I want to do now is a little unconventional for a historian, but I think that it will be effective: I want to tell a story about two women—one who is pro-choice and the other who believes that abortion kills a baby. The stories are fictional, but they are closely based on statistical profiles and a composite of real people, and I think they accurately portray the complexity of abortion politics today.

"Ashley" is a young white woman from a nonreligious, liberal, upper-middle-class family who is bound for an elite college. Both of her parents are graduate-educated professionals, and they have instilled in her the message that her own education and career must come before almost anything else. She knows that a pregnancy before marriage will be disastrous. Both because she is focused on her studies and because she and her friends are less likely than their parents were to get drivers' licenses early and to go out on dates (as opposed to texting and sending Instagram messages), Ashley is more likely than young people of the 1980s and 1990s were to postpone sex during her teen years. But in college, when Ashley gets a long-term boyfriend, she makes sure to follow the message that her parents and teachers have reiterated countless times: protect herself from pregnancy during sex. After one scare when she drank too much at a party and wound up in bed with someone who wasn't wearing proper protection, she immediately took a morning-after pill as soon as she was sober. But whenever she has been in a long-term relationship, she has used birth control pills religiously, and, when she was convinced that the IUD was right for her, she switched to that.

Ashley's mother, like 40 percent of women of her generation, actually had an abortion, and she raised her daughter to be strongly pro-choice. (Ashley's mother's abortion happened during her first year of law school, years before Ashley was born, at a time when she knew a pregnancy would be life-altering and unthinkable.) For Ashley, the pro-choice stance on abortion is obvious, since she and all her friends believe strongly in women's rights and always vote for Democrats. In fact, she even served as a campaign volunteer for a female Democratic candidate who made abortion rights a central issue. But Ashley is sure she will never need an abortion herself. And, while she insists that women who get abortions should never be judged for their decision, she privately thinks of them as somewhat irresponsible—or maybe the victim of Republicans and conservative Christians who want to keep them from getting access to free birth control. The best way to reduce abortions, she believes, is to make sure that every woman has the same opportunity that she has had: to use a reliable birth control method that will prevent her from ever having kids until the moment she's ready. And she knows that one day she will be ready. When she's in her very late twenties or early thirties, after she graduates from college, takes a year off to work for a nonprofit or an NGO in Africa, completes graduate school, and finishes the first year of her long-term career, she'll get married—probably after also sharing an apartment with her fiancé (who, of course, will also be a highly educated professional) for a couple years just to make sure they're right for each other. Ashley's parents will be very happy for her, and they will help pay for her wedding, which, if she's living in a northeastern city at the time, will probably cost between $35,000 and $75,000. After Ashley and her new husband settle into their marriage and make sure that their finances are in order, they might be ready to welcome a child into their family at about the time that Ashley is thirty-eight. The child will be carefully planned and wanted—which is what Ashley, her parents, and her pro-choice friends have always said: every child should be a wanted child.

In a much poorer neighborhood, another young woman is growing up who is the same age as Ashley. I'll call her "Jess." Jess watches some of the same TV shows as Ashley does, and she listens to some of the same music, but she doesn't go to the same high school or take the same type of classes, nor does she even know anyone like Ashley's family. In fact, she knows hardly anyone who lives in a two-parent home. Both her mother, who never married, and her grandmother, who was divorced, were single parents, and Jess is not even sure whether anyone in her family ever had a long-term marriage. She knows, though, that she would like to get married, because she has seen how difficult it is for her mother to take care of her and her two younger siblings. Her brother is always getting into fights at school, and her younger sister has been acting out—which is probably not surprising, since she was sexually abused in the past by one of her mother's live-in boyfriends. Jess dreams of a better life, and she knows that to do that, she will need to go to college, as her teachers have told her. In fact, she plans to become a doctor. She also dreams of having a family. Several of Jess's friends are having babies in high school, and Jess finds their babies adorable. But she also sees how difficult it is for her friends to care for their children, and she doesn't want to drop out of high school to become a mom. So, whenever she has a boyfriend in high school, she insists that he use a condom. She views herself as a very responsible person—a person who is a leader in her church youth group, a reasonably good student in school, and a person who has avoided the pitfalls of drugs, early pregnancy, and violence that have derailed the lives of some of her friends.

But she finishes high school without a realistic plan for the future. Her grades are too low for her to pursue her dream of becoming a doctor. She ends up at a technical college and signs up for a nursing degree program, but math and chemistry are a lot more difficult than she ever expected, and she begins thinking about dropping out. She's living with a boyfriend, and they're struggling to pay their bills. She's taking birth control pills, but one month she finds herself running short. She's beginning to think that maybe she doesn't belong in school anyway. Maybe she and her boyfriend should have a child and eventually get married. Without exactly planning to have a child—but without exactly planning not to, either—she finds herself pregnant and decides to drop out of school so she can focus on her two jobs: working as a retail clerk at Walmart and cutting hair. She is both nervous and excited about the arrival of her baby, and she wants to provide the very best life for her child that she can. The idea of getting an abortion so that she wouldn't have the child is unthinkable. She has been to church a lot more times than Ashley has, and unlike Ashley, she has no doubt that a baby in the womb is a real person. Her boyfriend leaves her a few months after her child is born, but she loves her baby, and she resolves to be as responsible as she can and provide for this child. But it is extremely difficult, especially since Jess has to work thirty-five to fifty hours a week and can still barely pay the bills.

At work Jess meets a man who she thinks would be a loving stepfather, and he soon moves in with her. Things progress at a rapid rate, and Jess finds herself dreaming once again of another baby and maybe even marriage. But one night her boyfriend comes home drunk and starts screaming at her during the argument that ensues. Then she discovers that he has been texting an old girlfriend on the side, and she starts to get suspicious. She kicks him out of their apartment. By that point, she's seven weeks pregnant. She feels that she cannot go on with this pregnancy. Marriage seems more elusive than ever, as does finishing college. It will be a challenge to provide for the child she already has, let alone another one. So, as much as she always thought she would never have an abortion, she scrapes together what little money she has, borrows an extra $200 from two of her girlfriends to cover the full price of a pregnancy termination, and has an abortion. Never again, she thinks. Never again.

The Democratic Party's rhetoric on abortion increasingly comes from people like Ashley (who will never have an abortion), but is directed toward people like Jess. If only someone like Jess could get access to contraception and government-subsidized education and child care, she could avoid the need for abortion, and she could finish her college degree and move forward with her career, they think—just as they themselves have done because of their access to contraception. Jess might welcome some of this. But the idea that contraception could be the main solution to her problems or that an economic plan that does not include marriage would be fulfilling is probably out of sync with Jess's values and practices. If she followed the message consistently, she might miss the chance to have a child altogether. The Republican Party's rhetoric on abortion perhaps recognizes the pain that abortion causes to women like Jess, but there is nothing in the Republican Party platform that offers much hope to a woman in Jess's economic situation. Jess already hates abortion. What would induce her to keep her second baby is probably not another abortion law—which might only prompt her to drive farther and pay more for an abortion—but rather a path forward in life. The path forward would include economic and educational assistance (which the Democratic Party would be happy to offer) and also a path to marriage (which perhaps neither party can provide).

What Does This Mean for a Political Strategy?

The pro-life movement has long had the goal of offering legal protection to unborn children from the moment of conception, but however noble that aim might be, very few people in the movement think that a constitutional amendment protecting human life is achievable at any point in the foreseeable future. Even among evangelicals who consider themselves pro-life, there is some reluctance to ban all destruction of embryonic life, as the popularity of in vitro fertilization (IVF) demonstrates. When Mississippi voters considered a referendum in 2011 to protect unborn human life from the moment of conception, they voted it down after realizing that it might affect popular means of birth control and fertility treatments.[45] Pro-lifers have the votes to pass increased restrictions on abortion in many states. And there is a chance that they could even overturn *Roe v. Wade*—though this is still somewhat doubtful. But because they have not succeeded in creating a changed cultural consensus on unborn human life, any gains that they make will probably lead to a political backlash that will ultimately hurt the movement. If they overturn *Roe v. Wade*, there is no question that the Democratic Party will be even more committed to mandating federal funding for abortions, which is already a promise in its platform. If they ban abortion in some states, other states with a pro-choice majority will likely expand abortion services. And the increasing availability of chemical abortions may make the debate over surgical abortions largely obsolete. We are not probably not far from the day when any woman in the United States who wants a first-trimester abortion will be able to order abortifacients over the internet without a prescription, because this is already the case in other countries.[46]

Roe was a disastrous decision on multiple levels. It was based on poor constitutional reasoning, tragic assumptions about the lack of value of fetal life, and a misguided notion that a judicial declaration would solve the abortion debate. Its legacy has been an exacerbation of political tensions on a scale that no one would have predicted in the early 1970s. I have long wished that it could be overturned, not only because of its effects, but because of the erroneous assumptions on which it was based. But overturning *Roe* at this moment—especially if it were done with five male justices voting against three women and one man—would not solve these problems. It would almost certainly lead to a pro-choice backlash that could expand abortion availability by expanding federal funding for abortions. It would galvanize a liberal movement to reverse the reversal with another Supreme Court decision upholding abortion rights. It would not produce a new cultural consensus in favor of the unborn, because it would be seen as a power play rather than as an act of justice. I suspect that Chief Justice John Roberts is aware of these issues, which is why a gradual erosion of *Roe* rather than a direct reversal is more likely. This is not exactly what the pro-life movement wanted, but it might be the best that can be obtained in the current political climate. What we really need is not merely a reversal of *Roe* and a limited prohibition on abortion in a few states, but a cultural change in people's views of sex, marriage, and unborn human life. This cannot be accomplished at the voting booth.

What we can do at the voting booth is choose candidates who will pursue economic policies that will help women like the fictional Jess and the real-life Erin care for their children. Legal protections for unborn children are desirable where they can be implemented and where they are supported by a broadly based cultural consensus, but a far more effective way to reduce the abortion rate and save unborn lives is to expand health-care availability and ensure that the working poor are given better wages and improved opportunities. Perhaps if the abortion rates continue to plummet, they will one day reach such low levels that a solid majority of Americans will be more comfortable with the idea of reversing *Roe* and providing legal protection for unborn children from the moment of conception. But even if this day never comes, any effort that we make to empower women to carry their pregnancies to term and care for their children is a step in the right direction. Sometimes this step can best be accomplished not by voting for a party that merely says that it is against abortion but by supporting a platform that shows genuine promise of saving lives.

A Christian who votes Republican should therefore realize that, while it is admirable that the party officially affirms the value of unborn life, the antiabortion policies that the GOP favors will never be effective unless they are coupled with efforts to help poor unmarried women carry their pregnancies to term. A Republican-voting Christian therefore has a particular obligation to do everything possible through churches, crisis pregnancy centers, and private charities to give impoverished women the resources they need to care for their children. A Republican-voting Christian should also work toward making marriage an option for these women.

A Christian who votes for Democrats might be able to take satisfaction in the idea that the Democratic Party supports some policies that will likely give low-income women the economic resources to carry their pregnancies to term. Expansions in Medicaid, universal health care, free college tuition, and federally funded day care will probably make childbirth a more viable economic option for low-income women. And reforms in the criminal justice system that reduce the incarceration rate, along with the economic expansion and job creation that both parties promise, might increase the number of economically self-sufficient marriage partners in the lower socioeconomic brackets. Even reforming the immigration system by offering a path to citizenship for the 11 million undocumented immigrants who are in the United States might promote family stability and increase the possibility of marriage among Hispanic women, whose out-of-wedlock pregnancy rate has soared in the last twenty or thirty years and who now are the second most likely demographic group to seek abortions, despite their pro-life Catholic and evangelical beliefs.[47] A Christian who supports the Democrats can be glad that the party offers policy proposals that might make a positive difference in the lives of women who are currently most at risk of getting an abortion.

But a Christian should be dismayed at the Democratic Party's strong insistence on keeping abortion legal, affirming abortion rights, and funding abortion with taxpayer money. The fact that the Democratic Party is now pledged to repeal the Hyde Amendment is a matter for serious concern, because this will make abortion far more readily accessible than it is now and may increase the abortion rate in addition to making taxpayers indirectly complicit in paying for abortions. Democrats are now committed to doing everything in their power to prevent the unborn from ever receiving legal protection in this country. This is not welcome news to a pro-life Christian. So, a Christian who votes Democratic has a special obligation to speak out in defense of the unborn and denounce the injustice of our current refusal as a nation to honor or protect human life from the moment of God's creation of it. That also means confronting the entire philosophical foundation on which the Democratic Party's position rests—a philosophical foundation that includes not only abortion rights but also an endorsement of an individualistic view of sexuality, a lack of interest in promoting heterosexual marriage, and a view that unplanned pregnancies are a social problem. This does not mean that a Christian cannot vote Democratic. But a Christian who does so needs to be fully aware that even if some of the party's policy proposals might save unborn lives, the party's stated principles on abortion are directly contrary to the values a Christian should hold.

Neither party, therefore, is really pro-life when it comes to abortion. One party is more committed to legal prohibitions and to the goal of overturning *Roe v. Wade*, and the other offers a broader array of policies that may actually address some of the root causes of abortion and potentially lower the abortion rate even while expanding legal access to abortion. But no matter which of these imperfect options a Christian chooses, a real pro-life strategy would require a much greater investment of resources outside of partisan politics. Perhaps that is not surprising. If Christians could have protected the unborn simply by checking a box in the voting booth, abortion likely would have ended a long time ago. Addressing the deeper human needs that have contributed to abortion means doing the messy work of confronting deeply rooted societal and personal sins. In other words, it requires the very sort of self-sacrifice that followers of a crucified Savior are divinely commissioned to do.

4

Marriage and Sexuality

"Haven't you read," he replied, "that at the beginning the Creator 'made them male and female,' and said, 'For this reason a man will leave his father and mother and be united to his wife, and the two will become one flesh'? So they are no longer two, but one flesh. Therefore what God has joined together, let no one separate."

—Matthew 19:4-6

Marriage should be honored by all, and the marriage bed kept pure, for God will judge the adulterer and all the sexually immoral.

—Hebrews 13:4

In 2004, the National Association of Evangelicals (NAE) joined Focus on the Family and the Family Research Council for "The Battle for Marriage" simulcast, an extravaganza of nationally known evangelical speakers that was filmed at NAE president Ted Haggard's church in Colorado Springs and carried live to five hundred churches across the country. The Massachusetts state supreme court had just mandated the legal recognition of same-sex marriage in the Bay State, and in response, the NAE leaders and their allies called for a constitutional amendment that would define marriage as a union between a man and a woman for every state in the nation. In James Dobson's view, this was possibly the most important battle line the Christian Right had ever drawn. Calling the fight "our D-Day, or Gettysburg or Stalingrad," he said, "The biggest threat to the family is the attack on the institution of marriage. . . . If that definition is changed and it becomes whatever some black-robed judge says it is, there is no returning from that precipice." Ted Haggard agreed. "Marriage is a foundational institution in society that should be protected," he declared.[1]

Two years later, Haggard was caught engaging in sexual activity with a male prostitute, a bombshell that forced his resignation as president of the NAE and at least temporarily ended his career as a megachurch pastor. Conservative evangelicals and their Catholic and Orthodox Jewish allies went on to lose their fight against same-sex marriage. The constitutional amendment proposal they supported never made it out of Congress, and public support for same-sex marriage rapidly increased. After a wave of states revised their marriage codes to allow gays to wed, the Supreme Court made same-sex marriage legal throughout the nation in 2015. By that point, Haggard himself was in favor of it. "We've reached a point where human dignity and mutual respect is so important," he said in 2012. "If someone is dealing with same-sex attraction or homosexuality, and they want someone to be their life partner of the same gender, though we would oppose that in our churches, it should be allowed by the state."[2]

The colossal defeat that evangelicals experienced in their fight against same-sex marriage followed a pattern that characterized nearly all their attempts to stop the sexual revolution. In the battles over divorce, premarital sex, out-of-wedlock pregnancy, and pornography, evangelicals' attempts to stop cultural trends through either sermonizing or political campaigns were quickly routed, and the sins that they had tried to fight in society found a home in their churches. Among younger evangelicals, there is widespread abandonment of traditional strictures against premarital sex, with several studies indicating that a majority of unmarried evangelicals in their mid- to late twenties are sexually active.[3] Even pastors are not immune; thirty years ago, a *Christianity Today* survey found that 23 percent of pastors admitted to a "sexually inappropriate" relationship while in ministry.[4] Nor has the evangelical church been effective in protecting its members from even the most heinous form of sexual sin: sexual abuse of minors by pastors or church staff. Perhaps it is no surprise that a church that has failed to protect its own flock from sexual temptation has also failed miserably in its political campaigns against the liberalization of sexual norms in society.

It would be easy at this point to throw up our hands in despair and renounce all political campaigns for the legal protection of Christian standards for marriage, gender, the family, and sexuality. If the past is any guide, and if current patterns hold, we can probably expect that in less than a decade, conservative evangelicals will decisively lose all their fights against transgender rights. They already have no discernible chance of reversing the legalization of same-sex marriage. And in the era of the internet, it may seem impossible to imagine how to stop the proliferation of pornography, especially when one of the nation's most popular porn sites is reporting 81 million viewers per day.[5]

But marriage is such an important divinely created societal foundation that Christians cannot afford to ignore cultural trends that undermine or threaten it. The strategy that Christians have used to defend marriage in the political sphere has not been effective, but perhaps there are other approaches that Christians could consider—options that perhaps neither political party has fully adopted. To figure out which alternative strategies might be effective, we need to find out why the strategies that Christians have already tried have not succeeded. And to do that, we need to begin our inquiry not with the early twenty-first-century battle over same-sex marriage or with the sexual revolution of the 1960s, but instead with a liberalization of cultural attitudes that began a century ago: the sexual revolution of the 1920s. As I will demonstrate from a historical survey of sexual mores in twentieth-century America, biblically minded Christians in the United States lost the battle for the preservation of marriage before the gay rights movement ever became a public force. The gay rights movement never should have been the primary target for Christians concerned about the preservation of marriage or Christian standards of sexual behavior. But now that conservative Christians have lost their battles both for the defense of marriage and for the preservation of heterosexual norms, where does that leave Christians who today want to promote biblically sanctioned marriage through public policy? Now that we have lost the battle against the sexual revolution, is there anything we can do in the political realm to protect marriage? I think there is. But perhaps before any discussion of a political defense of marriage, we need to go back to the Scriptures and ask what exactly it is that we think needs to be defended.

The Value of Marriage, according to the Scriptures

An emphasis on the value of marriage pervades the entire Bible. The Bible begins with a description of the marriage of the first man and woman, and it ends with a picture of the marriage of the Son of God to his church. In the two thousand or more pages between the opening chapters of Genesis and the closing verses of Revelation, the theme of marriage occurs again and again, whether it is the divinely orchestrated marriages of the patriarchs or the first miracle of Jesus, which he performed at a wedding feast. An entire book of the Old Testament (Song of Solomon) is devoted to a celebration of marital love, as is one of the Psalms (Ps. 45). Behind all the Bible's teaching on marriage is the theme of covenant love—a human relationship that mirrors God's relationship with his people.

Yet the Bible also gives repeated indications that marriages are threatened by sin. Among the consequences for the world's first sin were several disruptions between the relationship of husbands and wives. Instead of a loving harmony free of shame and a life lived in complete openness toward each other and God, husbands and wives would find their relationships plagued by a competitive power struggle (Gen. 3:16). And though the Bible's original pattern for marriage was faithful monogamy, disruptions to this pattern occurred not long after the entrance of sin into the world. By the end of the fourth chapter of Genesis, polygamy had already become normalized—a practice that would remain pervasive among wealthier members of God's covenant people, including Jacob, David, and, of course, Solomon. The tenth commandment included a warning about coveting a neighbor's wife, and the seventh commandment contained a direct prohibition of adultery—a crime that was punishable by death—but those commandments did not succeed in stopping either practice, as the example of King David and the repeated warnings in the Proverbs make clear. Divorce was never God's intention, as both the prophet Malachi and the words of Jesus indicate, but the presence of divorce, even among the covenant people of God, was a sign of how pervasive a "hardness of heart" was among the people who had received God's law and covenant blessings (Matt. 19:3–9).

What are we to make of all these passages? Why does marriage receive so much attention in Scripture—and why do we see such an inability of even God's covenant people to remain faithful to their spouses? If we look more closely at the Bible's passages on marriage, we find that the "meaning of marriage," as the title of one of Timothy Keller's books phrases it, is not primarily about the human parties involved; it is instead about God. God's relationship with his people is a type of marriage, as we learn in the Old

Testament Prophets (especially the book of Hosea). God has made an everlasting covenant with his people, and he relentlessly pursues their heart. When he created humans, he uniquely designed the original man and the original woman for a monogamous marriage that would mirror their relationship with God while also enabling them to participate in God's work of extending the reign of God throughout all the earth by filling the world with image-bearers of God. When sin entered the picture, marriage was damaged but not destroyed. Amidst all the human perversions of marriage and the sexual relationship, God continued to call his people back to the principle of marital fidelity, just as he called them back to covenant faithfulness in their relationship with himself. "Why do we profane the covenant of our ancestors by being unfaithful to one another?" the prophet Malachi asked the people of Judah approximately four hundred years before the coming of Jesus. "The Lord is the witness between you and the wife of your youth. You have been unfaithful to her, though she is your partner, the wife of your marriage covenant. Has not the one God made you? You belong to him in body and spirit. And what does the one God seek? Godly offspring. So be on your guard, and do not be unfaithful to the wife of your youth. 'The man who hates and divorces his wife,' says the Lord, the God of Israel, 'does violence to the one he should protect,' says the Lord Almighty. So be on your guard, and do not be unfaithful" (Mal. 2:10, 14-16). By faithfully loving another person in marriage, even in the midst of sin, we reenact on a small and imperfect scale the faithful love of God for his people. The failure of people to honor the marriage covenant, then, damages a picture of God's relationship with his people.[6]

The Old Testament includes some dramatic pictures of the reenactment of God's covenant love in marriage—perhaps nowhere more memorably than in the book of Hosea, in which God tells a prophet to take a prostitute as his wife and then pursue her relentlessly and buy her back when she runs away from her husband and sells herself into slavery. But as dramatic as these pictures are, they pale in comparison to the ultimate analogy between marital faithfulness and God's covenant love: the story of the cross. As Paul told the Ephesian Christians, marital unity is a "mystery" that portrays the union between Christ and his bride, the church—a union that was accomplished through Christ's atoning death on the cross (Eph. 5:22-33).

According to the Bible, marriage is of immense value not only because it is a divinely created institution for procreation and the rearing of children—though it certainly is that, as God's original command to Adam and Eve to "be fruitful and multiply" indicates. It is of immense value not only because it is God's gift for the realization of a more intense human intimacy than can be experienced in any other relationship—though it is certainly that as well, as the phrase "one flesh" suggests. It is of immense value because it is a picture of God's relationship with his people and a parallel to covenant faithfulness. When marriages are destroyed, a picture of the gospel is lost, which makes it more difficult for people to see God. Family dysfunction and spiritual disruption are closely connected. Before people would be ready for the revealing of the Lord in the incarnation, God said through his prophet Malachi, a prophet would need to "turn the hearts of the parents to their children, and the hearts of the children to their parents," or else God would "come and strike the land with total destruction" (Mal. 4:5).

The last phrase of that verse, which forms the concluding line of the Old Testament (at least in the arrangement of our modern Protestant English Bibles), has inspired American evangelicals for decades to attempt to save the nation from destruction by preserving marriages and families. "America will go as her homes go," one fundamentalist minister proclaimed in 1928, in a typical exhortation of the time. "If her homes are Christian, she and the world are safe. But if her homes are godless, Ichabod is already written on her flag."[7] Thirty years later, during the 1950s, Billy Graham preached a nearly identical message. Divorce "could ultimately lead to the destruction of our nation," he declared. "The home is the citadel of American life," he stated on another occasion, in a quotation that he borrowed from FBI director J. Edgar Hoover, a hero to many cultural conservatives at the time. "If the home is lost, all is lost."[8] And at the beginning of the twenty-first century, conservative evangelicals such as James Dobson reiterated this message, applying it to their fight against same-sex marriage. But while their concerns are rooted in biblical values, Christian attempts to save the nation by defending marriage have usually settled for only a partial defense of God's moral code. That is especially evident in the recent evangelical campaign against same-sex marriage, which strongly denounced homosexual unions while largely ignoring divorce and out-of-wedlock sex, both of which were also violations of God's covenant marital ideal.

A holistic approach to the issue would recognize that any model of marriage that does not treat marriage as a divinely orchestrated covenant is an unbiblical view and is therefore to some degree an attack on marriage. As Jesus said, it is God who joins husband and wife together—which means that marriage is not a human contract. And it is for that reason that humans do not have the right to separate two people whom God has joined. A biblical understanding of marriage would also recognize that sex is a marital sacrament that symbolizes and ratifies the "one flesh" that husbands and wives become in marriage. It is for that reason that New Testament writers view sex outside of marriage as both an attack on marriage and a sin against human bodies that, in the new covenant, are temples of the Holy Spirit (1 Cor. 6:12–20; Heb. 13:4). A biblical understanding of marriage recognizes that God created human beings as male and female, with different anatomies and different roles, for the purpose of procreation in marriage—which means that gender differentiations are not arbitrary human constructs but are instead reflections of God's creation order. Marriage, in other words, is a lifelong, divinely wrought, sexually faithful, covenant relationship between one man and one woman for the purpose of extending and proclaiming the reign of God through raising children and picturing the gospel to others.

Once we understand that a biblical defense of marriage goes far beyond insisting that marriages be heterosexual or even that divorces be made more difficult to obtain, we will understand that biblically minded Christians lost the battle for marriage not when the gay rights movement emerged, or even when the sexual revolution of the 1960s happened, but when Americans exchanged a covenant model of marriage for the idea that marriages are merely human contracts. This change occurred in the culture long before it was ratified into law. When Christians tried to reverse it through law, they failed, because moral regulation without heart changes has rarely been an effective tool for controlling people's sexual passions or enforcing marital fidelity. If even the divinely given Mosaic law code was unable to enforce God's creation ideal for marriage through legislation (Matt. 19:8), it is highly unrealistic to expect better results from American law. If the Bible is filled with examples of sinful violations of the marriage covenant among God's chosen people, surely we should not expect people who are outside of God's covenant to behave any better. Indeed, Christians who have attempted to preserve marriage through moral regulation have usually acknowledged the futility of expecting heart transformations through law and have therefore settled for a piecemeal approach to the issue by lobbying for a few surface-level laws while ignoring the deeper problem of a cultural rejection of biblical under-standings of covenant marriage.

For one hundred years, American cultural trends have been decidedly against the idea of marriage as a binding covenant created by God. Once we understand that, we will recognize that any further campaigns to "defend" marriage through lobbying campaigns against the latest attempt to liberalize marriage policy are almost certain to fail. This does not mean that Christians have to give up their quest to defend God's institution of marriage; it simply means that we have to quit expecting moral regulation to give us cultural victories when the root causes of the problem are much deeper than legisla-tion can address. The history of Christian attempts to protect marriage in the political realm is largely a century-long history of repeated defeats, because Christians underestimated the cultural forces that were arrayed against a biblical view of marriage, and they failed to address the root causes of the cultural shifts they opposed. An examination of this history may give us reasons to rethink our political strategy and to question whether we have expected more from politics than politics can possibly provide.

The Liberalization of America's Sexual Morals: A Hundred-Year Survey

"A wave of sex hysteria and sex discussion seems to have invaded this coun-try," *Current Opinion* magazine lamented in 1913. "Our former reticence on matters of sex is giving way to a frankness that would startle even Paris. Prostitution . . . is the chief topic of polite conversation." Then, in perhaps the most memorable line of the article—a line that the magazine borrowed from St. Louis editor William Marion Reedy—*Current Opinion* declared, "It has struck 'sex o'clock' in America."[9]

Like subsequent American sexual revolutions, the "wave of sex hysteria" in the early twentieth century challenged conventions in both sexual behav-ior and gender roles, and those changes in turn challenged long-standing assumptions about marriage. In the late nineteenth century, before the hour reached "sex o'clock," middle-class white Americans had treated any sexual behavior outside of marriage as scandalous, partly because they believed in marriage as an essential foundation for society and partly because they believed that sex outside of marriage harmed women. The purpose of federal government action against pornography in the 1870s, Mormon polygamy in the 1880s, and prostitution in the early twentieth century was both to protect women from abuse and to rein in men's lusts in order to channel their desires into monogamous marriage.[10]

The divorce laws of the late nineteenth century reflected the Protestant value of covenant marriage—or, as the Supreme Court phrased it, the idea that marriage was simultaneously a "sacred obligation" and a "civil contract."[11] Protestants of the nineteenth century—and especially those of the Reformed tradition—believed that marriage was a lifelong obligation whose premature dissolution was scandalous. But, unlike Catholics, they also generally believed that egregious violations of the marriage covenant could warrant the legal termination of a marriage. In Reformed Christian doctrine, grounds for divorce were limited to adultery and desertion, and some states, such as New York, accordingly granted divorces only when one party could prove that the other had been sexually unfaithful. Other states enlarged on this by allowing divorce for a few other specific violations of the marriage contract. One of the most liberal was California, which allowed divorce for six different reasons, including alcohol abuse, conviction of a felony, and either physical or mental cruelty—all of which were at least partly designed to protect women from abusive husbands. But even in California, the law assumed that marriage was designed to be a permanent contract and that only flagrant violations of that contract could justify its termination. When historian Elaine Tyler May reviewed California divorce records from the 1880s, she found that every person suing for divorce believed that the other party in the marriage had violated the marriage contract. They had entered the marriage believing that the other person would fulfill their vows, and when those vows were broken, they ended the marriage. Divorce in the late nineteenth-century United States was rare (at least by the standards of later decades) but hardly nonexistent. At the end of the nineteenth century, one out of every fifteen marriages in the United States ended in divorce.[12]

By the 1920s, just after "sex-o'clock" struck in America, a new generation of Americans had adopted a very different view of sexual morality and marriage. While still holding on to the general outlines of the traditional ideal of lifelong marriage, the generation that produced "flapper" culture and jazz dancing replaced courtship with recreational dating, and the marriage covenant with companionate marriage. In the late nineteenth century, a man who wanted to marry a woman would "court" her—preferably in her parents' parlor or during a daylight stroll in the park, but certainly not in the back seat of a buggy on a deserted moonlit road. If he was not ready to get married, he didn't ask a woman out. But by the 1920s, this changed with the invention of recreational dating, facilitated both by the automobile and by a rapid rise in attendance at residential colleges, where students could live for four years without having to worry about parental oversight. Before 1900, many people thought it was inappropriate for an unmarried couple to kiss before they were engaged. By the 1920s, no date was supposed to end without a kiss, and many did not end without extensive "petting," a practice that had the approval of the vast majority of college students, according to some of the writings of the time. The majority still retained the belief that sexual intercourse itself should be confined to marriage, but even in this area, standards were slipping; sex researchers of the 1940s and 1950s found that women born shortly after 1900 were twice as likely as those born in the late nineteenth century to have had sex before their wedding day.[13]

The new emphasis on recreational dating was also accompanied by new pressures on women to meet an ideal of beauty in order to catch and keep a man. Spending on cosmetics increased markedly during the 1920s; by the end of the decade, American women were spending $10 billion a year on beauty products, which was nearly as much as the annual expenditure of the federal government at the height of the First World War. Aided by the new phenomenon of movies, which created a national glamor culture that had never existed before, beauty pageants became a national craze, with the nation's largest and longest-enduring pageant, the Miss America beauty contest, debuting in 1921. Some women welcomed this change in their expected gender roles, while others—especially those who were middle-aged or who were religious conservatives—mourned the loss of womanly virtue. In the late nineteenth century—and even for the first decade or two of the twentieth century—middle-class women had presented themselves (and had been seen by men) as moral guardians. If they were married, they expected to exercise their moral influence in the home, primarily through motherhood but also through church activities and volunteer organizations. If they remained unmarried, they expected to be "housekeepers of society" through school teaching and social work. The most popular women's organization of the 1890s, the Women's Christian Temperance Union, modeled this middle-class female ideal of religiously inspired moral guardianship. But some of the women of the 1920s cast off this restraint. They wore much shorter dresses than their mothers had, and they started smoking cigarettes and going to dance halls. Instead of campaigning to rid society of alcohol, they tried drinking a little themselves. And they were much more overtly sexualized than their mothers had been. If they didn't engage in sex, they at least had to "pet" and go on dates. If such women no longer found their identity in moral guardianship or motherhood, it was now more important than ever to pursue the one area of self-identity that could win them attention: sexual beauty. Prostitution might have been on the wane, but sexual attraction was now more commodified than ever, both in the unprecedented extent of advertisers' use of feminine beauty to sell products and in women's desire to buy whatever might keep them looking young and beautiful.[14]

All of these changes had an effect on marriage. A generation that believed in dating several potential partners and engaging in sexual experimentation before marriage also began to believe that perhaps the marriage contract was not quite as binding as their parents had assumed. If Americans of the late nineteenth century divorced only when they perceived that a marriage contract had been broken, an increasing number of Americans of the early twentieth century believed that a marriage could be dissolved whenever it did not meet one's expectations. American couples of the 1920s often entered into marriage expecting to spend a lifetime of joy with the person with whom they had fallen in love while dating. When marriage failed to meet their expectations, some married people decided that it was acceptable to look for another partner. For the first time, a number of men said that they were divorcing their wives because the women they had married were losing their youthful beauty or gaining weight. Others said that they were leaving their spouses because of personality conflicts or different goals in the marriage. Some women said that they were getting out of marriages that they found too confining or controlling. The national divorce rate rose to one out of every seven marriages.[15]

For a long time, the nation's laws reflected an older set of marital ideals, despite shifting practices. Until the 1970s, no state granted no-fault divorce; every state required a person seeking a divorce to give a valid reason that would justify the dissolution of the marriage, and most often, states limited these reasons to a few egregious actions. No judge would grant a man a divorce merely because he thought his wife had gained too much weight. Though the rate of premarital sex continued to increase throughout the mid-twentieth century, with half of all women and a higher percentage of men having sex before their wedding day by the 1950s, public policies continued to reflect an older ideal. As late as the beginning of the 1960s, some state universities continued to discipline students for premarital sex. One unmarried pair at the University of Kansas who had the audacity to try to rent a hotel room in Lawrence for their escapade in 1960 were expelled from college, and a dorm monitor reported them to the police.[16]

Both political parties shared traditional notions about gender and sex in the mid-twentieth century. From the 1930s through the 1960s, the "breadwinner liberalism" of the New Deal was based on the ideal of a two-parent household, headed by a male breadwinner. Accordingly, the creation of jobs for men was given top priority in the New Deal; women's jobs took a distant second place. The government's policies were designed to encourage marriage and to discourage cohabiting out of wedlock. Until the 1960s, single mothers receiving benefits through Aid to Families with Dependent Children (AFDC) were subject to periodic unannounced visits from social workers who would check for signs that a man was living in the home. If they found such evidence, the family's welfare benefits would immediately be cut off.[17]

Imposing middle-class norms of sexual behavior on the poor was relatively easy, but sexual norms were more difficult to enforce when white middle-class Americans violated them. When *Playboy* magazine, which sold its first issue in 1953, reached a readership of one million by 1958, Congress reacted by asking the post office not to deliver issues one month. The Supreme Court ruled that the First Amendment prevented Congress from blocking the distribution of *Playboy*, but the fact that members of Congress tried to do this showed the standards by which they operated in the late 1950s.[18]

Of course, there was always a good deal of hypocrisy and double standards in enforcing these norms, but the fact that many people felt a desire to pretend to be more sexually pure than they really were is an indication of the degree to which conservative sexual standards still retained societal respect. But by the 1960s, the tension between a half century of increasing liberalization of personal sexual behavior and public policies that attempted to enforce a more traditional standard was nearing a breaking point.[19]

One of the points of tension was the sexual revolution's underlying current of male chauvinism masking itself as egalitarian liberalism. In the 1950s and 1960s, the men who embraced the *Playboy* ethos of nonmonogamous sex, wrapped in the package of unbridled consumerism and self-indulgence, often pictured themselves as liberated and enlightened people who wanted the same liberation for women. *Playboy* and some of its male allies were strong proponents of abortion rights for women, for instance—no doubt because of their belief that sexually liberated women should have a right to separate sex from pregnancy, just as sexually liberated men attempted to do. But the self-entitled attitudes of the liberal men who publicly championed an egalitarian ideal while privately using egalitarian language as an excuse for their boorish sexual behavior grated on some of the women who worked with them. Many of the leading feminists of the 1960s were New Left activists or liberals who were reacting not against the patriarchal views of conservative Christians (of which they had almost no first-hand experience) but rather the sexism of liberal men. Gloria Steinem worked briefly undercover as a Playboy bunny and was sharply critical of the sexism in Hugh Hefner's enterprise. Shulamith Firestone, Jo Freeman, and several other leading feminists of the late 1960s were members of New Left youth organizations controlled by male leaders who refused to share power with women—which is what prompted them to walk out in protest and launch their own women's movement. And Betty Friedan was a left-leaning freelance journalist who had enrolled in a graduate program in psychology at the University of California at Berkeley. Much of her book, *The Feminine Mystique*, was devoted to a critique of the sexism of Freudian psychology and other twentieth-century social science theories.[20]

As these women rightly pointed out, the sexual revolution of the early to mid-twentieth century was deeply sexist. Men judged women by their beauty, not their brains, and they expected women to forgo educational and career opportunities in order to serve their own convenience and lust. Women either had to confine themselves to the house as faithful homemakers while their husbands had adventurous careers (and possibly amorous escapades) in their absence or, if they attempted to advance themselves in the world of work and education, they had to tolerate boorish comments from men and even the direct demand for sexual favors.

Most of the leading feminists, however, did not renounce the sexual revolution, and they certainly did not advocate a return to an earlier set of gender norms as a remedy for the chauvinism of mid-twentieth-century liberalism. Instead, they advocated making the sexual revolution more egalitarian, which would mean a strong insistence on contraception and abortion rights, since women would need the absolute right to avoid unwanted pregnancy. Women would no longer find their primary identity in marriage, home, and family. Instead, the glass ceilings that kept women from advancing in the workforce, politics, and education would be broken, and women would have the freedom to pursue their own goals and define themselves in the way that they chose.

Conservative evangelicals viewed feminism as a threat to the family in the 1970s, and many of them—both women and men—supported Phyllis Schlafly's campaign against the Equal Rights Amendment (ERA). The proposed constitutional amendment, which would mandate equal treatment for men and women under the law, would, they feared, introduce a dangerous gender-neutral society that would include unisex restrooms, women drafted to serve in military combat, same-sex marriage, abortion rights, and an end to the legal privileges, such as alimony, that women had traditionally enjoyed. But beyond that, the ERA and the feminist movement were threats to the female homemaker ideal, family autonomy, and the long-standing social recognition of divinely created gender differences.[21] Social conservatives won their fight against the ERA, but it was a pyrrhic victory, because many of the legal and social changes that they feared soon became a reality because of court orders and public support for a greater degree of gender equality.

Conservative evangelicals also lost their fight against a public acceptance of premarital sex. Their fight against this trend, which was less public and less political than their battle against the ERA, was over almost as soon as it began, because societal attitudes about premarital sexual behavior experienced a sea change in less than ten years. As late as 1964, 77 percent of the women in the freshman class at the University of Kansas indicated that premarital sex was wrong even when a couple was engaged to be married, and 91 percent thought that sex between a couple who was not engaged was "unacceptable." But by 1975, 85 percent of college seniors nationwide said that they saw nothing wrong with premarital sex.[22] During the same interval, several mainline Protestant leaders, denominations, and educational institutions decided that they could accept premarital sexual activity as well.

State universities repealed the curfews and other regulations governing the interactions of men and women on campus. And in 1972, the Supreme Court struck down the last state laws against the distribution of contraceptives to unmarried women. Only seven years earlier, in 1965, the Supreme Court had explicitly limited the right to access contraceptives—and the corresponding right to privacy in sexual relationships—to married couples. Marriage was "intimate to the degree of being sacred," the court declared, and this was why the state could not regulate how married couples expressed their love for each other in the privacy of their bedroom and whether they used contraception while so doing. This right did not extend to unmarried people; the state did have the right to regulate their sexual behavior and prohibit "fornication," one of the concurring opinions in the case argued. But in 1972, the Supreme Court extended the right to privacy to the individual person, whether married or unmarried, and said that unmarried people had the same right as the married did to use contraception without interference from the state. In issuing this ruling, the Supreme Court was following public opinion more than leading it, because by the mid-1970s, the percentage of Americans who saw nothing wrong with premarital sex was higher than the percentage of those who thought it was sinful.[23]

The sweeping collapse of the societal taboo against premarital sex in less than a decade reflected the unstable foundation on which this taboo was based. By the early 1960s, biblical norms or Christian theological traditions had not been the primary foundation for mainline Protestant, governmental, or higher-educational policies on sex for a very long time. Instead, the primary foundation was a vague combination of tradition and reason. And by the 1960s, the usual reasons given for abstaining from premarital sex did not seem very compelling to many young people. The argument that premarital sex was a bad idea because it might lead to pregnancy no longer held the same weight after the invention of the birth control pill—and especially after the increased availability of legal abortion as a backup to contraceptive failure. The argument that it had a detrimental effect on one's future marriage or that a woman's loss of virginity would ruin her marriage prospects no longer sounded as persuasive as they had two or three generations earlier. At a time when liberal Protestant educators were encouraging students to figure out their own moral values by measuring them against the ultimate standard of universal love, many young people decided that the most loving thing to do was to have sex, regardless of whether they were married. And it was egalitarian, too, they believed. There would no longer be a double standard that punished women for sexual transgressions that men supposedly enjoyed without censure. Because the burden for maintaining chastity in a relationship had long fallen primarily on women rather than men—even if this did not accord very well with biblical norms—the campaign for women's equality in the 1960s and 1970s had the indirect effect of eroding some of the last vestiges of a system that attempted to protect female virginity. Even if many women ended up getting hurt by the new sexually permissive standards of the late 1960s and 1970s, a number of culturally progressive people of the time thought that all the trappings of the sexual revolution, including abortion, contraceptive access for the unmarried, easy divorce, and a new "swinging singles" culture of casual sex outside of marriage, went hand in hand with a commitment to women's rights. A few feminists who held onto traditional Christian values of sexuality objected. The pro-life, Catholic, self-identified feminist Juli Loesch said that the combination of easy premarital sex and the widespread availability of abortion reflected "the idea that a man can use a woman, vacuum her out, and she's ready to be used again. . . . It's like a rent-a-car or something."[24] But Loesch was in the minority among feminists on this issue.

The acceptance of premarital sex in the late 1960s was quickly followed by a rapid erosion of traditional community-decency standards. In 1968, a movie production code that had prohibited nudity and limited profanity was replaced by a movie rating system that gave a green light to the production of X-rated movies. By the end of 1970s, there were eight hundred adult movie theaters showing porn in the United States, with a weekly viewing audience of two to three million. Pornographic magazines became far racier. *Playboy* had created a sensation in the 1950s with its airbrushed nude centerfolds, but by the 1970s, customers looking for something more stimulating could go to their corner drugstore and buy copies of *Penthouse* or *Hustler*, with cartoons such as "Chester the Molester," photos of nude women in sexual poses with animals, or, in one particularly infamous picture from a 1978 *Hustler* cover, a woman being put through a meatgrinder. Some feminists objected, but the egalitarian-minded pornographers argued that the answer was not less porn but more; women should have their own erotic magazines, they said. The result was *Playgirl* (founded in 1973), a magazine with erotic photos of nude men that never became as popular as *Playboy*, but which served as an answer for people who complained that pornography was sexist or misogynistic.[25]

For a while in the 1970s, it seemed that every conventional sexual standard might be open for renegotiation. Bestselling novels now commonly featured a liberal use of sexualized profanity and graphic sex scenes. Television, which until the mid-1960s had been governed by rigid moral standards, now commonly featured frank discussions of sex, abortion, and divorce. If one looked hard enough, one could find a fringe group advocating for almost any sexual practice, no matter how perverse it might have once seemed. But most Americans did not change their views on all sexual matters. Rape, child molestation, and even adultery were still wrong, in their view. But what did change in the 1970s, in addition to a rapid acceptance of premarital sex and pornography among the younger generation, was a dramatic rise in the divorce rate.[26]

At the beginning of the 1970s, the national divorce rate was barely higher than 25 percent. By the end of the decade, there was one divorce for every two marriages. This near doubling of the divorce rate in only ten years alarmed many Americans at the time. Some blamed the phenomenon on no-fault divorce laws, which California adopted in 1970 and which then spread to most of the other states in the nation by the end of the decade. By making divorce far easier and less time-consuming, no-fault divorce laws certainly contributed to the trend of rising divorce rates. But the increase in demand for divorce started before the new laws were passed, and the liberalized laws were primarily a response to the large number of divorce cases that were clogging the courts. With the number of divorces in the United States increasing by 62 percent over the course of the 1960s, some people wanted to find a way to streamline the process.[27]

What was the main cause of the increasing number of divorces even before the laws were changed? There probably was no single factor; it was instead the result of several decades-long cultural trends that coincided to produce a perfect storm. For half a century before the 1970s, many American couples had believed that chronic unhappiness in marriage, not merely contractual violations, constituted grounds for divorce. There had been a few moments before the 1970s when the American divorce rate spiked—most notably, immediately after World War II, when returning veterans and the brides they had left behind to work in the nation's wartime factories found that putting a relationship back together after a multiyear absence might be more than they could handle. But even in those moments, the majority of couples had not divorced.

Perhaps there were two factors that kept the divorce rate lower in earlier decades, even as couples adopted expectations about marriage that might have otherwise caused the number of divorces to be much higher. Those two factors were the social stigma attached to divorce and the economic costs of divorce, especially for women. In earlier years, divorce was considered shameful, and those who dared to defy the taboo against it suffered social opprobrium. Only one major-party presidential candidate before 1980—Adlai Stevenson, who ran against Dwight Eisenhower in 1952 and 1956—had ever been divorced, and though his divorce was not the main reason for his landslide defeat, it was an issue for some voters. Nelson Rockefeller's divorce and remarriage in 1962 was considered so scandalous that it kept him from running for president in 1964—even though he had previously been viewed as the leading candidate for the Republican presidential nomination that year. The stigma attached to divorce was one reason why some women stayed with men who carried on decades-long affairs with another woman (as both Franklin D. Roosevelt and Lyndon Johnson did) or engaged in serial adultery with possibly dozens of partners (as was the case with John F. Kennedy and Martin Luther King Jr.). It was why women put up with emotional and physical abuse from their husbands or stayed in loveless relationships. And in addition to the anxiety about the social stigma about divorce, many couples who hated each other thought they nevertheless needed to stay together because of the kids.

In the 1970s, this changed. With the nation's change in sexual mores, the rise of the feminist movement, and a new individualism, both men and women felt less reticence in calling a divorce lawyer. In 1962, approximately 50 percent of American women agreed with the statement that a husband and wife who didn't "get along" should stay together if they had children, but by 1977, only 20 percent of women agreed with the statement.[28] Divorce did not damage children very much, psychological experts now said, and it had the potential to improve the happiness of everyone involved. The ranks of those now getting divorced included conservative men like Bob Dole, who may not have been carrying on affairs but who felt constrained in marriages they felt they had outgrown. They included people on the left, such as Jane

Fonda. They included television news anchors, Hollywood actors, and other national celebrities. They even included a few serial divorcees, like Elizabeth Taylor, who was in her sixth marriage by the late 1970s. But the ranks of the newly divorced also included culturally conservative Southern Baptists and others who had never imagined that their marriages would not last a lifetime. Most of all, the ranks included women who were fed up with troubled marriages. In an earlier decade, perhaps many of them would have stayed in a marriage, but now, because of the rapid rise in women's participation in the workforce, they had economic options they did not have before. Two-thirds of the people filing for divorce in the mid-1970s were women.[29]

Evangelical pastors preached against divorce in the 1970s, but beyond sermonizing, they did not take serious steps to stop the change in divorce laws or the shift in the national culture. Instead, by the end of the decade, the pastors associated with the emerging Christian Right were devoting more attention to homosexuality, which they treated as a greater threat to the family—and one that seemed easier to combat in the political and legal arenas.

Evangelicals' Failed Campaign against Gay Rights

Homosexuality seemed like an easy target in the late 1970s because, at the time, public sentiment seemed at least partly on conservative evangelicals' side. Only 43 percent of Americans in 1977 believed that "homosexual relations between consenting adults" should be legal. Only 13 percent of Americans believed that "homosexuality" was something that someone was "born with." (Today, about half of all Americans believe that sexual orientation is fixed at birth, and another 10 percent believe that it is a product of birth and environment).[30] For most of the twentieth century, a growing liberalization of attitudes toward premarital sexual behavior between opposite-sex couples was accompanied by *increasing* legal and social condemnation of homosexuality. Same-sex sexual relationships were illegal throughout the United States in the 1950s, and those suspected of being "homosexual" could lose their jobs. Psychologists considered homosexuality a mental illness and offered treatments to reverse it.[31]

But in the mid- to late 1960s, an emerging gay rights movement, with the support of a few liberal ministers, demanded an end to this discrimination.

In 1969, the movement burst into the open with a revolt against a police raid of a gay bar in New York known as the Stonewall Inn. In 1973, the American Psychiatric Association removed homosexuality from its list of mental illnesses. Twenty states repealed their laws against "sodomy" in the 1970s.[32] At the time, gay rights activists commonly linked their cause to the general climate of sexual liberation and gender equality, as well as the civil rights movement. And as a result, the movement faced a backlash from cultural conservatives—especially conservative evangelicals. With the support of Jerry Falwell and other evangelical pastors, Southern Baptist singer Anita Bryant successfully led a campaign in 1977 against a gay rights ordinance in Miami that would have protected gays' rights in employment, including their right to teach in public schools. The next year, conservative evangelicals lost their campaign in California for a referendum barring homosexuals from teaching in public schools, but won a smaller victory in Minnesota. The beginning of the AIDS crisis in 1983 set off a nationwide scare that temporarily increased fear of homosexuals and made it easier for opponents of gay rights to win their political battles. One of their most significant victories came in 1986, when the Supreme Court upheld the constitutionality of state sodomy laws, a severe setback to gay rights advocates. At the time, 57 percent of Americans believed that homosexuality should be illegal.[33]

But public support for gay rights increased in the 1990s, and evangelicals leading anti-gay rights campaigns found themselves on the defensive. The battle lines shifted. Instead of attempting to keep homosexuality illegal (which became impossible after the Supreme Court's ruling in *Lawrence v. Texas* in 2003), they focused instead on preserving the right of employers to refuse to hire gays. After 2004, their fight narrowed to the issue of same-sex marriage.

In their battle for the "defense of marriage," conservative evangelicals had the support of many conservative Catholics, who had not been leaders in the earlier campaigns against gay rights but who were mobilized by what they viewed as a redefinition of a foundational (and sacred) social institution. Public opinion was on the social conservatives' side for about seven years, but after 2011, more Americans supported same-sex marriage than opposed it. By the time the Supreme Court affirmed a national right to same-sex marriage in *Obergefell v. Hodges* (2015), most states outside the South had already legalized it—which is one reason why most opponents of the decision knew they had no realistic chance of reversing it.[34]

Conservative evangelicals lost their campaign against same-sex marriage because they failed to make a convincing case that gays wanted anything other than a basic American right. Some social conservatives argued that same-sex marriage should not be legalized because the state's primary interest in promoting marriage was its procreative function—which, they said, necessarily limited marriage to heterosexuals.[35] But the American cultural definition of marriage had been focused on a companionate ideal, rather than procreation, since the 1920s, and by the early twenty-first century, very few people outside socially conservative circles thought that the primary goal of marriage was to produce children. Some social conservatives argued that same-sex marriages were inherently unstable, because homosexuals were more promiscuous than heterosexuals. But by the early twenty-first century, same-sex romantic love appeared to a lot of people to be just like heterosexual romantic love: people dated around, slept with a few people, and then settled into a (mostly) monogamous marriage.

When evangelicals began their campaign against gay rights, in the late 1970s, most Americans did not view sexual orientation as an unchanging, inborn trait. Because sodomy was still illegal in most American states, and because homosexuality was still associated in many people's minds with mental illness or sexual deviancy, it was easy for them to win public support for an anti-gay rights campaign—especially if they argued that their main interest was protecting children from potential sexual predators. But by the twenty-first century, a new generation was coming of age with a completely different view of sexual orientation. Millennials viewed sexual orientation as a morally neutral, inborn biological trait that could not (and should not) be changed. They also viewed it as an essential part of one's identity, in the way that race or gender might be. Discrimination against gays, therefore, was a moral evil on a par with racism, sexism, or xenophobia. The result was an enormous generational divide on morality. Older evangelicals viewed same-sex marriage as an obvious evil. By contrast, younger Americans—and, to a certain extent, even younger evangelicals—believed that refusing to extend marriage rights was the real sin. Both sides believed that they had the moral high ground.

Part of the reason that the older generation of evangelicals lost credibility with the younger generation was that their defense of biblical morality had been too selective and too fraught with compromise. They quickly gave up the fight on divorce, perhaps because the issue affected their own churches, political allies, and families. Billy Graham, Jerry Falwell, and James Dobson all had children who divorced. One of the pastors on the executive board of the Moral Majority went through a painful divorce himself.[36]

Like many nonevangelicals, evangelical Christians came to view divorce as tragic and possibly even sinful in many cases—but not as something they could fight in the political sphere. Attempts to change the laws to make divorce more difficult proved to be a colossal failure. When Louisiana introduced a "covenant marriage" option that would allow couples going to the altar to voluntarily lock themselves into a pre-1970-style legal arrangement, where dissolving the marriage would be legally cumbersome and no-fault divorce would not be an option, only barely more than 1 percent of couples over a ten-year period agreed to submit to this.[37] Even among the most religious people in this socially conservative, traditionally Catholic and Baptist state, most people getting married recoiled at the idea of legally locking themselves into a permanent union.

And if evangelicals found themselves unable to prevent people either in their churches or outside them from getting divorced, they were equally unable to stop the widespread acceptance of premarital sex, even in their own congregations. By the second decade of the twenty-first century, more than half of all unmarried evangelicals had had sex by the time they were twenty-two, and among never-married evangelical adults of all ages the figure was more than 80 percent. More than half had had three or more sexual partners. Perhaps, for those who still subscribed to conservative sexual mores, it might have been at least slightly encouraging that 37 percent of evangelicals still thought that sex outside of marriage was "always wrong"— though 41 percent said it was "not wrong at all."[38] But with the overwhelming majority of young evangelicals failing to uphold traditional Christian standards in this area, and with nearly half not even claiming to believe in the standards, it certainly did not seem that evangelicals had won this battle in the culture wars. In fact, they had hardly tried. Although Christian books were filled with instructions on how to avoid sexual temptation, evangelicals' fight against premarital or extramarital sexual behavior, in the political realm, was limited mainly to campaigns to limit the sale of pornography—an effort that completely collapsed after online porn made campaigns against pornographic magazines obsolete.

Rediscovering a Biblical View of Sexuality

What could evangelicals have done differently? Perhaps they should have started by recognizing that the difference between a Christ-centered view of sexuality and the contemporary culture's standards was wider than they might have realized. The problem was not simply that the contemporary culture decided that a few behaviors that Christians had thought were wrong—such as homosexual sex or premarital sex—were actually okay. The problem was that contemporary Americans, like nearly all people who lacked a biblical worldview, had no understanding of the real purpose of sex. In the absence of Christian standards, various societies have imagined a wide variety of reasons for sex: procreation, pleasure, power displays, spiritual enlightenment, love, lust, manipulation, and a token of commitment, to name a few. The same has been true of non-Christian reasons for marriage. But no one outside Christian circles has imagined either marriage or sex in the way that the Bible describes it—that is, as a picture of the gospel. And few in today's secular culture see celibacy in the way that the Bible portrays it—that is, as a gift and a calling from God that can be used to God's glory and that in some settings is even preferable to marriage (1 Cor. 7:1-24).

This is the teaching that should have pervaded evangelical churches. If we understand the Bible's theology of sex and marriage, we will see that it is obvious that all sex outside of marriage is a violation of God's plan, because it is contrary to the picture of God's fidelity to his people that the Bible presents. And if we understand the Bible correctly, we will also see that marriage is not a human right but is instead a divine calling and a sacred trust—just as celibacy is. If this picture had been consistently presented, perhaps not nearly as many young evangelicals would have grown up thinking that the church was prejudiced against gays. Instead, they would have asked the same question about people experiencing same-sex attraction as they might have asked about any other group in the church: How can they best model the gospel picture in their own lives, regardless of their marital state? If the church had consistently insisted on marital faithfulness as a condition for service as an elder, deacon, or pastor, and if the church had acted quickly against all violations of the marital covenant on behalf of its leaders, perhaps a younger generation of evangelicals would have seen the beauty of

God's plan more clearly and would not have been as inclined to adopt the contemporary culture's standards for sexual behavior.

Similarly, if the church had adopted a biblical view of gender, a lot of current confusion among younger evangelicals could have been avoided. Social conservatives have often failed to effectively answer the charge from cultural liberals that rigidly conservative views of sexual behavior hurt women. Freedom for women, they say, can come only when female virginity is no longer treated as a fetish and women have the opportunity to negotiate sexual relationships on their own terms, without stigma or fear of pregnancy. Unfortunately, conservative evangelicals pushed back against these liberal arguments in the late twentieth century not with a thoughtful analysis of the purpose of gender and sexuality but with a ream of books that celebrated the physical ecstasy of marital sex while also defending complementarian gender roles by borrowing a great deal of outdated psychology from pre-1970 theories of gender, papered over with a thin veneer of Bible verses that supposedly supported these claims.[39] Perhaps it is no surprise that a younger generation of evangelicals found this thin reed of support for fixed complementarian gender roles less than compelling, and instead adopted not only a gender-egalitarian view of male-female relations in the church and the home but also an openness to premarital sex and gay and transgender rights claims. Perhaps a better starting point would have been the question of identity: Who determines a person's identity—God or the individual? Once we see that our primary identity is our relationship to Christ—not our sexual orientation, our gender, or any other quality—we can then work outward from that starting point to see how Christ can best be honored in the gendered bodies that God has given us. Rather than viewing gender as a fluid, self-defined construct, as our contemporary culture seems to do, we will ask the question why God chose to create people as male and female, and what God might have intended the relationship between the two to signify.

But very little of this can be translated into civil law. The reason that conservative Christians lost the fight against the sexual revolution regardless of whether they won political battles (as they did with the ERA and in the early stages of the gay rights movement) or lost them (as they ultimately did with same-sex marriage) is that the impetus for the social changes to which they objected came from the culture, not from the law. The Supreme Court was not the primary reason for the legalization of same-sex marriage in the United States. Rather, the legalization of same-sex marriage was the culmination of a century-long trend that included the separation of sex and marriage from procreation and lifelong commitment, the separation of sex from marriage, and an individualistic, rights-centered approach to both gender and sex. Most of all, it represented a belief that civil marriage was a contract, not a covenant—that is, a codified form of rights and obligations that reflected the interests of both parties, and not a binding vow before God that was subject to God's definitions. At this point, it is impossible to reverse these trends merely by fighting against same-sex marriage or by limiting the rights of transgender people.

Political Actions to Promote Marriage

Does this mean that Christians should not bring their views about sex and gender into the political sphere? Not at all. Christians do have a responsibility to promote biblical standards of sexuality and marriage to the extent that they can, because communities flourish when they have stable marriages. Even if the marriages of our non-Christian associates do not fully reflect a Christian view of the gospel, they nevertheless represent a positive good, both for the married couple and for other people in the community. Marriage tends, in most cases, to promote social stability. Children who grow up in two-parent households tend to have more economic resources, greater chances of academic success, and fewer emotional problems than children who grow up in single-parent families. Marriage restrains people's vices and selfishness, and channels people's energy toward concern for others, whether a spouse or children. Men who get married are less likely to go to prison or be sexually promiscuous.[40] Christians who care about their neighbors will want their community to adopt policies that promote lifelong marriage.

On this subject, the 2016 Republican Party platform is correct: "Every child deserves a married mom and dad." The family "is the foundation of civil society, and the cornerstone of the family is natural marriage, the union of one man and one woman."[41] Because of its commitment to pluralism, the Democratic Party refuses to affirm this.

But sadly, despite the Republican Party's affirmation of lifelong, heterosexual marriage and two-parent families, its own record in this area has been worse than that of liberals. Four of the last seven Republican presidential nominees have been divorced and remarried—two after being sexually unfaithful in their earlier marriages. Two of the five sitting Republican-appointed Supreme Court justices have been publicly accused of sexual harassment or sexual misconduct by multiple women. Of the four Republican Speakers of the House who have served during the past quarter century, only two gave credible evidence of being sexually faithfully to their wives; the other two included a serial adulterer who went through two divorces (including one that took place after an affair that he had while serving as Speaker and championing "family values" policies) and another who was subsequently sentenced to prison for sexually molesting several teen and preteen boys, despite being an alumnus of Wheaton College and a strong opponent of same-sex marriage.[42] The Democrats, of course, have had their own share of sex scandals and moral hypocrisy. But for a party that claims to stand for two-parent, monogamous, heterosexual marriage, Republican leaders' behavioral record has been particularly disappointing.

Even more disappointing, though, has been their policy record. Though Republicans have taken the lead in campaigning against same-sex marriage and ending the "marriage penalty" in the tax code, Republican economic policies that have hurt the working poor (such as an unwillingness to raise the minimum wage or extend the availability of federally funded health insurance to those barely above the poverty line) have probably hurt marriage rates, because there is a very close correlation between wealth and marriage—with poor people increasingly unlikely to marry at all.

Promoting Marriage by Helping the Poor

Although moral regulation has been an ineffective tool in fighting the cultural trends that undermine marriage, one policy tool might produce better results: poverty relief. Poor people and those with limited education are the least likely group in America today to get married and stay married. Before the late 1970s, the correlation between poverty (or low education) and divorce or between poverty and out-of-wedlock pregnancy was relatively low, but today it is stronger than it has ever been in American history. One 2010 study showed that 58 percent of forty-six-year-olds who had gotten married at some point in their lives but had never completed high school (and 49 percent of those who had only a high school diploma or who had attended some college but had not earned a four-year degree) had been divorced, while only 30 percent of those with a bachelor's degree had gone through a marital dissolution.[43] Baby boomers and older Gen-Xers who were poor or working class were far more likely to divorce than their middle- and upper-middle-class peers.

But now, among millennials, lower-income people are less likely to marry at all. One 2011 study showed that fewer than half of all adults with less than a four-year college education were currently married—compared to 64 percent of those with a BA degree. Although college graduates are likely to delay marriage until their late twenties or thirties, the vast majority eventually get married, and when they do marry, they are less likely than those with less education to get divorced or raise children in a single-parent home. But single-parent homes or live-in partnerships that lack the legal structure of marriage are now the norm for lower-income and less-educated Americans. The divorce rate has dropped slightly during the past forty years (it's now 39 percent), but the decrease in divorces has been more than offset by the increase in the percentage of children who experience the breakup of their unmarried parents' relationships. Fifty percent of children who are born into a home where their parents are cohabiting outside of wedlock will see their parents split up before they reach their ninth birthday. By contrast, only 20 percent of children born to married parents will experience this by age nine. And as marriage becomes the province of the educated middle class, the instability of cohabiting and single parenthood disproportionately affects the poor. The states that have the highest rates of single parenthood and divorce are the poorest states. Only 32 percent of children in Mississippi live in two-parent homes, compared to 52 percent in Massachusetts and 47 percent in California. The low marriage rates among the poor are not the result of choice. The majority of American adults who have never been married say that they would like to be.[44]

Christians should be concerned that marriage is increasingly becoming a privilege reserved for the middle class and the wealthy. While 56 percent of middle-class American adults between the ages of eighteen and fifty-five are currently married, only 39 percent of working-class Americans in this same age bracket are. For those below the poverty line, this number drops to only 26 percent.[45] In the past, cultural liberalism or the sexual revolution might have seemed to be the greatest threats to marriage, but today poverty is. To a certain extent, the sexual revolution has won among Americans of all social classes; no group has a consistently biblical approach to marriage and sexual behavior. Among the educated upper-middle class, delayed marriage, with a prolonged period of premarital sexual relationships, is now the norm. But once upper-middle-class people get married (usually sometime in their thirties), they tend to stay married. Since people from this group rarely have children outside of marriage, most children born into upper-middle-class professional homes will grow up in a two-parent family. Sixty-seven percent of children whose parents have four-year college degrees or graduate education are growing up in a home with two married biological parents. Among the lower-middle class and working class, early marriages and high levels of divorce are more common. And among younger members of the working class, as well as the vast majority of the poor, cohabitation and childrearing out of wedlock have become substitutes for marriage. Only 40 percent of the children of college dropouts—and only 33 percent of those whose parents have only a high school education or less—are living with two married parents. Among parents who are college dropouts, the majority have at least been married once—but have often gotten divorced—but among parents with a high school education or less, the majority have never been married at all.[46]

From a biblical standpoint, we know that the typical relationships for people in each of these three socioeconomic brackets fall far short of God's standard for marriage and sexuality. Premarital sex (with contraception, of course) has been the norm among the educated upper-middle class for the past half century. Their marriages are relatively stable, and their child-bearing is mostly confined to marriage, but there is no evidence that they are more likely than anyone else in America to view marriage as a binding, divinely authored covenant or a sacred obligation. They might be convinced that marriage is a desirable good and a social responsibility (at least when children are involved), and perhaps because of that view, they tend to put off a marital commitment until they have completed their education and become established financially—which often means that their late marriages might be preceded by nearly twenty years of out-of-wedlock sexual relationships. But they still view marriage as a dissolvable human contract, and they do not subscribe to the idea that sex is a divinely created marital sacrament that should be reserved for the covenant of marriage. The lower-middle class tends to marry earlier but also to divorce more frequently—which is why, among many lower-middle-class southern evangelicals, divorce rates are higher than they are for less religious (but better educated) members of the population and why divorce is no longer viewed as much of a sin, despite Jesus's statements on the subject.[47] And among the poorest Americans, the near-complete abandonment of marriage altogether—with cohabitation and single parenthood becoming far more common than marriage—is a sign of how far removed from the biblical ideal this group's behavior has become. No socioeconomic class is immune from the need for repentance in the area of sexuality and marriage. And no amount of moral regulation can solve this national moral crisis. But even if we recognize the limitations of public policy, there is still substantial social value in promoting marriage among the poor. Giving the poorest members of our society a path to marriage will not necessarily reduce the amount of out-of-wedlock sex in America, but it will increase the percentage of children growing up in two-parent homes, and it will give the poor an opportunity for family stability that is currently reserved primarily for those who are wealthier or better educated.

Conservatives and liberals frequently engage in a chicken-and-the-egg argument over which came first: poverty or low marriage rates. Are people poor because they choose to have children out of wedlock instead of getting married? Or do they feel unable to get married because they're poor? Perhaps both phenomena are at work. Many poor people now expect to have children before marriage, a choice that makes it less likely that they will be able to escape poverty. But on the other hand, one of the primary reasons that lower-income unmarried people give for not being married is financial insecurity; 47 percent of those making less than $30,000 a year and 40 percent of those earning between $30,000 and $75,000 cited financial issues as a "major" reason for their unmarried state.[48] If they felt more financially secure, they would be much more likely to get married and stay married.

What is needed is both a cultural change in the understanding of marriage and economic security for the working poor. Marriage rates would be much higher if we could return to the view that Americans had of marriage in the 1950s, 1960s, and early 1970s, when there was almost no difference between the marriage habits of the poor and those of the wealthy. Both the poor and the middle class married at young ages half a century ago, and neither group was much more likely than the other to get divorced.[49] Marriage rates may be low because millennials and the emerging Generation Z believe that they have to delay marriage until they finish their college education and attain an income level that the poor might never achieve. This expectation needs to change. But at the same time, we could probably also increase marriage rates by increasing income levels for the working poor. The Democratic Party's support for higher minimum wages and universal health insurance are not usually billed as pro-marriage proposals, but by reducing poverty, they will probably increase marriage rates and family stability and reduce the number of children growing up in single-parent homes.[50]

Other promising policy proposals that might improve marital and family stability by helping the poor, the marginalized, and the vulnerable (including especially vulnerable women) include the following.

Prison Reform

Proposals to reduce incarceration rates or replace prison sentences with other penalties would likely have a positive effect on marriage rates, because prison has a devastating effect on marriages. Men who have spent time in prison are only about half as likely to marry as men of the same age who have never spent time behind bars—yet they are just as likely to have children. And for prisoners who are already married at the time of their sentencing, imprisonment is a marriage-killer. One study indicated that for every year one partner in a marriage remained in prison, the chance of the marriage ending in divorce increased by 32 percent.[51]

Maternity Leave

The first federal mandate requiring American employers to give new mothers twelve weeks of unpaid leave so that they could care for their children was passed by a Democratic Congress and signed into law by President Bill Clinton. At the time, this was not on the Christian Right's list of priorities, perhaps partly because it amounted to a federal regulation of business (which the right has generally opposed) and perhaps also because it might have encouraged mothers of young children to remain in the workforce—a phenomenon that worried some conservative evangelicals who believed that children needed to receive care from their mothers, not a daycare facility. Conservative evangelicals may have had reason for this concern, but today, with 70 percent of mothers of children under age eighteen participating in the workforce, one might ask whether the most family-friendly strategy is to oppose family-leave policies on the grounds that mothers need to be at home full-time with their children or support measures that will allow working mothers to balance their work with family responsibilities and spend more time with their children without losing needed income. Today the Democratic Party supports converting unpaid family leave to paid leave by offering "all workers at least 12 weeks of paid leave to care for a new child."[52] Some progressives also want to find ways to make the workplace more family-friendly by offering parents flexible working hours, child-friendly work spaces, and opportunities to work from home.

Reunion of Undocumented Immigrant Families

The Trump administration has separated thousands of children from their families at the border and has placed those children in federal detention centers. As of April 2019, it appeared that it would take about two years for the government to complete the family reunification process for those children, and some children will never be reunited with their parents. But as bad as this is, a far more egregious family-separation policy is likely to take place if the Trump administration presses forward with its plan to deport a substantial percentage of the 11 million undocumented immigrants who are currently in the United States illegally. These families, which include more than 4 million children who were born in the United States and are therefore US citizens who cannot legally be forcibly deported, have often been in the United States for two decades or more. To deport these immigrants now would break up family units, separating children from parents and sometimes husbands from wives. As of 2011, there were five thousand children who ended up in the foster-care system because their undocumented parent had been deported or detained by immigration authorities. This number will likely increase significantly if the Trump administration is able to proceed with its proposal for large-scale deportations of "millions" of undocumented immigrants. In fact, the number of children left behind is probably already much higher than it was in 2011, because between 2015 and 2017, the US government deported 87,351 undocumented immigrants who claimed to have at least one US-born child.[53] The Democratic Party has proposed a path to citizenship for these immigrants and their families, a move that will prevent the broken homes that will be created with deportations.

Sexual Harassment Laws

Conservative Christians who care about God's standard of sexual behavior should rejoice in a zero-tolerance policy toward sexual harassment in the workplace and the college campus. However, the main impetus for these laws has come from liberals, with conservative Christians often turning a blind eye to calls for justice in this area. The first significant call for sexual harassment legislation came in the wake of Anita Hill's testimony during the Senate confirmation hearings for Clarence Thomas's nomination to the Supreme Court in 1991. At the time, Christian Right organizations supported Thomas and dismissed Hill's allegations, because they wanted another conservative justice on the Supreme Court. In the aftermath of the hearings, they did not include sexual harassment legislation in their list of political priorities.[54] Then, in 2016, most evangelical leaders associated with the Christian Right, with only a few rare exceptions, dismissed concerns about Donald Trump's crude comments about women. Again, the Supreme Court was a higher priority for them. In 2017, they gave only mixed support to the #MeToo movement's effort to force men who had engaged in sexual harassment to be held accountable for their behavior.[55] And in 2018, they defended Judge Brett Kavanaugh against allegations of sexual misconduct brought forward by multiple women—just as the majority of white evangelical voters in Alabama had done the previous year, when several women accused Republican Senate candidate Roy Moore of sexual misconduct and rape. Liberals, of course, have not had a perfectly clean record on this matter either (as Bill Clinton's affairs and Democrats' reactions to them in the 1990s demonstrated), but it is sad that when Democrats, prompted by the demands of a grassroots women's movement, have taken new steps to hold men accountable for sexual behavior that evangelicals have always known is wrong, Republican evangelicals have chosen party over principle and have consistently defended political allies against all charges. It is even more unfortunate that they have shown so little interest in strengthening policies against sexual harassment—even though this would seem to be a rare opportunity to bring civil law or workplace policy into closer harmony with God's standards.

What Is a Christian Response to the Marriage Crisis?

Christians who want to honor God's standards of sexual behavior and value marriage in the way that God intended will have to take a countercultural stance that aligns with neither political party. Americans of both parties have largely accepted the legitimacy of sex outside of marriage. Both groups have seen marriage as a contractual partnership rather than an inviolable, divinely ordered covenant. Faithful Christians will have to stand against these cultural trends in their own lives and practice lifelong fidelity to a single partner even when the cultural pressures for a different choice seem overwhelming. If most unmarried adults are having sex, biblically minded single Christians will need to be part of the minority who wait until marriage. If the vast majority of their associates are using pornography, Christians will need to live counterculturally and rely on the Spirit's gift of self-control to resist sinful opportunities that may be only a finger-click away. If a Christian married couple is part of a culture that accepts divorce as an option of last resort, they will need to stand against that cultural trend and rely on God's grace to persevere in loving each other even through difficult times. If millions of low-income Americans are cohabiting rather than getting married because they find the financial pressures overwhelming, low-income Christians who are dating a prospective partner may have to defy expectations, budget as carefully as they can, and then take a step of faith by getting married even when they know that money will be tight. If millions of highly educated Americans are postponing marriage until their thirties even as they engage in long-term sexual relationships before going to the altar, college-educated Christians who have found a prospective spouse and are determined to remain sexually pure may have to make a countercultural choice by getting married in their early twenties, even if they haven't yet completed graduate school or achieved the expected level of financial stability. And if tens of millions of people are saying that there is nothing wrong with sex between two people of the same gender, a Christian who experiences same-sex attraction will have to rely on God's strength in fighting against an overwhelming cultural pressure to give in to those desires. In all these areas, Christians who are resolved to live counterculturally should look first to their own lives—and, second, to fellow believers in their churches—before attempting to change the culture. If we fail to confess our own sins and take the sexual motes out of our own eyes before speaking to the larger culture on these issues, we will only further damage the cause we seek to promote.

But if our own house is in order and we have honestly confessed our own failings before seeking to change others, we can then assess how we can promote marriage and sexual morality in the public square. And we might find that, despite all the confusion that exists in our culture because of a century-long sexual revolution, there is at least one reason to remain hopeful: the vast majority of Americans value marriage. This might seem like a strange statement in view of the fact that the vast majority of Americans have sex outside of marriage, view marriage as an impermanent contract whose definition can be changed at will, and, in the case of many people, raise children outside of marriage. But public-opinion polls show that most Americans want to be married, and their behavior indicates the same. The decades-long campaign for same-sex marriage was a sign of how much many gays and lesbians wanted to be a part of an institution that most Americans view as an essential component of adult life and a source of lasting joy. Politicians of both political parties frequently affirm the value of marriage on the campaign trail, whether in speaking of their policy proposals or talking about their own experiences with a spouse. The high value that Americans place on marriage—with most unmarried adults saying that they want to get married and most people saying that divorce is a problem, even if they view it as necessary in some cases—is not necessarily shared by people in some regions of the world, such as Scandinavia, where unmarried cohabiting is common even among the highly educated. But in the United States, there is enough vestigial memory of a Christian standard to make people long for a lifelong, happy marriage, even when the dream might seem unattainable.

Christians can rely on this cultural ethos, as imperfect as it might be, and pursue policies that will help people pursue their dream of marriage. Perhaps in our current society, the best way to fight the effects of the sexual revolution is not with legal regulations of immoral behavior but rather with economic policies that will give people the tools they need to get married and experience its blessings for themselves. The greatest threat to a culture of marriage in the United States is probably not a change in definition of marriage, or even a culture of divorce, but rather the rise of a society in which a growing number of people believe that they are cut off from the blessing of marriage because of their economic circumstances. Changing this mindset will probably be a work of the church more than a project of the state. But if there is something that we can do at the voting booth to give economically marginalized people the financial ability to choose marriage or to keep their marital union intact, why would we pass up this opportunity?

Same-Sex Marriage and Religious Liberty

In the view of some conservative Christians, everything that I have said about marriage policy up to this point has failed to address the real issue involved in the contemporary political battle over marriage: the right of Christians to refuse to endorse same-sex marriages that they consider to be sinful. Until 2015, conservative Christians' fight against same-sex marriage was primarily a battle to keep the state from giving its imprimatur to unions that they considered sinful and not true marriages at all. But since the Supreme Court's *Obergefell v. Hodges* decision of 2015 rendered this battle futile and irrelevant, conservative Christians have turned their attention to an issue that they consider equally important: the battle to protect individual Christians from being compelled to violate their consciences by endorsing these marriages.

In 2017, the Supreme Court issued a narrowly defined decision that barely prevented the state of Colorado from forcing a baker to decorate a cake for a same-sex couple. Colorado claimed that the baker was discriminating against the couple on the basis of their sexual orientation, which is a violation of civil rights law. The baker claimed that he was exercising his right to free speech and freedom of religion. By siding with the baker on the narrowest grounds imaginable (that is, a mere technicality of Colorado's motivations in the matter), the Supreme Court left open the broader question of whether a businessperson's right of conscience or freedom of religion trumps the civil rights of LGBT people to equal accommodations and equal opportunity for commercial transactions. Both sides in this controversy expect continued court challenges in this contest between two competing sets of rights. The Democratic Party's platform has sided firmly with LGBT rights in this matter; religious freedom, Democrats argue, cannot be used as an excuse for discrimination against gays. The Republican Party platform, by contrast, calls for the maximum protection of religious liberty in this matter. Which side is right? How should a Christian decide this question?

From one perspective, at least, the Bible's guidance on this question is clear: no right is more important than the right to freely obey God. As Peter told the Sanhedrin council in the fifth chapter of Acts, Christians believe that when there is a conflict between civil law and God's law, "we must obey God rather than human beings" (Acts 5:29). If a Christian realizes that all rights come from God, and that our duty to God supersedes every other responsibility, it would seem that the right to freely worship God and follow the commands of God would be greater than every other right. The early Christians sometimes had to suffer imprisonment and death because of their refusal to follow state laws, but in the United States, we have often had the privilege to avoid punishment because of our nation's expansive view of religious freedom. Indeed, the United States has traditionally taken a more expansive view of religious freedom than most other democracies (let alone totalitarian states), and this is a tradition that is worth guarding carefully—as other Christian groups, especially the Catholic Church in recent years, have noted. "Freedom of conscience and of religion," Pope John Paul II declared in 1980, "is a primary and inalienable right of the human person; what is more, insofar as it touches the innermost sphere of the spirit, one can even say that it upholds the justification, deeply rooted in each individual, of all other liberties."[56] From this perspective, the Democratic Party's willingness to subvert religious freedom to LGBT rights is alarming.

In the view of a large number of Democrats today, LGBT rights are civil rights, and they deserve just as much legal protection as African Americans' right to equal treatment under the law. Because the Supreme Court ruled in 1983 that the First Amendment did not protect religious colleges from the consequences of violating federal civil rights statutes even if they opposed interracial marriage on religious grounds, many observers on both sides of the debate over same-sex marriage believe that the inclusion of LGBT rights in state or federal civil rights policy will not leave much room for religious exemptions except in the narrowest of circumstances.[57] Currently, liberal supporters of same-sex marriage generally believe that religious institutions (e.g., churches, synagogues, temples, or mosques) could claim exemptions from being compelled to perform same-sex marriages, but beyond this narrowest of concessions to religious freedom in the case of churches' right to uphold their beliefs on their own property, they do not believe that the First Amendment's free exercise clause can give any protection to religiously based violation of LGBT civil rights.[58] They have argued that an individual—whether an employee or a small-business owner—does not have the freedom to opt out of servicing same-sex weddings on grounds of conscience, and a number of lower courts have upheld this argument. Even theological seminaries may not be exempt from this requirement. Two Fuller Theological Seminary students who were expelled for marrying same-sex partners in violation of the seminary's statement of beliefs are now suing the seminary for violation of their civil rights.[59] Whether they will win their lawsuit is still undetermined, but the fact that they have taken Fuller Theological Seminary to court is an indication of how far some proponents of LGBT rights are willing to go in their effort to narrow the grounds of religious exemptions to state or federal LGBT civil rights policy.

Many Christians who value freedom of religion have allied with conservative politicians who promise to protect the right of individuals, businesses, and institutions to act on their religious convictions, not only in the area of LGBT rights but also in regard to abortion and other matters. Traditionally, conservatives have shown more interest in individual rights than in the right to equality for minority groups, so it is not surprising that the Republican Party has sided with religious liberty in the current battle between marriage equality and religious freedom. There was a time, a few decades ago, when liberal Democrats also supported the right of conscience to a greater degree. In the early 1970s, for instance, at a time when many liberals opposed the Vietnam War on grounds of conscience, there was widespread support among liberals for legislation to protect the rights of doctors and nurses who refused on religious grounds to participate in abortions.[60] But today the mainstream liberal Democratic position is that the right to equality—whether the right to equal access to abortion and contraception, the right to marriage equality, or the right of LGBT people to equal treatment under the law—cannot be curtailed by appeals to religious freedom or the First Amendment's free exercise clause. In the view of many contemporary

Christians, therefore, the Republican Party is their only hope of protecting not only their own religious liberty but also the religious liberty of their neighbors, including (but not limited to) fellow Christians. If they were to surrender on this issue, numerous religious colleges, hospitals, seminaries, and other institutions might be forced to close or, at the very least, would be subjected to expensive lawsuits and the loss of tax exemptions or other privileges. And the nation itself would suffer, because one of the most important foundational human rights would be restricted.[61]

But before we jump to the conclusion that the only way to defend the cause of the gospel and human rights is to support the Republican Party on this issue, there is another question that we need to consider: the question of whether it is reasonable to expect the courts to protect Christians from the consequences of a cultural shift that has already mostly occurred. What we are seeing from the Democratic Party is not so much an unprecedented assault on religious liberty but rather a ratification of a long-standing principle in American law that religious freedom does not give people the right to violate the rights of others. Even the most ardent defenders of religious liberty have admitted that the principle of religious freedom does not invariably trump every other human right—including the right to equality. Pope John Paul II himself conceded this. As he defended religious liberty in the strongest terms, he added, as a caveat, "Of course, such freedom can only be exercised in a responsible way, that is, in accordance with ethical principles and by respecting equality and justice."[62] The American legal system has adopted a similar position. While courts have nearly always recognized that people have an absolute freedom to participate in the religious worship services of their choice or to opt out of officially organized religion altogether, the courts have generally not allowed people to use their religious beliefs as a justification for behavior that is generally considered morally objectionable or dangerous. In *Reynolds v. United States* (1879), the Supreme Court ruled that Mormons' freedom of religion did not give them the right to engage in polygamy. In *Employment Division v. Smith* (1990), the Supreme Court declared that appeals to religious freedom could not exempt Native Americans from the consequences for violations of state drug policies when they smoked peyote in religious ceremonies. And in *Bob Jones University v. United States* (1983), the Supreme Court ruled that the First Amendment's guarantee of religious freedom could not protect the South Carolina fundamentalist university from having its tax exemption denied because it violated federal civil rights policy through its religiously motivated ban on interracial dating among its students.[63] Perhaps some of these cases were wrongly decided, but regardless of whether we agree with the Supreme Court's reasoning, it is clear that long before LGBT rights became an issue, the court was perfectly comfortable saying that while people in the United States had the right to believe whatever they wanted when it came to religion and to go to any place of worship they chose, the right of free religious practice did not give them the right to practice polygamy, use illicit drugs, or violate federal civil rights policy.

In at least some of those cases, conservative evangelicals were not particularly concerned, because their religiously motivated practices did not yet violate social norms in the way that polygamy, illicit drug use, or racial discrimination did. Today we are on the verge of seeing alleged discrimination against LGBT people treated as tantamount to racial or gender discrimination, and when that happens, we cannot expect the courts to give any more preference to the religious liberty defense than the Supreme Court did in these other cases.

In general, the Supreme Court is willing to grant religious liberty or free-speech exemptions when the behavior in question is not viewed as socially disruptive—which is why, for instance, the court ruled in favor of the Amish people's right to withdraw their children from school after eighth grade and why the court similarly upheld the right of Jehovah's Witnesses to exempt their children from mandatory school pledge-of-allegiance drills.[64] But we cannot realistically expect the court to do this for conservative evangelicals once objections to same-sex marriage become as socially unacceptable as objections to interracial marriage. The Supreme Court tends to follow prevailing cultural opinion on these sorts of issues, so when the culture shifts, we can expect the court to follow sooner or later.

What should a Christian do in the face of this? If we have lost the cultural battle for the definition of marriage, we cannot expect the courts to protect us forever. This means, I think, that instead of fighting for what I believe is ultimately going to be another failed cause, we need to think about how to use whatever resources we have not to protect our rights at all costs but rather to love our neighbors and gain a hearing for the gospel. When Paul thought that he could win a hearing for the gospel by suffering, he was willing to be beaten for the sake of the gospel, even when it violated his rights as a Roman citizen (Acts 16). On the other hand, when he thought that he could win a hearing for the gospel by exercising his rights, he did so. He did all things "for the sake of the gospel," he said (1 Cor. 9:23). Christians today should do the same thing.

How individual Christians decide to do this may vary, but if we decide to embark on a political campaign or a legal challenge to protect our religious liberty, we need to make sure that doing so will advance the gospel rather than merely protect us from having to suffer for the cause of Christ. Some Christians may decide that they can best advance the gospel by protecting their fellow Christians' right to act on their convictions without losing their jobs, businesses, or personal savings, and by ensuring that the United States will continue to honor religious liberty as an inviolable, foundational right—a position that they may view as the best way of ensuring that the rights directly pertaining to a person's relationship with God will receive more protection than any right merely governing interpersonal relationships. But if we take this position, we need to make sure that we are not merely seeking to protect our own interests. Only if we are just as zealous to defend the religious freedom of Muslims or Sikhs as we are to speak up for the rights of Christians can we say that we are consistent advocates of religious liberty. And even then, we need to be sure that our advocacy of religious liberty is genuinely advancing the gospel. I question whether the cause of the gospel is advanced when Christians make headlines for winning the right to practice what others believe is discrimination or when they attend political rallies where they give hearty applause to politicians who promise to protect their rights. Such behavior does not strike non-Christians as loving or unselfish—probably because, in some cases, the behavior really is more self-interested than self-sacrificial. Ideally, a defense of our own religious liberty will be coupled with a willingness to protect the rights of those with whom we disagree, including both non-Christian religious minorities and people who self-identify as LGBT—because even if we know from Scripture that their beliefs and behavior are wrong, we still have a responsibility to protect their human dignity and right to equality under the law.

Some Christians are opposed to any new legal protections for LGBT individuals, both because they believe (with some justification) that these protections will restrict their own religious liberty to act on their convictions and because they believe that these legal protections would amount to an endorsement of sin. And so, for decades Christians have waged unsuccessful defensive political campaigns that have not only failed in their original objective but have also resulted in ill will toward conservative Christians from defenders of LGBT rights. I am not sure that a defense of the Bible's standards of sexuality required Christians to engage in these political campaigns or to oppose all gay rights measures. I think that Christians could have supported stronger measures to protect the human dignity of people who self-identify as LGBT without necessarily endorsing sinful sexual behavior and without compromising their own freedom to act on their Christian convictions. In a morally pluralistic society, Christians need to remember that biblical law cannot (and should not) always be enshrined in American law. The principle that God sends his blessings on both the righteous and the unrighteous (Matt. 5:45) should, in at least some cases, guide our understanding of how we can best promote justice and win a hearing for the gospel among people who are skeptical about Christians' commitment to equality.

One recent approach that seeks to extend an olive branch to LGBT rights advocates while also protecting conservative Christians' religious liberty is a proposal from a Republican congressman to add LGBT rights to federal civil rights policy (which congressional Democrats support), but only on condition that individuals, small businesses, and religious institutions (including religious schools) will receive exemptions from this law and be given the right to act on their own convictions. Unfortunately, this proposal currently has very little chance of ever becoming law in our polarized political climate, because advocates of LGBT rights are unlikely to concede this much ground to religious conservatives who oppose same-sex marriage, and some religious conservatives are reluctant to enshrine LGBT rights in federal civil rights policy, a move that they believe would be a compromise with sin.[65] Therefore, no political compromise is in sight that will resolve the conflict between LGBT rights and religious liberty. In this polarized political culture, many conservative Christians have adopted an all-or-nothing approach to this issue, but this approach is highly unlikely to win—and even if it does, it will likely damage the reputation of the gospel among people who view Christians as opponents of equal rights.

The way of the cross will certainly not compromise God's standards of sexuality or of marriage, but neither will it engage in a worldly rights-based politics that seeks to use the courts to protect ourselves against a hostile culture. Real victories in the culture will come not through the courts but through a quiet witness of love and self-sacrifice. What will this look like in practice? It may mean something very different from what either the Democratic or Republican Party offers. It may mean using public policy to empower people to get married and stay married, while at the same time bearing countercultural witness of marital faithfulness in our own lives. It may mean genuine repentance when we fall short of God's standards ourselves and a humble trust in God when our stances strike others as objectionable or anachronistic. And when it comes to voting, it may mean that we will support candidates whose policies are most likely to promote marital stability—not merely candidates who appeal to our own self-interest or who offer a promise of cultural victories that politics can never provide.

Some Christians may decide that they can best preserve a witness for the gospel by supporting the Republican Party's advocacy of religious freedom and the sanctity of the two-parent family, but when they do so, they need to also remember that defending biblical marriage means a lot more than merely speaking out against homosexuality. They need to consider the possibility that the party's stances on immigration, economics, and other issues may be contributing to the disintegration of two-parent families—and that if that is the case, they have a responsibility to work to change these policies. Other Christians may decide to support the Democratic Party because of its advocacy for the poor, but if they do so, they also have a responsibility to speak out against the party's official abandonment of biblical standards of marriage. The Democratic Party has endorsed a sinful philosophy, and Christians who are Democrats have a particular duty to oppose it. They also need to speak up for the right of Christians to act on their convictions when it comes to opposing same-sex marriage—a right that current Democratic Party policy seems unlikely to fully protect. But in defending religious liberty, all Christians—whether Democrats or Republicans—need to make sure that they are not merely acting out of self-interest, and that they are genuinely attempting to win a hearing for the gospel. They need to pray for the wisdom that Paul demonstrated in determining when to exercise his legal rights and when to suffer a wrong without complaint for the sake of Christ.

Religious freedom and biblical marriage are important values, but neither is as important as the glory of God and the gospel. Regardless of what political strategy we adopt on these issues, we need to make sure that it will result in the gospel winning a hearing among our neighbors. Sometimes the gospel may be magnified if the freedom for Christians to act on their religious convictions is protected, but there are also times when the glory of the gospel will be most evident if Christians show more concern for their neighbors' rights than for their own and if they are willing to suffer for their beliefs without complaint.

5

Race

From one man he made all the nations, that they should inhabit the whole earth.

—Acts 17:26a

After this I looked, and there before me was a great multitude that no one could count, from every nation, tribe, people and language, standing before the throne and before the Lamb. They were wearing white robes and were holding palm branches in their hands. And they cried out in a loud voice: "Salvation belongs to our God, who sits on the throne, and to the Lamb."

—Revelation 7:9–10

This is what the Lord says: Do what is just and right. Rescue from the hand of the oppressor the one who has been robbed. Do no wrong or violence to the foreigner, the fatherless or the widow, and do not shed innocent blood in this place.

—Jeremiah 22:3

April 23, 1899, was a Sunday afternoon in Newnan, Georgia, but the righteous-minded residents of the town had something other than church on their minds when they paraded Sam Hose through the streets in preparation for his lynching. For weeks, the Atlanta newspapers had issued scathing indictments of Hose's crimes, and the city's most prominent paper, the *Atlanta Constitution*, had even offered a $500 reward for his arrest. Hose, a young black man who, like most African Americans of his generation, worked for a white property owner instead of being able to own his own land, had murdered his boss, Alfred Cranford, with an axe, the papers declared. Even worse, he had raped his employer's wife immediately after the axe-murder, they reported. His crime was "of such a revolting nature as to sicken the heart of the most hardened person," the *Atlanta Constitution* editorialized, under a headline that read, "Negro Will Probably Be Burned."[1]

Hose was indeed burned to death. After eluding his pursuers for two weeks, he was finally caught, but instead of facing a jury—which surely would have condemned him to execution, albeit in a possibly more humane manner—he experienced the wrath of a lynch mob. In front of nearly two thousand people, the lynch mob stripped Hose of his clothes, bound him with a heavy chain, and then cut off his ears, followed by his fingers. Having mutilated their victim, they then doused him in oil and set him on fire. Immediately after his death, they scrambled to cut up his bone fragments, which some marketed as souvenirs. Pieces of bone were sold for twenty-five cents, while portions of Hose's liver "crisply cooked" went for a dime. Some of the four thousand people who had taken special trains from Atlanta to witness the lynching, but who had arrived too late to see it, were especially eager to buy "pieces of flesh" as a prize for their Sunday outing.[2]

Because Hose, in a vain attempt to ward off the lynch mob, had told the crowd that a nearby black preacher named Elijah Strickland had paid him $12 to murder his employer, the mob then rounded up Strickland. The sixty-year-old preacher insisted on his innocence and brought character witnesses to testify in his favor, but to no avail. Despite the dubiousness of Hose's claim, the mob murdered Strickland and then cut him up as well—likely only a few hours after the clergyman delivered his last Sunday sermon.[3]

Brushing aside the lynching of Strickland—which embarrassed some southern whites, including the editors of the *Louisville Courier-Journal*, who called it "weird"—the white leaders of Georgia focused instead on Hose's crime and insisted that he deserved the retaliation that he had received. Hose's act of murder and rape was "the most diabolical in the history of crime," the governor declared. While the governor insisted that he wanted to protect the black citizens of his state against mob violence, he also warned blacks that if they wanted "to secure protection against lawless whites, they must show a disposition to protect the white people against the lawless blacks." The *Atlanta Constitution* adopted a nearly identical position. If people were disturbed by the thought of the "ravisher in flames," they needed to remember "the darker picture of Mrs. Cranford outraged [i.e., raped] in the blood of her murdered husband," the *Constitution* declared. "The wife was seized, choked, thrown upon the floor, where her clothing lay in the blood of her husband, and ravished," the paper asserted. "Remember the slain husband, and, above all, remember that shocking degradation which was inflicted by the black beast, his victim swimming in her husband's warm blood as the brute held her to the floor."[4] This view extended to some of the clergy as well. Sam Jones, a popular southern Methodist evangelist, defended the lynching as an appropriate penalty for rape. "The man, white or black, who commits an outrage on a virtuous woman, deserves death," he declared. "Sam Hose deserved to be burnt."[5]

Black Christians saw the matter very differently. Ida B. Wells, a civil rights activist who had edited a newspaper in Memphis before the threat of mob violence forced her to flee the South for Chicago, wondered why whites who professed be so concerned about sexual violence against women did not call for the death of white men who raped black women. In 1892 in Nashville, she pointed out, a lynch mob that invaded a jail and hanged a black man for merely visiting a white woman rushed past a white man who was in the same jail for raping an eight-year-old black girl and left him unharmed. In fact, most of the black men who were lynched were not rapists, she argued. When a group of Chicago African Americans, headed by a local minister, hired a private investigator to travel to Georgia to collect the facts about the lynching of Sam Hose, the detective concluded that Hose had actually never raped Mrs. Cranford at all, and his murder of her husband had nothing to do with sex and everything to do with economics and power. In the heat of an argument about wages, Cranford had threatened Hose, who then, in a moment of misjudgment, threw an axe at his employer, killing him. As the detective noted at a mass meeting of African Americans at Chicago's Bethel Church, Mrs. Cranford "says herself that Hose did not say a word to her or in any way touch her."[6]

In April 2015, three white police officers patrolling a low-income, predominantly black neighborhood in Baltimore that, in the words of the *New York Times*, was "known for drug dealing," looked a young man in the eye—twenty-five-year-old Freddie Gray—who was not doing anything noticeably wrong at the time but who became nervous and ran. The chase did not last long. When the police caught Gray, they threw him to the ground and crushed his larynx. Gray, who was asthmatic, did not resist arrest, but his compliance came too late. He asked for his inhaler, but since he did not have it with him, the officers did not give him one. Instead, they handcuffed him and, in violation of police protocol, did not fasten his seatbelt when they placed him in a police van—an omission that ensured that a handcuffed person would receive what was colloquially known as a "rough ride." By the end of the ride, the officers had put Gray in leg irons, which probably exacerbated his pain. After being jostled in the van for forty minutes, Gray quit breathing and was no longer able to speak. When doctors examined him, they found that his spine was 80 percent severed at the neck. They were unable to save him, and Gray died a week later. The officers never charged Gray with anything except attempting to elude the police and possessing a small switchblade that some thought might be long enough to be a violation of a Baltimore city ordinance—though the Maryland state attorney asserted that the blade length of Gray's pocketknife was within legal limits. He died because of police treatment that he received merely for attempting to run away.[7]

The police officers were put on trial for homicide but found not guilty. The Trump administration's Justice Department declared that it would not bring federal charges against the officers. And in many (though, thankfully, not all) predominantly white evangelical churches throughout the country, black Christians who talked about police violence against blacks or who used the slogan "Black Lives Matter" were told that such talk was divisive. Just as with the lynching of Sam Hose, the deaths of Freddie Gray and a host of other young black men at the hands of police divided Christians, with many black churches expressing outrage and demanding justice and many white churches remaining silent or even showing support for the police.[8]

On May 25, 2020, a white police officer in Minneapolis pressed his knee into the neck of the handcuffed forty-six-year-old George Floyd for nearly nine minutes and killed him, ignoring his pleas for his life and the entreaties of bystanders who were outraged to see what the officer was doing with the support of two of his colleagues. Like Gray, Floyd had had a difficult life. He had spent time in prison in Houston for armed robbery more than a decade earlier, and after moving to Minneapolis and taking two jobs to make ends meet, he had lost those jobs due to the economic disruptions of COVID-19. Like Gray, he posed no threat to the police or to anyone else at the time of his arrest. He was arrested for allegedly trying to give a counterfeit bill to a store clerk, and he died, it seems, merely because a police officer decided in anger to give him a taste of "street justice." Like Gray, he left behind many friends and family members who could not make sense of the tragedy. One of those was his six-year-old daughter.[9]

This time, hundreds of thousands of people across the country decided that they had had enough, and they took to the streets in protest. Within days of Floyd's killing, the nation became engulfed in race-related demonstrations on a scale that had not occurred since 1968. Cities across the United States, from Atlanta to Los Angeles, felt compelled to impose curfews because of the massive unrest. It was clear that many people shared the sentiment of Floyd's closest friend, Christopher Harris: "When you try so hard to put faith in this system, a system that you know isn't designed for you, when you constantly seek justice by lawful means and you can't get it, you begin to take the law into your own hands."[10] If those of us who are white Christians genuinely want to understand the rage against racial injustice, we have to find out how this "system" of structural racism operates and why Floyd's friend and numerous other African Americans are convinced that it has always been biased against them. Issues of race, of course, involve more than interactions between blacks and whites, but because whites' use of blacks as a controlled labor force has shaped the nation's perceptions of race for the past four centuries, this chapter will focus mainly on this story and its continuing effects on Americans today.

How Should We Understand These Attacks on Black Lives?

The deaths of Hose, Gray, and Floyd were not isolated cases but were instead part of a much larger pattern. In the year in which Hose was lynched, twenty-six other blacks in Georgia also met their deaths at the hands of a lynch mob—as did more than 4,500 American blacks between 1882 and 1935. In the year in which Gray died, American police fatally shot 995 people—23 percent of whom were black men, in a nation in which black males account for only 6.4 percent of the population. Only 54 percent of the people fatally shot were even carrying a gun, let alone using it to endanger someone else's life.[11]

But as disturbing as racial discrimination in law enforcement or white fears of black crime might be, these issues are not the only reasons for the violent deaths of blacks at the hands of whites. To find the root cause of their deaths, we have to look at American racial injustice as a system of economic exploitation of the black labor force, with law enforcement or vigilante violence used to control blacks who are kept in poverty through policy decisions that have deprived them of a chance to get ahead. Like the vast majority of young black men of his generation, Sam Hose was denied the opportunity to be a free, independent farmer. Blacks accounted for 56 percent of the population of Coweta County, Georgia, at the time, but they owned only forty-four of the county's 2,855 farms—that is, less than 2 percent of the farms.[12] Because Hose was denied the opportunity to own land of his own, both his livelihood and his life depended on the whim of his employer. When he asked his employer for a higher wage, his employer answered his question with a gun, prompting Hose to fear for his life. And when Hose threw an axe at his employer in self-defense, he knew that he would receive no mercy from all-white law enforcement or an all-white jury. Indeed, he probably knew that he would be lynched before his case even went to trial, because during the two months before his own lynching, seven blacks in Coweta County and nearby Campbell County met their deaths at the hands of lynch mobs.[13] Hose's death was not simply the product of individual white hatred; it was the product of systematic economic exploitation, racial injustice in the legal system, and a pervasive white fear of black revolt and black sexual violence. It was not surprising that the story of a young black man killing his employer would quickly be distorted into the sensational story of black-on-white rape, or that, for many white churchgoing Christians in the region, this story would seem to be a justifiable reason for violent retaliation against Hose.

The deaths of Freddie Gray and George Floyd were also rooted in economic injustice, because today in the twenty-first century, just as in the late nineteenth and twentieth centuries, blacks who live in lower-income neighborhoods are especially vulnerable to police violence. Gray was born prematurely to a Baltimore mother who was a heroin addict and middle-school dropout who could not read. After coming home from the hospital, he was taken to a cheap apartment where lead paint was peeling off the walls. For decades, many of the poorest blacks in Baltimore and other major urban areas in America had lived in decrepit apartments that were owned by white landlords who jeopardized the lives and health of their black tenants by violating safety standards. When Gray was three, the lead level in his body was more than seven times as high as the CDC-approved limits; in fact, it was high enough to justify a lawsuit against the apartment owner. When Gray went to school, he was diagnosed with attention deficit hyperactivity disorder (ADHD)—which some thought might have been caused by the high lead levels in his body—and he had to repeat several grades. By the time he was a young adult, he was living a life in and out of prison—mostly for possession of heroin and marijuana, as well as for other related crimes.[14] When the police looked him in the eye on the day they were patrolling his neighborhood, they assumed that Gray and other young black men like him were likely to be causing trouble. And the solution for which white Americans had settled decades earlier was the only solution they knew: lock people like Gray up. Had they simply taken him to jail for another round of imprisonment, his case never would have made headlines. He would have been merely one of the hundreds of thousands of young black men who would spend much of their lives in prison. Gray's life became a matter of public scrutiny only because police went too far in this case by shackling him in a van, causing his spinal cord to snap and killing him. But the problem that Gray faced was not solely a result of police misjudgment; instead, his entire twenty-five-year life was shaped by racialized poverty—a structure that included poor schools, unsafe apartments, abundant drugs, limited job opportunities, and the lack of a stable, two-parent family. Floyd's early life may have been marginally better, but it was still a story of struggling to survive. It is perhaps no coincidence that at the time of his death, he had recently lost his job and was out of work—like 17 percent of other black workers, the group with the highest unemployment rate in the United States.[15]

Fighting racial injustice, therefore, will mean more than simply decrying particular abuses of power on the part of police or anyone else. It will certainly include this—and I, for one, am glad that conversations about racial discrimination in policing or ways to discourage police officers from using excessive force have entered the national conversation. These matters understandably anger many African Americans, especially African American men who are repeatedly harassed by random police stops and who sense with each encounter with the police that their lives could be in danger. But fighting the racial injustice that led to decades of lynching, followed by decades of mass incarceration and police brutality against African Americans, will also mean confronting the long history and continuing reality of economic exploitation based on race—an exploitation that not only affects the large numbers of African Americans who are poor but that also contributes to white racism against even the comparatively few African Americans who defy the statistical odds to become wealthy. For white Christians, it will also mean learning to see racial issues from the point of view of our black brothers and sisters in Christ rather than through the assumptions that have shaped the political circles in which we might have traveled in the past. I am thankful to see that many white Christians are now rightly disturbed by the police killings of unarmed black people, but even those who have begun to say that "black lives matter" might not fully understand the larger racist structures of economic exploitation that have shaped the social backdrop to these murders. We are living in a nation that was founded—and that continues to exist—on stolen goods. Those stolen goods include the labor, the human dignity, and, far too often, the very lives of African Americans. Those of us who are white cannot hope to achieve racial justice or racial reconciliation in our churches, communities, or nation until we acknowledge this situation and the ways in which we might have personally benefited from it and unknowingly perpetuated it. But to oppose this racist economic exploitation from a distinctively Christian framework—instead of merely a secular framework based on contemporary notions of social justice—we need to first look at what the Bible says about God's vision of racial unity and the dignity of each divinely created person.

The Bible's Vision of Racial Unity and Justice

When we turn our eyes from the streets of our nation's cities to the soaring vision of racial unity in the final pages of Scripture, the contrast is so jarring that it may be hard at first to fully grasp. The heavenly scene in Revelation 7, in which people from "every nation, tribe, people and language" stand in their redeemed heavenly glory and bring honor to the Lamb who has purchased them for himself (Rev. 7:9), is one of the most compelling pictures of racial unity in the Bible. John Piper has used this passage as a central theme in explaining his own journey from white southern racism to a passionate commitment to racial equality. The passage has been quoted in articles against racism from a wide range of evangelical ministries, ranging from Intervarsity Christian Fellowship blogs to *Charisma* magazine articles.[16] And indeed, the passage is worth reading and rereading, because it offers us a glimpse of God's equal love for people from every racial and ethnic group, and his relentless pursuit of those people through the cross. Just as people from every race constitute one humanity that is created by God in his image (Acts 17:26), so the redeemed people of God consist of one new humanity (2 Cor. 5:17), with each individual member equally purchased by God for himself so that people of every race will enjoy full fellowship with each other in a glorified state of heartfelt worship of the Savior that will last for eternity. God has adopted people of every race into his eternal family, purchasing them with the blood of his Son and honoring them with eternal glorification in his throne room.

When we as Christians see people of another race, we therefore see divine image bearers—the face of God in the face of another person. When we look at Christians of another race, we see people who are on their way to glorification in the presence of the living God. They have been purchased with the blood of the Lamb, just as we have, and their struggles are therefore our struggles and their sorrows our sorrows (Rom. 12:15). That is why racial justice should matter to a Christian. We should grieve when divine image bearers are treated unjustly, because it does not reflect the intention of God's created order, and it does not reflect the eschatological reality that Revelation 7 portrays. We should especially grieve when the racial injustice in our society is so egregious that it snuffs out the lives of divine image bearers.

Blacks in the United States today are three times more likely than whites to grow up in poverty; in 2016, 31 percent of African American children lived in a household below the poverty line (that is, a household earning less than $25,000 a year, if the family included two children), while fewer than 11 percent of white children lived in such a household. As adults, blacks are nearly six times as likely to end up in prison as whites are, and they are far more likely to be arrested for drug possession, even though their drug use rates are approximately the same as those of whites. Even among the millions who do not go to prison, many blacks lack the average white person's access to health care, income, and wealth. White

American households have, on average, about ten times as much wealth as black American families. White Americans also live longer. Black American men will die, on average, about four years earlier than white American men, and black women will die three years earlier than their white female counterparts.[17]

In a society in which racial differences closely correlate with differences in health, wealth, and life expectancy, what does it mean for a Christian to live in light of the Bible's eschatological vision of full racial equality? For the past four decades, many conservatives have argued that racial justice means pursuing color-blind policies that treat all people equally under the law, without regard for racial differences. Many liberals have argued, by contrast, that racial justice means pursuing race-conscious policies that correct the injustices of the past and level the playing field. White evangelicals have generally sided with conservatives on this question. Most black Christians, by contrast, believe that a color-blind strategy will only perpetuate discrimination. To get to the eschatological vision of Revelation 7:9, we might have to spend some time doing what Jeremiah 22:3 requires: rescuing from the hand of the oppressor the one who has been robbed.

For white Americans—especially for those who identify as politically or religiously conservative—the color-blind strategy has enormous appeal, because it appears on its surface to be perfectly fair and race-neutral. It also has the advantage of being cost-free to most whites. A strategy of racial justice, by contrast, would demand a lot more from those of us who are white. It might require an uncomfortable acknowledgment that we have benefited from a racially discriminatory system and that we may even have inadvertently helped to perpetuate it. It might require us to give up some of our privileges—to sacrifice our own interests for the sake of others. Indeed, it might require the politics of the cross rather than the politics of privilege or the status quo. We might find, for instance, that in seeking to "rescue from the hand of the oppressor the one who has been robbed" (Jer. 22:3) that we have inadvertently done a bit of robbing ourselves and therefore have to give up some things that we have wrongly believed were ours. But before we can determine exactly what sacrifices this might entail, we will have to determine how much racial injustice currently exists in American society—and what might be required to correct it.

Learning to See Racial Injustice

White evangelicals are one of the least likely groups in contemporary America to acknowledge the presence of contemporary racial injustice. According to a 2018 PRRI poll, 53 percent of white evangelical Protestants believe that "socioeconomic disparities between black and white Americans are due to lack of effort by black Americans"—a statement with which 72 percent of nonwhite Christians and 70 percent of religious "nones" disagree.[18] While 57 percent of all Americans agree that black Americans today face "a lot of discrimination," only 36 percent of white evangelicals believe this, and 60 percent say that blacks "do not face a lot of discrimination." By contrast, 86 percent of black Protestants believe that African Americans today experience "a lot of discrimination."[19]

For those of us who are middle-class white Christians (a category that includes myself), one of the first steps in learning to approach the politics of race with love, compassion, and understanding is to learn to see the racial injustice around us—something that apparently, according to the recent PRRI survey data, most of the people in our religious tradition have not been very good at doing. Closing our eyes to racial injustice or minimizing its extent is easier than we might think. If we are enjoying some degree of economic security, it may be very difficult for us to fully realize the economic insecurity of others. It is even more difficult for us to admit that whatever privileges or comforts we enjoy may be the result of injustices done to another group of people. This is probably something that we cannot do on our own strength, without asking for the Spirit's help. So, before delving into the difficult question of whether those of us who are white and middle class might be benefiting from racial injustices that we inadvertently perpetuate, we might do well to open the word of God and reread the parable of the rich man and Lazarus with an eye to asking which person in the parable we most resemble:

> There was a rich man who was dressed in purple and fine linen and lived in luxury every day. At his gate was laid a beggar named Lazarus, covered with sores and longing to eat what fell from the rich man's table. Even the dogs came and licked his sores.
>
> The time came when the beggar died and the angels carried him to Abraham's side. The rich man also died and was buried. In Hades, where

he was in torment, he looked up and saw Abraham far away, with Lazarus by his side. So he called to him, "Father Abraham, have pity on me and send Lazarus to dip the tip of his finger in water and cool my tongue, because I am in agony in this fire."

But Abraham replied, "Son, remember that in your lifetime you received your good things, while Lazarus received bad things, but now he is comforted here and you are in agony. And besides all this, between us and you a great chasm has been set in place, so that those who want to go from here to you cannot, nor can anyone cross over from there to us."

He answered, "Then I beg you, father, send Lazarus to my family, for I have five brothers. Let him warn them, so that they will not also come to this place of torment."

Abraham replied, "They have Moses and the Prophets; let them listen to them."

"No, father Abraham," he said, "but if someone from the dead goes to them, they will repent."

He said to him, "If they do not listen to Moses and the Prophets, they will not be convinced even if someone rises from the dead." (Luke 16:19-31)

One of the sobering things about this parable is that it connects our treatment of the poor and the marginalized with our faith in Jesus (as the last verse, with its reference to someone rising from the dead, suggests) and with our eternal destiny. But for me, as a white middle-class Christian with an above-average income, the most alarming thing about this parable is my own resemblance to the rich man. Like the rich man, I have not consciously made poor people's lives worse. But also, like the rich man, I have spent much of my life blind to the injustices that many people around me were experiencing and oblivious to the way I was perpetuating those injustices by enjoying the benefits of my own privileged life while doing little to help those who were suffering.

For most of my early life, I saw racial injustice primarily as a matter of personal prejudice. I knew that some people hated others of a different skin color, and since I was sure that I treated everybody equally, regardless of race, I assumed that I was not guilty of the sin of racial injustice. But eventually, I came to realize, partly as a result of my graduate study in American history, that racial injustice in the United States has usually been closely connected to economic exploitation, and that it is quite possible for someone (myself included) to benefit from systems of economic injustice and perpetuate those systems even while sincerely believing that they are free of racial prejudice. A genuine commitment to being "anti-racist," as the author Ibram X. Kendi describes it, requires a conscious commitment to end systems of racially based economic exploitation, not merely an affirmation of being unprejudiced.[20]

It is inspiring to me to hear the personal testimonies of white Christians who began their lives as complacent participants in racial injustice but whose lives were changed and whose eyes were opened to racism as a result of the gospel. John Piper, for instance, has movingly described his own repentance from his youthful sins of acceptance of the system of racial segregation and discrimination, and his decision to adopt an African American child and make racial justice a priority in his preaching.[21] Russell Moore has likewise made racial reconciliation and racial justice key priorities in his work as president of the Southern Baptist Convention's Ethics and Religious Liberty Commission—a clear repudiation of the racism that plagued his denomination and his cultural environment when he was growing up in Mississippi.[22] A commitment to racial justice begins with a Spirit-led conviction of sin, but once this conviction pervades every area of our lives, it will extend to the voting booth as well.

There are policy proposals that can protect people's dignity in ways that are not currently being realized, but in order to understand what these policies might be and why they are needed, we must first examine the deep roots and widespread pervasiveness of the structural economic racial injustices that affect African Americans. Many whites think of racism primarily as a matter of personal hatred toward members of another race, but actually, the most damaging aspects of racial injustice are not personal but structural, and they are rooted in a centuries-long economic exploitation of people that still persists.[23] The process of seeking racial justice in the political sphere is the process of reversing the policies that have perpetuated the economic exploitation of people based on their race and replacing these policies with new political initiatives that honor people's God-given human dignity by protecting their lives and health and offering them an opportunity to provide for their families, with jobs that pay sustainable wages for meaningful work.

A History of Economic Exploitation and Denial of Human Dignity

The ongoing economic exploitation of large numbers of African Americans is rooted in a four-hundred-year history that began with slavery and continued with other forms of coerced labor. The vast majority of African Americans in the United States today are descended from people who were kidnapped from their homes, sold by slave traders, and forcibly brought to the Americas (either the Caribbean islands, South America, or the port cities of the North American coast) to work under the command of white overlords who believed they owned both the labor and the bodies of the people they had purchased.

The Africans who were forcibly brought to America were not the first people to be kidnapped, forcibly traded, and enslaved, but they were the first—and, so far, only—group of people to be put into a centuries-long dehumanizing racial caste system of economic and political exploitation in order to justify the indignities to which they were subjected. For millennia before the African slave trade, various people groups from around the world enslaved captives in war or people who could not pay their debts. The Bible is filled with references to enslaved people, because slavery was ubiquitous in the ancient Near East and Mediterranean world. Historians estimate that at least 20 percent of the people in the ancient Roman Empire were slaves.[24] Forced labor was an essential component of the civilizations of ancient Egypt, medieval Europe, and early modern Africa. Faced with a system in which slave labor was a foundational component of the economy, the Old Testament regulated slavery, prohibiting some of the worst abuses of the system—including kidnapping (a capital crime in ancient Israel) as well as permanent enslavement of fellow Israelites. The New Testament required Christian masters to treat their slaves as fellow brothers and sisters in the Lord (Eph. 6:9; Philem. 15-16). Slavery in the ancient world could be brutal, and Paul advised Christians not to give up their freedom by becoming slaves if they had any choice in the matter (1 Cor. 7:23). But it was not until the advent of modern capitalism and the transatlantic slave trade that the full horrors of the commodification of human beings became evident. With the advent of the transatlantic slave trade, what had been a local or regional system of exploitation became global. Ancient slavery had often been temporary in nature; slaves frequently had opportunity to earn their freedom or at least receive a job promotion and an increased status while enslaved. But the African slave trade removed 12 million people from their homes and brought them to the Americas to become a permanent slave caste.[25]

The dehumanization of enslaved people for the sake of profit began on the slave ships, which were deliberately filled to overcapacity on the assumption that about 15 percent of the human cargo would die and have to be thrown overboard before reaching their destination. Each enslaved person was chained to a bunk that had only eighteen inches of headroom. The lack of sanitation on slave ships—in which toilet facilities for the captured people consisted of, at best, only an open tub—meant that dysentery was a constant plague. And when the slaves arrived at their destination, which was usually a Caribbean island port, the commodification only continued.[26]

Most enslaved Africans during the first few generations of the transatlantic slave trade were brought to Caribbean sugar plantations and forcibly worked to death in the span of only a few years. Because the supply of new slaves was plentiful, the white sugar plantation owners who purchased slaves saw no need to protect their slaves from an early death; they expected to have to replace slaves about as often as contemporary American families replace cars. Slaves on the early eighteenth-century Caribbean sugar plantations rarely lasted longer than five or ten years in the hot sun and brutal work conditions (nearly a third died within only three years), but when they passed away, fresh arrivals from Africa took their place.[27]

In North American colonies such as Virginia and South Carolina, the slaves usually lived long enough to reproduce and, in some cases, reach a moderately old age, but this did not save them from exploitation. Instead of being worked to death while still in their twenties, slaves were often forced to participate in a "breeding" system that treated them like animals. Enslaved women were legally raped. In an attempt to produce more of what they considered the best stock, slave breeders maximized their profits by ordering particular enslaved men to sleep with particular enslaved women. And in a sign of how often slavery provided an excuse for white men to indulge their own lusts, the highest-priced slaves in the antebellum United States were not strong young men but were instead the beautiful young women sold at the "fancy girl" market in New Orleans.[28] The property right of a slave owner to sexually exploit his slaves was legally recognized, but slave marriages were not—which meant that the law allowed slave families to routinely be broken up at auctions, with husbands separated from wives, parents from children, and brothers from sisters. And regardless of whether they were sold, all slaves—including children, women, old men, and young men—could be (and often were) legally whipped or subjected to bodily mutilation.

White Americans' economic dependence on slavery led them to adopt a racist ideology to justify the permanent enslavement and exploitation of a particular people group. In early seventeenth-century Virginia, some of the people who bought African slaves did not yet think of slavery in strictly racial categories, because they also traded in white indentured servants and frequently sent their African slaves to work in fields alongside indentured whites and enslaved American Indians. It is not entirely clear that all the slave owners in the first generation of slavery in Virginia necessarily viewed enslavement as a permanent condition for Africans; between 1619, when the first enslaved Africans were brought to Virginia, and 1662, when the Virginia legislature legally codified the enslavement of Africans as a hereditary (and presumably lifelong) condition, the presence of a sizeable number of free blacks in the colony suggests that a number of African slaves found a path to emancipation. But this was very short-lived. Before the mid-seventeenth century, some white Europeans had justified slavery on the grounds that its subjects were non-Christian. But as African slaves began converting to Christianity, the Virginia legislature responded with a series of laws that both encouraged the evangelization of slaves and explicitly decreed that "baptism does not alter the condition of the person as to his bondage or freedom." Christians could be legally enslaved as long as they were black. And "black" was a category broad enough to include mixed-race children born to a black mother through sexual relations with her white overseer. As the Virginia legislature stated in 1662, "Whereas some doubts have arisen whether children got by any Englishman upon a Negro woman should be slave or free, be it therefore enacted and declared by this present Grand Assembly, that all children born in this country shall be held bond or free only according to the condition of the mother."[29]

Once slavery was equated with a hereditary condition tied to race, it became more important than ever to provide rationales for why one particular race—the African—was uniquely suited to slavery. Some of the early justifications were religious; the "curse of Ham" was a popular justification in some Christian circles for the enslavement of people of African descent, from the seventeenth century through the nineteenth. But by the end of the eighteenth century—and especially in the nineteenth century—scientific racism became the preferred justification among many educated whites. Thomas Jefferson devoted an extensive amount of space in his *Notes on the State of Virginia* to discussing the scientific basis for assuming that blacks were inferior to whites; the author of the line "all men are created equal" apparently felt the need to qualify that statement with an explanation of why his own slaves were not biologically equal to him. During the next few generations, scientific racism became even more virulent and widespread, with cranial studies, evolutionary explanations, and numerous other pieces of evidence marshalled in support of the idea that "Negroes" were biologically inferior to whites.[30]

By 1860, on the eve of the Civil War, the most valuable commodity in the United States was not cotton, wheat, textiles, railroads, or any manufactured good; it was human lives: the 4 million enslaved people who were collectively valued at $3 billion. Slaves were such a valuable commodity that they determined the fortunes of white people in the South; it was impossible to become rich in the South without being a slaveholder, and the more slaves a person owned, the richer a person was. For that reason, 90 to 95 percent of the wealth in the South was concentrated in the hands of the 1 percent of the white population that owned a hundred or more slaves each. Because of the wealth that came from owning slaves, more millionaires lived in the Mississippi Valley than anywhere else in the United States.[31]

Slaves were such a valuable economic resource that many white southerners were willing to risk their lives to preserve the institution. In 1860, when northern antislavery advocates elected the first Republican president (Abraham Lincoln) on a platform of keeping slavery out of the western territories, southern defenders of slavery saw the handwriting on the wall; they feared that if free states outnumbered slave states, the day was not far off when Congress would vote to ban slavery entirely. Without even waiting for President-elect Lincoln to be inaugurated, several states in the Deep South, led by South Carolina (the majority of whose population consisted of enslaved people), seceded from the Union.

The South lost the gamble, and it suffered catastrophic economic consequences as a result. For the next hundred years, the South lagged behind the North in per capita income. Because of increased global competition during the 1860s, cotton would never again produce the fabulous fortunes that it did before the Civil War. And, of course, $3 billion in human assets disappeared from the ledger books when slaves were emancipated.[32] White southerners were determined to recoup these losses.

For the next century, the white South treated nominally free blacks as a labor supply that needed to be tightly controlled. Within months of the end of the Civil War, several southern states enacted Black Codes, which required African Americans to enter into work contracts that obligated them to work for a particular employer for the next twelve months. A decade later, the South embarked on a longer-term experiment with sharecropping and tenant farming, both of which left African Americans propertyless and usually penniless. In a worst-case scenario—which was not uncommon—sharecroppers could end a year of work in debt to the landowner and legally obligated to remain on the land to work off the debt. Because cotton prices were declining throughout the late nineteenth century, sharecroppers who were legally required to plant and harvest cotton for the landowner often never saw the shares of the profits they had expected; landowners commonly balanced their books by depriving the sharecroppers of any money and, to add insult to injury, charging them rent for their farm implements and housing. For three generations after the Civil War, many black southern farmers were tied to the land without getting an opportunity to own it. Even when they were able to save up enough money to buy land—which was not often—whites sometimes refused to sell. In 1900, only 22 percent of blacks (compared to 49 percent of whites) owned the homes they lived in. African Americans' prospects for education were even lower. Only 38 percent of black males between the ages of six and thirteen were attending school in 1900—compared with 72 percent of American white males of the same age. The South did not have a single publicly funded black high school until 1920. As late as 1940, the average African American adult in Georgia had only a fourth-grade education.[33] And blacks were also largely deprived of the right to vote in all states south of the Mason-Dixon Line. As late as the early 1960s, blacks in Mississippi who attempted to register to vote experienced violent retaliation, including, in some cases, police beatings with a blackjack.[34] Throughout the century-long era from the end of the Civil War to the beginning of the civil rights movement, white law enforcement officers worked in tandem with vigilante executioners to police any African

Americans who challenged the legal system of racial segregation that had denied them educational opportunities and had kept them tied to low-wage menial jobs. In thousands of cases, these efforts to enforce the racial caste system included executing blacks, even when they had not killed or threatened anyone else.

Because much of this discrimination occurred in the South (where 90 percent of African Americans lived as late as 1900), it might be tempting to imagine that racism was merely regional and that blacks who were able to move to a northern city would be able to better their opportunities. But this was not necessarily the case. More than a million African Americans did move to the North—especially to major industrial eastern and midwestern cities such as New York, Chicago, Philadelphia, and Detroit—between 1915 and 1930. And millions more left the South during World War II and the following two decades. These African Americans escaped some of the worst aspects of southern racial discrimination; they gained the opportunity to vote and to attend public high schools. But most never escaped poverty. Because of the housing discrimination that was pervasive in the North, they were not able to buy houses on the white side of town; instead, they were confined to overcrowded, overpriced black districts of the city where most residents were forced to be tenants rather than owners. The Federal Housing Administration (FHA) refused to underwrite loans for homebuyers who were purchasing houses in black neighborhoods—the only neighborhoods where blacks could buy. As a result, blacks often found it very difficult to purchase property. And with a low tax base, schools in black-majority areas of a city were often badly underfunded—which meant that graduates were often unprepared for college and, in many cases, did not even bother to apply. Many who attended these schools, in fact, never graduated at all. In 1970, only 31 percent of blacks—and only 44 percent of those in the labor force—had completed high school. (By comparison, 55 percent of whites at the time had a high school diploma.)[35]

Having been cut off from most of the resources that whites used to acquire wealth—resources such as property, government-subsidized loans, quality education, and good jobs—blacks remained disproportionately poor. As late as 1965, 66 percent of African American children—and 63 percent of those over the age of sixty-five—lived below the poverty line. This changed dramatically for at least some African Americans in the late 1960s, after the passage of landmark civil rights legislation and poverty relief programs; by 1970, only 42 percent of African American children remained below the poverty line.[36] The Civil Rights Act of 1964—which, among other things, prohibited discrimination in employment and education on the basis of race—helped to create a new black professional middle class. The first federal funding provisions for underresourced public schools also helped many African Americans, as did federal prohibitions on discrimination in housing. Some African Americans experienced dramatic gains during the 1960s and 1970s, when the combination of civil rights legislation and affirmative action policies opened up new educational and career opportunities that had previously been closed. Michelle Obama, who lived in a low-income, majority-black area of Chicago where her grandfather had moved from the South a half century earlier, was able to attend a charter school and then go from there to Princeton University, after which she earned a law degree. For the daughter of a boiler-room worker and the great-great-granddaughter of a sharecropper who had been born in slavery, this was a substantial rise in socioeconomic status.[37]

But the gains were tenuous for most blacks. At the very moment that new educational and career opportunities were opening up for some African Americans, many traditional career paths were closing. Several of the cities to which African Americans had moved during the Great Migrations of the twentieth century experienced severe economic declines in the 1970s, when a combination of foreign competition, automation, and an energy crisis shuttered factories and threw people out of work. Detroit, which was a majority-black city by the 1960s, was hit especially hard, but a number of other northern cities that had been popular destinations for African Americans also experienced employment declines. The percentage of African American children who lived in poverty in 1995 was exactly what it had been twenty-five years earlier, in 1970: 42 percent.[38]

While far more blacks did go to college in the late twentieth and early twenty-first century (63 percent of blacks in the labor force had at least some college by 2018), those who did not fared far worse than their parents' generation had. In 2011, in the midst of the Great Recession, 25 percent of blacks aged twenty-five and older who lacked a high school diploma were unemployed, and even in 2018, when the national unemployment rate was only 3 percent, more than 10 percent of blacks without a high school diploma were out of work—as were nearly 7 percent of black high school graduates who had not attended college. Largely because of the low job prospects for blacks without a college education, the black unemployment rate has generally been twice as high as the rate for whites for the past several decades. Whites who drop out of school do not face job prospects that are quite as dim; among all races, the unemployment rate for adults who lacked a high school diploma was less than 6 percent in 2018. And even among college graduates, black graduates had a slightly higher unemployment rate than white graduates.[39] For blacks who want to survive economically, college is an absolute necessity, but even a BA degree is not a guarantee of escaping poverty.

Mass Incarceration of Low-Income African Americans

As the black unemployment rate rose in the 1970s and early 1980s, another government policy devastated the black community: increased police targeting of young African American men and a massive rise in the incarceration rate. In 1980, the total number of Americans of all races in jail or prison was barely over 500,000. But because of President Ronald Reagan's War on Drugs and the implementation of new minimum sentencing guidelines, judges and police forces cooperated to lock up a new generation of suspected criminals. By 1990, the number of Americans in jail or prison had increased to over a million; by 2000, it had reached 2 million. African Americans were far more likely than members of other races to go to prison. In 1970, only 133,000 African American men were in prison; by 2000, more than 600,000 were. By 2004, 30 percent of black men born in the late 1960s who had not gone to college had spent time in prison. And by 2008, one of every nine African American men aged twenty to thirty-four was currently in prison. A statistician at the US Department of Justice estimated in 2003 that a black male had a 32 percent chance of going to prison at some point during his life. During the past decade, this trend has begun to reverse; the number of African American men in prison has decreased somewhat, even as the likelihood of women, whites, and Hispanics going to prison has increased. But for the period between the early 1980s and the first decade of the twenty-first century, the mass incarceration of young black men had catastrophic effects on the black community. Studies indicated that blacks were no more likely than whites to smoke marijuana, but they were far more likely to be arrested for it, because they were more likely to be stopped and searched. And if they were sent to prison, their chance of getting a job was severely reduced. Among ex-prisoners of all races, 27 percent were unemployed in 2008—an unemployment rate that was five times higher than the general unemployment rate at the time. But among black ex-prisoners, the unemployment rate was even higher; 35 percent of black male ex-prisoners and 44 percent of black ex-prisoners who were female were unemployed. And this was *before* the Great Recession made jobs extremely scarce for everyone.[40]

The high rate of incarceration among African Americans has affected the families and children of those who go to prison. Incarcerated men were far less likely than others to get married or stay married—and yet they were just as likely to father children. In 2000, one out of every ten black children had a father incarcerated. By 2014, that number would increase to one out of nine. Altogether, there are 10 million children in the United States with a parent who has gone to jail or prison.[41]

Most people who go to prison also lose their voting rights and thus their opportunity to participate in the nation's democracy. Only two states—Maine and Vermont—do not deprive convicted felons of their voting rights, and, perhaps not coincidently, those two small states are some of the whitest in the nation. In many states, convicted felons can at least regain their voting rights after the completion of their sentences, but in several states—including heavily black areas of the South, such as the states of Alabama, Mississippi, and Tennessee—those convicted of certain crimes can lose their voting rights permanently, even after release. High incarceration rates among blacks thus lead to higher rates of disfranchisement in a pattern that some have called a "new Jim Crow."[42]

Just as some whites in the past justified lynching on the supposition that those who were executed by lynch mobs were rapists who deserved their fate, so a new generation of whites has excused mass incarceration and the loss of voting rights on the grounds that the country needs "law and order" to be safe from black criminals. As more blacks entered the prison system, white stereotypes of blacks as criminals were confirmed, and whites have found it easier to excuse news reports of police brutality toward blacks, racial disparities in the use of the death penalty, and the massive gap between the imprisonment rates of whites and blacks. Most whites do not realize that the racial disparity in arrest rates is partly the result of ongoing economic disparities and the longstanding neighborhood segregation that isolates low-income blacks in urban neighborhoods that lack good job prospects. Neighborhood segregation has made it easy for police to target neighborhoods that are considered high crime areas—which are invariably low-income and, not coincidentally, often majority-black. While commonly leaving most high-income or middle-class neighborhoods alone and ignoring most illegal drug use that occurs there, police regularly patrol low-income minority neighborhoods, looking for people who they assume likely have drugs or guns in their possession. And when they find such evidence, they lock up the perpetrators or, in a few extreme cases, kill them on the street.[43]

The Economic Struggles of Middle-Class African Americans

African Americans who escape this cycle of poverty and stay out of prison still find that their hold on a middle-class standard of living is extremely tenuous, because their only path to a middle-class life requires taking on a massive amount of debt early in life. Most black college students have to borrow their way to a degree; they cannot depend on resources from their families. In 2017, 73 percent of white households owned a house, but only 43 percent of black households did. As home prices have increased faster than the rate of inflation, blacks have fallen further behind, with the prospect of buying a home now more elusive for them than it has been in decades. Twenty percent of black applicants were denied a conventional home loan in 2017—compared to only 8 percent of white applicants. Without the opportunity to own a house, the majority of blacks lack the assets and nonliquid capital investment that the white middle class takes for granted. In a 2017 survey, fewer than half of black heads of households said they believed they could get $3,000 in an emergency even if they borrowed from family and friends. The median net worth of a black family in America today is only $17,000; this includes the value of a car, savings account, checking account, retirement savings, television, and all other assets, both liquid and nonliquid. Nineteen percent of black households (but only 9 percent of white households) have a net worth of zero or below. By comparison, the median net worth of a white household is $171,000. The vast majority of black college students thus start their lives with substantially fewer resources than whites; in fact, whatever financial resources they have are probably borrowed against their future. Before the Great Recession of 2008, blacks' rate of home ownership and net wealth were increasing, but after a wave of foreclosures on black-owned homes, blacks have still not recovered from this financial catastrophe. The Great Recession wiped out decades of black economic gains, and by 2019, a smaller percentage of blacks owned homes than at any point since 1968. Even before the outbreak of COVID-19 exacerbated the economic distress of African Americans, median black wealth was decreasing.[44]

When blacks enter the job market, they not only enter with substantial college-loan and personal debt, but they also arrive with the knowledge that if they attain a middle-class standard of living, they will probably want to help support an aging parent, who most likely is going to be entirely dependent on a meager Social Security paycheck that will not pay for their health-care expenses. This, in fact, was what happened to Stacey Abrams, the former minority leader of the Georgia House of Representatives and the 2018 Democratic nominee for governor. Abrams holds a BA from Spelman College and a JD from Yale Law School, but like many African American professionals, she borrowed nearly all the amount that she needed for private school tuition and struggled financially throughout her time in school. She used her credit card to pay for school supplies and help her family with expenses—a strategy that proved costly when she missed a credit card payment as an undergraduate college student. She was then hit with a massive credit charge and a severe drop in her credit score; a $100 purchase led to a series of fines and interest payments that cost her, according to her estimate, nearly $3,000 over the course of seven years. Her first professional job after law school came with a $95,000 a year salary, but at that point she already owed tens of thousands of dollars in student loans and college credit-card debt. As soon as she graduated from law school, she made paying off the credit card debt a top priority and succeeded. But then, when she was thirty-three and still paying back her student loans, her younger brother and his girlfriend had a child removed from their home because of their drug addictions, and her parents then began raising the child—which they could not afford to do. (Abrams's parents were Mississippi Methodist ministers whom she described as "genteel poor.") A few months later, Hurricane Katrina devastated their Mississippi home. Abrams then began supporting her parents while still struggling to pay off student loans. And when she had to help her parents with their growing medical expenses, she was forced to request a deferment on her taxes, which resulted in an additional $54,000 debt to the government. As late as 2018, when she was running for governor of Georgia, she still owed $96,000 in student loans and another $76,000 in credit card debt that she had taken on in order to help her parents. Only in 2019, at the age of forty-five, did Abrams finally pay off the last of her student loan and tax bills—and then only with the help of a $150,000 book advance and a stringent personal budget that made getting out of debt a top priority. If it took more than two decades for one of the most prominent young African American Democrats in the country—a woman who delivered the Democrats' official response to the 2019 State of the Union address and who was widely mentioned as a possible vice presidential candidate—to pay off her debt, is it any wonder that most African Americans today (even the most educated and highest paid ones) are struggling financially or are only a step or two away from poverty? "I suspect my situation will sound familiar to others who are the first in their families to earn real money," Abrams said.[45]

If a generation is approximately twenty-five years, and if most African Americans in the United States today are descended from slaves who arrived in America in the mid-eighteenth century, an African American of Abrams's generation is likely descended from at least five generations of people born into slavery, three generations of sharecroppers and impoverished tenant farmers who were denied the chance to get more than an elementary or middle school education, and one generation of parents who were barely living above the poverty line. For this reason, there is very little real wealth in the black community, even among high income earners. Less than 2 percent of the wealth in the United States belongs to African Americans. Blacks own less than 1 percent of rural land in the United States; in fact, their holdings are so small that five individual white large landowners own more acres than all black landowners in the United States combined. The fact that in 2018, even before the COVID-19 crisis made African Americans' economic situation still more precarious, the percentage of blacks who owned their own home was as low as it had been in the year of Martin Luther King Jr.'s assassination, a half century earlier, is an indication of how many economic setbacks African Americans have experienced in recent years.[46]

These economic setbacks will affect the educational and career prospects of the next generation of African Americans who are attempting to enter the middle class. Most African Americans who attend college are poor. Seventy-two percent of African American college students receive Pell Grants, compared to only 34 percent of white students. (The median annual family income for recipients of a Pell Grant, a form of federal financial aid that is based solely on financial need, is less than $30,000.) Seventy-one percent of African American college students receive federal loans. While upper-middle-class white Americans can usually depend on their parents' financial support to get them through college and started in a career, people from low-income families not only lack access to parental resources but are also often burdened with the responsibility to provide both financial and emotional assistance for their impoverished relatives—which may include taking care of a sibling's children, helping provide for a parent, or assisting with a grandparent's healthcare—all while trying to get through college on borrowed money. Perhaps partly because of this financial stress, the majority of African Americans who begin college will never finish their degree. Black high school graduates are now nearly as likely as their white counterparts to enroll in college, but they are about 50 percent less likely to graduate. In 2018, only 23 percent of African Americans in their late twenties had a four-year college degree, compared to 44 percent of whites.[47]

Despite the presence of a black middle class (and even black upper-middle class), most blacks are not part of it: the median household income for a black family of three today is only $43,000—compared to $71,000 for whites. Blacks are more than twice as likely as whites to live in poverty, and black children are even more so; 33 percent of black children were living below the poverty line in 2017, compared to only 11 percent of non-Hispanic white children.[48] White households, on average, are 70 percent more likely to own a house and nearly twice as likely to have a retirement savings account. Sixty-two percent of black households have no retirement savings—compared to only 37 percent of whites.[49] This means that the majority of blacks will enter their seventies, after working long hours in often back-breaking jobs for their entire lives, with no house, no retirement savings, and, at most, only a few hundred or thousand dollars in a bank account. This problem is likely to only get worse over the next few years, because the rate of black home ownership is declining.

Because even middle-class blacks are usually only one or two generations removed from poverty—and are themselves often in danger of falling back into a low-income bracket if misfortune strikes—they consistently vote for the party that they perceive offers the best protections for the poor and marginalized. In the view of the vast majority of blacks, the Republican Party has a poor track record on these issues. This was especially true of President Ronald Reagan's administration in the 1980s. By raising payroll taxes—which especially hurt the working poor—while refusing to raise the minimum wage, Reagan made the poorest Americans poorer. Worse, his incarceration policies devastated the black community for the next generation by leaving hundreds of thousands of young black men with a prison record that would make it very difficult for them to get a job. At the same time, the Reagan administration's Justice Department worked hard to dismantle affirmative action programs that had provided a rare moment of opportunity for ambitious young blacks who were seeking educational and career opportunities that had been denied to their parents. Perhaps it is no surprise, therefore, that when Reagan won election by a landslide in 1984—a landslide in which he carried forty-nine states because of his overwhelming popularity among middle-class whites—he received only 9 percent of the African American vote.[50] In subsequent presidential elections, Democratic presidential candidates have continued to receive approximately 90 percent or more of the African American vote, largely because most black voters perceive that the Republican Party proposals of the last few decades—including initiatives to privatize Social Security, restrict the scope of national health insurance programs, and oppose Democratic efforts to expand federal subsidies for college tuition—will have a disproportionately negative effect on their families. In addition, they believe that Republican-enacted voting restrictions disfranchise many people of color, depriving them of the limited opportunity they have to reform the system.

Most of the people affected by policies that hurt low-income blacks are Christians, because African Americans—especially African American women—are, according to social science surveys, the most devoted Bible readers, faithful church attenders, and committed people of prayer in the country today.[51] One might ask the question: How should white Christians respond to the economic plight of their fellow brothers and sisters in the Lord? In particular, how should we respond at the voting booth? Should we follow the lead of most black Christians and vote Democratic? Perhaps before answering this question, it would be useful to think about what the Bible says about social justice—and what this might mean for public policy today.

Seeking Racial Justice Today

The meaning of justice in social relationships is encapsulated in God's instructions for the covenant people of Israel in Jeremiah 22: "This is what the Lord says: Do what is just and right. Rescue from the hand of the oppressor the one who has been robbed. Do no wrong or violence to the foreigner, the fatherless or the widow, and do not shed innocent blood in this place" (Jer. 22:3). If we take this passage at face value, it seems to offer a clear set of political priorities: We should pursue policies that will protect life instead of shedding innocent blood. We should pursue policies that protect the well-being and rights of the economically marginalized and vulnerable—especially the "fatherless," the single mother, and the "foreigner" or anyone else who has been deprived of the full benefits of citizenship. We should seek to right the wrongs of those who have been unjustly deprived of their property. Although the original setting for this verse was the covenant nation of Israel (not the United States), and although its original audience had no concept of race in the modern sense, it does not require a great deal of imagination to apply this verse to contemporary questions of race. Have blacks, as a class of people, been deprived of their property in the United States? Have they been unjustly deprived of their lives? Are there any policies that would protect the fatherless, the single mothers, and the strangers who are marginalized because they are part of racial groups that have historically faced unequal treatment in the law? If so, we have a mandate to pursue those policies.

One of the best ways to right racial injustices, empower African Americans to get out of poverty, and protect African American lives is to expand access to health insurance, affordable housing, college, and retirement plans. Right now, blacks are heavily dependent on public-option health insurance, because only 56 percent of blacks (compared to 75 percent of non-Hispanic whites) have private health insurance. Any proposal to trim public health insurance programs will have a severe effect on African Americans. Obamacare helped millions of African Americans get health insurance for the first time; it reduced the percent of nonelderly blacks who were uninsured from 19 percent to 12 percent. But blacks are still at greater risk than whites of having no health insurance, which makes the preservation and expansion of federal health insurance a critical issue for them.[52] When we deprive people of access to affordable health care, we jeopardize their lives and their ability to survive economically. With medical debt now the leading cause of bankruptcy in the United States, the working poor are especially vulnerable to any reductions in their access to comprehensive, affordable health insurance.

Similarly, we should seek policies that will reduce the incarceration rate. In a country that for decades has reacted to crime by locking people up for increasingly longer periods while depriving them of the ability to reintegrate themselves into the workforce and society, we should seek a more biblically grounded model of restorative justice—that is, policies that encourage lawbreakers to make restitution for their offenses rather than simply being incarcerated for their crimes. Some of these proposals have come from conservative evangelicals. Prison Fellowship, founded by Charles Colson after his own imprisonment and conversion, has promoted rehabilitation and restorative justice policies for decades, as have other faith-based organizations.

We need to find ways to make jobs more available to the economically marginalized—that is, those who are most vulnerable to being unemployed or underemployed, even when the national unemployment rate is low. If the black unemployment rate has consistently been approximately twice as high as the white unemployment rate for half a century, this is a social justice problem that we cannot ignore. White conservatives have traditionally opposed the most common remedy to address this: affirmative action in hiring. Christians can, of course, debate whether affirmative action is the best remedy for the racial disparity in employment, but regardless of whether we support this particular policy, we must commit ourselves to seeking solutions that will close this racial gap—whether it means tax incentives to encourage businesses to relocate in economically marginalized, heavily black areas, or perhaps more government financial assistance to low-income college students who are trying to earn degrees that will make them more competitive in the job market. When it comes to jobs, blacks in this nation have been in the equivalent of a long-term economic recession even in the best of times—and, in the worst of times, a severe economic depression on a scale that whites faced in the 1930s. If we love our neighbor, we have a responsibility to make their economic well-being a priority.

Not surprisingly, African Americans have also identified an increase in the minimum wage as a high political priority. Ninety-three percent of African Americans support increasing the minimum wage to $15 an hour—a move that most Democrats, but only 30 percent of self-described conservative Republicans, favor.[53] Fifty-four percent of African American workers—and nearly 60 percent of Hispanic workers—are currently earning less than $15 an hour (which equals $30,000 a year for those who work forty hours a week).[54] Increasing the national minimum wage to $15 an hour would therefore increase the wages of more than half of all black workers in the nation. Of course, increases in the minimum wage do not come without economic costs, and a Christian may decide that such costs—which might include increased unemployment or increases in the prices of goods and services—outweigh the benefits for the poor. But again, if we care about our neighbor, we will seek solutions to a low-wage economy in which more than half of all black and Hispanic workers are earning less than $30,000 a year. Many black families have only a single wage-earner, which means that a wage of less than $15 an hour might have to accommodate the needs of several children. Indeed, 54 percent of black children live with a single parent. And women—who are far more likely than men to be single parents—are also the workers most likely to be trapped in low-wage jobs; 63 percent of minimum-wage workers are women.[55] Many of these women struggle to care for children on wages that are not high enough to lift their families above the poverty line.

Some African Americans have also proposed more race-specific solutions to the problems of racial economic inequality. Reparations for slavery, which Ta-Nehisi Coates has championed, are one such solution.[56] Needless to say, reparations are controversial and would probably require a national, widespread white acknowledgment of responsibility for racial injustice before they would be accepted. Whether any amount of money could begin to compensate for the vast amount of harm that African Americans have experienced at the hands of whites over the past four centuries is questionable. Perhaps white Christians should be willing to acknowledge their complicity in racial injustice, but in any case, the political solutions that would bring the greatest economic relief to black voters do not necessarily require a national admission of white guilt; they merely require white middle-class voters to cast ballots with the interests of the poor in mind. For Christians who take biblical teachings about poverty seriously, this should not be too much to ask.

What about the Black Family?

Social conservatives have suggested for more than fifty years that the only real solution to the problem of black poverty is to increase marriage rates in the black community.[57] If more than half of black children are born out of wedlock or grow up in single-parent homes—and if single-parent families are far more likely than married families to be in poverty—shouldn't we advocate marriage and responsible sexual behavior as the key to reducing poverty rates?

When this argument was first made, in the mid-1960s, it was racially divisive, and for decades it remained so, because it seemed as if white conservatives were blaming blacks for their own poverty. Some African Americans considered the argument racist, because they thought that white conservatives were accusing blacks of being sexually promiscuous and irresponsible as a race (and, in fact, some white conservatives were saying this).[58] But in the last twenty years, the percentage of white children born out of wedlock has increased by nearly 50 percent, while the percentage among blacks has been stable. Black women are still more likely than white women to give birth out of wedlock, but the gap is narrowing, especially in comparison with lower-income and lower-educated whites. In 2016, 52 percent of all births to white mothers with only a high school diploma were out of wedlock—up from only 18 percent in 1990. Single parenthood and out-of-wedlock pregnancy may be somewhat correlated with race, but they are even more closely correlated with poverty and low educational levels. Women who earn a college degree before having children are more likely to be married than unmarried, regardless of race, while a majority of mothers who never go to college are likely to give birth out of wedlock, regardless of whether they are white, black, or Hispanic.[59] Single parents are more likely than others to remain poor, but poor people are also more likely to become single parents.

From a Christian perspective, of course, we should want to reduce out-of-wedlock pregnancy rates and single parenthood, and we should seek to promote marriage. But how can we promote marriage through public policy?

Too often, conservatives' approach has been either to attack social welfare programs that they claim reward single parenthood and discourage marriage or to offer tax cuts for married couples. But the most effective policies to promote marriage rates, Harvard sociologist William Julius Wilson has argued, might be focused on creating jobs in low-income, high-minority areas, because if young men have jobs that can support a family, they are much more likely to get married.[60]

Perhaps as Christians, we should be open to multiple approaches to the promotion of marriage. In our churches, we should help individuals get the spiritual and material resources they need to get married and stay married. In our public policy proposals, perhaps we should concentrate on creating economic policies that will improve the well-being of people who are most economically vulnerable—and therefore most likely not to get married before having children. We do not have to choose between economic relief for the poor and promotion of marriage, because the public policies that will help the material well-being for the poor may also indirectly lead to improved family stability and higher marriage rates.

What about Poor Whites?

I teach at a second-tier regional university in rural Georgia that has almost as many black students as whites. The two groups belong to different political parties, and their view of the history of race relations and racial policy is very different. But most of them, regardless of race, have at least one thing in common: a long family history of working-class poverty and a present continuing struggle to earn enough to pay their bills. When I have given my classes family history assignments, I have found that nearly all of my black students have ancestors who were sharecroppers or tenant farmers and who lived well below the poverty line for the first half of the twentieth century. But I have also found that many of my white students likewise have early twentieth-century ancestors who were sharecroppers, tenant farmers, or southern textile mill workers, and who, in some cases, had never been to school and could not read and write. They earned hardly any more money than some of their black counterparts did, and they barely had any more schooling. Today the descendants of these white mill workers and sharecroppers are sitting in the same classrooms as the descendants of black sharecroppers and field hands, and they will soon be struggling to pay off similar amounts of student debt and compete for the same jobs. Why, some conservatives have asked, should my white students be penalized through affirmative action programs or other liberal measures to correct alleged racial injustice, when they have clearly not experienced any sort of "white privilege," at least when it comes to their bank account? In recent years, conservatives have made substantial gains among white working-class voters by railing against programs that they claimed were designed by "limousine liberals" to privilege blacks at the expense of working-class whites.[61] As Christians, how should we respond to this? Which side is right—the liberals who demand justice for African Americans or the conservatives who say that working-class whites should not be unjustly made to pay for a supposed "white privilege" that they never experienced?

I think that the best approach is to acknowledge that the patterns of injustice in American society have penalized people by class, as well as by race, and the two are related. Racial oppression, including violence against African Americans, developed as a way to control a labor force—that is, to keep blacks confined to a particular social class in order to extract their labor. Sharecropping, which included both blacks and whites, was another way to control the labor force. Company-owned, textile mill towns that offered workers only rented housing, subsistence wages, and hardly any opportunities for education, were another way to control a labor force. All of these were methods of robbing the poor. Some were certainly more egregious forms of injustice than others. Textile mill managers, for instance, never engaged in the same gross human rights abuses that slave breeders did. And white sharecroppers were not nearly as likely to be lynched as black sharecroppers. But the end result of the exploitation that both groups of workers experienced left a similar lasting economic effect, in the sense that the great-great grandchildren of white sharecroppers and white mill workers who were trapped in cycles of debt and poverty may have had no more opportunity to acquire savings and education than the great-great grandchildren of black sharecroppers. It is true that the unique forms of racial injustice that African Americans experience leave many blacks of all income levels at risk of police brutality and color-based discrimination, because the racial stereotypes that emerged from centuries of white efforts to confine blacks to a low-wage or unpaid labor force continue to haunt our society and affect even those relatively few African Americans who manage to reach the upper middle class. The experience of low-income whites has been very different in this regard; their perceived socioeconomic status is not stamped on their skin, nor have they generally experienced the same dangers from law enforcement. Most low-income whites who own guns are not at risk of being shot by police merely for honestly answering a police officer's question, as Philando Castile was in Minnesota in 2016. But rather than pit one group's claims against the other, perhaps we should ask what policies might bring justice to both blacks and whites whose families were sinned against in the past and who have therefore been denied the opportunity to enter the workforce without a great deal of debt. Proposals to make health care more accessible, move our society closer toward paying a living wage, and make college more affordable are likely to benefit low-income workers of all races. Rather than use the claims of poor or working-class whites to evade our responsibility for correcting racial injustice, those of us who are white Christians should seek justice for all people who have been robbed in the past. And if there is any group that has been robbed en masse, surely it is the people whose ancestors were stolen from Africa and whose wages were then robbed for generations, in ways that still affect their economic plight today.

Opposing a New Racism: Prejudice against Hispanic Immigrants

For decades, most writing on race focused on black-white race relations, just as most of this chapter has. But today another closely related form of racial discrimination has received a great deal of support from white evangelicals who would never classify themselves as racist: discrimination against Hispanic immigrants, especially those from Mexico. Indeed, the pattern of discrimination that Hispanics currently face closely parallels the discrimination that African Americans have historically experienced, because both groups have been trapped in low-wage jobs by structural barriers that confined them to second-class status.

Mexican Americans have faced barriers to equality in the United States ever since the Mexican War of 1846–1848. The Mexican War, which was fought over a boundary dispute over Texas, resulted in the United States taking one-third of Mexico. Abraham Lincoln and many other members of his political party condemned the war as unjust at the time, but the Democratic president James Knox Polk, who subscribed to the ideology of "Manifest Destiny," celebrated these territorial gains. In fact, he contemplated taking over all of Mexico but ultimately decided against it on the grounds that the country would be too difficult to administer. Instead, he settled for one-third of the country. This 500,000-square-mile area, which stretched from California to Texas and north to Colorado and Utah, included what would become the entire Southwest of the United States. Mexicans who lived there were welcome to live in the United States, and some of them found jobs as ranch hands because of their expertise in cattle herding. But they were not treated as equals to white American citizens. In the early twentieth century, the state of Texas created racially segregated schools for Mexicans, just as it created racially segregated schools for blacks. In the early 1930s, during the early years of the Great Depression, the government tried to protect the jobs of native-born Anglo-Americans by forcibly deporting half a million Mexican workers. When the United States entered World War II, though, the country suddenly needed Mexican agricultural workers to replace American men who had been drafted, so in 1942 the country began the *"bracero"* program, which brought thousands of Mexicans to southern California each year to work on the fruit and vegetable farms—but then sent them back to Mexico whenever harvest season was over. Some of the Mexicans who arrived experienced a great deal of discrimination and even violence. In 1943, Los Angeles experienced several days of race riots that were primarily directed against Mexican American young people. Despite the racial backlash, the temporary worker program expanded after the war was over, because the California fruit and vegetable industry began depending on low-wage Mexican workers. By the 1950s, the *bracero* program was bringing 400,000 Mexican workers into the United States each year. But journalistic exposés in the early 1960s led to bad publicity for the program. The Mexican workers were mistreated, journalists argued, but they were also reducing wages for native-born American workers. The program ended in 1964.[62]

After 1964, there was no easy way for most Mexican workers to legally enter the United States, because immigration quotas were set at a level far too low to accommodate the number of people who wanted to come. The Immigration Act of 1965 allowed only 170,000 immigrants per year to enter from the entire Western Hemisphere—far less than the 400,000 or more

Mexicans who had crossed the border each year during the 1950s. And after 1978, immigration quotas for the Western Hemisphere were set at only 20,000 per country, and immigrants with immediate family ties or professional skills were given preference—which meant that the hundreds of thousands of Mexican workers who wanted to enter California to work on the fruit and vegetable farms had no chance of getting a visa. The American agricultural industry could not sustain itself without these workers, and many Mexicans, in turn, believed that they could not sustain their families without American wages. In the absence of opportunities to enter the United States legally, they turned to illegal means.[63]

Instead of making it easier for Mexican workers to immigrate to the United States, the American government invested in increased border enforcement. Between 1980 and 2000, the number of border patrol agents increased from 2,500 to 9,200; by 2009, it had increased to more than 20,000. This increased enforcement cost an enormous amount of money. In 1980, the United States spent only $83 million per year on border security, but by the second decade of the twenty-first century, it was spending $18 billion per year.[64] While the number of deportations rose dramatically with increased border enforcement, the enforcement was not enough to deter desperate Mexicans from attempting to cross the border to escape gang violence and take manual labor jobs that often paid eight times as much as equivalent work in Mexico. The food and construction industries depended on these workers. Half of the nation's farmworkers are undocumented immigrants, according to the estimates of the US Department of Agriculture. Undocumented immigrants also comprise 15 percent of the nation's construction workers and 24 percent of the nation's maids and cleaners. Currently, most of these industries face a labor shortage, so the argument that undocumented immigrants are taking American jobs is hard to support.[65]

The US economy needs Mexican immigrants, and many Mexican workers need American jobs, but instead of offering these jobs to Mexican immigrants openly and honestly, the United States has exploited their labor in ways that are reminiscent of the decades-long exploitation of the black labor force under Jim Crow. Since 1986, approximately 11 million undocumented immigrants—most of whom are Mexican—have lived in a state of legal limbo, unable to legally establish residency, and yet continuing to work and establish families in the United States. When they reach old age, they will be unable to collect Social Security or retirement benefits. And if they brought young children to the United States at the time of their arrival, those children will be unable to legally get a job in the US, receive federal financial aid for college, or establish legal residency. Perhaps it is not too surprising that Hispanic immigrants who face few options are trapped in poverty. The US government has dealt with some of these young Hispanics in the same way that it dealt with many young blacks: by locking them up. Hispanics now comprise 23 percent of the total prison population and 32 percent of the people held in federal prisons—even though they account for only 16 percent of the US adult population.[66]

The jobs to which undocumented immigrants are confined are often brutal, and companies have deliberately exploited their workers' undocumented status to induce them to accept dangerous work conditions without complaint. This is especially true in southern chicken-processing plants, which embarked on a campaign to hire Hispanic workers (many of whom they knew were undocumented) in the mid-1990s. At one such plant—a facility in Guntersville, Alabama, affiliated with Farm Fresh Foods—Miguel Gonzalez filed a complaint with OSHA in 2016 that alleged, in the words of two journalists who summarized the complaint, that the plant's employees "were forced to work at punishing speeds in ankle-deep water with floating fat and chicken guts. They were enclosed in poorly ventilated rooms with chlorinated cleaning products wafting in the air, severely limited in bathroom and water breaks. . . . Several workers had to seek medical help. Workers who didn't keep up the pace were moved to an extremely cold area of the plant as punishment."[67] Thirty years ago, when most of those jobs would have gone to American blacks, they were the focus of civil rights protests led by Jesse Jackson. Today these jobs are going to undocumented immigrants, who are easier to exploit. Miguel Gonzalez complained to OSHA about the conditions he experienced, but most undocumented immigrants are too fearful of retaliation to report the abuse.

If, like me, you eat food produced in America, there is a high probability that the fruit, vegetables, and meat on your table have been brought to you through the labor of undocumented immigrants, who are likely trapped in exploitative work conditions. We have watched a racially based labor caste system emerge, in which 11 million people are prevented from ever receiving a path to citizenship and legal-resident status, while the entire nation has become dependent on their low-wage labor. Instead of reforming the immigration laws to give these people an opportunity to legally work in the United States and retain their human dignity by earning the right to speak up against abusive work situations, we have denied them a path to citizenship even while daily enjoying the products of their labor. And, to make matters worse, we as a society have justified this by speaking disparagingly of undocumented immigrants as the "illegals" who pose a threat to our safety—phrases that are eerily reminiscent of the charges that white Americans leveled against blacks, even while profiting from their low-wage work.

As Christians, we have a responsibility to "welcome the stranger," as many progressive evangelicals have pointed out. But our responsibility also goes beyond this. If we live in the United States, we are consuming the products of people whose labor is being exploited—that is, people who are subject to inhumane work conditions precisely because they are undocumented. We are living in a nation that has, for the past fifty years, maintained immigration quotas that are far too low to support our economy—and, as a result, has regularly exploited the labor of undocumented workers even while the public denounces them. We have a responsibility to end this injustice.

Ending the injustice will not come through increased border security or further investments in immigration raids. It may come when we treat the 11 million undocumented immigrants in our nation as human beings who are entitled to the same humane work conditions that we would expect for ourselves. In other words, they need a path to citizenship and legal protection. Those who were brought to this country as children especially need a path to citizenship, so that they can legally attend college and take jobs. Ending the injustice may also require us to look at the hypocrisy of our past actions toward Mexico and reassess whether it was right for us to profit for decades from the low-wage labor of Mexican migrants while depriving them of the opportunity for citizenship—and, to add insult to injury, doing all of this on land that the United States took from Mexico under extremely dubious circumstances in a nineteenth-century war that many Americans considered unjust, even at the time.

How Should We Vote If We Care about Racial Justice?

In 2012, 96 percent of black women voters cast their ballots for Democratic presidential candidate Barack Obama. In 2016, at least 94 percent—and possibly as many as 98 percent—voted for Hillary Clinton in her race against Donald Trump. The Pew Research Center survey found that African American women's support for Trump was so low that it was statistically zero.[68]

Black women are the demographic group that is most likely to be among the working poor. They are also the most likely people in the United States to be believing, Bible-reading, churchgoing Christians. Fifty-nine percent go to church every week. Eighty-seven percent say that they rely on their faith to get through difficult times.[69] Many of them even have reservations about abortion; one 2007 survey found that 51 percent of African American weekly churchgoers said that they wanted to see abortion made illegal.[70] But regardless of their views on abortion, almost no black women vote Republican. Their economic condition, their race, and their desire for economic justice have made them loyal Democrats for decades.

The same is increasingly true of Hispanics. Sixty-seven percent of Hispanic women voters supported Clinton in 2016; only 28 percent voted for Trump. Sixty-five percent of Hispanic men (and 81 percent of black men) also supported Clinton.[71]

How should a white Christian respond to these statistics? If nonwhite Christians who are most likely to experience economic vulnerability are voting overwhelmingly for Democratic candidates and refusing to support Republicans, should we say that they are misguided and do not understand which party will really protect their interests? Or should we recognize that perhaps on issues of race and poverty, the Republican Party is not the best choice for people who are not white? And if that is the case, do those of us who are white Christians have an obligation to stand with the oppressed and vote Democratic? After all, if we are voting with the nonwhite poor, we will not be voting Republican.

This is something that should give all middle-class white Christians pause, because in both the Old and New Testaments, God repeatedly states that he is on the side of the poor and the oppressed. If the poor and oppressed—especially the poor and oppressed who are followers of Jesus—are overwhelmingly voting for one particular party despite its stance on abortion, we need to think very carefully before casting a ballot for the party that an overwhelming number of the oppressed and economically marginalized view as the party of oppression. If, after examining our own position, we remain convinced that we have a moral duty to vote Republican for other reasons, we at least need to acknowledge the possibility that the Republican Party's policies on economics and race are not in the best interests of most blacks and Hispanics. And if that is the case, we may have an obligation to do what we can to change the party's policy or at least counteract it by finding other ways to challenge the structures of racial and economic injustice in our nation.

But if we decide to vote for Democrats, that does not relieve us of the responsibility of working for racial and economic justice in ways that may go against the grain of the party. Numerous progressive white Democrats believe they have the policy solutions for economic and racial justice, but their lack of religious values alienates them from black voters. In the 2020 southern Democratic presidential primaries where blacks predominated, the candidate who won the overwhelming majority of black votes (Joe Biden) was not the presidential aspirant with the most comprehensive, detailed policy solutions or the most economically progressive platform. Instead, he was someone who is comfortable talking about his Christian faith and speaking in black churches while demonstrating a record of service and empathy that many black voters respected.

When I talk to the black students who take my classes on American history, and when I read the works of black Christians or listen to black pastors talk about racial injustice, I find that very rarely do I hear a call for whites to embrace a set of policy solutions. Instead, what I hear repeatedly is that blacks would like those of us who are white to repent and acknowledge the racial injustice that exists and the extent to which we have played a role in perpetuating it.[72] This repentance will likely lead to a change in how we understand public policy and perhaps even in how we vote. But if we embrace a new set of progressive policies without repentance, nothing of lasting value will have been accomplished, even in the eyes of the people whom we are supposedly trying to help. In other words, we cannot assume—as I once wrongly did—that changing our party registration to align with marginalized groups of people accomplishes something of spiritual value. Something of lasting spiritual value will be accomplished only when we surrender ourselves to God on issues of race and poverty and acknowledge the extent to which those of us who are white might have been a lot more like the rich man than Lazarus in the parable that Jesus told. But once we do that, we may find that we vote in a different way.

If we vote Democratic, though, we will not do so out of a smug self-righteousness or a disdain for our Republican brothers and sisters in the faith as racists. Instead, we will do so in humility as we realize that those of us who are white were likely once blind to issues of race (and perhaps still are to a larger degree than we realize). We will also mourn the Democratic Party's growing secularism and lament the fact that its positions on some issues (such as transgender rights or abortion) are not only morally wrong but at odds with the views of some of the very people that the party claims to represent in its quest for racial justice. The Democratic Party is a very imperfect vehicle for racial justice. It cannot substitute for the gospel. This means that even if we vote Democratic, we will realize that we have far more in common with Christians who have the gospel but vote Republican than we do with secular Democrats who vote the way we do but lack the gospel.

In the end, it will be the gospel—not the Democratic Party—that leads us to the racial reconciliation of Revelation 7:9. White evangelicals have sometimes used such statements to excuse their own lack of support for the cause of civil rights for African Americans, but that is not my intention here. Instead, I am affirming the power of the gospel in order to caution politically progressive evangelicals not to make an idol of their progressive political stances on racial issues, which we are likely doing whenever we make a particular political stance a litmus test for Christian fellowship or an excuse for leaving a body of believers whom we consider racially unenlightened. Racial injustice is a serious sin, but it is not the only sin about which we should be concerned, and it is not an unforgivable sin even when we find it in the church among believers. It is possible that Jesus is doing more for the cause of racial reconciliation through the work of gospel-believing, misguided white Christians who vote for racially unjust policies than he is through unbelievers who get the policy right but reject the gospel.

But even as we wait for the consummation of Jesus's kingdom and the genuine racial reconciliation that it will bring, we have a responsibility to work for racial justice in a broken world, and we have a duty to bring that quest into the voting booth. Regardless of which party we choose to support, racial justice must be an important goal of our ballot choices. White Christians who vote Republican need to be honest with themselves about the effect that their vote will have on African Americans, Hispanics, and the cause of racial reconciliation—just as Christians who vote Democratic need to be honest with themselves about the effect that their vote will have on this and other moral causes. If, in a world of imperfect choices, we choose the less racially inclusive candidate because of our concern about other moral issues, we need to recognize the obligation that this places on us to devote even more effort to the cause of racial justice in other areas of life. The eschatological vision of the Scripture and the Bible's call for justice demand that we do no less.

6

Wealth and Poverty

*Whoever oppresses the poor shows contempt for their Maker,
but whoever is kind to the needy honors God.*

          −Proverbs 14:31

*Woe to those who make unjust laws, to those who issue oppressive
decrees, to deprive the poor of their rights and withhold justice
from the oppressed of my people, making widows their prey and
robbing the fatherless. What will you do on the day of reckoning,
when disaster comes from afar? To whom will you run for help?
Where will you leave your riches?*

          −Isaiah 10:1-3

*Looking at his disciples, he said: "Blessed are you who are poor,
for yours is the kingdom of God."*

          −Luke 6:20

The Bible mentions the concerns of the poor more than two thousand times, according to the tally compiled by the progressive evangelical magazine *Sojourners*.[1] In the Old Testament, God provided for the impoverished by telling the ancient Israelites to leave some grain in their field for the landless poor to collect for themselves (and the prophets then strongly rebuked the people when they instead abused the poor), and in the New Testament, early Christians were told that "true religion" consisted partly of "look[ing] after the orphan and widow in their distress" (James 1:27). Collections to care for the poor were a central part of the early church's ministry. And some of

Jesus's most famous parables, such as the good Samaritan and the story of the rich man and Lazarus, centered on people's attitude toward the poor or less fortunate. Throughout the church's two-thousand-year history, Christians of all theological persuasions have agreed that Jesus's followers have a responsibility to care for the poor. But they have not agreed on exactly how to do this.

For decades, Democrats have appealed to the Bible's injunctions about caring for the poor and have asked why Republican Christians who oppose expansions in social welfare programs and support tax cuts for the rich are not concerned about these verses. Christians who are politically conservative have countered that genuine concern for the poor is not shown in government handouts but in real economic opportunity, which they believe the capitalist system offers. And when charitable giving is needed, churches and private organizations are much better equipped than the government to provide it—which is why they have historically opposed government healthcare policies and federal antipoverty programs while also supporting proposals to privatize Social Security, introduce work requirements for welfare recipients, and outsource some of the government's social welfare programs to federally funded faith-based charities.[2] Which side is correct? Does the Bible's ethic of caring for the poor require Christians to support government programs to alleviate poverty? Or are political conservatives correct in their charge that government antipoverty initiatives hurt the poor, and that real efforts to help lower-income people will have to come from private organizations working within the capitalist system? Before we can weigh in on this debate, we need to look closely at the nation's poor and the nation's rich both in the present and in the past with an eye to determining whether the nation's economic policies are helping the poor provide for their families or instead are hurting the people whom God wants us to protect.

Biblical Principles

One of the Bible's most important principles regarding the poor is that people's human dignity is preserved when they have an opportunity to provide for their families through work and when they are protected from falling into long-term debt. The Mosaic law code's provision for debt forgiveness in the Year of Jubilee ensured that no person falling into economic misfortune permanently lost their land (which, in an agricultural economy, served as people's only means of production) and that no greedy person could amass large landholdings for himself at the expense of others. In other ancient Mediterranean societies, vast wealth inequality led to slave revolts, political revolutions, and other attempts by the poor to even the playing field and take vengeance on the rich. But in ancient Israel, God established a system to ensure that no one would be able to create a long-term monopoly in land and power. While a family might temporarily lose their land, go into debt, and even fall into short-term slavery, a year of restoration every half century would ensure that this situation would never be permanent (Lev. 25:8-55). In addition, those who temporarily fell into debt had additional protections. Even while landless, they had the right to harvest from the corners of their neighbors' fields—which meant that they would never have to go hungry (Lev. 19:9-10; 23:22). While working as day laborers, they had the right to be paid their wages on a daily basis. If they had to borrow money, they could not be deprived of their only set of clothing as a surety for their debt, and if they had to sell themselves into slavery, they could not legally be enslaved for more than seven years. Creditors were not allowed to charge interest on their loans—a provision that might sound quaint or unworkable in a modern capitalist economy, but which was an important safeguard for the poor in an agriculturally based economy where the lack of opportunity to amass additional wealth meant that even the lowest rates of interest could be crippling (Exod. 21:2; 22:25-27). Together, all of these protections for the less fortunate meant that if people followed God's law, they could be assured that God's promise that "there need be no poor people among you" would be fulfilled (Deut. 15:4).

As we know from the rest of the Old Testament, the ancient Israelites broke every provision in God's law. They did not honor the required Sabbaths or the Years of Jubilee. They subjected their brothers and sisters to permanent slavery. They found ways to illegally move ancient boundary markers and deprive the poor of their land. They charged usurious interest on loans to the poor and then seized the children of the poor as slaves when they could not pay. All of this incurred a strong rebuke from God and ultimately led to a divine judgment on the ancient Israelite nation as a way to right the wrongs done against the poor.

The modern United States is not an ancient agricultural economy, and very little of the wealth that we hold consists of arable land. The precise guidelines that the Old Testament gives for caring for the poor will not directly apply to our situation. In fact, some of these guidelines did not even apply to the urban economies of the New Testament era—which may explain why Jesus seemed to accept the validity of earning interest on investments even though the Old Testament had forbidden the practice and why the primary economic relief that the poor needed in the early church consisted of money rather than land (Luke 19:23; 1 Cor. 16:1–3). But if God went to such great lengths to create a just economic system for his covenant people under the Mosaic system and if he issued numerous rebukes through his prophets when his people violated those economic injunctions, we can safely assume that when we vote on issues pertaining to an economic system today, God is concerned about how that system affects the poor. Will the economic system that we support give the poor more opportunity to get out of debt and participate fully as productive, well-paid workers? Or will the system instead make the lives of the poor even harder? If the latter is the case, we are likely on very dangerous ground.

The History of Wealth and Poverty in the United States

Has the United States ensured that all members of society have opportunities to take jobs that will allow them to provide for their families without falling into debt? If we confine our examination to the present, the answer is clearly no. And even in the past, America's record in this area was, for the most part, mixed at best. But there have been a few eras in American history when the nation has demonstrated a stronger commitment toward ensuring equal economic opportunity for citizens of all socioeconomic levels.

As long as the United States remained heavily agricultural, the government could keep people from falling into poverty by providing more land for each new generation, so that every family could be assured of having a farm. Immediately after the Revolutionary War, the newly created US government settled its debts to war veterans by offering them free land on the frontier. Two generations later, the US government began selling western land at a discount to anyone who wanted it. And in 1862, the Homestead Act promised a free 160-acre plot to anyone willing to settle it for five years. Of course, this free-land program came at a tremendous cost in human lives, since the army had to drive out and kill the Native Americans who were living on the western prairie in order to take their land and give it to white settlers. And African Americans, who were forcibly brought to this country to work on land owned by whites, were largely prevented in most cases from ever owning the crops that they planted and harvested or the farmland that they tilled. Though a few made it to the West and became free, independent homesteaders, the vast majority worked as tenant farmers, day laborers, or sharecroppers in the South, a situation that kept them permanently in debt and deprived of nearly all economic and political rights.[3] But for white citizens, the government's land-distribution programs amounted to a highly effective antipoverty measure. As long as free land was available in the West, most whites had a realistic chance of becoming independent farmers. There was always the risk, of course, that drought, insects, or blight could destroy their land investments, but if they survived, they could provide for their families with plots of ground that they owned themselves.

The industrialization of the nation's economy changed this situation. While industrialization improved average living standards overall and enabled a few people to make spectacular fortunes, it also made the lives of the poor more uncertain than ever. In the industrial economy, most factory workers owned no land and almost no capital. They lived paycheck to paycheck, which meant that if they were laid off in a time of economic downturn, they had no safety net. Throughout the nineteenth century, the industrial economy went through cycles of booms and busts, and during the "busts," some people were on the verge of starvation. During the depression of 1893, when as much as 20 or 25 percent of the workforce may have been unemployed, and when many of those who remained employed faced steep wage cuts that made it impossible for them to pay their bills, angry workers turned to strikes and marches to get the attention of the government or their employers. Some of the strikes turned violent. In Illinois and other parts of the Midwest, a 28 percent wage reduction at the Pullman Palace Car Company prompted more than 100,000 railroad workers to go on strike or refuse to service Pullman cars. Pitched battles ensued after the Illinois governor sent in the state militia and the US president dispatched the army. Workers destroyed railcars, while soldiers fired on the striking workers. This was not an isolated case (there were numerous other incidents of labor violence in the late nineteenth century), but it was galvanizing for many of the people who lived through it. As a result of his experiences with the Pullman Company, one of the leaders of the strike, Eugene Debs, who was jailed for his activities, became a lifelong socialist and received nearly one million votes (6 percent of the total) as a Socialist Party candidate for president in 1912.[4]

Meanwhile, those at the top of the nation's economy earned massive fortunes that have never been surpassed. John D. Rockefeller, the nation's first billionaire, personally owned about 1.5 percent of the GDP because of his control of the nation's oil supply. If translated into modern dollars, his wealth, by some measures, would have been equivalent to more than $300 billion—a figure somewhat larger than even Jeff Bezos or Bill Gates controls today. Several other Gilded Age tycoons also surpassed Bezos and Gates in real wealth, or at least came close to it. Andrew Carnegie, the nation's leading steel magnate, accumulated a fortune that would be worth more than $200 billion in early twenty-first-century dollars, as did Cornelius Vanderbilt, who made his money in railroads and shipping.[5]

Before the industrialized economy of the Gilded Age (the period from 1865 to 1900), these fortunes were impossible to achieve in the United States, but by the late nineteenth century, industrialization enabled a handful of people who controlled a new technology to earn enough money to live lives of opulence that had never before been seen in America. Both Rockefeller, a strict-minded northern Baptist who abstained from alcohol and disliked ostentatious displays of wealth, and Carnegie, a Scottish immigrant who believed in a self-help philosophy and never forgot his working-class roots, lived frugally and eventually gave away much of their fortunes to charitable and educational enterprises, but the Vanderbilts built a string of mansions across the Eastern Seaboard and threw fashionable parties that were the talk of the society gossip pages. One of the Vanderbilts' "summer cottages" on the Newport, Rhode Island, beach was a seventy-room sumptuous display that was built to look like a Renaissance Italian palace. Another, which was William Vanderbilt's present to his wife for her thirty-ninth birthday, was built with 500,000 cubic feet of marble. (Incidentally, the couple divorced only three years after the house was completed.) The most spectacular Vanderbilt residence, the Biltmore Estate in Asheville, North Carolina, was a 250-room behemoth that stretched over four acres of floor space and included a medieval-looking seventy-foot-high banquet hall decorated with sixteenth-century tapestries. Meanwhile, in New York City, only a few blocks away from the Vanderbilts' six-story Fifth Avenue mansion, crowded tenement houses that packed as many as a dozen people into a single bedroom and provided only a single basement toilet for nearly 150 people housed some of the hundreds of thousands of southern and eastern European immigrant workers who arrived in New York City each year and who labored in the factories that earned the wealth for the Gilded Age tycoons. And these were the fortunate ones. Those who lost their jobs—or, in the worst case, lost their parents, as some unfortunate orphans did—might have to move out onto the street. Some of the most shocking photos from the Gilded Age are of barefoot young boys sleeping on steam grates in New York City in a desperate attempt to keep warm. Even many western farmers, who had become dependent on the market economy, credit, and the railroads, and who were no longer the free, independent entrepreneurs that they had dreamed of becoming, were in desperate straits and were looking for the monetization of silver to increase the money supply and make it easier to pay off their loans to the eastern bankers whose control of their lives they had come to hate. The nearly one million votes that Eugene Debs received as the Socialist Party nominee for president in 1912 were a sign of the anger that many people felt over the great wealth disparity in America.[6]

Yet what America adopted as an antidote to wealth inequality was not socialism but rather Progressivism. The Progressives of the early twentieth century were overwhelmingly Protestant, and for many of them, their concern about wealth inequality was rooted at least partly in the religion of the social gospel. They believed in hard work and capitalism, but they also believed that the Gilded Age tycoons had rigged the system by establishing monopolies that unfairly kept competitors out of the market and by making political contributions that ensured that their industries would remain free from government regulation. This was a threat to American democracy, they believed, and it was morally wrong. If the behavior of the rich remained unregulated, the rich would destroy the nation's moral values and its democratic political order. Accordingly, the first constitutional amendment that the Progressives enacted once they gained control of government was an amendment giving the federal government the right to tax personal incomes. At first, only the wealthiest 2 percent of households paid a federal income tax, and the tax rates varied from only 1 percent to a maximum of 6 percent.[7] With taxation set at such modest levels, the measure did almost nothing to lessen the growing divide between the rich and the poor. Nor did the Progressives' other measures, such as antitrust legislation, child labor laws, and federal regulation of railroad rates, have much discernible effect on poverty or the political power of the wealthy.

At the end of the Progressive era, in the 1920s, business-friendly Republican presidential administrations cut taxes, and the divide between the rich and poor, which was already high, increased still further. By the end of the 1920s, the wealthiest 0.1 percent owned 25 percent of the nation's wealth and the top 1 percent owned more than 50 percent, while the bottom 90 percent of Americans owned barely more than 15 percent of the nation's wealth. In terms of real dollars, the bottom 90 percent were slightly poorer in 1929 (just before the onset of the Great Depression) than they had been in 1917, while the wealthiest 10 percent were substantially richer.[8] But unlike the Gilded Age, relatively few people in the 1920s expressed concern about wealth disparity, because, thanks to the new availability of consumer credit, most white working-class and middle-class Americans were now able to borrow their way to a higher standard of living and enjoy the "good life," even if their real wealth was decreasing. By the end of the 1920s, more than half of all automobile sales were financed with credit. Americans now routinely used credit to buy houses and, with the new availability of department store credit cards, even consumer goods. This could be risky, of course, especially when interest rates for borrowing were often as high as 30 percent. One slight economic hiccup could throw a borrower into deep poverty. Even in 1926, at the height of the prosperity of the "roaring twenties," more than one out of twenty farms in Minnesota and South Dakota experienced foreclosure in just a single year. Outside the farm belt, urban Americans lived similarly precariously, as they purchased more on credit than their incomes suggested they could afford. This is one reason why the Great Depression of the 1930s was so devastating for Americans who lost their jobs: They had been far more financially insecure before the depression than they realized, so as soon as they lost their income source, they often ended up homeless and destitute almost instantly. By 1933, at the nadir of the depression, 25 percent of Americans were unemployed, and many of them were desperate for a political revolution.[9]

The political revolution they received was rather modest compared to most of the solutions that were adopted in Europe, which was equally desperate for economic relief. The United States did not adopt fascism, communism, socialism, or totalitarianism. Nor did it experience a political coup. But it did create a social welfare state, with social safety-net programs such as Social Security pensions, Aid to Families with Dependent Children (AFDC), and unemployment insurance to protect people who were out of the workforce through no fault of their own. And in the early 1940s, during the Second World War, the United States implemented a steeply progressive income tax, with a maximum marginal tax rate of 94 percent for incomes over $200,000 (equivalent to about $3 million in 2020).[10]

From the 1930s through the 1970s, a coalition of both Republicans and Democrats accepted the principle that although every wage earner had the responsibility to contribute to their country through taxes, the rich had an obligation to pay a much larger percentage of their income, since they had more resources. A majority of Americans who remembered the depression also accepted the necessity of a government-provided social safety net both to alleviate the suffering of the poor and to offer opportunity to the middle class. During this period, the government funded the construction of federal highways, subsidized home mortgages, provided the first federal financial assistance to public schools in low-income areas, and offered the first federal college loans. Even more importantly, the high rate of government spending on the military during the Cold War provided both blue-collar and white-collar jobs to millions of Americans who worked in the military-industrial complex, and it fueled the high economic growth rates of the era—growth rates that have never been equaled since the 1960s. Due in part to this high rate of economic growth, low unemployment, and high taxes on the rich, the wages and real wealth of working-class and middle-class Americans increased, while the disparity between the rich and poor decreased.[11]

Wealthier Americans were willing to accept higher taxes partly because of an ethic of shared sacrifice that pervaded the era. At a time when there was a near-continuous military draft and when many Americans believed that no sacrifice was too great to protect the nation from nuclear annihilation or from taking second place to the Soviet Union in the Cold War, high tax rates were simply part of the responsibility that Americans had to "ask what you can do for your country," as President John F. Kennedy famously phrased it. Fiscally conservative Republicans such as President Dwight Eisenhower would have liked to cut taxes, but because of their commitment to a balanced budget, they refused to do so unless they could offset every tax cut with an equivalent spending cut. And Democrats such as Kennedy and Lyndon Johnson did cut taxes when they thought they could do so without incurring high budget deficits, but then raised them again when they thought the budget required it. By raising taxes, Johnson managed to balance the budget in his last year in office—the last time this would happen for nearly thirty years.[12]

The principle of progressive taxation and a social safety net was rooted partly in a Christian consensus. American Catholic clergy advocated a "living wage" since the beginning of the twentieth century, because they argued that it was immoral to pay a male breadwinner less than what he needed to support his family. Both liberal Protestants and Catholics supported the principle of Social Security, unemployment insurance, and President Lyndon Johnson's "War on Poverty." The idea that the American capitalist system would be fair only if the nation demonstrated concern for the less fortunate reflected the biblical injunction to care for the poor, many Christians believed. Of course, at least a few Christians, especially those who were politically conservative, thought differently. Critics of the government's social welfare programs (who were a minority for much of the mid-twentieth century) called these programs, along with the accompanying high tax rates, "socialism," but in reality, the programs aided the capitalist system by providing the research and development money for private industry and ameliorating the harsher effects of an unregulated economy that had prevailed in the Gilded Age and the 1920s.[13] A thoroughgoing socialist system, which is usually defined as government ownership of industry, never had much support in the mid-twentieth-century United States.

However, as memories of the depression and the shared sacrifices of the Second World War and the early Cold War began to fade, so did support for highly progressive taxation and a strong social safety net. Conservative critiques of this system increased in the 1960s and 1970s, and in the 1980s, the Reagan administration began dismantling much of this apparatus. The reasons for white middle-class Americans' disillusionment with the social welfare state were varied and complex, but they essentially came down to this: many Americans began to believe that the social welfare state was inefficient, harmful to the economy and the nation's morals, and a threat to their wallets. They also began to have much greater confidence in the private market as a substitute for government action.[14]

This was not entirely a bad thing, although many liberals thought it was. Private organizations had provided a social safety net long before the government took over this function. In the 1920s, private employers had introduced the first retirement pension system in the United States, and even after the advent of Social Security, the benefits negotiated by labor unions or offered by private corporations continued to be an important supplement to the nation's government-administered retirement pension program. Similarly, private charitable efforts funded public libraries, hospitals for the poor, and the expansion of educational opportunities for African Americans in the early twentieth century. Some discussion of whether private entities could do a better job than the government in providing a social safety net might not have been a bad idea. And some critiques of the outcomes of the government's welfare programs might also have been justified. Conservatives in the 1970s frequently blamed AFDC, arguably the most oft criticized social welfare program of the time, for encouraging laziness, sexual irresponsibility, and marital disintegration. While these criticisms were often greatly exaggerated and racially charged, the critiques did point to a disturbing shift in public views of welfare assistance from a last resort to a fundamental right. In the early 1960s, only about 33 percent of eligible people chose to apply for AFDC, but by 1971, more than 90 percent did.[15] During the second half of the twentieth century, the percentage of AFDC recipients who were single mothers who had never married also increased. Although conservatives probably greatly overestimated the degree to which AFDC was responsible for the rise in the out-of-wedlock birthrate, some discussion of the values that the AFDC policies encouraged—and the question of whether the policies could be revised to encourage other values—was probably merited. In fact, this did happen in the mid-1990s, when AFDC was replaced with Temporary Assistance for Needy Families (TANF), which imposed work or educational requirements for recipients and limited the time people could remain enrolled in the program.

But unfortunately, reasonable critiques that could have functioned as suggestions for policy revision became instead, in the hands of a new generation of conservatives, a justification for both the dismantling of the entire social welfare state and the progressive tax rates that had supported it. Ronald Reagan was elected in 1980 on a promise to cut taxes, which he did. When he entered office, the top marginal income tax rate was 70 percent; when he left, it was 28 percent.[16]

Before Reagan entered office, nearly all Republican presidents of the past half century, from Herbert Hoover to Gerald Ford, had been deficit hawks who believed that balancing the budget took priority over cutting taxes. Reagan reversed these goals. Cutting taxes should happen before balancing the budget, he thought, because, in accordance with the new supply-side theories of conservative economists, he thought that tax cuts for investors and business entrepreneurs would stimulate economic growth to such a degree that not only would everyone have a lot more money to spend but the tax revenues from the increased salaries would surpass the revenues that would have been collected if the higher tax rates had been left in place. To some, the theory sounded too good to be true (George Bush called it "voodoo economics"), and it was. When Reagan cut taxes, the budget deficit nearly tripled—from $79 billion a year during his first year in office to $221 billion a year only five years later. Wealth inequality also increased. Between 1977 and 1989, the pretax income of the richest 1 percent grew by 77 percent, while the bottom 40 percent experienced an income decline. The uneven effect of the tax cuts left more wealth in the hands of the already wealthy, but a new public acceptance of higher salaries for the rich—especially those who were top corporate executives—also contributed. In the mid-1970s, the average CEO of any of the nation's largest 350 publicly traded firms earned just over thirty times as much as the average nonsupervisory worker—which meant that in 1978 a CEO's compensation would have been equivalent to about $1.5 million today. By the end of the 1980s, that increased to 120 times. Today the average CEO of one of these large firms earns more than three hundred times the salary of an average private-sector nonsupervisory worker. While average salaries, when adjusted for inflation, increased less than 11 percent between 1978 and 2014, CEO salaries and compensation packages at the nation's largest companies increased by 997 percent to reach more than $16 million a year.[17]

The poor struggled during the 1980s. Reagan refused to raise the minimum wage, so as a result, people working minimum-wage jobs earned one-third less in real dollars at the end of Reagan's presidency than at the beginning, since their paychecks did not keep pace with inflation. Reagan cut money for school lunch programs. He also signed into law legislation that increased the FICA tax, a flat tax that paid for Social Security and disproportionately hurt the working poor. His drug policies put more of the poor—especially the minority poor—in prison, branding them with a felony record that often prevented them from finding work after they were released. Overall, the poorest 20 percent of Americans experienced a 10 percent reduction in their after-tax income between 1977 and 1988—even as the richest 20 percent experienced a 34 percent increase in their after-tax income during the same period.[18]

The increase in wealth inequality was probably not due to any one policy—not even to tax cuts that disproportionately benefited the wealthy, although this policy certainly exacerbated the increase in wealth disparity. Due to a confluence of factors, the struggles of the working poor continued long after Reagan and Bush left office. The cost of housing, health care, and college tuition increased at much faster rates than wages (which were largely stagnant). As a result, the working poor and even much of the middle class became increasingly reliant on credit. By 2019, 41 percent of American households were carrying credit card debt; collectively, Americans owed more than $1 trillion on credit card purchases alone. Collectively, they also owed more than $1.6 trillion in student loan debt, an amount distributed among 44 million people, at the rate of $28,000 per person for the class of 2017. More than 11 percent of student loan borrowers miss payments and fall into arrears on that debt, with devastating effects to their credit scores. Most Americans—whether middle class or working poor—are living paycheck to paycheck. Only 39 percent say they have $1,000 in the bank to cover an unexpected emergency.[19]

Currently, the wealth divide between the haves and have-nots is about what it was between 1927 and 1929.[20] We have returned to a level of wealth inequality in this country that we have not seen in ninety years. And, like the 1920s, we are covering up this wealth inequality with massive amounts of consumer debt—though, for reasons that we will examine, this dependence on credit is even greater than it was on the eve of the Great Depression.

Why Is the Gap between Rich and Poor Increasing?

It is tempting to say that the working poor and the increasingly indebted middle class simply need to practice wise financial principles. Maybe what they need to get out of debt is not a new government policy but rather a course in managing personal finances, some might think. No doubt good financial management principles would help many individuals, but financial management principles alone will not be enough to solve our massive debt problem. Instead, the problem is a combination of stagnant wages and massive increases in the price of housing, education, and health care.

Home prices are currently rising faster than wages in 80 percent of the counties in the United States, according to a 2019 analysis of federal government data. In 1965, the median new home price in the United States was only $20,000 (which would translate into about $110,000 in 2000 dollars or the equivalent of $164,000 in 2020), but by 2000 the median cost was $169,000 ($250,000 in 2020 dollars), and by the summer of 2019, it had reached $325,000. Part of the problem is that developers rarely build small, affordable houses anymore. By the beginning of the twenty-first century, new houses were, on average, more than twice as large as homes constructed in the 1950s. But this is only one component of the problem. Due to increased demand for housing in certain areas, the prices of even older, smaller homes are increasing faster than the rate of inflation. This is largely because, as jobs and thus populations shift to urban areas, increasing numbers of people want to live in the same space, thus driving up both home prices and the cost of apartment rentals. In some cities, this has been catastrophic. Average mortgage payments in New York and San Francisco now run between 95 and 120 percent of the average salary in those cities—which means that the majority of people working there can afford nothing more than a small apartment rental and perhaps not even that. In two hundred American cities, median home prices have now exceeded $1 million. Even in cities that have historically been more affordable, such as Atlanta, population pressures have resulted in a rapid upsurge in rent, which places enormous pressures on the working poor. By 2016, the cost of rent had become so high that nearly 7 million Americans had to pay more than 50 percent of their income for rent alone. One-third of all households currently pay more than 30 percent of their income for housing.[21]

The price of college has also become a major source of debt for the middle class and even some of the working poor. Only a generation or two ago, most people did not go to college, but today some form of post-high school education has become a requirement for nearly every career—even for many entry-level jobs in fields such as truck driving, hairstyling, and midlevel manager positions at local grocery stores. As a result, people who once could have entered the workforce without a college degree now have to borrow money in order to get this entrance ticket to the world of work. And this ticket has now become more expensive than ever. Even when adjusted for inflation, the cost in real dollars for attending both public and private four-year colleges and universities doubled between 1985 and 2016, and the cost of a year of community college nearly doubled. Seventy percent of students have to take out loans to cover these costs. Now that more than two-thirds of high school graduates are going to either a two-year or four-year college, the majority of young adults are likely to contract substantial debt even before they get their first full-time job. Even worse, approximately 40 percent of all people who start a four-year college program drop out before finishing their degree—which means, in many cases, that they owe large amounts of money for a degree that they will never complete and therefore can never use. In 1989, only 9 percent of American families were trying to pay off student loan debts; by 2010, 19 percent were. Collectively, Americans now owe more than $1.6 trillion in student loan debt, with the average undergraduate borrower owing more than $37,000 on graduation day. For most borrowers, repaying these loans will be a twenty-year project.[22]

But the major crisis that the working poor and many in the middle class face is health care. For the working poor or those who are struggling to remain in the middle class, a medical emergency can mean the difference between remaining financially solvent and going bankrupt. More than half of all bankruptcies in the United States (about half a million per year) are caused at least in part by medical bills.[23] This means that in the past five years alone, several million Americans have had their financial lives ruined at least partly because of unforeseen medical bills.

As costs of these three necessities—a place to live, a ticket to a job, and lifesaving health care—increased exponentially, the federal government simultaneously rolled back its social services. The minimum wage has not been raised in ten years and is currently set at only $7.25—a rate so low that minimum-wage earners working forty hours a week earn less than $15,000 a year, leaving them below the poverty line if they have to support any dependents. Food stamps, which were once the key for poor people to escape food insecurity, are insufficient to cover an adequate diet for most families. The Supplemental Nutrition Assistance Program (SNAP), the current moniker for what was once popularly known as the "food stamp" program, gives a four-person family only $465 of food per month on average—which amounts to only $27.35 per person per week. Individuals receive, on average, only $134 in food per month. And even this small benefit is available only to the working poor who can find a job, because after the welfare reform of 1996, adult households without children lose their SNAP benefits after three months unless they find work or enroll in job training. The myth of lazy, able-bodied adults living off of welfare is badly out of touch with the current reality. The truth is that most of the poor who are not disabled are trapped in low-income jobs that do not pay enough for them even to put food on the table. Even as welfare programs have been trimmed, taxes on the poor have continued to increase. After raising the FICA tax in the 1980s—a flat tax that disproportionately affects lower-income workers—the government also increased the charges for Medicare that seniors must pay. Similarly, as increases in the costs of college education have continued to outpace inflation, many state and local governments have economized by reducing their financial commitments to their state university systems, thus exacerbating the cycle of tuition increases in public universities that were once much more affordable.[24]

In the area of housing assistance, the government has also cut back. Eager to replace the crime-ridden "projects" with low-crime, revenue-generating condos, cities such as Atlanta have entirely discontinued their public housing programs and replaced them with housing vouchers for low-income residents. But in a tight housing market, where in some cities there might be fifteen or twenty applicants for every one person who is given an apartment, many landlords refuse to take the vouchers, since they would instead prefer to rent only to tenants who can afford to pay the full price out of their own pockets. And cities that are overwhelmed with the requests of hundreds of thousands of residents who cannot afford housing have often run out of vouchers and quit issuing them. Besides, there are increasingly fewer inexpensive apartments available for low-income people, regardless of whether they have vouchers. If replacing older, cheaper housing with high-end luxury condos or sleek office space is more profitable, few property owners will pass up an opportunity to increase the value of their holdings, even if poorer tenants are hurt in the process. The nation lost four million low-income apartments between 2011 and 2017.[25]

The United States now has the fourth highest rate of income inequality among industrialized nations, ranking behind only Mexico, Chile, and Turkey in the contest for this dubious honor. And as the divide between the rich and the poor has grown, income segregation has also increased. Fewer Americans rub shoulders with people outside their own income bracket. Neighborhoods have become more economically homogenous, and Americans are now less likely to marry across socioeconomic class lines. As the majority of the nation's housing has become less affordable for people with lower incomes, poor people have become increasingly concentrated in low-income neighborhoods, some of which are "food deserts" that lack convenient and affordable sources of fresh fruit and vegetables. They have also become increasingly invisible to middle- and upper-middle-class Americans, who are less likely than ever to personally know someone who is poor.[26]

As a result, if we are upper-middle class, we may no longer see the poor, and we may underestimate how many low-income wage earners there really are and how much they are struggling. Because we routinely say that the United States is the richest nation in the world, we may underestimate how much of that wealth is concentrated at the top—and how few people share in its benefits. Perhaps it is time to take a quick tour of the American population, as separated by income brackets known as "quintiles." Each quintile represents 20 percent of American households.

A Quick Tour of the American Economy by Quintiles

The Poorest Quintile

Twenty percent of American households earn less than $25,600 a year, with the average amount totaling only $13,775.[27] More than half of the adults in this quintile are out of the labor force—often not by choice, since more than 20 percent of the working-age adults in this quintile are disabled, and others are jobless people who would desperately like to find work. But about 38 percent of these households (and a majority of the households whose total annual income is slightly more than $20,000) are headed by the "working poor." Despite working hard at minimum-wage or low-income jobs, these householders are unable to lift their families over the poverty line. Most typically, low-income families are headed by single mothers without college degrees; in fact, 30 percent of all female-headed households in the United

States fall below the poverty line. The poorest quintile includes a disproportionately high number of children: 13 million, to be exact. And many of these children are struggling. Six million American children (and 14 percent of households with children under the age of six) are "food insecure." For many Americans, poverty can be an early death sentence. The nation's poorest states have the highest infant mortality rates, and those deaths are concentrated disproportionately among African Americans living below the poverty line. A baby born in Mississippi is more than twice as likely as a baby in Massachusetts to die at birth. And among older adult women nationwide, those in the poorest quintile can expect to live thirteen fewer years than those in the wealthiest quintile. In some conservative states that refused to participate in the federal government's expansion of Medicaid during the Obama administration, some of these families might also lack health insurance. Disproportionately likely to be in single-parent homes, this group is much more likely to vote Democratic than Republican (if they vote at all), because they see federal assistance programs as their only hope of paying their rent and putting food on the table or getting the health care that can make a difference between life and death.[28]

Children born into the poorest quintile do not have a particularly high probability of ever escaping poverty, since fewer than 40 percent will earn any college credit (even from a two-year technical college) by the time they are twenty-two—and fewer than 15 percent will enroll at a four-year college or university.[29]

The Second Quintile: The Struggling Working Class (20th to 40th Percentile)

Twenty percent of American households earn between $25,600 and $50,000 per year, with the average amount totaling just over $37,000. These households have a particularly difficult struggle, because they earn too much to be eligible for Medicaid, food assistance programs, and other welfare assistance, but not enough to be able to save. Most of these households—which include a mix of single-parent families, married couples with only one income, and a few single adults—are living paycheck to paycheck and hoping that their credit card debt will not bankrupt them. By 2004 (before the financial crisis of 2008), 44 percent of families in the second-lowest income quintile were carrying credit card debt that they could not immediately pay off, and there is every reason to believe that this percentage has only continued to increase since then. By 2013, the average family in Alabama, for instance—a state where approximately half of all households are in the nation's lowest two income quintiles—owed more than $15,000 in nonmortgage debt. Two generations ago, labor unions negotiated comfortable wages and pension benefits for blue-collar workers, but with unionized workers now accounting for less than 7 percent of the private-sector workforce (down from approximately one-third of all wage and salary workers in the 1950s), those days are long gone. Because many of the people in the struggling working class do not have jobs with retirement benefits, they will have to depend mainly on Social Security checks for their retirement, even though the average Social Security beneficiary receives only $17,000 per year, before Medicare fees are deducted. As a result, an increasing number of elderly people remain in the workforce, taking on low-income jobs until they become too feeble to continue. Twenty-seven percent of Americans over the age of sixty-five are now in the workforce, as are 8 percent of those over seventy-five.[30]

The Third Quintile: The Indebted Stagnant Middle Class (40th to 60th Percentile)

The 20 percent of American households in the middle quintile earn between $50,000 and $80,000 per year, with an average income of slightly less than $64,000. In inflation-adjusted real dollars, the income level of this middle group is almost exactly the same as it was twenty years ago, even as some of their key expenses—housing, college, and health care—have increased much faster than the rate of inflation. People in this group are likely to go to college—though they have only a 50 percent chance of finishing a degree program that they start, with fewer than a third of recent high school graduates from this group likely to ever obtain a bachelor's degree—and they probably have health insurance and quite likely a house. But middle-class Americans are financing almost all of this on credit, even into old age. Nearly three million over the age of sixty are still paying off student loans—mostly for children who defaulted on their obligations years before, but sometimes on their own behalf for degrees that they felt they needed to complete to change careers, perhaps after a job layoff. Collectively, Americans over the age of fifty owe $260 billion in student loans—up from $36 billion only fifteen years ago. Younger middle-income Americans are even more deeply in debt. At any given moment, the average US household now owes more than $16,000 in credit card bills, $29,000 in auto loans, and $50,000 in student loans—not to mention $182,000 on a home mortgage.[31]

The Fourth Quintile: The Upper-Middle Class (60th to 80th Percentile)

The 20 percent of American households in the slightly upper-middle-class range earned between $80,000 and $130,000 a year, with an average income of nearly $102,000. How well this group is faring depends largely on where they live. In a rural, exurban, or affordable suburban market, they might be comfortably able to meet their financial obligations, assuming that an unexpected medical crisis or other emergency does not set them back. But if they are in one of the nation's major cities, they are likely wondering how far their salary will stretch. With more than 80 percent of Americans currently in debt, most of the members of the upper-middle class are, like their less wealthy peers, financing their middle-class lifestyles at least partly through credit. Even among Americans between the ages of fifty-five and sixty-four, 41 percent are carrying credit card debt, as are 32 percent between the ages of sixty-five and seventy-four.[32] And while this group has experienced modest growth in real earnings in recent years, much of this is because of a commitment to two-income professional careers that did not exist a half century ago—not because of a real increase in wages over the past few decades. Most of the people in this income group are married, and in most cases, both spouses are working a full-time job; only 20 percent of these homes include an adult who is out of the workforce, and fewer than 10 percent include someone who works only part-time.[33]

This means that in addition to all their other expenses, many upper-middle-class couples with young children also have to pay substantial amounts for childcare—or, in some cases, choose to limit their number of children or forgo having them altogether because, after contracting massive educational loans that may take two decades to pay off, they decide that they cannot afford to have kids. Fertility rates in the United States are now the lowest they have ever been and have fallen below replacement levels. Educated professional couples are now the most likely to forgo having children. The main reason they give for this choice is not convenience but economics: a 2018 *New York Times* poll showed that 64 percent of people who said that they were having "fewer children than they considered ideal" cited the high cost of childcare as a reason for their decision, with others mentioning inadequate paid family leave or concerns about the economy as related factors.[34]

The Fifth Quintile: The Upper-Income Earners (80th to 90th Percentile)

American households in this range earn between $130,000 and just under $185,000. In some areas of the country, households with this income are living comfortably, but in the two hundred cities where median house prices exceed $1 million, even some of these people probably struggle—especially if they are trying to balance high mortgage payments with student loan debt and possibly private school tuition for their children. Eighteen percent of people in households earning more than $100,000 per year are currently repaying college loan debt—and 36 percent of these debtholders are "worried" about their ability to repay. By no stretch of the imagination can they be considered poor, but they are also not likely to advance themselves as quickly as they might have expected. Like members of the fourth quintile, this quintile consists mostly of dual-income couples. During the past fifteen years, this income group has experienced only modest income gains, even as their expenses have increased. Many have reacted mainly by demanding tax cuts. Outside of a few liberal coastal areas and university enclaves, this group is disproportionately Republican. But even if they are Democrats, they are not likely to see themselves as wealthy people who should be paying more taxes. Instead, nearly every major Democratic proposal for tax increases has been limited to households earning more than $250,000 a year. Households below the 95th percentile—and perhaps even 99th percentile—would be unaffected.[35]

The Wealthy (90th to 95th Percentile)

Earning between $185,000 and $249,000 a year, households in this range usually come from the ranks of educated professionals or successful small-business owners, and they are doing at least modestly well. But rising educational and housing costs have hit this group especially hard. The average educational debt for a law school graduate is now $113,000. And that does not factor in interest on the loan. A graduate of one of the most elite law schools who borrows his or her entire way through the program will likely end up having to pay $550,000 over the course of the next twenty years—a debt that does not include a spouse's educational loans, which might also be substantial.[36] So, even this group of "wealthy" Americans may spend the first half of their professional careers deeply in debt. Getting into the right college, no matter the cost, is important to this group: 25 percent of their children attend Ivy League or elite colleges, and nearly 70 percent attend a college that is at least considered "selective."[37]

The Richest 5 Percent (95th to 99th Percentile)

Earning between $249,000 and $422,000 a year, this group has experienced some of the most rapid income gains of any American group in the past few years. In real, inflation-adjusted dollars, the average pretax income level of this group is nearly twice as high as it was in 1980.[38] And because of changes in the tax law that benefit higher-income earners more than lower ones, this group's take-home pay has increased even more substantially.

The 1 Percent (99th Percentile)

The income levels for this group are rapidly increasing. In 1995, the 1 percent earned 15 percent of all income in the United States, but by 2015, their earnings accounted for 22 percent of the whole. And as the incomes of these richest Americans increased, the salary level required to get into the 1 percent grew rapidly as well. In 2014, an annual income of $386,000 would be enough to put a household in the richest 1 percent, but by 2018, that figure had increased to $422,000.[39] As their incomes have risen, their share of the national wealth has also increased.

Who are these people? Most of them are medium-sized-business owners, with the average business employing about fifty-seven people. They make it a priority to send their children to the best colleges; nearly 80 percent of the children from these families attend selective, elite, or Ivy League schools.

In fact, many of the leading private universities and liberal arts colleges in America, including five of the eight Ivies, enroll more students from the top 1 percent than from all of the bottom 60 percent combined. Furthermore, despite elite colleges' concerted efforts to diversify, the percentage of their students who come from the top 1 percent has increased over the past decade and a half, while the percentage who come from the bottom 40 percent has declined—perhaps partly because rapid increases in college tuition have put elite colleges even further out of the price range of the vast majority of Americans.[40]

The Richest 0.1 Percent and the 0.01 Percent

In 2015, an annual household income of $1.6 million was the minimum threshold to put a family in the richest one-thousandth (the 0.1 percent) of American households, and an annual income of $7 million was required to get into the 0.01 percent. On average, households in the 0.1 percent earn just under $3 million per year, and those in the elite 0.01 percent—a total of 16,000 households—earn an average of nearly $19 million a year, with an average net worth per family of $111 million. Although a few celebrities in the sports or entertainment world might be included, most people in the top 0.1 percent are bankers, CEOs of businesses that employ at least 150 people, or possibly an extremely successful lawyer. And among the top 0.01 percent, hedge fund managers, technology company founders, and other spectacularly successful business owners dominate the list.[41]

The Richest Billionaires

The four hundred richest Americans are collectively worth nearly $3 trillion—more than the entire GDP of Canada and Mexico combined and more than the collective wealth of all forty-two million African Americans in the United States. The wealth of these four hundred uber-rich (all of whom were worth at least $2 billion) increased by 59 percent between 2012 and 2017, even as most of the rest of the American population experienced stagnant wages and long-term declines in wealth.[42]

If income distribution is uneven in American society (with the highest-earning 20 percent of Americans earning more than 60 percent of all income in the United States), wealth distribution is even more badly skewed. The bottom 60 percent of the American population own less than 5 percent of the nation's wealth, and the bottom 80 percent own barely more than 10 percent. By the time we reach the 80th and 90th percentile of income earners—all of whom have six-figure annual household incomes—we find people who are starting to accrue real capital through 401(k)s, home ownership, and investments, and that is why nearly 50 percent of America's wealth is held by people in the 80th to 98th percentile. But even by the time we reach the 99th percentile, we have still accounted for only 60 percent of the wealth in the United States, because the top 1 percent owns a full 40 percent of America's wealth. And even among the top 1 percent, much of the wealth is concentrated at the very top of the pyramid. In fact, three American individuals—Microsoft founder Bill Gates, investment guru Warren Buffett, and Amazon founder Jeff Bezos—collectively own as much wealth as 160 million Americans combined. In other words, the combined wealth of the three richest people in the nation (which totaled $263 billion at the end of 2017) is equal to the combined savings, assets, retirement holdings, and all other forms of wealth of 50 percent of the American population.[43]

What Principles Should Guide Christians in Thinking about the Economy?

Should it bother a Christian that three men in the United States own as much as 160 million other Americans combined? Or should it bother a Christian that wages have been stagnant for most people, or that millions of poor people lack health insurance? Should it disturb a Christian that the prices of housing, health care, and college are increasing faster than the rate of inflation?

The answers to these questions are not easy, because no Bible verses directly suggest a limit on the amount of money that one person should be allowed to earn, nor does Scripture state what housing or other necessities should cost. Nevertheless, biblical principles can guide us in thinking about these issues.

For Christians, wealth is neither good nor evil in itself but is rather a tool for accomplishing the work of the kingdom of God. A primary purpose of earning money is to share with those who are in need (Eph. 4:28; 1 Tim.

6:17-19). In the church, Christians should do everything they can to ensure that no one is in need. At the same time, all able-bodied people, including the poor, are expected to work for a living and to take care of their families themselves rather than live off the generosity of others (2 Thess. 3:6-13; 1 Tim. 5:4-8). So, a billionaire's fortune is neither good nor evil in itself, and there is no categorical reason why it would be wrong for three individuals in the nation to earn as much as 160 million other Americans combined. Those wealthy individuals would be personally sinning if they did not use their money to help others in need for the glory of God, but simply acquiring the wealth, if it is done honestly and fairly, is not categorically wrong. Nevertheless, there is a principle that "from everyone who has been given much, much will be demanded" (Luke 12:48). Suggesting that the rich have a greater responsibility to care for others than the poor do is a basic application of biblical teaching that has been accepted for centuries in the West, and that formed the basis for the system of progressive taxation in the early twentieth century.

But this principle also applies to those who are considerably less wealthy. If you are a typical American, you probably do not feel rich, and you might even feel cash-strapped, but if you noticed, while reading through the description of the various income quintiles, that your family has an above-average income, you have a particular obligation to be generous. After all, if Paul commended the Macedonian Christians for giving to others despite their own "extreme poverty" (2 Cor. 8:2), can we as upper-middle-class Americans justify doing any less? It is in this area that we as Christians can set ourselves apart from the typical partisan discussions of tax policy. While Republicans seek tax cuts that disproportionately benefit the wealthy, and Democrats seek to place the vast majority of the tax burden on the rich, a Christian can live counterculturally by setting an example of personal sacrifice and seeking to give away money to benefit those who are poorer. And if we practice this self-sacrifice and generosity in our personal lives, we will likely find that these attitudes lead us to seek similar policy initiatives at the voting booth. Instead of demanding a reduction in taxes for ourselves, we will seek ways to make sure that poorer people are not burdened even further.

The Bible contains numerous commands to give the poor "justice." What exactly justice for the poor entails in the twenty-first century may be a matter of debate, but it seems that, at the very least, policies that deprive the poor of life-saving health care, leave children "food insecure" even when their mothers are working, or force people to borrow tens of thousands of dollars simply for a ticket to enter the workforce may not meet the standard of justice. Using the principles of the Mosaic law code as a guide, we can say that it seems that God wants everyone to be able to provide food for their families and to do so without accruing long-term debt. Economic policies that move our society closer to this goal deserve our support, while those that move us further away from it should be rejected. Or, to put it another way, policies are not wrong simply because they might benefit the rich, but if a policy hurts the poor by making it more difficult for them to provide for their families or increasing the likelihood that they will fall into long-term debt, it is wrong. By this definition, many of the economic policies that white evangelical Christians have supported in recent decades are morally wrong.

Tax Cuts and Government Deficits

Both the Democrats and the Republicans commonly promise tax cuts for the middle class. The sticking point, though, is the richest 5 percent or 1 percent; Republican presidential administrations consistently cut taxes for this group, while Democrats raise them. Which is the more moral strategy?

Drawing on the assumptions of supply-side economics, Republicans argue that cutting taxes on the wealthy will free up more money for investment, which will in turn generate economic growth. Democrats, by contrast, draw on the assumptions of Keynesian economics, which says that while tax cuts for the wealthy might result in modest economic growth, at least in the short term, substantial long-term economic growth is driven by demand, not investment—which means that the real key to economic growth is putting more money in the pockets of lower-income consumers, who will use it to buy goods and services and generate economic growth. The debates between Keynesian and supply-side economists are complex and cannot be fully resolved here. Nevertheless, after three rounds of supply-side Republican tax cuts (one under Ronald Reagan in the 1980s, another under George W. Bush at the beginning of the twenty-first century, and a third under Donald Trump in 2017), some facts are clear: Tax cuts for the wealthy do generate some economic growth, but not enough to offset the massive increases in deficit spending that also result. And they exacerbate income inequality that is already high.

Reagan's tax cuts, combined with an increased rate of military spending, caused the budget deficit to balloon from less than $100 billion a year to more than $200 billion. Similarly, when George W. Bush took office, he inherited a budget surplus from Bill Clinton, but the combination of a tax cut, a mild economic downturn, and the increased spending needed after the 9/11 terrorist attacks caused the budget deficit to balloon once more, from $158 billion during his first year in office to $413 billion only two years later. When President Donald Trump cut taxes during his first year in office, the results were similar: the budget deficit of $665 billion, which he inherited from Obama, increased to nearly $1 trillion in 2019, even during a time of high economic growth.[44]

The problem with economic deficits that result simply from tax cuts for the rich is that they pass on debt to a future generation, forcing them to pay the cost for our economic joyride. Right now, the country has a debt of $22 trillion. In 2019 alone, the government spent $394 billion solely on interest on the debt. This yearly amount will continue to rise as the debt continues to snowball and interest rates increase. To put things in perspective, $394 billion is more than 12 million times the median per capita income in the United States for 2017 (which was $31,786). This means that in 2019, the federal government made an interest payment that amounted to the total annual income of more than 12 million "average" American workers. And its annual deficit that year—the amount by which spending exceeded revenue—equaled the total annual income of about thirty-one million "average" people.[45]

There are times of crisis when high deficit spending might be justified. During the worst financial crisis since the Great Depression, Barack Obama's deficits exceeded $1 trillion at times—though they decreased markedly during his second term in office, when the economy improved. The United States also ran up record-level deficits during the Second World War, when the government frantically borrowed whatever it could to win the war. But in the early 1940s, the government also raised taxes to an eye-popping 94 percent for the top marginal income bracket, and tax revenues dramatically increased. The economy grew, too, since all of the government's spending was plowed back into military contracts that benefited American workers.

When the war ended, deficit spending dropped as well, and balanced budgets returned in the 1950s. By 2019, though, we were running deficits that, when calculated as a percentage of the GDP, were just as high as they were during the Second World War and higher than they had ever been since. And no longer was the debt held almost entirely by American citizens, as it was during World War II. Instead, the US government depended on a bevy of foreign creditors (mainly China and Japan, but also wealthy investors from other countries), along with raids on the Social Security trust fund, to keep itself financially solvent.[46] Deficit spending is not a problem per se if it addresses national crises or leads to long-term economic growth that offsets initial deficit spending. But this did not happen with most of the Republican tax cuts, especially those created in 2017. They were implemented when the economy was already relatively healthy, they did not produce long-term growth that was sufficient to offset the decline in tax revenue, and they did not produce an infrastructure that would benefit the United States in the long term. They also exacerbated the divide between the rich and poor.

Because so much of the nation's wealth is concentrated at the top, tax cuts that do not directly exclude the wealthiest people will always primarily benefit the rich, because the poor do not earn enough to pay much in income tax. Currently, the bottom 50 percent of income earners pay only 3 percent of the taxes in the United States. Those earning between the 75th and 90th percentile pay 17 percent of the taxes, those between the 90th and 95th percentile pay 11 percent, those between the 95th and 99th pay 21 percent, and those in the 99th pay 37 percent. With more than 50 percent of taxes being paid by the upper 10 percent of income earners (that is, those who earn more than $178,000 a year), any across-the-board tax cut will primarily benefit the wealthy. Defenders of tax cuts for the rich say that the wealthy deserve a tax cut, because their tax burdens exceed their share of the income. But this is not entirely true. The rich pay most of the income taxes because they earn and control most of the money. The upper 10 percent of Americans earn 47 percent of the income and own almost 90 percent of the wealth. The top 1 percent earn 20 percent of the income and own 40 percent of the wealth. If the richest 1 percent pay 37 percent of the nation's income taxes, as they currently do, are they really shouldering an unfair burden? Right now, the top marginal tax rate of 37 percent, which affects people earning more than $500,000 a year, is lower than the *average* income tax rate that people pay in several European countries.[47] Furthermore, since the super rich earn much of their money through investments, not salaries, and since capital gains are subject to a tax rate of only 24 percent, their effective tax rate is much lower.

While any across-the-board tax cut will benefit the wealthy more than the poor, Trump's tax plan did not even pretend to be an across-the-board cut; it cut rates on the rich more than those on the poor. The top 5 percent of income earners received a 2.2 percent increase in after-tax income, while those with incomes ranging from the 20th to the 80th percentile received an increased income of only 0.4 percent. The only group whose personal income tax rate was left unchanged (at 10 percent) were the very poorest Americans: those earning less than $10,000 a year.[48] Furthermore, as with all previous tax cuts, the Trump tax cuts left FICA tax rates unchanged, and since the FICA tax is a flat tax that has no minimum income exemption and that disproportionately affects the poor, the working poor were left with just as much of a tax burden as ever.

Though the jolt to the economy that resulted from these tax cuts might have contributed to the record-high hiring spree and the lowest unemployment rate in decades, these gains were not evenly distributed, nor were they likely to address the real economic problems of the working poor and middle class. Instead, they resulted in higher deficits that future generations will continue to pay for, or that will become an excuse for cutting government social programs that the poorest Americans depend on.

Modest tax increases on the rich do not automatically result in economic slowdowns; they instead produce balanced budgets. At the beginning of his presidency, Bill Clinton raised the income tax rate for the top 1.2 percent of income-earners from 31 percent to 39.6 percent, and, when coupled with modest spending cuts and tax cuts in other areas, this tax increase on the rich did nothing to stop several years of sustained economic growth, and the increased revenue led to three years of balanced federal budgets. Barack Obama raised the top rate to 43 percent, and once again, the deficit was reduced, while a gradual economic recovery continued.[49] While there is no question that if taxes on the rich are decreased sufficiently, the economy will improve, there is also no evidence to suggest that such tax cuts are the only (or indeed, even the best) way to produce economic growth. When faced with the evidence that tax cuts on the rich cause budget deficits that are a tax on the future, and that they exacerbate income inequality while depriving the government of revenue that it could use for needed programs that would address the problems of the poor and the working class, it seems impossible to justify these tax cuts—especially when taxes on the rich are already low by international standards and when the richest 1 percent are currently paying only 37 percent of the income taxes in the United States even though they own 40 percent of the wealth.[50]

One note of caution, though: While I think a Christian would do well to support higher taxes on the wealthy, we need to be careful about our motivation for doing so. If our motivation is anger at the rich and a desire to confiscate their fortunes—as I fear that it might be, among some on the left—it is probably wrong. This was the motivation of some people on the left at the beginning of the twentieth century and again during the Great Depression of the 1930s, and at a time when the early twentieth-century level of wealth inequality has returned, the same attitudes have resurfaced. These attitudes are understandable but not necessarily godly. A more Christian approach would be to say that because the rich have benefited disproportionately from the American economic and legal system, they have an increased obligation to contribute to society from their surplus. This was the view that most Americans took during the mid-twentieth century, from the 1940s to the 1970s, when politicians from both parties supported top marginal tax rates of 70 percent or more. We have lost the sense of collective sacrifice that influenced this era, and as a result, the debate over taxes too often pits a selfish desire on the right to protect private assets and show little concern for the poor versus a selfish desire on the left to redistribute wealth and punish the rich. If we had a better understanding of social obligations, the discussion of tax rates would be less acrimonious.

But a change in tax structure alone will not solve the problems of the nation's poor or address the debt burden that even members of the upper-middle class are facing. Instead, we will need to see sweeping structural reforms in the areas of college costs, housing costs, and health-care costs. Neither political party is currently fully addressing the structural reforms that will be needed in these areas to bring the nation into line with biblical values regarding debt and concern for the poor.

College Costs

The $1.6 trillion that Americans owe in college loans is a crisis. A system that requires people to borrow tens of thousands of dollars merely for the right to enter the workforce and take a job that will pay enough for them to take care of their families is contrary to the biblical mandate to keep the poor from falling into long-term debt. The opportunity to earn a living should not depend on a person's willingness to mortgage their future by borrowing money that will take one or two decades to repay.

But educational debt is only one part of this crisis. The real crisis—which hardly any politicians are discussing—is that college is no longer a ticket to socioeconomic mobility, even though this is the main reason why students go to college. (Eighty-eight percent of college freshmen in 2012 said that they were going to college "to be able to get a better job," according to a national survey.)[51] With only a few exceptions, most people going to college will end up in exactly the same income bracket as their parents—but they will often accrue a debt of tens of thousands of dollars in order to do this. College has become a highly expensive sorting mechanism that, for the most part, restricts rather than expands socioeconomic mobility—while charging students and their families for a process that will, in most cases, leave them in exactly the same socioeconomic position as they were before. This does not mean that a student should not attend college; in fact, the economic prospects for someone without a college degree are dismal, with the median earnings of a high school graduate with no college credit totaling only 60 percent of the median earnings of someone with a four-year college degree.[52] But if a college education is now a necessity to keep from falling into poverty, it is no longer a ticket to a higher socioeconomic position. Most middle-class students go to colleges designed for the middle class and spend large amounts of money to enter careers that will pay them about the same amount of money as their parents earned. Most upper-income students go to elite colleges and pay large amounts of money for credentials that allow them to remain in the upper-income bracket. And the poor who do not go to college are left even further behind.

This is not necessarily the fault of the colleges. Nor is it the fault of any single entity or person. Instead, as access to college expanded—first because of the free college tuition benefits resulting from the GI Bill at the end of

World War II and then later because the economic growth of the 1950s and 1960s enabled more World War II generation parents to send their baby boomer children to college—white-collar employers who had not previously required a college degree began expecting that their applicants would have one, so a college degree became both a sorting mechanism and a sine qua non for a larger number of jobs. In the early twentieth century, when the percentage of Americans with a college degree was in the low single digits and when only a minority of adults had even a high school diploma, college was not a prerequisite for most white-collar jobs—let alone blue-collar ones. Even high school teachers were not required to have a college degree at the end of the nineteenth century. Because a college degree was still considered a rare commodity in the mid-twentieth century, the first generation of people to attend college in large numbers—the World War II veterans who went to college for free on the GI Bill—experienced enormous socioeconomic benefits, because with a college degree (especially a degree in engineering or business), they could immediately enter the white-collar upper-middle class. Convinced of the benefits of college, they then strongly encouraged their children to get a college education, which resulted in a massive increase in student enrollment and a rapid expansion of state universities and colleges in the 1960s, when the baby boomers entered. By 1970, nearly 60 percent of all eighteen-to-twenty-one-year-olds in the United States were going to college.[53] Colleges could hardly hire professors quickly enough to fill the demand. But the economic gains that baby boomers expected from college did not immediately materialize. The over-supply of bachelor's degrees in the 1970s and the economic downturn of the era combined to cause the real wages of males with a four-year college degree to decrease. In the economic expansion of the 1980s, college graduates once again did well, and by 1991, their real earnings had once again reached the level of college graduates in the late 1950s, when adjusted for inflation.[54] By that point, a college degree had become essential for all members of the middle class, since the traditional paths to good jobs without college that had once existed—such as military service, labor union trade certification, and apprenticeships—were no longer worth much when not accompanied by at least a technical-college degree. So, middle-class baby boomers sent their children to college, and now the grandchildren of the baby boomers are beginning, in some cases, to take their place on college campuses.

But these college students now face a financial reality very different from the one the baby boomers faced. Because college was far less expensive a half century ago, most baby boomers paid for it without taking out long-term loans. In 1965, the national average for annual tuition at public four-year colleges was only $257 ($2,089 in 2019 dollars); today it is $10,230, or nearly five times the 1965 rate when adjusted for inflation.[55] In 1965, a baby boomer college student could have paid a full year's in-state tuition at a public university by working for 205 hours (just over five weeks of full-time work) at a minimum-wage summer job. Today, the cost of a full year's tuition at an average-priced public college would require 1,411 hours of minimum-wage work (which is thirty-five weeks of full-time work), and this does not even include the money required for books and living expenses, all of which would make it impossible for a typical student at even the lowest-priced colleges in the country to pay the full cost of college while working their way through school, as working-class students who could not rely on parents' contributions frequently did during the 1960s and 1970s.[56]

For the past half century, more than half of all high school graduates have gone to college, so at this point, a college degree is no longer exceptional but is instead expected even for many entry-level, low-paying jobs. This hurts families at all income levels.

The poorest quintile is hurt because jobs for people with only a high school diploma or less have almost entirely disappeared—or, at least, those that pay enough for a person to live on have disappeared. With even low-level management jobs at local grocery or retail stores now usually requiring a college education, those who lack this are trapped in a cycle of very low-wage, entry-level jobs, with no real opportunity for advancement. One of the reasons that marriage rates are so low for this group is that few in this quintile feel that they can earn enough to support a family. With fewer than 15 percent of the college-aged population in this quintile attending a four-year college—and fewer than 40 percent attending any type of post-high school educational institution at all, whether two-year or four-year—an economy that has largely made college a required ticket to enter the workforce hurts this group enormously, and this is one reason among several why members of this quintile are frequently jobless.[57]

The shift toward making college a required ticket of entry to the workforce has also hurt the struggling middle class. A majority of children from this income group go to college, but the degrees they earn are not a ticket to a better life but are instead simply the price of entry for the type of jobs that their parents might have been able to get with less cost and possibly lower credentials. The university where I teach, the University of West Georgia (UWG), is an example of this, because our students come mainly from the struggling middle class. The median household income for a family sending their child to UWG is $68,100—which puts them at the 58th percentile for all household incomes. At age thirty-four, a few years after graduation, the median *individual* income for a UWG alum is only $37,500—which puts one in the 58th percentile for *individual* incomes. If the graduate is married—as 57 percent of our thirty-four-year-old graduates were in 2014—it is reasonably likely that the income from a spouse would put their household income somewhere around the $68,000 needed to stay in the 58th percentile for family income. And though this data extends only to age thirty-four, other data compilations show that nationwide, the income percentile that a person is in at age thirty-six is likely to be the same income percentile at age sixty. So, after acquiring $21,000 in debt on average, our students end up at the end of their four, five, or six years in college in exactly the same income bracket their parents are in. Fewer than 2 percent will move from the bottom quintile to the top quintile, and only 16 percent will move up two or more income quintiles. For every student who moves up in socioeconomic status, another student will experience downward mobility. Eleven percent of our incoming students come from families in the bottom quintile, and 11 percent of our graduates will remain in the bottom quintile at the age of thirty-four—which means that the economic mobility of our students, on average, is approximately zero.[58] Most of our graduates would almost certainly have been far worse off economically if they had never gone to college, so the decision to attend college was a wise one. But it is also an expensive choice that offers fewer opportunities for economic advancement than they might have hoped. Many students are charged tens of thousands of dollars for the privilege of entering the workforce and remaining in the same socioeconomic bracket in which they grew up.

This is not necessarily UWG's fault, and it is certainly not a story unique to our university. UWG, which is considered a moderately "selective" (though not a "highly selective") regional public university, is typical of hundreds of other similar public four-year regional institutions. A nearly identical story could be told at any such school in the country, whether it is Emporia State University, Idaho State University, or Indiana State University (all of which have similar income demographics and social mobility indexes). These schools might offer many benefits to students, and there might be numerous compelling reasons to attend, but one thing they are not doing is moving people out of the working class and lower-middle class into the upper-income echelons in any sizeable numbers.[59]

College has become a required ticket to jobs that a generation or two ago often went to people with only a high school diploma. Now many members of the middle class are having to mortgage their future simply for the right to remain in the same socioeconomic bracket that their less-educated parents were in. And because the prices of housing, health care, and college are far higher than the costs that their parents faced a generation ago, these struggling middle-class graduates will almost certainly have more debt and less disposable income than their parents had at their age. This may be one reason why the marriage rate of our alumni who are in their mid-thirties is less than 60 percent. Trapped in a mounting cycle of debt and unable to get ahead in life with a job that pays less than $40,000 a year, they may not feel ready to take on the responsibilities of a family.

The struggling middle class has been especially hurt by the cuts in state funding to public colleges. After the financial crisis of 2008, states across the nation slashed their funding to their state-university systems, because they could not afford to subsidize them, and as a result, public universities had to substantially raise tuition at the very moment when the struggling middle class could least afford it. In Georgia, where the state slashed funding for public colleges and universities by about 40 percent during a four-year period, tuition and fees increased by 65 percent at state universities between 2006 and 2016, and by 59 percent at technical colleges.[60] Students from the struggling middle class met that cost by taking out even more loans, which meant that they entered the workforce even more in debt than they otherwise would have been.

Some states, including Georgia, have tried to offset these costs by offering lottery-funded merit-based scholarships, but these scholarships disproportionately benefit students from higher income brackets. Economically struggling students, who often enter college with lower high school GPAs than their upper-middle-class peers, are less likely to receive a merit-based scholarship, and even if they do receive it in their freshman year, they are highly likely to lose it sometime during their college career, since the sacrifices that they make to work their way through college often cause their college GPAs to fall below the level required to keep these scholarships. In 2016, 79 percent of students (and 98 percent of in-state freshmen) at Georgia's highly selective flagship school, the University of Georgia, received the state's lottery-funded, merit-based HOPE Scholarship or the even more prestigious Zell Miller Scholarship, but only 16 percent of students at the much poorer, less selective Albany State University received either form of state merit-based aid. The median household income for UGA students was $130,000, compared to only $31,000 for Albany State students. Georgia's HOPE Scholarship, while widely touted as a ticket to an affordable college education, is largely a transfer of wealth from the state's poorest 40 percent to the richest 20 percent, while bypassing much of the struggling middle class. Poor people are the ones buying most lottery tickets. Nationally, people who earn less than $30,000 a year spend four times as much on the lottery as people earning more than $75,000. And upper-middle-class homes are the ones receiving the greatest benefits from the lottery-funded scholarships. In South Carolina, majority-black Orangeburg County, which has a poverty rate of 23 percent and a median household income of $35,000, received on average about forty-one cents in lottery-funded scholarships and other educational funds for every $1 that residents spent on the lottery from 2008 to 2018. By contrast, majority-white Pickens County, which has an 18 percent poverty rate and a median household income of $45,000, received $3.26 in scholarship and educational funds for every $1 residents spent on the lottery.[61] Merit-based scholarships (unlike need-based scholarships) benefit wealthier people far more than the poor, and lottery-funded scholarships especially hurt the poor. A far more equitable system of funding would have been a progressive income or property tax to subsidize state universities and lower tuition costs.

What can a Christian voter do about this? The real solutions for all of this may be beyond the capability of any political party. In the long term, we need to find ways to end the process of degree inflation by making sure that students get a better value for their money for every degree that they earn and a clearer path to the workforce for those who want it—which might mean making career-building measures such as internships a central part of the college curriculum in the many institutions that students view primarily as a path to a white-collar job. If colleges can connect students to employers at an earlier point in the educational process, fewer students might feel the need to add even more degrees to their resume in a seemingly endless quest to beat the degree inflation that too often hinders them from getting a satisfying job with merely a four-year college degree.

But we also need to keep students from falling deeper into debt. The current model of college education, in which the price of tuition continues to rise faster than inflation, is unsustainable. We cannot continue to impose this burden on the struggling middle class. In the short term, we need to give students financial aid that does not simply amount to a pile of interest-bearing loans. In the long term, we need to pursue structural reforms that will keep college costs down. One reason that college costs continue to increase exponentially is that education is a labor-intensive industry that so far has defied most cost-saving measures. Professors, who are often compensated with costly health plans and reasonably competitive salaries, are expensive, and administrators are even more so. But community colleges, which require instructors to carry heavier teaching loads because they do not expect their faculty to combine teaching with research, have significantly lower costs—and therefore lower tuition. One possible plan, which some Democratic presidential candidates have floated in the recent past, would be to provide free community college throughout the United States, as the state of Tennessee already does. Others have suggested going beyond this and making four-year public colleges free for everyone in the nation, just as public schools at the K–12 level are.[62]

Although these proposals might appear promising, there are valid arguments against them, and Christians should avoid the temptation to link any particular stance on the issue of college with the cause of the gospel. Critics may be correct in noting that one danger with any proposal to expand access to higher education and reduce its costs is that it will likely lead to degree inflation, because employers will have to adopt a more selective sorting mechanism to differentiate between potential job applicants. In the late nineteenth century, when the percentage of Americans with high school diplomas was lower than the percentage with four-year college degrees today, a high school diploma opened doors that today are available only to people with master's degrees. As the number of people with high school diplomas expanded, the value of that degree decreased. The same is likely to happen with college degrees—as indeed, it already has. In my own opinion—speaking not as a Christian or even as a policy expert on the matter, but as an educator who has given the matter some consideration—the benefits of making at least vocationally oriented community colleges free for all students will probably outweigh the risks, since it would substantially reduce the debt burdens for the population in greatest need of debt relief. Of course, this is a matter of individual judgment, and Christians may differ in their views of the wisdom of "free college." But while Christians are certainly not under a biblical mandate to support this particular policy, they need to be prepared to offer reasonable alternatives if they reject this. The massive educational debt burden that millennials are experiencing—and that Generation Z will soon experience—is a moral issue, and we have a Christian duty to address it, even if we may not agree on exactly how to do so.

Health Care

If medical bills are the leading cause of bankruptcy in the United States, and if millions of Americans remain uninsured or underinsured, is it right for American Christians to oppose policies that would expand access to affordable health care for the poor—especially when health care can be a matter of life and death?

Because only 58 percent of working-age Americans get health insurance through their jobs, millions of people who are disproportionately likely to be in the lower income brackets are dependent on government-subsidized health insurance. President Barack Obama made insuring these people one of his highest priorities. Under the Affordable Care Act (dubbed "Obamacare"), states were given federal subsidies to give the working poor with annual incomes up to 138 percent of the poverty level free medical insurance under Medicaid. The lower-middle class who earned slightly more than this (up to 400 percent of the poverty line for their family) could receive federal subsidies for insurance; the cutoff for subsidies was $47,000 for an individual salary in 2015. And those who earned more than this, but who were not given health insurance through their employer, could buy insurance on government health exchanges. The results were dramatic: the number of uninsured Americans dropped from forty-five million (17 percent of all nonelderly Americans) to fewer than twenty-seven million in 2016 (10 percent of the nonelderly population).[63] A national health insurance plan had been a central goal of the Democratic Party since the 1940s, and although Obamacare did not fully achieve its aim of insuring every person in the United States, it came closer than any previous attempt.

However, Republicans complained immediately about the cost and alleged governmental overreach of Obamacare. During Obama's presidency, the Republican-controlled House of Representatives made dozens of unsuccessful attempts to repeal, modify, or block funding for the program, and then, under President Donald Trump, Republicans made a concerted effort to replace Obamacare with a new health-care plan of their own. The bill they attempted to pass would have achieved most of its cost savings by radically shrinking Medicaid funding—that is, health insurance for the poor.[64]

Actually, despite conservative beliefs to the contrary, Obamacare succeeded in greatly reducing the rate of growth in health-care spending. From the 1960s to the present, spending on health care has always greatly outpaced the rate of inflation. From 1960 to 2007, the nation's annual rate of increased spending on health care never fell below 5.2 percent, and it was sometimes as high as 16 percent. From 2010 to 2017, the annual rate of increase never exceeded 5.8 percent, and it was sometimes as low as 2.9 percent; the average rate of increase during this time was only 4.2 percent—a rate never seen even once from John F. Kennedy's presidency to the end of George W. Bush's.[65]

But while Obamacare has resulted in cost savings for the nation as a whole, most middle-class workers have had to spend more, because health insurance companies have transferred cost burdens to workers by charging them higher premiums and even higher deductibles. Between 2008 and 2018, the average deductible for employer-provided health insurance increased by 212 percent—eight times faster than wages and twelve times the inflation rate. Most middle-class workers now fork over thousands of dollars per year for insurance and medical bills, despite having employer-provided health insurance. Insurance premiums are increasing faster than the rate of inflation as well. The average annual premium for an employer-provided family health insurance plan in 2018 was $19,616 (55 percent higher than in 2008), though workers paid only $5,547 of this, with employers picking up the rest of the tab.[66] All of this has made professional workers more expensive for companies to subsidize, which means that the cost for labor-intensive professional services, including college education (where tenured professors and administrators are routinely given some of the best health insurance plans on the market), have continued to increase faster than wages or inflation.

Revolting at this transfer of costs to the professional middle class, many middle-class and upper-middle-class workers voted for Republicans who promised to repeal Obamacare. Had the Republicans succeeded in their plan—which they nearly did, failing by only a single Senate vote—they would have wiped out the health insurance coverage of millions of poor people who benefited from Obamacare's expansion in Medicaid. But what they could not do at the federal level has been done at the state level in some conservative regions. Currently, fourteen states—all solidly Republican, and mostly in the South, but with a few scattered in the upper Midwest and Mountain West—have refused a federally funded subsidy that would allow people whose annual income is up to 130 percent of the poverty line to get free health care under Medicaid.[67] Several of these states have recently passed highly restrictive abortion laws, but if they are serious about reducing abortion rates, they could probably do so by giving lower-income women the affordable health care they need to carry their babies to term and provide for their well-being after birth.

What should a Christian think about all of this? Should a Christian support proposals to solve the increased burden of health-care costs for middle-class and upper-middle-class workers by taking away health coverage from the working poor who lack coverage through their jobs? Or should a Christian support plans such as Obamacare, which expanded lower-income Americans' access to affordable health care, even as health care became more expensive for people with employer-provided health insurance?

Given what the Bible teaches about the importance of caring for the poor, it seems clear that if higher health-care premiums and deductibles for middle-class professionals are the only way that we can offset the cost of providing health-care coverage to millions of the working poor for the first time and potentially save some of them from an early death or at least a cycle of medical debt from which they can never escape, the cost is worth it. Trying to save money for ourselves by playing with the lives of the poor is the very opposite of what the Bible teaches about economic justice.

But at the same time, the rising health-care costs that middle-class professionals face is a genuine crisis that should not be ignored. What can be done about this? While the economics of health care have been debated for decades, and while opinions differ widely, I think there is good evidence to suggest that expanding the federal government's control over the health-care process will likely give the government the power to rein in medical costs and experience the benefits of economies of scale in a way that has not yet occurred in the United States. Canada, which has had universal health insurance for decades, spends 11 percent of its GDP on health care, with a per capita cost of $4,826 in US dollars for every Canadian citizen. The United Kingdom spends $4,246 per person. Sweden spends $5,511. The United States spends $10,209 per person (18 percent of its GDP)—more than any other country in the world.[68] Defenders of the American system argue that these high costs are necessary to pay for drug research, or that they result from the high cost of litigation, or that they are required to give hospitals and doctors an incentive to stay in the business, or that they prevent chronically ill and elderly people from being denied health care altogether in a cost-conscious government-run system. The evidence for any of these claims is mixed at best. Instead, what seems to be the case is that when a single entity that is accountable to the people oversees the entire health-care system, it will finally acquire the financial and political muscle to contain costs—as has happened in nearly every other industrialized country around the world. If I am correct in this, a national health-care plan—a concept that the nation's Catholic bishops have supported, at least in the abstract, for decades—will help not only the working poor but also middle-class professionals, and the savings that result will in turn free companies to hire more professional workers. The reduction in health insurance costs might even reduce the cost of labor-intensive professional services, such as college—thereby solving multiple economic problems.

But even if I am wrong about this—and, of course, health-care economics can be debated at length—certain moral principles seem clear. It is wrong to take health care away from the poor in order to save money for those who are richer. It is wrong to treat life-saving care as a commodity given only to those who have the ability to pay—while leaving those without that ability the choice between risking death or plunging themselves into a debt from which they might never escape. Twenty-five percent of Americans, according to a 2019 Gallup poll, said that they or a family member had "put off" medical treatment for a "serious" condition during the past twelve months because of cost. Each year, another 530,000 Americans declare bankruptcy at least partly because they could not pay their medical bills. One in six Americans are behind on payments on their medical debt—a debt that currently totals $81 billion.[69] Christians might disagree with each other on the precise solutions to these issues, but we need to at least agree that solving these problems is a moral imperative.

In many ways, funding others' health care with our hard-earned tax dollars may seem like an unfair imposition, but as Christians, we have the worldview to see it in a different light. The most expensive people to care for are those who are chronically ill and those who are in the final months of life. The healthiest 50 percent of the population incurs only 3 percent of the health-care costs.[70] So why are the healthiest 50 percent asked to pay for the medical care for those who are constantly sick—especially when those who most need medical treatment are often the least likely to have the financial resources to provide it for themselves and must therefore take the hard-earned money of healthier people? What gives them this right? The answer, I think, becomes apparent when we realize the social responsibility that we have to protect the lives of other human beings who are made in the image of God. The Catholic Church, which has long championed this principle, has advocated for national health insurance programs for more than seventy years. When we realize that whatever health and monetary resources we enjoy are gifts from God, we will have less compunction about spending our money to save the lives and health of people whom we might never meet—but who need our resources in order to survive.

How Is Money Earned in the United States?

For most Americans, real wages have been stagnant for nearly a half century; in 1964, the average wage in the United States, in 2018 inflation-adjusted dollars, was $20.27, and in 2018, it was $22.65 (which would amount to about $45,000 a year for people who work forty hours a week). And with payroll (FICA) taxes now 6.2 percent instead of 3.6 percent (as they were in 1964), the very slight increase in pretax wage rates during the past fifty years might barely be noticed in workers' paychecks.[71] Meanwhile, the costs of housing, health care, and education have increased exponentially. Why have wages not experienced a corresponding increase?

Economists are divided in their answers to this question, because no one really knows for sure what accounts for the historically anomalous long-term stagnation in wages. Some attribute the long-term stagnation to the decline in the power of labor unions, which succeeded in the 1940s and 1950s in securing wage increases for their members. Others have suggested that automation or the export of manufacturing jobs to other countries has resulted in a long-term wage stagnation. These explanations are probably at least partly correct, but they may overlook a more central factor: the shift from manufacturing to services in our society. Today fewer than 9 percent of nonfarm payroll employees in the United States are engaged in manufacturing, while 71 percent are in the service sector. In 1960, by contrast, about a third of the workforce was employed in manufacturing. This shift over the past half century has had a significant effect on depressing wages, because in a free-market economy, people's salaries will tend to increase only to the extent that their productivity increases, which is difficult to achieve in the service sector. In a manufacturing job that relies on technology to increase worker productivity, the amount of goods that each worker produces might increase over time. But in a service-based economy, there will probably be very little productivity gains for most workers—especially those who are employed in low-wage jobs in retail and food service, industries that together account for a much larger contingent of the workforce than are employed in manufacturing. Sixty or seventy years ago, engineering innovations might have made an automobile worker on an assembly line more productive, and with the help of union negotiations, that worker would therefore have received a comfortable wage increase each year. But today, engineering innovations in manufacturing are probably more likely to replace workers with automation than to make them more productive. The average auto plant now features one thousand robots, with far fewer human workers than before. The number of auto manufacturing jobs in the United States declined by more than 300,000 between 2000 and 2016.[72] Seventy years ago, a high school or even middle school graduate could have taken a manufacturing job that would have given them consistent wage increases over time, but today, even many college-educated workers are more likely to end up in relatively low-paying service jobs that offer no substantial real wage increases over the course of a worker's career. Those who are enterprising go into health care, a field that now employs 12 percent of all workers in the United States. Of the top ten jobs for community college graduates (according to *US News and World Report*), eight are in health care. While these jobs pay comparatively well, their salaries are also very flat over time, as most service jobs are. A radiation technologist, for instance, might start out with an average salary of $29 an hour, but after five to nine years of experience, will receive a pay increase of only $4.[73] And most service-sector jobs for community college graduates will not pay as high a starting salary as careers in radiation technology. Community college and university graduates who end up working in retail, customer service, or one of any number of other service jobs will probably experience relatively stagnant wages that might be substantially less than $29 an hour.

This is not true at the top of the income distribution, however. Salaries for executives have increased exponentially during the past forty years, with the average CEO pay increasing 90 times faster than average worker pay between 1978 and 2015. In inflation-adjusted dollars, CEOs of the top 350 companies in the United States earned an average of $1.5 million a year in 1978 and $16.3 million in 2015. Why is this? As we have shifted away from manufacturing, the fortunes that can be made in the United States have come less from figuring out how to make things than from moving people and money around. Of the ten richest people in the United States today, one earned his billions entirely through investing, another earned his fortune by creating Facebook, and two acquired their wealth by cofounding Google. Among other billionaires, a similar pattern emerges: nearly 25 percent of the four hundred richest Americans earned their fortunes in hedge funds, private equity, or other forms of finance, and another 15 percent came from technology-based companies. If we look at multimillionaires rather than billionaires, a similar pattern of overrepresentation of the financial sector or nonmanufacturing sources of wealth is also apparent. About 20 percent of people in the top 0.1 percent earn their money in finance. By 2008, 28 percent of newly minted Harvard graduates were employed in finance, because this was the field they thought would make them even wealthier.[74]

In other words, the people whom we reward the most as a society are people who know how to move money around. To be sure, this is a highly useful service, because it ensures that capital will be available to brilliant people who have ideas for improving people's lives. But the downside is that very little of this wealth will trickle down to the average worker. A typical hedge fund uses money from millionaires to invest in high-risk start-up technology companies that employ almost exclusively educated workers, and if this succeeds, it then makes the investors even wealthier, with spectacular gains going to the hedge fund manager. This grows the American economy but does not necessarily improve wages. Yet because investment is a primary generator of economic growth, we reward it in our tax code. People who earn more than half a million dollars a year in long-term investment will pay a maximum capital gains tax of only 20 percent—whereas, if they had earned this money through salaried work, they would have paid a top marginal tax rate of nearly 38 percent. In fact, a tax rate of only 20 percent on long-term capital gains is lower than the 22 percent income tax rate that an individual earning $40,000 a year pays on wages.[75] And, if President Trump had had his way, he would have cut capital gains taxes even more, as he suggested doing in both 2019 and 2020.

While I do not think that the Old Testament prohibitions on charging interest to fellow members of the covenant community apply in exactly the same fashion to people in a nonagricultural economy, it should perhaps concern Christians that a leading source of personal wealth in our economy—and an exacerbator of the growing wealth divide between the rich and the poor—is the very activity that God repeatedly warned his people against in the Old Testament. This is not to suggest that we do not need investment. Instead, I merely want to note that investment does not do much to improve an average worker's wages—yet investment is primarily what our tax code and our society reward.

A long-term solution to this problem may be beyond the reach of any presidential candidate, because it would require economic structural changes that the government cannot dictate. Attempts to preserve manufacturing jobs through the implementation of tariffs or the abandonment of international trade agreements have not been successful. But there are at least two things that the government could do to redress the growing income imbalance between the rich and the lower-middle class: The government could raise the minimum wage, and it could increase the capital gains tax rate. It was a Democratic president (Bill Clinton) who decreased the top long-term capital gains tax rate from 28 to 20 percent, and no Democratic or Republican president has dared to raise it since, because the decrease in capital gains tax rates in the mid-1990s is widely credited with helping to produce the economic boom of the late 1990s. But perhaps Christians who care about the poor should ask whether it is right to continue to pursue an economic growth strategy in which most workers will continue to fall further behind, as their wages stagnate and their debt increases. If the price of producing an uneven economic growth that will offer very little to lower-wage workers is a tax code that takes less from a millionaire investor than it does from a Walmart floor manager earning $46,000 a year, we need to ask whether we want to pay this price.

The Conservative Defense of Marriage as an Antidote to Poverty

Much of what I have said so far would suggest that Democrats offer better solutions than Republicans to the problem of poverty and declining opportunities for the middle class. In several policy areas, I think that is undoubtedly the case. On tax policy, there is no question that Republican policy proposals will further increase the divide between the rich and the poor. In health care, Republicans have not suggested a solution that will expand health-care access to the poor. (Republicans claim that if they can reduce health-care costs overall, the poor will be able to afford to buy their own health insurance, but this certainly will not happen in the short term, and it is highly doubtful that it will happen in the long term, either.)

But there is one area where conservatives have an edge over liberals: the promotion of marriage as an antipoverty measure. In 2017, 41 percent of children living with a single mother were poor, compared to only 8 percent who lived with two married parents.[76] Any antipoverty strategy should include a strategy to promote marriage. But even if this is a conservative proposal, the best way to promote marriage through the political realm may involve the same measures that liberals favor, such as a universal health-care system, better job security, and a solution to the college debt crisis, because for many people, financial barriers are one of the greatest obstacles to marriage. If it is true that we can fight poverty by promoting marriage, it might be even more true that we can promote marriage by fighting poverty.

Where Does This Leave Us?

I wrote nearly all of this chapter before the outbreak of COVID-19. At that time, the United States was experiencing some of the lowest levels of unemployment in half a century, and yet even then our nation was not economically healthy. Among the middle class, most young adults faced greater economic challenges than their parents, despite acquiring more education. Among the working poor, millions of children experienced food insecurity, and millions of adults faced a health-care crisis that left them only one step away from bankruptcy. If this was the case in a time of perceived economic prosperity, what long-term economic outcome can we expect now that COVID-19 and the ensuing shelter-in-place orders have resulted in the highest levels of unemployment that the United States has experienced since the 1930s? It is probably too early to say, but one thing is nearly certain: Unless government policy changes radically, we can expect that the growing divide between the rich and the poor, along with the systemic economic problems described in this chapter, will continue to grow worse. The income gap between the rich and the poor increased markedly during the prosperity of the 1980s and 1990s, but it became even more pronounced during the 2008 financial crisis, when many lower-income Americans (especially African Americans) lost their homes. One might have expected the collapse of the housing market in 2008 to result in more affordable housing for the poor by reducing the cost of home mortgages, but instead tighter restrictions on lending seemed only to move the possibility of obtaining a mortgage loan further out of reach. One might have expected the financial crisis to slow the growth of college tuition increases, but instead large cuts in state funding to education prompted state colleges and universities to increase tuition and fees at a faster rate. Thus, no matter what happens to the economy in the next few years, the issues outlined in this chapter will still be relevant for the Christian voter—especially if a prolonged economic downturn has the same negative impact on lower-income workers that the 2008 financial crisis did.

In my view, typical conservative economic proposals make our nation's long-term crisis worse by hurting the poor in order to protect the upper-middle class. If Christians vote for Republican candidates who exacerbate the wealth gap, those Christians need to be committed to finding compassionate ways to help the poor in every other area of their lives. Christians always have a responsibility to use their wealth to help others, but if we know that the money that we have received as a tax refund comes primarily from a tax cut that has disproportionately aided the wealthy and will burden a future generation with debt, we have an even greater responsibility not to spend the extra money on ourselves but rather in the service of the kingdom of God. Conservatives can aid the poor by practicing generosity, helping those around them learn wise financial-management principles that will reduce their debt, and supporting private-market solutions that promise to reduce health-care costs for those least able to pay—as many faithful Christians are doing.

But what about a Christian who votes Democratic, in the belief that the Democrats will do a better job than the Republicans in helping the poor? Here a note of caution is in order. It may be true, as I have suggested, that most current Democratic economic proposals are better attuned to the needs of the poor than most Republican proposals. But even if that is the case, a Christian needs to guard against the economic selfishness that appears in a lot of Democratic rhetoric on wealth and taxes. Calling for higher taxes on the ultrarich in order to help the poor requires no self-sacrifice whatsoever for those who are not ultrarich. As Christians who follow the way of the cross, we should be suspicious of the idea that we can do good to others without inconveniencing ourselves. Indeed, it is striking that the people with the highest rates of personal giving are not secular liberal Democrats but are instead conservative Christians who are often Republicans.[77] This should be a convicting statistic for Democrats. If we vote Democratic in order to help the poor, we need to make sure that our actions on behalf of the poor extend far beyond the voting booth. We need to make sure that moral outrage against greed, expressed in voting choices or in progressive political activism, does not become a substitute for genuine charity.

But perhaps even more importantly, we need to resist the temptation to become materialistic in our thinking about poverty. The Democratic Party's proposals to reduce the wealth gap are inherently materialistic, in that they assume that what the poor need is material resources. But while Christians should strive to ensure that the poor have material resources (James 2:16), a Christian will also realize that "life [is] more than food, and the body more than clothes" (Matt. 6:25). We should fight against structural injustices that burden the poor, but not merely to give people economic resources; instead, we do so in order to treat people as image bearers of a heavenly Father who loves them more than any human—let alone government program—ever could.[78] We need to avoid the temptation to think that the full solutions to the problems that the poor face can come through politics.

However, we also need to avoid the temptation of thinking that Christians have no obligation to help the poor through their political choices. Political solutions can never fully alleviate poverty. They cannot substitute for personal action in the private sphere, which is often far more effective than government programs in meeting the real needs of the poor. Political solutions can certainly never substitute for the gospel. But at the same time, Christians have an obligation to avoid voting for political proposals that will make the lives of the poor more difficult and more unfair. We might not be able to eradicate poverty through politics, but we should certainly do everything that we can to avoid enacting policies that will make the problem worse. If Christians become convinced, as I have, that our national policies are burdening the poor with extraordinary debt and, in some cases, depriving them of their very lives because of a lack of access to affordable health care, we have an obligation to act. The two thousand Bible verses on concern for the poor might have something to say to us.

Afterword

The Politics of the Cross and the Preservation of the Nation

Also, seek the peace and prosperity of the city to which I have carried you into exile. Pray to the Lord for it, because if it prospers, you too will prosper.

—Jeremiah 29:7

Do nothing out of selfish ambition or vain conceit. Rather, in humility value others above yourselves, not looking to your own interests but each of you to the interests of others.

—Philippians 2:3-4

Harvard University history professor James Kloppenberg concluded his seven-hundred-page global history of democracies by noting that democracies are more fragile than we might think. Most democratic experiments have failed. A democracy will succeed only if a critical mass of voters consistently engage in what he called "reciprocity"—that is, the willingness to sacrifice their own self-interest for the good of others. That has happened in America, he said, because of the nation's liberal Protestant heritage. When that heritage disappears, democracy might disappear with it.[1]

The willingness to sacrifice our own interests for the sake of others, which Kloppenberg said was the key to sustaining democracies, sounds very much like the message of Philippians 2:3-4: "Do nothing out of selfish ambition or vain conceit. Rather, in humility value others above yourselves, not looking to your own interests but each of you to the interests of others." While this passage might apply primarily to our behavior within the family of God, the attitude of giving up our own desires for the sake of others should characterize our actions in every sphere of life. If there is any group of voters who should take this message with them into the voting booth, it should be gospel-believing evangelical Christians. What if instead of being known as a political interest group, evangelical Christians in the United States were known as the people who cared enough about the nation and the well-being of their neighbors to sacrifice their own interests at the voting booth and cast ballots primarily with the good of others in mind?

But, in fact, white evangelical Christians' political behavior has generally not been characterized by this attitude. Rather than voting out of concern for the democratic order and the interests of all members of the community (especially the economically or racially marginalized who might be among those Jesus called the "least of these"), white evangelicals have generally entered the voting booth concerned first and foremost with a moral cause. In past decades, that cause might have been a crusade against sexual immorality or Communism. Today the cause is most likely to be the religious liberty of Christians or, above all, the defense of unborn lives. These causes are not wrong. But there is a danger when cause-driven politics blinds us to other needs that our neighbors might have. Unborn lives are vitally important. But so are black lives. So are the lives of immigrant children detained on the border. Rather than engage in single-issue voting, we need to ask the questions: How can I sacrifice my own interests to do the most good for the cause of the kingdom of God? And how can I bring the kingdom of God to bear on my neighbor's life by showing God's love to my neighbor through my vote?

When we open our eyes to all the ways that the justice and mercy of the kingdom of God can be applied to the social issues around us, we will probably realize that the amount of evil in our society vastly exceeds what evangelical single-issue voting might be able to address. This has always been the case. In eighteenth-century England or America, for example, an evangelical Christian with contemporary moral priorities might have assumed that the international slave trade—with its kidnapping and its sacrifice of human life—was the era's most egregious social evil. But the eighteenth-century wars against Native Americans—which, in at least one case, involved the deliberate use of smallpox germs to infect a native population—were not much better. And dueling, which was legal in many places and which some thought was hardly wrong at all, was also a legitimate concern. So which of these evils should Christians of the time have been most concerned about? A single-issue voter would have risked ignoring a lot of social evil for the sake of fighting one particularly egregious example of it. And if our hypothetical single-issue voter of the late eighteenth century had a contemporary evangelical political mindset, the voter probably would have expected moral regulation to solve problems that moral regulation alone, in fact, did not. This, of course, was the case with the international slave trade. When the kidnapping and transatlantic transport of African slaves was finally outlawed in the United States in 1808—thanks, in part, to people of conscience who spoke up—it was replaced by a domestic slave trade, with forced breeding of enslaved women and the sale of children on the auction block, that was arguably equally heinous.

Because there is never a moment when there is only one major sin in a society, an excessive focus on one single injustice can blind us to the amount of evil both in our present milieu and in the past. The contemporary legal abortion industry is certainly not the only time that Americans en masse have callously disregarded human life (including the lives of children), as a quick glance back at the slave trade and other evils of the eighteenth or nineteenth centuries might tell us. Nor is it the only example of callous disregard for human life today. As important as the abortion issue is, if we are not careful, we can risk allowing a single-minded focus on this one evil to blind us to the many other contemporary instances of disrespect for human life and disregard for the people whom God has created in his image. And we also risk assuming that a quick and simple moral regulation will solve the problem. If outlawing the international slave trade did nothing to prevent the slave breeding and slave auctions that grew in its wake, we can probably assume that merely outlawing abortion, without a widespread heart change, will probably not be sufficient to solve the underlying problem. It may not even do much to protect human life.

But does this mean that we should passively accept the injustices around us? Not at all. Rather than be surprised at the extent of injustice in our society, a Christian who subscribes to the doctrine of original sin will expect that injustice will be pervasive. But a Christian who understands the power of the cross will also welcome the opportunity to bring the light of Jesus's kingdom to bear on these injustices. We will do so with humility, knowing that we cannot do the Spirit's work of changing hearts. But we will also do so with confidence, knowing that Jesus wants us to do good to all people (Gal. 6:10)—including the people who are affected by our votes. As I have tried to show throughout this book, there are real policy solutions that might address the social evils of our generation (including abortion), but because these policy solutions do not conform to the regulatory paradigm that has long shaped white conservative evangelicals' approach to politics, they may not be part of our current political agenda. The pursuit of these policy solutions may even require us to cross party lines at times and support candidates whose philosophy we disagree with, but whose policies we think will probably result in a reduction of injustice.

In the end, we as Christians may not come to an agreement on exactly which party offers the best opportunity to do good and promote justice at any given moment. We know that even at best, any political party will inadequately represent the priorities of God's kingdom, and at worst, the party may be a form of Christian heresy. But when we transcend partisanship and seek the good of our neighbor, that may not matter, because our real loyalty will not be to a particular political party. We may worship with those who check a different box on the ballot than we do, but if both Democratic and Republican Christians vote with a Christlike determination to put others' interests before their own, both will be practicing Christian politics. True Christian politics is not about passing a litmus test or embracing a particular partisan identity. It is not even about subscribing to a particular political agenda. Instead, true Christian politics comes when we as individual followers of Jesus prayerfully make a determination to submit our voting choices to the lordship of Christ by sacrificing our own agenda for the sake of others and showing love to our neighbor through our policy choices. Regardless of the political choices that we ultimately make, we know that when our choices are shaped by a selfless reflection of Jesus's love for others, we will catch a glimpse of what it really means to bring the cross into politics. If we do this, as Kloppenberg suggested, we might play a role in preserving American democracy—which could be the modern equivalent of "seeking the peace and prosperity of the city" (Jer. 29:7). But more importantly, we will bear witness to the glory of the cross.

Introduction: A Different Kind of Politics

Some of the many thoughtful books examining how Christians should respond to contemporary political issues and our current partisan political divide include Charles D. Drew's *Surprised by Community: Republicans and Democrats in the Same Pew* (self-published, 2019), Amy E. Black's *Honoring God in Red or Blue: Approaching Politics with Humility, Grace, and Reason* (Chicago: Moody, 2012), Lisa Sharon Harper's *Evangelical Does Not Equal Republican . . . or Democrat* (New York: New Press, 2008), and Ronald J. Sider's *Just Politics: A Guide for Christian Engagement* (Grand Rapids: Brazos, 2012). Drew and Black focus on how Christians should respond in a loving manner to other believers with whom they disagree politically, and both also discuss reasons why different groups of Christians might line up on different sides of the political debate. Sider, a progressive evangelical who generally leans toward the political left but who is also pro-life on abortion, offers thoughtful theological insight on the major hot-button issues of the moment from the perspective of social-justice-oriented evangelicalism. Philip Yancey's *Christians and Politics: Uneasy Partners* (Creative Trust Digital, 2012) is an excellent, succinct analysis of the temptation that political power poses to contemporary Christians. Mark A. Noll's *Adding Cross to Crown: The Political Significance of Christ's Passion* (Grand Rapids: Baker, 1996) calls for Christians to adopt a cross-shaped humility in their approach to politics.

Readers who are seeking a guide to the way that various Christian theological traditions might differ in their approach to politics might want to consult *Five Views of the Church and Politics*, edited by Amy E. Black (Grand Rapids: Zondervan, 2015). Joshua D. Chatraw and Karen Swallow Prior's *Cultural Engagement: A Crash Course in Contemporary Issues* (Grand Rapids: Zondervan, 2019) is a thoughtful and comprehensive anthology of contrasting perspectives on a wide range of hot-button American political issues, with essays from competing viewpoints from across the contemporary Christian theological spectrum. The citations in Sider's *Just Politics* also offer a wide-ranging guide to some of the best works of political theology from Anabaptist, Reformed, and Wesleyan perspectives.

For an insightful secular critique of both political parties (albeit a critique that is heavily influenced by the liberal Catholic social justice theology of its author), E. J. Dionne Jr.'s *Why Americans Hate Politics*, 2nd ed. (New York: Simon & Schuster, 2004), offers useful historical information and a perceptive analysis.

Theologically conservative evangelical Christians who wonder whether the Bible contains an imperative for social justice might find it useful to read Timothy Keller's *Generous Justice: How God's Grace Makes Us Just* (New York: Viking, 2010), which offers a compelling argument for the connection between cross-centered grace and a commitment to justice.

Several recent books by evangelicals have lamented the current political direction of American white evangelicalism and suggested a corrective. John Fea's *Believe Me: The Evangelical Road to Donald Trump* (Grand Rapids: Eerdmans, 2018) offers a sympathetic critique of the modern white evangelical alliance with Donald Trump, written by an American historian who is himself an evangelical Christian. Thomas Kidd's *Who Is an Evangelical? The History of a Movement in Crisis* (New Haven: Yale University Press, 2019) laments the conflation of contemporary American white evangelical conservatism with evangelicalism itself and argues that, at its best, American evangelicalism has been politically diverse and not firmly identified with any particular political party. And Russell Moore's *Onward: Engaging the Culture without Losing the Gospel* (Nashville: Broadman & Holman, 2015) suggests that perhaps Christians should replace partisan political strategies with gospel-centered outreach that combines an acknowledgment that Christians have largely lost the culture wars with an awareness of opportunities for missional living in a post-Christian, morally pluralistic society.

Finally, *To Change the World: The Irony, Tragedy, and Possibility of Christianity in the Late Modern World* (New York: Oxford University Press, 2010), by sociology professor James Davison Hunter, offers a detailed corrective to the Christian pursuit of political power, whether it comes from the right or the left.

Chapter 1: The Protestant Moralism of the Republican Party

There are several good academic histories of the Republican Party. Lewis L. Gould's *The Republicans: A History of the Grand Old Party* (New York: Oxford University Press, 2014) may be the most comprehensive, evenhanded survey. Heather Cox Richardson's *To Make Men Free: A History of the Republican Party* (New York: Basic Books, 2014) offers a critical appraisal of the GOP's shift from the antislavery politics of the 1860s to the party's long history of support for monied interests from the Gilded Age to the present. One of the best histories of the last half century of the GOP, with a focus on conservatives who moved the party to the right, is Donald T. Critchlow's *The Republican Ascendancy: How the Republican Right Rose to Power in Modern America*, 2nd ed. (Lawrence: University Press of Kansas, 2011). E. J. Dionne Jr.'s *Why the Right Went Wrong: Conservatism—From Goldwater to Trump and Beyond* (New York: Simon & Schuster, 2016) presents a more critical appraisal of this same half century of GOP history.

David Farber's *The Rise and Fall of Modern American Conservatism: A Short History* (Princeton: Princeton University Press, 2010) insightfully describes the philosophy and assumptions of twentieth-century American conservatives, and also offers a series of fascinating biographical portraits of several politicians and movement activists who represented the various ideological strands of modern American conservatism, including libertarianism, neoconservatism, and social conservatism. The best intellectual history of mid-twentieth-century American conservatism is still George H. Nash's classic work, *The Conservative Intellectual Movement in America since 1945*, 2nd ed. (Wilmington, DE: ISI, 2006).

For earlier eras of moral regulation (much of which was conducted through the Republican Party), Gaines M. Foster's *Moral Reconstruction: Christian Lobbyists and the Federal Legislation of Morality, 1865–1920* (Chapel Hill: University of North Carolina Press, 2002) and Michael McGerr's *A Fierce Discontent: The Rise and Fall of the Progressive Movement in America* (New York: Oxford University Press, 2003) are useful historical surveys. Thomas R. Pegram's *Battling Demon Rum: The Struggle for a Dry America, 1800–1933* (Chicago: Ivan R. Dee, 1999) and W. J. Rorabaugh's *Prohibition: A Concise History* (New York: Oxford University Press, 2018) chronicle the rise and fall of what was perhaps American Protestants' most prominent moral crusade after the Civil War.

Matthew Avery Sutton traces the connection between conservative evangelical dispensationalist theology and opposition to the New Deal in *American Apocalypse: A History of Modern Evangelicalism* (Cambridge, MA: Harvard University Press, 2014). For an analysis of the connection between church, state, and the Republican Party during the Cold War, see Kevin M. Kruse's *One Nation under God: How Corporate America Invented Christian America* (New York: Basic Books, 2015). The development of conservative evangelicals' alliance with the Republican Party is traced in Darren Dochuk's *From Bible Belt to Sunbelt: Plain-Folk Religion, Grassroots Politics, and the Rise of Evangelical Conservatism* (New York: W. W. Norton, 2011) and my own *God's Own Party: The Making of the Christian Right* (New York: Oxford University Press, 2010). Seth Dowland's *Family Values and the Rise of the Christian Right* (Philadelphia: University of Pennsylvania Press, 2015) surveys the cultural flashpoints that have shaped recent American cultural conservatism. Andrew Hartman's *A War for the Soul of America: A History of the Culture Wars*, 2nd ed. (Chicago: University of Chicago Press, 2019), presents an intellectual history of the conflicts that have energized many cultural conservatives since the 1960s and explains why social conservatives have lost nearly all their fights. David T. Courtwright's *No Right Turn: Conservative Politics in a Liberal America* (Cambridge, MA: Harvard University Press, 2010) focuses on popular culture and national politics rather than intellectual history but reaches a similar conclusion: social conservatives' alliance with the right has not stopped the liberalization of American cultural values.

A few prominent conservative activists who have left the Christian Right have come to similar conclusions. For their assessment of why the evangelical alliance with the Republican Party failed to change the direction of American culture, see Cal Thomas and Ed Dobson's *Blinded by Might: Can the Religious Right Save America?* (Grand Rapids: Zondervan, 1999) and David Kuo's *Tempting Faith: An Inside Story of Political Seduction* (New York: Free Press, 2006).

Most of the books listed above present a critical assessment of the Christian Right, political conservatism, and the Republican Party, but for a thoughtful defense of conservative ideas from a Catholic natural-law perspective, see Robert P. George's *Conscience and Its Enemies: Confronting the Dogmas of Liberal Secularism* (Wilmington, DE: ISI, 2013) and *The Clash of Orthodoxies: Law, Religion, and Morality in Crisis* (Wilmington, DE:

ISI, 2001). Readers are also encouraged to look at some of the classic mid-twentieth-century works of intellectual conservatism, such as Russell Kirk's *The Conservative Mind* (1953), Richard M. Weaver's *Ideas Have Consequences* (1948), and William F. Buckley Jr.'s *God and Man at Yale* (1951).

Chapter 2: The Secularized Liberal Protestantism of the Democratic Party

The most comprehensive, engagingly written history of the Democratic Party currently available is probably Jules Witcover's *Party of the People: A History of the Democrats* (New York: Random House, 2003).

Unfortunately, there is as yet no single work that comprehensively traces the religious heritage of the Democratic Party, but several useful studies touch on aspects of this history. Michael Kazin's *A Godly Hero: The Life of William Jennings Bryan* (New York: Alfred A. Knopf, 2006) examines Bryan's blend of evangelical Christian faith and commitment to a progressive politics that championed the rights of the "commoner." Barry Hankins's *Woodrow Wilson: Ruling Elder, Spiritual President* (New York: Oxford University Press, 2016) and Cara Lea Burnidge's *A Peaceful Conquest: Woodrow Wilson, Religion, and the New World Order* (Chicago: University of Chicago Press, 2016) explore the influence of Wilson's theological beliefs on his political ideology. The influence of liberal Protestant Christianity on President Franklin D. Roosevelt's social consciousness is explored in John F. Woolverton and James D. Bratt's *A Christian and a Democrat: A Religious Biography of Franklin D. Roosevelt* (Grand Rapids: Eerdmans, 2019). For Christianity's influence on the Cold War foreign policy of President Harry S. Truman, see William Inboden's *Religion and American Foreign Policy, 1945–1960: The Soul of Containment* (New York: Cambridge University Press, 2008). Robert Bauman's *Fighting to Preserve a Nation's Soul: America's Ecumenical War on Poverty* (Athens: University of Georgia Press, 2019) analyzes liberal Christian support for President Lyndon Johnson's social policies. The Christian roots of George McGovern's liberal political commitments are the subject of Mark A. Lempke's *My Brother's Keeper: George McGovern and Progressive Christianity* (Amherst: University of Massachusetts Press, 2017). For Democratic president Jimmy Carter's Christian faith, see Randall Balmer's *Redeemer: The Life of Jimmy Carter* (New York: Basic Books, 2014) and Carter's own *Faith: A Journey for All* (New York: Simon & Schuster, 2018). Barack Obama discussed his own liberal Protestant faith at some length in *The Audacity of Hope* (New York: Three Rivers, 2006).

For the early twentieth-century social gospel and the connection between liberal Protestantism and progressive politics, see Christopher H. Evans's *The Social Gospel in American Religion: A History* (New York: New York University Press, 2017) and Heath W. Carter's *Union Made: Working People and the Rise of Social Christianity in Chicago* (New York: Oxford University Press, 2015). For liberal Protestant support for the civil rights and antiwar movements of the mid-twentieth century, see Michael B. Friedland, *Lift Up Your Voice Like a Trumpet: White Clergy and the Civil Rights and Antiwar Movements, 1954–1973* (Chapel Hill: University of North Carolina Press, 1998), James F. Findlay Jr.'s *Church People in the Struggle: The National Council of Churches and the Black Freedom Movement, 1950–1970* (New York: Oxford University Press, 1993), Sarah Azaransky's *This Worldwide Struggle: Religion and the International Roots of the Civil Rights Movement* (New York: Oxford University Press, 2017), and Doug Rossinow's *The Politics of Authenticity: Liberalism, Christianity, and the New Left in America* (New York: Columbia University Press, 1998). Charles Marsh's *The Beloved Community: How Faith Shapes Social Justice from the Civil Rights Movement to Today* (New York: Basic Books, 2004) brings this story up to the twenty-first century.

For discussions of Catholic support for the New Deal and the social welfare state in the mid-twentieth century, see George J. Marlin's *The American Catholic Voter: 200 Years of Political Impact*, 2nd ed. (South Bend, IN: St. Augustine's Press, 2006), and Kenneth J. Heineman's *A Catholic New Deal: Religion and Reform in Depression Pittsburgh* (University Park: Pennsylvania State University Press, 1999). John T. McGreevy's *Catholicism and American Freedom: A History* (New York: W. W. Norton, 2003) is an exceptionally insightful and detailed analysis of points of both agreement and difference between Catholicism and American liberalism in the twentieth century. For Catholic social teaching and its points of agreement and disagreement with the contemporary Democratic Party, see Thomas Massaro's *Living Justice: Catholic Social Teaching in Action*, 3rd ed. (Lanham, MD: Rowman & Littlefield, 2016).

For progressive evangelical theologies of social justice in the late twentieth and early twenty-first centuries, see David R. Swartz's *Moral Minority:*

The Evangelical Left in an Age of Conservatism (Philadelphia: University of Pennsylvania Press, 2012), Brantley W. Gassaway's *Progressive Evangelicals and the Pursuit of Social Justice* (Chapel Hill: University of North Carolina Press, 2014), and Philip Goff and Brian Steenland's anthology *The New Evangelical Social Engagement* (New York: Oxford University Press, 2014). All three of these books are academic histories written by sympathetic observers, but for a progressive evangelical's own perspective, see Jim Wallis's *God's Politics: Why the Right Gets It Wrong and the Left Doesn't Get It* (New York: HarperCollins, 2005). Erik S. Gellman and Jarod Roll's *The Gospel of the Working Class: Labor's Southern Prophets in New Deal America* (Urbana: University of Illinois Press, 2011) as well as Roll's *Spirit of Rebellion: Labor and Religion in the New Cotton South* (Urbana: University of Illinois Press, 2010) chronicle evangelical social justice activism among economically marginalized southerners in the 1930s. And Robert H. Abzug's *Cosmos Crumbling: American Reform and the Religious Imagination* (New York: Oxford University Press, 1994) discusses the optimistic millennial vision and social activism of the early nineteenth-century northern evangelicals who brought their commitment to societal reform into the political sphere.

In recent years, several books lamenting the Democratic Party's secularization and abandonment of the priorities of its Christian supporters have been published. For complaints about the Democratic Party's secular turn, see Michael Sean Winters's *Left at the Altar: How the Democrats Lost the Catholics and the Catholics Can Save the Democrats* (New York: Basic Books, 2008) and Mark Stricherz's *Why the Democrats Are Blue: Secular Liberalism and the Decline of the People's Party* (New York: Encounter Books, 2007). For a thoughtful critique of contemporary American liberalism's focus on individual rights, see Mary Ann Glendon's *Rights Talk: The Impoverishment of Political Discourse* (New York: Free Press, 1991). James Davison Hunter's *Culture Wars: The Struggle to Control the Family, Art, Education, Law, and Politics in America* (New York: Basic Books, 1991) offers additional insights on the moral relativism of contemporary cultural liberalism.

Chapter 3: Abortion

Most histories of abortion in America are written from a pro-choice perspective and present a similar narrative—namely, that prohibitions on abortion were repressive, misogynistic, and ineffective, and that the legalization of abortion was a victory for women's rights and the right to sexual privacy. Variations of this argument can be found in James C. Mohr's *Abortion in America: The Origins of National Policy, 1800–1900* (New York: Oxford University Press, 1978), Leslie J. Reagan's *When Abortion Was a Crime: Women, Medicine, and Law in the United States, 1867–1973* (Berkeley: University of California Press, 1997), N. E. H. Hull and Peter Charles Hoffer's *Roe v. Wade: The Abortion Rights Controversy in American History* (Lawrence: University Press of Kansas, 2001), and David J. Garrow's *Liberty and Sexuality: The Right to Privacy and the Making of Roe v. Wade*, 2nd ed. (Berkeley: University of California Press, 1998). For a discussion of what the enactment of new prohibitions on abortion will likely mean, see Michelle Oberman's *Her Body, Our Laws: On the Front Lines of the Abortion War, from El Salvador to Oklahoma* (Boston: Beacon, 2018). Unfortunately, pro-lifers who have rejected the philosophy behind many of these books have too often dismissed the evidence that laws against abortion in early twentieth-century America really were ineffectively enforced. Marvin Olasky's *Abortion Rites: A Social History of Abortion in America* (Wheaton, IL: Crossway, 1992), written from a conservative Christian pro-life perspective, presents a thoughtful, nuanced history of the pre-*Roe* era that resists this temptation and instead acknowledges gaps in enforcement of the law, as well as reasons why American attitudes toward abortion changed over time. Olasky's thoughtful history is essential reading for any Christian who wants to understand the long history of abortion in the United States.

For the early history of the American pro-life movement and the development of pro-life arguments, see John T. McGreevy's *Catholicism and American Freedom: A History* (New York: W. W. Norton, 2003) and my own *Defenders of the Unborn: The Pro-Life Movement before Roe v. Wade* (New York: Oxford University Press, 2016), which also includes a lot of information about *Roe v. Wade* and the reasons why the Republican and Democratic Party adopted different positions on abortion after the mid-1970s. For the abortion debate after 1973, with a focus on legal history, see Mary Ziegler's *After Roe: The Lost History of the Abortion Debate* (Cambridge, MA: Harvard University Press, 2015) and *Abortion and the Law in America: Roe v. Wade to the Present* (New York: Cambridge University Press, 2020). Andrew R. Lewis's

The Rights Turn in Conservative Christian Politics: How Abortion Transformed the Culture Wars (New York: Cambridge University Press, 2017) argues that conservative evangelicals' pro-life political commitments have made them more supportive of other social justice issues.

For histories of the Christian tradition's view of the sanctity of unborn human life, see John R. Connery's *Abortion: The Development of the Roman Catholic Perspective* (Chicago: Loyola University Press, 1977) and David Albert Jones's *The Soul of the Embryo: An Enquiry into the Status of the Human Embryo in the Christian Tradition* (London: Continuum, 2004). For philosophical and scientific arguments in defense of the value of unborn human life, see Robert P. George and Christopher Tollefsen's *Embryo: A Defense of Human Life* (New York: Doubleday, 2008) and Francis J. Beckwith's *Defending Life: A Moral and Legal Case against Abortion Choice* (New York: Cambridge University Press, 2007). For comprehensive pro-life arguments, see also Pope John Paul II's *Evangelium Vitae* (1995). For those who would like to read the perspective of a Protestant ethicist and New Testament scholar, Richard B. Hays's *The Moral Vision of the New Testament: A Contemporary Introduction to New Testament Ethics* (New York: HarperCollins, 1996) offers an insightful, nuanced overview of the New Testament's implications for discussions of abortion. Discussions of this issue can also be found in Glen H. Stassen and David P. Gushee's *Kingdom Ethics: Following Jesus in Contemporary Context* (Downers Grove, IL: InterVarsity, 2003), Ronald Sider's *Just Politics*, and John Stott's *Issues Facing Christians Today*, 4th ed. (Grand Rapids: Zondervan, 2006). Sider's *Completely Pro-Life: Abortion, the Family, Nuclear Weapons, the Poor* (Downers Grove, IL: InterVarsity, 1987) defends a comprehensive pro-life ethic for the protection of human life before and after birth. Charles C. Camosy's *Beyond the Abortion Wars: A Way Forward for a New Generation* (Grand Rapids: Eerdmans, 2015) and *Resisting Throwaway Culture: How a Consistent Life Ethic Can Unite a Fractured People* (Hyde Park, NY: New City Press, 2019) suggest ways to apply the consistent life ethic across the political divide. No political party in the United States fully reflects this perspective, as I point out in my essay, "Pro-Lifers of the Left: Progressive Evangelicals' Campaign against Abortion," in *The New Evangelical Social Engagement*, ed. Philip Goff and Brian Steensland (New York: Oxford University Press, 2014).

Chapter 4: Marriage and Sexuality

Numerous academic and journalistic accounts chronicle the twentieth-century American sexual revolution, the gay rights movement, changes in cultural and legal definitions of marriage, and the reasons why conservative opponents of these changes lost their battles. The vast majority of these books are written from a culturally liberal, secular perspective that takes a generally positive view of the liberalization of sexual norms, but biblically minded Christians can still benefit from reading these works to understand why these cultural changes occurred—and why conservative Christians' strategies to thwart these changes did not succeed. Beth Bailey's *From Front Porch to Back Seat: Courtship in Twentieth-Century America* (Baltimore: Johns Hopkins University Press, 1988) and *Sex in the Heartland* (Cambridge, MA: Harvard University Press, 1999) explore the causes of the sexual revolution and its effects on heterosexual young people over the course of the twentieth century. Leigh Ann Wheeler's *How Sex Became a Civil Liberty* (New York: Oxford University Press, 2013) is a legal history of the sexual revolution throughout the twentieth century, with a focus on the American Civil Liberties Union (ACLU) and the Supreme Court. Paula S. Fass's *The Damned and the Beautiful: American Youth in the 1920s* (New York: Oxford University Press, 1977) and Joshua Zeitz's *Flapper: A Madcap Story of Sex, Style, Celebrity, and the Women Who Made America Modern* (New York: Three Rivers, 2007) celebrate the sexual rebellion of young people during the "Roaring Twenties"; Barry Hankins's *Jesus and Gin: Evangelicalism, the Roaring Twenties and Today's Culture Wars* (New York: St. Martin's Press, 2010) offers a more nuanced perspective that takes evangelical critiques of the cultural changes of the era far more seriously. Nancy F. Cott's *Public Vows: A History of Marriage and the Nation* (Cambridge, MA: Harvard University Press, 2000) chronicles changing definitions of marriage in public law during the nineteenth and twentieth centuries, while Stephanie Coontz's *Marriage, a History: How Love Conquered Marriage* (New York: Penguin, 2005) traces the cultural history of changing American expectations of marriage during the same period. Elaine Tyler May's *Great Expectations: Marriage and Divorce in Post-Victorian America* (Chicago: University of Chicago Press, 1980) is a highly insightful comparative study of the reasons for divorce in California in the 1880s and 1920s—a study that reveals a great deal about changing attitudes toward marriage in the early twentieth century. Another informative history of divorce in the United States is J. Herbie DiFonzo's *Beneath the Fault Line: The Popular and Legal Culture of Divorce in Twentieth-Century America* (Charlottesville: University Press of Virginia, 1997).

There are numerous histories of the gay rights movement, but one of the most readable and comprehensive (though now somewhat out-of-date) is Dudley Clendinen and Adam Nagourney's *Out for Good: The Struggle to Build a Gay Rights Movement in America* (New York: Simon & Schuster, 1999). Lillian Faderman's *The Gay Revolution: The Story of the Struggle* (New York: Simon & Schuster, 2015) brings the story up to the second decade of the twenty-first century. Margot Canaday's *The Straight State: Sexuality and Citizenship in Twentieth-Century America* (Princeton: Princeton University Press, 2009) details the regulation of homosexuality in mid-twentieth-century America. Joanne Meyerowitz's *How Sex Changed: A History of Transsexuality in the United States* (Cambridge, MA: Harvard University Press, 2002) sheds light on why psychologists and others began to consider gender and sexuality fluid, malleable categories in the mid-twentieth century. Michael J. Klarman's *From the Closet to the Altar: Courts, Backlash, and the Struggle for Same-Sex Marriage* (New York: Oxford University Press, 2013) is a legal history that sheds light on why the argument for legalization of same-sex marriage rapidly won acceptance in the nation's courts.

Several books chronicle the acceptance of the sexual revolution among Christians—at least theologically liberal Christians and, at times, evangelicals. R. Marie Griffith's *Moral Combat: How Sex Divided American Christians and Fractured American Politics* (New York: Basic Books, 2017) offers a lot of insight on liberal Protestant attitudes toward sexuality from the 1920s to the late twentieth century. Heather R. White's *Reforming Sodom: Protestants and the Rise of Gay Rights* (Chapel Hill: University of North Carolina Press, 2015) examines the liberal Protestant ministers who supported gay rights in the 1960s and 1970s. Tom Davis's *Sacred Work: Planned Parenthood and Its Clergy Alliances* (New Brunswick, NJ: Rutgers University Press, 2004) and Doris Andrea Dirks and Patricia A. Relf's *To Offer Compassion: A History of the Clergy Consultation Service on Abortion* (Madison: University of Wisconsin Press, 2017) chronicle liberal Protestant ministerial support for Planned Parenthood, birth control, and abortion rights.

Evangelicals' cultural and political opposition to the sexual revolution receives extensive attention in Sara Moslener's *Virgin Nation: Sexual Purity and American Adolescence* (New York: Oxford University Press, 2015), Hilde Lovdal Stephens's *Family Matters: James Dobson and Focus on the Family's Crusade for the Christian Home* (Tuscaloosa: University of Alabama Press, 2019), and Seth Dowland's *Family Values and the Rise of the Christian Right* (Philadelphia: University of Pennsylvania Press, 2015). Amy DeRogatis's *Saving Sex: Sexuality and Salvation in American Evangelicalism* (New York: Oxford University Press, 2015) and Christine J. Gardner's *Making Chastity Sexy: The Rhetoric of Evangelical Abstinence Campaigns* (Berkeley: University of California Press, 2011) present a critical (but also insightful) analysis of evangelical purity culture. My own essay, "Sex and the Evangelicals: Gender Issues, the Sexual Revolution, and Abortion in the 1960s," in *American Evangelicals and the 1960s: Revisiting the "Backlash,"* ed. Axel Schaefer (University of Wisconsin Press, 2013), suggests that evangelicals adopted far more of the prevailing culture's view of sexuality in the 1960s than they were willing to admit. Alan Petigny's *The Permissive Society: 1941–1965* (New York: Cambridge University Press, 2009) likewise suggests that evangelicals, like other Americans, experienced a liberalization of sexual attitudes and other cultural values during the supposedly conservative 1950s. Allan C. Carlson's *Godly Seed: American Evangelicals Confront Birth Control, 1873–1973* (New York: Transaction, 2012) argues that American evangelicals' acceptance of contraception in the mid-twentieth century was at odds with Protestants' historic opposition to the practice. And for evidence that evangelical teaching on sex has not deterred evangelical teens from sexual experimentation, see Mark D. Regnerus's *Forbidden Fruit: Sex and Religion in the Lives of American Teenagers* (New York: Oxford University Press, 2007).

While most histories of the sexual revolution are written from a culturally liberal perspective, there are at least a few good conservative scholarly analyses of the negative aspects of this cultural shift. Mary Eberstadt's *Adam and Eve after the Pill: Paradoxes of the Sexual Revolution* (San Francisco: Ignatius, 2012) and *Primal Screams: How the Sexual Revolution Created Identity Politics* (West Conshocken, PA: Templeton, 2019) offer perceptive historical overviews and cultural critiques from a conservative Catholic perspective. Elizabeth Fox-Genovese's *Marriage: The Dream That Refuses to Die* (Wilmington, DE: ISI, 2008) is a historical survey and defense of traditional marriage written by a leading academic historian who was also a Catholic convert. Mark Regnerus's *Cheap Sex: The Transformation of Men, Marriage, and Monogamy* (New York: Oxford University Press, 2017) argues that the sexual revolution did not advance women's rights (as cultural liberals often claim) but instead privileged men's sexual desires at women's expense.

For conservative arguments in favor of defending traditional marriage and gender norms in the political arena, a good place to start is *What Is Marriage? Man and Woman: A Defense*, written by Sherif Girgis, Ryan T. Anderson, and Robert P. George (New York: Encounter Books, 2012), which presents a natural-law perspective. Anderson's *When Harry Became Sally: Responding to the Transgender Moment* (New York: Encounter Books, 2018) applies a similar analysis to the debate over transgender rights and public policy.

The influence of poverty and social class on marriage practices and attitudes toward marriage is explored in Kathryn Edin and Maria Kefalas's *Promises I Can Keep: Why Poor Women Put Motherhood before Marriage* (Berkeley: University of California Press, 2005) and William Julius Wilson's *More Than Just Race: Being Black and Poor in the Inner City* (New York: W. W. Norton, 2009). Edin, Kefalas, and Wilson explain why the poorest Americans are unlikely to marry, but W. Bradford Wilcox's scholarship presents social science arguments to demonstrate why the lives of the poor improve when they do marry. For some of Wilcox's findings and arguments, see *Why Marriage Matters: Thirty Conclusions from the Social Sciences*, 3rd ed. (New York: Broadway Books, 2011).

For a gospel-centered, evangelical theology of marriage, an excellent resource is *The Meaning of Marriage: Facing the Complexities of Commitment with the Wisdom of God*, written by Timothy Keller with Kathy Keller (New York: Dutton, 2011). Keller's book reminds us of what marriage is, according to the Bible, and why even conservative defenses of marriage have sometimes lost sight of its real, gospel-based significance. *Sexual Brokenness and the Hope of the Gospel*, ed. Russell Moore (Nashville: Leland House, 2014), applies a gospel-centered ethic to a wide variety of sexual sins in contemporary American culture. There are far too many other thoughtful evangelical books on sexuality to list here, but one that should certainly be mentioned is Christopher Yuan's *Holy Sexuality and the Gospel: Sex, Desire, and Relationships Shaped by God's Grand Story* (Colorado Springs: Multnomah, 2018).

Chapter 5: Race

Books on the history of the African American experience number in the thousands and cannot possibly be listed comprehensively here. For a classic comprehensive survey of African American history, see John Hope Franklin and Evelyn Brooks Higginbotham's *From Slavery to Freedom: A History of African Americans*, now in its ninth edition (New York: McGraw-Hill, 2011), or, for a more popularly oriented (but still academically sound) treatment, Henry Louis Gates Jr. and Donald Yacovone's *The African Americans: Many Rivers to Cross* (New York: Smiley Books, 2013).

A few of the titles that I would recommend on the history of slavery and the origins of racism in America and the Western world include Peter Kolchin's *American Slavery, 1619-1877*, 2nd ed. (New York: Hill and Wang, 2003), Ira Berlin's *Generations of Captivity: A History of African-American Slaves* (Cambridge, MA: Harvard University Press, 2003), Marcus Rediker's *The Slave Ship: A Human History* (New York: Viking, 2007), Hugh Thomas's *The Slave Trade: The Story of the Atlantic Slave Trade, 1440-1870* (New York: Simon & Schuster, 1997), George M. Fredrickson's *Racism: A Short History* (Princeton: Princeton University Press, 2002), Winthrop D. Jordan's *White over Black: American Attitudes toward the Negro, 1550-1812* (Chapel Hill: University of North Carolina Press, 1968), Edmund S. Morgan's *American Slavery, American Freedom* (New York: W. W. Norton, 1975), Eugene D. Genovese's *Roll, Jordan, Roll: The World the Slaves Made* (New York: Random House, 1974), Edward E. Baptist's *The Half Has Never Been Told: Slavery and the Making of American Capitalism* (New York: Basic Books, 2014), and Ibram X. Kendi's *Stamped from the Beginning: The Definitive History of Racist Ideas in America* (New York: Nation Books, 2016).

For segregation, racial discrimination, and the African American experience after 1865, see Jacqueline Jones's *Labor of Love, Labor of Sorrow: Black Women, Work, and the Family, from Slavery to the Present*, 2nd ed. (New York: Basic Books, 1985), Leon F. Litwack's *Trouble in Mind: Black Southerners in the Age of Jim Crow* (New York: Alfred A. Knopf, 1998), Douglas A. Blackmon's *Slavery by Another Name: The Re-Enslavement of Black Americans from the Civil War to World War II* (New York: Anchor Books, 2008), and Thomas J. Sugrue's *Sweet Land of Liberty: The Forgotten Struggle for Civil Rights in the North* (New York: Random House, 2008).

For structural racism in American housing and economic development after the Second World War, see Thomas J. Sugrue's *The Origins of the Urban Crisis: Race and Inequality in Postwar Detroit*, 2nd ed. (Princeton: Princeton University Press, 2005). Richard Rothstein's *The Color of Law: The Forgotten History of How Our Government Segregated America* (New York: Liveright, 2017) and Ira Katznelson's *When Affirmative Action Was White: An Untold History of Racial Inequality in Twentieth-Century America* (New York: W. W. Norton, 2005) offer excellent historical analysis of the codification of structural racism into American law in the twentieth century.

For analyses of contemporary structural racism, see Michelle Alexander's *The New Jim Crow: Mass Incarceration in the Age of Colorblindness* (New York: New Press, 2010), Elizabeth Hinton's *From the War on Poverty to the War on Crime: The Making of Mass Incarceration in America* (Cambridge, MA: Harvard University Press, 2016), James Foreman Jr.'s *Locking Up Our Own: Crime and Punishment in Black America* (New York: Farrar, Straus and Giroux, 2017), and Dorothy Roberts's *Killing the Black Body: Race, Reproduction, and the Meaning of Liberty*, 2nd ed. (New York: Vintage Books, 2016). Personal reflections by contemporary African Americans on the persistent effects of racism in twenty-first-century America include Ta-Nehisi Coates's *Between the World and Me* (New York: Spiegel & Grau, 2015) and Ibram X. Kendi's *How to Be an Antiracist* (New York: One World, 2019). Both of these books are written by non-Christians, and I would not give a complete endorsement to their entire analysis, but they offer useful food for thought, especially for white Christians who are attempting to understand the contemporary African American experience. Christians who want to know what policy proposals they can support that might address the issues of structural racism and mass incarceration highlighted in these works might be interested in Dominique DuBois Gilliard's *Rethinking Incarceration: Advocating for Justice That Restores* (Downers Grove, IL: InterVarsity, 2018).

African Americans' development of a Christian theology of suffering and liberation is succinctly chronicled in Albert J. Raboteau's *Canaan Land: A Religious History of African Americans* (New York: Oxford University Press, 1999). For primary sources from black Christians of the eighteenth, nineteenth, and twentieth centuries, see Milton C. Sernett's *African American Religious History: A Documentary Reader* (Durham, NC: Duke University Press, 1999). One of the most widely circulated black Christian theological reflections of the mid-twentieth century was Howard Thurman's *Jesus and the Disinherited*, first published in 1949 (repr., Boston: Beacon, 1996). Martin Luther King Jr.'s *Strength to Love* (repr., Minneapolis: Fortress, 2010), a collection of his sermons, is another useful guide to the black Christian theology that guided the civil rights movement. For the influence of Christianity on the civil rights movement, see David L. Chappell's *A Stone of Hope: Prophetic Religion and the Death of Jim Crow* (Chapel Hill: University of North Carolina Press, 2004), David J. Garrow's *Bearing the Cross: Martin Luther King, Jr., and the Southern Christian Leadership Conference* (New York: HarperCollins, 1986), and Charles Marsh's *God's Long Summer: Stories of Faith and Civil Rights* (Princeton: Princeton University Press, 1997). Biographies of civil rights activists who were motivated by their Christian faith include Andrew M. Manis's *A Fire You Can't Put Out: The Civil Rights Life of Birmingham's Reverend Fred Shuttlesworth* (Tuscaloosa: University of Alabama Press, 1999) and Kay Mills's *This Little Light of Mine: The Life of Fannie Lou Hamer* (New York: Dutton, 1993). John M. Perkins's *Let Justice Roll Down*, rev. ed. (Grand Rapids: Baker Books, 2014; originally published in 1976), is an autobiographical account of an African American Christian from Mississippi who found the ability to forgive in the power of the gospel and who worked closely with conservative white evangelicals to bring a commitment to racial justice to the church. For a white Reformed evangelical pastor's account of his own journey of repentance of the sin of cooperation in perpetuating racial injustice, see John Piper's *Bloodlines: Race, Cross, and the Christian* (Wheaton, IL: Crossway, 2011).

For a black Christian's historical critique of white evangelicalism's racism and alliances with conservative political causes that hurt black Americans, see Jemar Tisby's *The Color of Compromise: The Truth about the American Church's Complicity in Racism* (Grand Rapids: Zondervan, 2019). Other books that touch on the challenges that white evangelicals face in understanding African Americans' experiences and working toward racial justice include Michael O. Emerson and Christian Smith's *Divided by Faith: Evangelical Religion and the Problem of Race in America* (New York: Oxford University Press, 2000) and J. Russell Hawkins and Philip Luke Sinitiere's *Christians and the Color Line: Race and Religion after Divided by Faith* (New York: Oxford University Press, 2014). A lot has been published on this topic in the two decades since Emerson and Smith's work first appeared, but *Divided by Faith* as well as Hawkins and

Sinitiere's anthology of scholarship remain useful introductions. Mark Noll's scholarship on race and religion—especially his *God and Race in American Politics: A Short History* (Princeton: Princeton University Press, 2008)—is also a highly useful guide to the historical reasons why black and white American Christians have very different understandings of race and politics.

Readers who want to explore the reasons for the unpopularity of the Republican Party among most African Americans can consult Michael K. Fauntroy's *Republicans and the Black Vote* (Boulder, CO: Lynne Rienner, 2007) and Jeremy D. Mayer's *Running on Race: Racial Politics in Presidential Campaigns, 1960-2000* (New York: Random House, 2002). Thomas Byrne Edsall and Mary D. Edsall's *Chain Reaction: The Impact of Race, Rights, and Taxes on American Politics* (New York: W. W. Norton, 1991) examines the racial backlash associated with some conservative campaigns against high taxes and social welfare programs.

Many of the books listed above focus on structural racism as the explanation for the wealth divide between blacks and whites, but for an analysis of the roles that marriage and family, as well as poverty, play in this phenomenon, see James T. Patterson's *Freedom Is Not Enough: The Moynihan Report and America's Struggle over Black Family Life from LBJ to Obama* (New York: Basic Books, 2010) and William Julius Wilson's *The Truly Disadvantaged: The Inner City, the Underclass, and Public Policy*, 2nd ed. (Chicago: University of Chicago Press, 2012). Stephan Thernstrom and Abigail Thernstrom's *America in Black and White: One Nation, Indivisible: Race in Modern America* (New York: Simon & Schuster, 1997) also examines the connection between family life, race, and poverty and advances an argument for conservative color-blind policies—an argument that is at odds with the views presented in most of the other books listed here.

For surveys of the challenges confronting Hispanic immigrants in low-wage industries, see Angela Stuesse's *Scratching Out a Living: Latinos, Race, and Work in the Deep South* (Berkeley: University of California Press, 2016) and Helen B. Marrow's *New Destination Dreaming: Immigration, Race, and Legal Status in the Rural American South* (Stanford, CA: Stanford University Press, 2011). Paul Ganster and David E. Lorey's *The U.S.-Mexican Border into the Twenty-First Century*, 2nd ed. (Lanham, MD: Rowman & Littlefield, 2008), is a historical survey of changes in American policy toward Mexican immigration and the country's border with Mexico. Marisa Abrajano and

Zoltan L. Hajnal's *White Backlash: Immigration, Race, and American Politics* (Princeton: Princeton University Press, 2015) examines the role that opposition to Latino immigration has played in hardening racial attitudes and converting whites to the Republican Party. For thoughtful Christian reflections on American immigration policy, see Robert W. Heimburger's *God and the Illegal Alien: United States Immigration Law and a Theology of Politics* (New York: Cambridge University Press, 2018) and M. Daniel Carroll R.'s *Christians at the Border: Immigration, the Church, and the Bible*, 2nd ed. (Grand Rapids: Brazos, 2013).

Chapter 6: Wealth and Poverty

James T. Patterson's *America's Struggle against Poverty in the Twentieth Century*, rev. ed. (Cambridge, MA: Harvard University Press, 2000), Michael B. Katz's *The Undeserving Poor: America's Enduring Confrontation with Poverty*, 2nd ed. (New York: Oxford University Press, 2013), and Frank Stricker's *Why America Lost the War on Poverty—and How to Win It* (Chapel Hill: University of North Carolina Press, 2007) offer detailed, scholarly analyses of the effect that both the Great Society programs of the 1960s and the cuts in social welfare programs during the late twentieth century had on poverty rates in the United States. Edward N. Wolff's *A Century of Wealth in America* (Cambridge, MA: Harvard University Press, 2017) is a lengthy, data-rich analysis of wealth inequality from the early twentieth century through the beginning of the twenty-first-century Great Recession. Matthew P. Drennan's *Income Inequality: Why It Matters and Why Most Economists Don't Notice* (New Haven: Yale University Press, 2015) and Paul Krugman's *The Conscience of a Liberal* (New York: W. W. Norton, 2007) present concise overviews of the trends that Wolff examines in detail, and most readers will probably find them more accessible. Most of these works focus primarily on income inequality or poverty, but for a detailed study of the economics of the middle class, see Robert J. Gordon's *The Rise and Fall of American Growth: The U.S. Standard of Living Since the Civil War* (Princeton: Princeton University Press, 2016). For the American economy before World War II, Jeremy Atack and Peter Passell's *A New Economic View of American History: From Colonial Times to 1940*, 2nd ed. (New York: W. W. Norton, 1994), is a useful guide. For the history of debates over health insurance in the United States, see Paul Starr's *Remedy and Reaction: The Peculiar American Struggle over Health Care Reform* (New Haven: Yale University Press, 2011). For Social Security, see Daniel Béland's *Social Security: History and Politics from the New Deal to the Privatization Debate* (Lawrence: University Press of Kansas, 2005). For the nation's punitive treatment of the poor after the 1970s, see Julilly Kohler-Hausmann's *Getting Tough: Welfare and Imprisonment in 1970s America* (Princeton: Princeton University Press, 2017). The reasons why conservative defenses of the free market became an article of faith for many middle-class white Americans in the late twentieth century is explored in the first chapter of Daniel T. Rodgers's *Age of Fracture* (Cambridge, MA: Harvard University Press, 2011).

Books are useful guides to the history of wealth and poverty in the United States, but for the latest economic data, online resources are indispensable. The Kaiser Family Foundation (www.kff.org) offers nonpartisan, data-driven analyses of the current state of health care in the United States. The US Bureau of Labor Statistics (www.bls.gov) and the US Census Bureau (www.census.gov) offer comprehensive, reliable data on American income, wealth, and employment by race, age, and gender. The *New York Times*, the *Washington Post*, the *Wall Street Journal*, the *Atlantic*, and the *Economist* also regularly cover these topics and are useful guides to summaries and analyses of the latest data and research.

For evangelical Christian reflections on how followers of Jesus should think about poverty, two widely read books offer useful guides: Ronald J. Sider's *Rich Christians in an Age of Hunger: Moving from Affluence to Generosity*, rev. ed. (Nashville: Thomas Nelson, 2015), and Steve Corbett and Brian Fikkert's *When Helping Hurts: How to Alleviate Poverty without Hurting the Poor . . . and Yourself*, 2nd ed. (Chicago: Moody, 2012). The two books differ in their perspective, and neither deals precisely with the issues covered in this volume, but both are filled with biblically grounded insights on the responsibility that Christians have to love the economically impoverished (whether in the United States or the developing world) and how they can best do that by thinking and acting counterculturally.

Afterword: The Politics of the Cross and the Preservation of the Nation

James T. Kloppenberg's *Toward Democracy: The Struggle for Self-Rule in European and American Thought* (New York: Oxford University Press, 2016) is far from the only book published within the past five years on the fragility of democracy and the reasons for its success or failure, but its emphasis on the altruistic or religious grounding of successful democracies makes it especially useful for Christian reflection—even though it is not in any way a religious book. Steven Zablitsky and Daniel Ziblatt's *How Democracies Die* (New York: Broadway Books, 2018) pinpoints the decline of unwritten institutional norms as a leading cause of democracy's failure internationally and offers a sober assessment of the current state of democracy in the United States. For a Christian reflection on the value of democracy, see Nicholas Wolterstorff's essay "Do Christians Have Good Reasons for Supporting Liberal Democracy?," in Wolterstorff and Terence Cuneo's *Understanding Liberal Democracy: Essays in Political Philosophy* (New York: Oxford University Press, 2012), 305–28. D. A. Carson's *Christ and Culture Revisited* (Grand Rapids: Eerdmans, 2008) points out the reasons why Christians should work to preserve both social justice and the democratic political order, even while recognizing that the promotion of democracy is not our ultimate aim.

Notes

Introduction

1. Timothy Keller, "How Do Christians Fit into the Two-Party System? They Don't," *New York Times*, September 29, 2018. For a similar perspective, see also Russell Moore, *Onward: Engaging the Culture without Losing the Gospel* (Nashville: Broadman & Holman, 2015).

2. Charles D. Drew, *Surprised by Community: Republicans and Democrats in the Same Pew* (self-published, 2019); John Fea, *Believe Me: The Evangelical Road to Donald Trump* (Grand Rapids: Eerdmans, 2018); Philip Yancey, *Christians and Politics: Uneasy Partners* (Creative Trust Digital, 2012); Amy E. Black, *Honoring God in Red or Blue: Approaching Politics with Humility, Grace, and Reason* (Chicago: Moody, 2012); Benjamin P. Dixon, *God Is Not a Republican* (Jacksonville, FL: East & 42nd, 2012); Lisa Sharon Harper, *Evangelical Does Not Equal Republican . . . or Democrat* (New York: New Press, 2008); Cal Thomas and Ed Dobson, *Blinded by Might: Can the Religious Right Save America?* (Grand Rapids: Zondervan, 1999); David Kuo, *Tempting Faith: An Inside Story of Political Seduction* (New York: Free Press, 2006); Charles Colson, *Kingdoms in Conflict* (Grand Rapids: Zondervan, 1989). For representative samples of Wallis, Sider, and Campolo's critiques, see Ronald J. Sider, *Just Politics: A Guide for Christian Engagement* (Grand Rapids: Brazos, 2012); Tony Campolo, *Red Letter Christians: A Citizen's Guide to Faith and Politics* (Ventura, CA: Regal, 2008); and Jim Wallis, *God's Politics: Why the Right Gets It Wrong and the Left Doesn't Get It* (New York: Harper, 2005).

3. Robert D. Putnam and David E. Campbell's *American Grace: How Religion Divides and Unites Us* (New York: Simon & Schuster, 2010) presents social science survey data demonstrating that white millennials who leave evangelicalism often do so mainly because of their political and ethical views: they identify the evangelical Christian tradition with a conservative political movement and intolerance toward gays.

4. Katelyn Beaty, "I Was an Evangelical Magazine Editor, but Now I Can't Defend My Evangelical Community," *Washington Post*, November 14, 2016.

5. Audio recording of James Dobson's prayer at the Intercessors for America conference, January 5, 2018, in "Dr. Dobson Calls for Prayer for the President," Intercessors for America, January 11, 2018, www.ifapray.org/blog/dr-dobson-calls-prayer-president.

6. Kim Hart, "Exclusive Poll: Most Democrats See Republicans as Racist, Sexist," Axios, November 12, 2018, https://www.axios.com/poll-democrats-and-republicans-hate-each -other-racist-ignorant-evil-99ae7afc-5a51-42be-8ee2-3959e43ce320.html; A. W. Geiger and Gretchen Livingston, "8 Facts about Love and Marriage in America," Pew Research Center,

February 13, 2019, https://www.pewresearch.org/fact-tank/2019/02/13/8-facts-about-love -and-marriage.

7. Readers' comments on Keller, "How Do Christians Fit into the Two-Party System?," https://www.nytimes.com/2018/09/29/opinion/sunday/christians-politics-belief.html #commentsContainer.

8. John Piper, "Jesus Died to End Abortion and Racism," *Desiring God*, October 20, 2011, www.desiringgod.org/articles/jesus-died-to-end-abortion-and-racism.

9. For evangelical and historical critiques of Christian nationalism, see John Fea, *Was America Founded as a Christian Nation? A Historical Introduction*, 2nd ed. (Louisville: Westminster John Knox, 2016); John D. Wilsey, *American Exceptionalism and Civil Religion: Reassessing the History of an Idea* (Downers Grove, IL: InterVarsity, 2015).

10. For divorce laws, see J. Herbie DiFonzo, *Beneath the Fault Line: The Popular and Legal Culture of Divorce in Twentieth-Century America* (Charlottesville: University Press of Virginia, 1997). For Prohibition, see W. J. Rorabaugh, *Prohibition: A Concise History* (New York: Oxford University Press, 2018); and Thomas R. Pegram, *Battling Demon Rum: The Struggle for a Dry America, 1800–1933* (New York: Ivan R. Dee, 1998).

11. For a discussion of how Christians should define social justice and why they should pursue it, see Timothy Keller, *Generous Justice: How God's Grace Makes Us Just* (New York: Viking, 2010).

12. This statement is in accordance with chapter 1 of the Westminster Confession of Faith, which affirms both the Old and New Testaments as the supreme "rule of faith and life" and notes the "consent of all the parts" of the complete written word of God. In keeping with this, the Westminster Shorter and Larger Catechisms highlight the Ten Commandments' applicability to modern Christians, since they are where God's "moral law" is "summarily comprehended."

Chapter 1

1. Not all Republicans (and perhaps not even a majority of them) were motivated by a religiously inspired opposition to slavery, but many were. For the influence of evangelical antislavery activism on the Republican Party of the 1850s and early 1860s, see Eric Foner, *Free Soil, Free Labor, Free Men: The Ideology of the Republican Party before the Civil War*, 2nd ed. (New York: Oxford University Press, 1995), 103–48. Foner wrote, "It is well known that the areas of New England settlement were swept in the 1820's and 1830's by a series of religious revivals, which strongly influenced the reformism of the ensuing years. The 'burned-over' districts of upstate New York, the Western Reserve, and other areas became centers of abolitionism in the 1830's, and of radical Republicanism in the 1850's. The evangelical revivalists instilled in them a commitment to reform the evils they saw in society, and fostered a view of the world in which compromise with sin was itself a sin" (*Free Soil*, 108).

2. "Congratulatory Speeches of Edward Everett and Charles Sumner," *The Liberator*, November 18, 1864, www.lincolnandthecivilwar.com. For the role of religion in Americans' understanding of the Civil War and the antislavery cause, see Harry S. Stout, *Upon the Altar of the Nation: A Moral History of the Civil War* (New York: Viking, 2006).

3. Mark Wahlgren Summers, *Rum, Romanism, and Rebellion: The Making of a President, 1884* (Chapel Hill: University of North Carolina Press, 2000), 282–83; Republican Party

platforms of 1880, 1884, and 1888, archived online at the American Presidency Project, https://www.presidency.ucsb.edu/documents.

4. Richard F. Hamilton, *President McKinley, War and Empire* (New Brunswick, NJ: Transaction, 2007), 81. For an analysis of McKinley's Methodist faith, see Gary Scott Smith, *Religion in the Oval Office: The Religious Lives of American Presidents* (New York: Oxford University Press, 2015), 159–95.

5. For a more detailed exposition of these differences, see Andrea L. Turpin, *A New Moral Vision: Gender, Religion, and the Changing Purposes of American Higher Education, 1837–1917* (Ithaca, NY: Cornell University Press, 2016), 14–20.

6. Republican Party Platform of 1928, https://www.presidency.ucsb.edu/documents /republican-party-platform-1928.

7. Republican Party Platform of 1956, https://www.presidency.ucsb.edu/documents /republican-party-platform-1956. For the civil religion of President Eisenhower and conservative Republicans in the 1950s, see Stephen J. Whitfield, *The Culture of the Cold War*, 2nd ed. (Baltimore: Johns Hopkins University Press, 1996), 77–100; and Kevin M. Kruse, *One Nation under God: How Corporate America Invented Christian America* (New York: Basic Books, 2015), 67–93.

8. For white American evangelicals' alliance with the Eisenhower administration and the Republican Party in the 1950s and 1960s, see Daniel K. Williams, *God's Own Party: The Making of the Christian Right* (New York: Oxford University Press, 2010), 11–67. For Eisenhower's view of religion as a bulwark of morality and patriotism in the Cold War, see Gary Scott Smith, *Faith and the Presidency: From George Washington to George W. Bush* (New York: Oxford University Press, 2006), 221–58. For Nixon, see Daniel K. Williams, "Richard Nixon's Religious Right: Catholics, Evangelicals, and the Creation of an Antisecular Alliance," in *The Right Side of the Sixties: Reimagining Conservatism's Decade of Transformation*, ed. Laura Jane Gifford and Daniel K. Williams (New York: Palgrave Macmillan, 2012), 141–58.

9. Joel A. Carpenter, *Revive Us Again: The Reawakening of American Fundamentalism* (New York: Oxford University Press, 1997), 63. For dispensational premillennialists' political conservatism in the early twentieth century, see Matthew Avery Sutton, *American Apocalypse: A History of Modern Evangelicalism* (Cambridge, MA: Harvard University Press, 2014), especially 232–61.

10. George M. Marsden, *Reforming Fundamentalism: Fuller Seminary and the New Evangelicalism* (Grand Rapids: Eerdmans, 1987), 153–61; Williams, *God's Own Party*, 27. For the political views of *Christianity Today* magazine, see Robert Booth Fowler, *A New Engagement: Evangelical Political Thought, 1966–1976* (Grand Rapids: Eerdmans, 1982). For California evangelicals' political conservatism in the early postwar years, see Darren Dochuk, *From Bible Belt to Sunbelt: Plain-Folk Religion, Grassroots Politics, and the Rise of Evangelical Conservatism* (New York: W. W. Norton, 2011).

11. Williams, *God's Own Party*, 26; Whitfield, *Culture of the Cold War*, 83.

12. Roy L. Laurin, "Are 'Reds' Hiding in Our Churches?," *United Evangelical Action*, December 1, 1953, 10; "Ministers Favor Eisenhower 8 to 1," *Christianity Today*, October 29, 1956, 28; "How Will America Vote?," *Christianity Today*, October 24, 1960, 25; AP, "Kennedy Is Attacked," *New York Times*, July 4, 1960.

13. William Martin, *A Prophet with Honor: The Billy Graham Story* (New York: William

Morrow, 1991), 344–48, 422–24; Michael Jay Sider-Rose, "Between Heaven and Earth: Moody Bible Institute and the Politics of the Moderate Christian Right, 1945–1985" (PhD diss., University of Pittsburgh, 2000), 187; "The W.C.C. and Vietnam," *Christianity Today*, March 4, 1966. For one of several examples of J. Edgar Hoover's published editorials in *Christianity Today*, see J. Edgar Hoover, "The Faith of Our Fathers," *Christianity Today*, September 11, 1964.

14. NAE resolutions of 1951, listed in *United Evangelical Action*, July 1, 1951, 6; Republican Party platforms of 1948 and 1956.

15. NAE, Resolution on Human Rights, 1956, www.nae.net/human-rights; Nancy Gibbs and Michael Duffy, *The Preacher and the Presidents: Billy Graham in the White House* (New York: Center Street, 2007), 74–75.

16. "Civil Rights and Christian Concern," *Christianity Today*, May 8, 1964, 28–29; "To Tell the Truth," *Christianity Today*, December 4, 1964, 32; "Murder Is Murder—Anywhere," *Christianity Today*, August 28, 1964, 31.

17. Republican Party platform of 1964, https://www.presidency.ucsb.edu/documents /republican-party-platform-1964. For Graham's call for "law and order," see Williams, *God's Own Party*, 87–88; and Steven P. Miller, *Billy Graham and the Rise of the Republican South* (Philadelphia: University of Pennsylvania Press, 2009). For an analysis of white evangelical opposition to the civil rights movement and complicity in racism, see Jemar Tisby, *The Color of Compromise: The Truth about the American Church's Complicity in Racism* (Grand Rapids: Zondervan, 2019).

18. Republican Party platform of 1964; Mark Galli, "Where We Got It Wrong," *Christianity Today*, December 2018, 27.

19. Book review, *Moody Monthly*, July 1933, 481; Jerry Falwell, *Listen, America!* (Garden City, NY: Doubleday, 1980), 77–78; Robert David Sullivan, "Charitable Giving Is Highest among the Most Religious," *America*, January 7, 2016, https://www.america magazine.org/content/unconventional-wisdom/blue-states-get-dinged-almanac-american -philanthropy.

20. Some of the most thoughtful evangelical proposals for private solutions to the problem of poverty include Marvin Olasky, *The Tragedy of American Compassion* (Wheaton, IL: Crossway, 1992); and Marvin Olasky, *Compassionate Conservatism: What It Is, What It Does, and How It Can Transform America* (New York: Free Press, 2000). For a brief survey of poverty rates since the 1960s, with an analysis that generally suggests the moderate effectiveness of President Lyndon Johnson's antipoverty social welfare programs, see Drew Desilver, "Who's Poor in America? 50 Years into the 'War on Poverty,' a Data Portrait," Pew Research Center, January 13, 2014, www.pewresearch.org/fact-tank/2014/01/13/whos-poor -in-america-50-years-into-the-war-on-poverty-a-data-portrait.

21. Lyman Kellstedt et al., "Faith Transformed: Religion and American Politics from FDR to George W. Bush," in *Religion and American Politics: From the Colonial Period to the Present*, ed. Mark A. Noll and Luke E. Harlow, 2nd ed. (New York: Oxford University Press, 2007), 272–73; *Christianity Today*, December 22, 1972, 39; Harold J. Ockenga, "McGovern vs. Nixon," *Hamilton-Wenham [MA] Chronicle*, November 2, 1972; *Eternity*, January 1973, 7; RNS, "Graham Says Nixon Not in Watergate," *Baptist Standard*, February 16, 1973, 18; Martin, *Prophet with Honor*, 399.

22. Carl F. H. Henry, "Open Letter to President Ford," *Eternity*, January 1976, 22.

23. "Interviews and Issues," *Christianity Today*, October 8, 1976; "Campaign Countdown: 'Bloc Busters,'" *Christianity Today*, October 22, 1976; "The Political Peak Is Also the Brink," *Christianity Today*, November 19, 1976.

24. US Department of Health, Education, and Welfare, *Vital Statistics of the United States, 1965*, vol. 3: *Marriage and Divorce* (Washington, DC, 1968); George A. Akerlof and Janet L. Yellen, "An Analysis of Out-of-Wedlock Births in the United States," Brookings, August 1, 1996, www.brookings.edu/research/an-analysis-of-out-of-wedlock-births-in-the -united-states; John Needham, "Gone with the Sin: Closure of Adult Theater in Santa Ana Reflects Trend Credited to—or Blamed on—the Videocassette Revolution," *Los Angeles Times*, August 14, 1990; Daniel K. Williams, *Defenders of the Unborn: The Pro-Life Movement before Roe v. Wade* (New York: Oxford University Press, 2016), 212; Kenneth L. Woodward, "Born Again! The Evangelicals," *Newsweek*, October 25, 1976, 68–78; "Mobilizing the Moral Majority," *Conservative Digest*, August 1979, 14.

25. Williams, *God's Own Party*, 163–64.

26. For more on these campaigns, see Williams, *God's Own Party*, 133–85.

27. For Falwell's conservative views on free enterprise, as well as social issues, see Daniel K. Williams, "Jerry Falwell's Sunbelt Politics: The Regional Origins of the Moral Majority," *Journal of Policy History* 22 (2010): 125–47.

28. Glenn H. Utter and John W. Storey, *The Religious Right: A Reference Handbook*, 2nd ed. (Santa Barbara, CA: ABC-CLIO, 2001), 12.

29. Kenneth A. Briggs, "Dispute on Religion Raised by Campaign," *New York Times*, November 9, 1980. For evangelicals' alliance with Reagan, see Daniel K. Williams, "Reagan's Religious Right: The Unlikely Alliance between Southern Evangelicals and a California Conservative," in *Ronald Reagan and the 1980s: Perceptions, Policies, Legacies*, ed. Cheryl Hudson and Gareth Davies (New York: Palgrave Macmillan, 2008), 135–49.

30. See Williams, *Defenders of the Unborn*, 244–47, for more on the development of the pro-life movement's judicial strategy.

31. Williams, *God's Own Party*, 207–10.

32. Charles E. Shepard, "Operation Rescue's Mission to Save Itself," *Washington Post*, November 24, 1991; Gayle White, "Falwell Will Lead 'Summit on Rescue' at Omni Hotel in Anti-Abortion Fight," *Atlanta Journal-Constitution*, November 22, 1988; Lorri Denise Booker, "250 Protest Falwell Talk on Abortion," *Atlanta Journal-Constitution*, December 10, 1988. For the influence of Christian contemporary music on young evangelicals' political views in the 1980s, see Eileen Luhr, *Witnessing Suburbia: Conservatives and Christian Youth Culture* (Berkeley: University of California Press, 2009).

33. Stuart Rothenberg, "Anti-Abortion Activist Randall Terry Runs for Congress in N.Y.," CNN, March 24, 1998, https://www.cnn.com/ALLPOLITICS/1998/03/24/spotlight /rothenberg.

34. Paige L. Schneider, "The Impact of the Christian Right Social Movement on Republican Party Development in the South" (PhD diss., Emory University, 2000), 116–17, 140; Christopher Ingraham, "The Stark Racial and Religious Divide between Democrats and Republicans, in One Chart," *Washington Post*, September 6, 2017; David E. Rosenbaum, "G.O.P.'s Moderates Accept an Accord on Abortion Issue," *New York Times*, August 8, 1996; Elisabeth Bumiller, "Palin Disclosures Raise Questions on Vetting," *New York Times*, Sep-

tember 1, 2008; David D. Kirkpatrick, "McCain's Effort to Woo Conservatives Is Paying Off," *New York Times*, September 2, 2008.

35. Republican Party platform of 2016, https://www.presidency.ucsb.edu/documents /2016-republican-party-platform.

36. Pew Research Center, "Attitudes on Same-Sex Marriage," May 14, 2019, www.pew forum.org/fact-sheet/changing-attitudes-on-gay-marriage.

37. NPR, "Abortion Rate Falls to Lowest Level since *Roe v. Wade*," January 17, 2017, www .npr.org/sections/thetwo-way/2017/01/17/509734620/u-s-abortion-rate-falls-to-lowest-level -since-roe-v-wade; Rod Dreher, *The Benedict Option: A Strategy for Christians in a Post-Christian Nation* (New York: Sentinel, 2017).

38. Cal Thomas and Ed Dobson, *Blinded by Might: Can the Religious Right Save America?* (Grand Rapids: Zondervan, 1999).

39. For a historical study of this shift in the Christian Right's goals in the 1990s, see Justin Watson, *The Christian Coalition: Dreams of Restoration, Demands for Recognition* (New York: St. Martin's Press, 1997).

40. "James Dobson: Why I Am Voting for Donald Trump," *Christianity Today*, October 2016. For an analysis of the fears that drove white evangelicals to vote for Trump, see John Fea, *Believe Me: The Evangelical Road to Donald Trump* (Grand Rapids: Eerdmans, 2018).

41. For Harding's escapades, see Barry Hankins, *Jesus and Gin: Evangelicalism, the Roaring Twenties and Today's Culture Wars* (New York: Palgrave Macmillan, 2010), 5–19.

42. CDC, "Number and Percent of Births to Unmarried Women, by Race and Hispanic Origin: United States, 1940–2000," www.cdc.gov/nchs/data/statab/t001x17.pdf; Riley Griffin, "Almost Half of U.S. Births Happen outside Marriage, Signaling Cultural Shift," *Bloomberg News*, October 17, 2018, www.bloomberg.com/news/articles/2018-10-17/almost -half-of-u-s-births-happen-outside-marriage-signaling-cultural-shift.

43. "Oath on the Bible Used by Reagan's Mother," *New York Times*, January 21, 1981.

44. For a history of these warnings, see Andrew R. Murphy, *Prodigal Nation: Moral Decline and Divine Punishment from New England to 9/11* (New York: Oxford University Press, 2009).

45. Fea, *Believe Me*, especially chapter 1, "The Evangelical Politics of Fear."

46. Alec Tyson and Shiva Maniam, "Behind Trump's Victory: Divisions by Race, Gender, Education," Pew Research Center, November 9, 2016, pewresearch.org/fact-tank/2016 /11/09/behind-trumps-victory-divisions-by-race-gender-education.

47. Ross Douthat, "The G.O.P. at a Crossroads," *New York Times*, December 17, 2015.

48. Leo P. Ribuffo, *The Old Christian Right: The Protestant Far Right from the Great Depression to the Cold War* (Philadelphia: Temple University Press, 1983), 80–177.

49. Dan T. Carter, *The Politics of Rage: George Wallace, the Origins of the New Conservatism, and the Transformation of American Politics* (New York: Simon & Schuster, 1995), 424; Lloyd Rohler, *George Wallace: Conservative Populist* (Westport, CT: Praeger, 2004), 97.

50. Anthony M. Orum, "Religion and the Rise of the Radical White: The Case of Southern Wallace Support in 1968," *Social Science Quarterly* 51 (1970): 676; Geoffrey Layman, "Where Is Trump's Base? Not in Church," *Washington Post*, March 29, 2016.

51. Brendan Cole, "Pastor Robert Jeffress Says Trump Is Christian 'Warrior' and Democrats Worship Pagan God Moloch 'Who Allowed for Child Sacrifice,'" *Newsweek*, October 2, 2019.

Chapter 2

1. William Jennings Bryan, "Cross of Gold" speech, July 9, 1896, http://historymatters .gmu.edu/d/5354. For Bryan's evangelicalism and political appeal to other evangelical Protestants, see Michael Kazin, *A Godly Hero: The Life of William Jennings Bryan* (New York: Alfred A. Knopf, 2006).

2. Philip Goff et al., "Introduction," in *The Bible in American Life*, ed. Philip Goff et al. (New York: Oxford University Press, 2017), 14–16.

3. For an engagingly written account of Jackson's life and politics, see H. W. Brands, *Andrew Jackson: His Life and Times* (New York: Doubleday, 2005).

4. Lawrence Frederick Kohl, *The Politics of Individualism: Parties and the American Character in the Jacksonian Era* (New York: Oxford University Press, 1989), 48–49; Harry L. Watson, *Liberty and Power: The Politics of Jacksonian America*, 2nd ed. (New York: Hill and Wang, 2006), 231–53; John Hope Franklin, *The Militant South, 1800–1861*, 2nd ed. (Urbana: University of Illinois Press, 2002), 33–62; Daniel Walker Howe, *What Hath God Wrought: The Transformation of America, 1815–1848* (New York: Oxford University Press, 2007), 435–36, 478–79, 579–86.

5. Kohl, *Politics of Individualism*, 44.

6. Jules Witcover, *Party of the People: A History of the Democrats* (New York: Random House, 2003), 237–357; David Burner, *The Politics of Provincialism: The Democratic Party in Transition, 1918–1932* (New York: Alfred A. Knopf, 1968).

7. Jacob Riis, *How the Other Half Lives: Studies among the Tenements of New York* (repr., Cambridge, MA: Harvard University Press, 1970).

8. Christopher H. Evans, *The Social Gospel in American Religion: A History* (New York: New York University Press, 2017), 78–85; Paul M. Minus, *Walter Rauschenbusch: American Reformer* (New York: Macmillan, 1988).

9. Evans, *Social Gospel in American Religion*, 21–85; Gary Dorrien, *The Making of American Liberal Theology: Imagining Progressive Religion, 1805–1900* (Louisville: Westminster John Knox, 2001), 261–334, especially 311–13; Sydney E. Ahlstrom, *A Religious History of the American People* (New Haven: Yale University Press, 1972), 802–4.

10. Federal Council of Churches of Christ, "The Social Creed of the Churches," December 4, 1908, nationalcouncilofchurches.us/common-witness/1908/social-creed.php.

11. Michael McGerr, *A Fierce Discontent: The Rise and Fall of the Progressive Movement in America, 1870–1920* (New York: Free Press, 2003), 79–104; Evans, *Social Gospel in American Religion*, 48–51; Lewis L. Gould, *Four Hats in the Ring: The 1912 Election and the Birth of Modern American Politics* (Lawrence: University Press of Kansas, 2008), 70, 144.

12. Barry Hankins, *Woodrow Wilson: Ruling Elder, Spiritual President* (New York: Oxford University Press, 2016).

13. Doug Rossinow, *Visions of Progress: The Left-Liberal Tradition in America* (Philadelphia: University of Pennsylvania Press, 2008), 21–28; Alan Brinkley, *The End of Reform: New Deal Liberalism in Recession and War* (New York: Alfred A. Knopf, 1995), 8–11.

14. Franklin D. Roosevelt, Remarks to Visiting Protestant Ministers, January 31, 1938, https://www.presidency.ucsb.edu/documents/remarks-visiting-protestant-ministers -washington-dc.

15. Franklin D. Roosevelt, Second Inaugural Address, January 20, 1937, http://history

matters.gmu.edu/d/5105; Franklin D. Roosevelt, First Inaugural Address, March 4, 1933, http://avalon.law.yale.edu/20th_century/froos1.asp.

16. Eleanor Roosevelt, "The Moral Basis of Democracy" (1940), in *Courage in a Dangerous World: The Political Writings of Eleanor Roosevelt*, ed. Allida M. Black (New York: Columbia University Press, 1999), 50, 58.

17. Franklin D. Roosevelt, address announcing the Second New Deal, October 31, 1936, docs.fdrlibrary.marist.edu/od2ndst.html.

18. James T. Fisher, *Communion of Immigrants: A History of Catholics in America*, 3rd ed. (New York: Oxford University Press, 2008), 94–98; John T. McGreevy, *Catholicism and American Freedom: A History* (New York: W. W. Norton, 2003), 127–65.

19. Samuel Moyn, *Christian Human Rights* (Philadelphia: University of Pennsylvania Press, 2015), 65–100; "Catholics Draft Human-Rights Aim," *New York Times*, February 2, 1947.

20. McGreevy, *Catholicism and American Freedom*, 150–65.

21. *Annual of the Alabama Baptist Convention* (1933), 55; Kenneth K. Bailey, *Southern White Protestantism in the Twentieth Century* (New York: Harper & Row, 1964), 114; Daniel K. Williams, *God's Own Party: The Making of the Christian Right* (New York: Oxford University Press, 2010), 14–38. For northern fundamentalist political conservatism in the early twentieth century and opposition to the New Deal, see Matthew Avery Sutton, *American Apocalypse: A History of Modern Evangelicalism* (Cambridge, MA: Harvard University Press, 2014), especially 232–62.

22. Harry S. Truman, Inaugural Address, January 20, 1949, https://avalon.law.yale.edu/20th_century/truman.asp. For the religious foundation of Truman's view of American foreign policy at the beginning of the Cold War, see William Inboden, *Religion and American Foreign Policy, 1945–1960: The Soul of Containment* (New York: Cambridge University Press, 2008), especially 105–56.

23. Kevin M. Schultz, *Tri-Faith America: How Catholics and Jews Held Postwar America to Its Protestant Promise* (New York: Oxford University Press, 2011), 15–96.

24. David L. Chappell, "Religious Revivalism in the Civil Rights Movement," *African American Review* 36 (2002): 581–95.

25. For a study of the young liberal Protestant ministers who embraced the civil rights and antiwar movements in the 1960s, see Michael B. Friedland, *Lift Up Your Voice Like a Trumpet: White Clergy and the Civil Rights and Antiwar Movements, 1954–1973* (Chapel Hill: University of North Carolina Press, 1998).

26. For the connection between liberal Protestant Christianity and the secular left in the 1960s, see Doug Rossinow, *The Politics of Authenticity: Liberalism, Christianity, and the New Left in America* (New York: Columbia University Press, 1998).

27. Mark A. Lempke, *My Brother's Keeper: George McGovern and Progressive Christianity* (Amherst: University of Massachusetts Press, 2017); Randall Balmer, *Redeemer: The Life of Jimmy Carter* (New York: Basic Books, 2014); Jimmy Carter, *Faith: A Journey for All* (New York: Simon & Schuster, 2018); David Harris, "Understanding Mondale," *New York Times*, June 19, 1983; Peter Steinfels, "Beliefs: In a Wide-Ranging Talk, Al Gore Reveals the Evangelical and Intellectual Roots of His Faith," *New York Times*, May 29, 1999; Barack Obama, *The Audacity of Hope: Thoughts on Reclaiming the American Dream* (New York: Crown, 2006), 195–226; Katherine Weber, "Hillary Clinton Shares Why She Likes

Methodist Church, Talks about Social Gospel," *Christian Post*, April 29, 2014, https://www
.christianpost.com/news/hillary-clinton-shares-why-she-likes-methodist-church-talks
-about-social-gospel.html.

28. Frances Stead Sellers and John Wagner, "Why Bernie Sanders Doesn't Participate
in Organized Religion," *Washington Post*, January 27, 2016. For Carter's values and commitment to pluralism, see Carter, *Faith*, 18–21.

29. Jessica Martinez and Gregory A. Smith, "How the Faithful Voted: A Preliminary
2016 Analysis," Pew Research Center, November 9, 2016, https://www.pewresearch.org
/fact-tank/2016/11/09/how-the-faithful-voted-a-preliminary-2016-analysis; Elizabeth Po-
drebarac Sciupac and Gregory A. Smith, "How Religious Groups Voted in the Midterm
Elections," Pew Research Center, November 7, 2018, https://www.pewresearch.org/fact
-tank/2018/11/07/how-religious-groups-voted-in-the-midterm-elections; Gregory A. Smith,
"Among White Evangelicals, Regular Churchgoers Are the Most Supportive of Trump,"
Pew Research Center, April 26, 2017, https://www.pewresearch.org/fact-tank/2017/04/26
/among-white-evangelicals-regular-churchgoers-are-the-most-supportive-of-trump.

30. Frank Newport, "Church Attendance and Party Identification," Gallup, May 18,
2005, https://news.gallup.com/poll/16381/church-attendance-party-identification.aspx.

31. For black Christian political theology and the black church's use of the Exodus narrative, see Gary S. Selby, *Martin Luther King and the Rhetoric of Freedom: The Exodus Narrative
in America's Struggle for Civil Rights* (Waco, TX: Baylor University Press, 2008); Howard
Thurman, *Jesus and the Disinherited*, 2nd ed. (Boston: Beacon, 1996); J. Deotis Roberts,
A Black Political Theology (Louisville: Westminster John Knox, 1974); Albert J. Raboteau,
Canaan Land: A Religious History of African Americans (New York: Oxford University Press,
1999).

32. Cleve R. Wootson Jr., "Rev. William Barber Builds a Moral Movement," *Washington
Post*, June 29, 2017.

33. Martinez and Smith, "How the Faithful Voted."

34. Mark Pattison, "On Abortion, Hispanic and White Catholics Differ in Their Views,"
America, August 13, 2019, americamagazine.org/politics-society/2019/08/13/abortion
-hispanic-and-white-catholics-differ-their-views; Stephen Beale, "Polls: Most Latino Catholics Lean Democrat," *National Catholic Register*, October 21, 2016.

35. Kayla Fontenot, Jessica Semega, and Melissa Kollar, "Income and Poverty in the
United States: 2017," United States Census Bureau, September 2018, www.census.gov
/content/dam/Census/library/publications/2018/demo/p60-263.pdf; Angela Hanks,
Danyelle Solomon, and Christian E. Weller, "Systematic Inequality: How America's Structural Racism Created the Black-White Wealth Gap," Center for American Progress, February 21, 2018, www.americanprogress.org/issues/race/reports/2018/02/21/447051/systematic
-inequality.

36. The figure of two thousand Bible verses on poverty and social justice comes from
Sojourners, sojo.net/sites/default/files/2000verses.pdf.

37. United States Conference of Catholic Bishops, "Forming Consciences for Faithful Citizenship," 2015, www.usccb.org/issues-and-action/faithful-citizenship/forming
-consciences-for-faithful-citizenship-title.cfm.

38. United States Conference of Catholic Bishops, "Forming Consciences for Faithful
Citizenship," 2015.

39. "Dozens of Nuns, Other Catholics Arrested Advocating for Immigrants," Religion News Service, February 27, 2018, religionnews.com/2018/02/27/dozens-of-nuns-other -catholics-arrested-advocating-for-immigrants; "Detaining Migrant Children 'Immoral and Inhumane,' Says Catholic Group Joining Lawsuit," *Catholic World Report*, January 27, 2019, www.catholicworldreport.com/2019/01/27/detaining-migrant-children-immoral -and-inhumane-says-catholic-group-joining-lawsuit; Julia Jacobs, "U.S. Says It Could Take 2 Years to Identify up to Thousands of Separated Immigrant Families," *New York Times*, April 6, 2019.

40. George Gallup Jr., "Public Closely Divided on Abortion Issue," Gallup Poll, March 18, 1976; Daniel K. Williams, *Defenders of the Unborn: The Pro-Life Movement before Roe v. Wade* (New York: Oxford University Press, 2016), 227–29.

41. Democratic Party Platform of 1980, presidency.ucsb.edu/documents/1980-demo cratic-party-platform; United Church of Christ, Tenth General Synod, "A Pronouncement: Civil Liberties without Discrimination Related to Affectional or Sexual Preference," June 27–July 2, 1975, http://d3n8a8pro7vhmx.cloudfront.net/unitedchurchofchrist/legacy_url /6047/1975-A-PRONOUNCEMENT-CIVIL-LIBERTIES-WITHOUT-DISCRIMINATION.pdf ?1418430279.

42. Michael Sean Winters, *Left at the Altar: How the Democrats Lost the Catholics and How the Catholics Can Save the Democrats* (New York: Basic Books, 2008).

43. Jonathan V. Last, "Weekly Standard: Obamacare vs. the Catholics," NPR, February 7, 2012, npr.org/2012/02/07/146511839/weekly-standard-obamacare-vs-the-catholics; *Burwell v. Hobby Lobby Stores* 573 US 682 (2014), oyez.org/cases/2013/13-354.

44. Democratic Party Platform of 2016, presidency.ucsb.edu/documents/2016-demo cratic-party-platform.

45. Jonathan Martin, "Canceled Fund-Raiser Prompts a Question: Can a Democrat Oppose Abortion?," *New York Times*, May 22, 2019.

46. Dave Andrusko, "Pro-Life Democrats Fight Uphill Battle in Congress," *National Right to Life News*, April 28, 1992; Ruth Graham, "This Could Be the End of the Road for Pro-Life Democrats in Congress," *Slate*, November 7, 2018, https://slate.com/news-and-politics/2018 /11/joe-donnelly-pro-life-democrats-congress-midterms.html.

47. Democratic Party Platform of 2000, presidency.ucsb.edu/documents/2000-demo cratic-party-platform.

48. Democratic Party Platform of 2008, presidency.ucsb.edu/documents/2008-demo cratic-party-platform.

49. "Abortion Trends by Party Identification," Gallup, news.gallup.com/poll/246278 /abortion-trends-party.aspx. Survey data on Democratic voters' opinions on abortion comes from 2019 Gallup polls. For views on abortion from the contenders for the 2020 Democratic presidential nomination, see Maggie Astor, "How the 2020 Democrats Responded to an Abortion Survey," *New York Times*, November 25, 2019.

50. Pew Research Center, "Religious Landscape Study: Democrats and Democratic Leaners Who Identify as Black," https://www.pewforum.org/religious-landscape-study /racial-and-ethnic-composition/black/party-affiliation/democrat-lean-dem; Pew Research Center, "Religious Landscape Study: Democrats and Democratic Leaners Who Identify as White," https://www.pewforum.org/religious-landscape-study/racial-and-ethnic

-composition/white/party-affiliation/democrat-lean-dem; Martinez and Smith, "How the Faithful Voted."

51. Ron Sider, "Ron Sider: Why I Am Voting for Hillary Clinton," *Christianity Today*, October 2016, 54. Sider said that he had voted for George W. Bush, but in 2016 he was so strongly opposed to Donald Trump that he endorsed Hillary Clinton, despite believing that the Democratic Party platform was "wrong on abortion—period."

52. "Transcript of Speech by Clinton Accepting Democratic Nomination," *New York Times*, July 17, 1992.

53. J. Peter Nixon, "What Is Subsidiarity?," *U.S. Catholic*, September 2018, 49; Pontifical Council for Justice and Peace, "Compendium of the Social Doctrine of the Church: Chapter Four," 2004, catholicculture.org/culture/library/view.cfm?id=7214#PartIV.

Chapter 3

1. The National Right to Life Committee predicted in early June 1992 that *Roe v. Wade* would be overturned within a year ("Bush Loses: A Horror Story for 1992," *National Right to Life News*, June 23, 1992, 6). Instead, the Supreme Court reaffirmed the main tenets of *Roe* in *Planned Parenthood v. Casey* later that month.

2. Robert P. Jones, "Committed to Availability, Conflicted about Morality," PRRI, June 9, 2011, prri.org/research/committed-to-availability-conflicted-about-morality-what-the -millennial-generation-tells-us-about-the-future-of-the-abortion-debate-and-the-culture -wars.

3. Pew Research Center, "Public Opinion on Abortion: Views on Abortion, 1995–2018," October 15, 2018, www.pewforum.org/fact-sheet/public-opinion-on-abortion; David Masci, "American Religious Groups Vary Widely in Their Views of Abortion," Pew Research Center, January 22, 2018, www.pewresearch.org/fact-tank/2018/01/22/american-religious -groups-vary-widely-in-their-views-of-abortion.

4. For ancient Christian denunciations of abortion, see Didache 2 ("You shall not murder a child by abortion nor kill that which is born"); Barnabas 19:5 (which uses nearly identical language as the Didache); Athenagoras of Athens, *A Plea for the Christians* 35, trans. B. B. Pratten ("And when we say that those women who use drugs to bring on abortion commit murder, and will have to give an account to God for the abortion, on what principle should we commit murder? For it does not belong to the same person to regard the very foetus in the womb as a created being, and therefore an object of God's care, and when it has passed into life, to kill it"); Tertullian, *Apology* 9.8, trans. S. Thelwall ("In our case, murder being once for all forbidden, we may destroy even the foetus in the womb, while as yet the human being derives blood from other parts of the body for its sustenance. To hinder a birth is merely a speedier man-killing, nor does it matter whether you take away a life that is born, or destroy one that is coming to the birth. That is a man which is going to be one; you have the fruit already in its seed"). For a thoughtful historical analysis of medieval scholastic and early modern Catholic opinion about ensoulment and the beginning of human personhood, see John R. Connery, *Abortion: The Development of the Roman Catholic Perspective* (Chicago: Loyola University Press, 1977); and David Albert Jones, *The Soul of the Embryo: An Enquiry into the Status of the Human Embryo in the Christian Tradition* (London: Continuum, 2004).

5. Martin Luther, "Lectures on Genesis," chapter 25, in *Luther's Works*, ed. Jaroslav

Pelikan, vol. 4 (St. Louis: Concordia, 1964); John Calvin, Commentary on Exodus 21:22, in *The John Calvin Bible Commentaries: The Harmony of the Law*, vol. 3: *Commentaries on the Four Last Books of Moses*, trans. Charles William Bingham (reprint edition, CreateSpace, 2015).

6. Ted Olsen, "From Jesus to Mary and Back Again: The History of the Annunciation," Christian History website of *Christianity Today*, March 2010, www.christianitytoday .com/history/2010/march/from-jesus-to-mary-and-back-again-history-of-annunciation .html.

7. For the scientific and philosophical case for the right to life from the moment of conception, see Robert P. George and Christopher Tollefsen, *Embryo: A Defense of Human Life* (New York: Doubleday, 2008); and Francis J. Beckwith, *Defending Life: A Moral and Legal Case against Abortion Choice* (New York: Cambridge University Press, 2007).

8. For an early expression of this argument, see Lester Kinsolving, "Therapeutic Abortion—Past and Current Views," *San Francisco Chronicle*, April 2, 1966. This argument has been repeated in numerous pro-choice sources. For a recent reiteration of it aimed for an evangelical audience, see Jonathan Dudley, *Broken Words: The Abuse of Science and Faith in American Politics* (New York: Crown, 2011).

9. For a more detailed discussion of this history, see Daniel K. Williams, *Defenders of the Unborn: The Pro-Life Movement before Roe v. Wade* (New York: Oxford University Press, 2016).

10. For liberal Protestants' endorsement of contraception in the mid-twentieth century, see Tom Davis, *Sacred Work: Planned Parenthood and Its Clergy Alliances* (New Brunswick, NJ: Rutgers University Press, 2005). For their new openness to women in senior ministry positions, see Alan Petigny, *The Permissive Society, 1941–1965* (New York: Cambridge University Press, 2009). For the liberal Protestant emphasis on social justice and structural sin in the 1960s, see Michael B. Friedland, *Lift Up Your Voice Like a Trumpet: White Clergy and the Civil Rights and Antiwar Movements, 1954–1973* (Chapel Hill: University of North Carolina Press, 1998). For Fletcher's ideas and changing views of sexual ethics and morality in general among liberal Protestants in the 1960s, see Heather R. White, *Reforming Sodom: Protestants and the Rise of Gay Rights* (Chapel Hill: University of North Carolina Press, 2015), 117–19.

11. American Baptist Convention, Resolution on Abortion, May 1968; United Presbyterian Church in the USA, Resolution on Abortion, 1970; General Conference of the United Methodist Church, Resolution on Abortion, April 1970; United Church of Christ, "Freedom of Choice Concerning Abortion: A Proposal for Action Adopted by the Eighth General Synod," June 29, 1971; Pew Research Center, "Views about Abortion among Mainline Protestants by Religious Denomination" (2014), https://www.pewforum.org/religious -landscape-study/compare/views-about-abortion/by/religious-denomination/among /religious-tradition/mainline-protestant.

12. John R. Rice, "The Murder of the Helpless Unborn," *Sword of the Lord*, October 22, 1971; RNS, "The Supreme Court's Decision on Abortion: Dr. Criswell Says He Agrees with It," *Baptist Bible Tribune*, February 16, 1973, 1; "A Protestant Affirmation on the Control of Human Reproduction," *Christianity Today*, November 8, 1968, 18; Billy Graham, "Any Abortion Method Violation of God's Law," *Atlanta Constitution*, November 27, 1972; Carl F. H. Henry, "Is Life Ever Cheap?," *Eternity*, February 1971, 20–21; National Association of

Evangelicals, Resolution on Abortion, 1973; L. Nelson Bell, "An Alternative to Abortion," *Christianity Today*, June 18, 1971, 17. For a detailed history of evangelical debates about contraception and abortion, see Allan C. Carlson, *Godly Seed: American Evangelicals Confront Birth Control, 1873–1973* (New York: Transaction, 2011). For a Reformed evangelical rebuttal to a pro-choice interpretation of Exodus 21:22, see Presbyterian Church in America, Report of the Ad Interim Committee on Abortion, 1978, http://pcahistory.org/pca/studies/2-015 .html.

13. For evangelicals' cautious endorsements of limited abortion liberalization bills in the late 1960s, see S. I. McMillen, "Abortion: Is It Moral?," *Christian Life*, September 1967, 50, 53; Nancy Hardesty, "Should Anyone Who Wants an Abortion Have One?," *Eternity*, June 1967, 32–34; Robert D. Visscher, "Therapeutic Abortion: Blessing or Murder?," *Christianity Today*, September 27, 1968, 6–8; and "A Protestant Affirmation on the Control of Human Reproduction," *Christianity Today*, November 8, 1968, 18. All of these articles opposed "abortion on demand" but cautiously accepted the legitimacy of abortion in cases of medical necessity. For examples of the hardening of evangelical opinion against abortion in reaction to the legalization of elective abortion at the beginning of the 1970s, see "The War on the Womb," *Christianity Today*, June 5, 1970, 24–25; Bell, "Alternative to Abortion"; and Henry, "Is Life Ever Cheap?" For *Christianity Today*'s opposition to *Roe*, see "Abortion and the Court," *Christianity Today*, February 16, 1973, 33.

14. Southern Baptist Convention, Resolution on Abortion, 1971; SBC, Resolution on Abortion, 1974. In 1976, the Southern Baptist Convention shifted away from its moderate position on abortion by adopting a resolution declaring that all abortions "terminate the life of an innocent human being" (SBC, Resolution on Abortion, 1976). In 1980, the convention endorsed a "constitutional amendment prohibiting abortion except to save the life of the mother" (SBC, Resolution on Abortion, 1980). For Carl Henry's political priorities in 1976 (which included abortion, but not necessarily as the most urgent political cause), see Carl F. H. Henry, "An Open Letter to President Ford," *Eternity*, January 1976, 23.

15. Jesse L. Jackson, "How We Respect Life Is Over-Riding Moral Issue," *National Right to Life News*, January 1977; Louise Lague, "Youth Pro-Life Rally Has Anti-Abortion Theme," *Washington Star*, September 4, 1972; Norman McCarthy, "Monument Rally Stresses Rights of the Unborn," *Catholic Standard*, September 7, 1972.

16. Williams, *Defenders of the Unborn*, 156–74, 205.

17. "The Kennedy Who Could Be President (If She Weren't a Woman)," *Ladies Home Journal*, March 1976; James M. Perry, "Shriver Falls Victim to His Own Church," *National Observer*, January 31, 1976.

18. "Abortion Ruling Praised, Rapped," *Lancaster (PA) New Era*, January 24, 1973; "30,000 at Life Rally in St. Louis," *National Right to Life News*, November 1973, 2.

19. Williams, *Defenders of the Unborn*, 219–29, 244–47.

20. Francis A. Schaeffer, *How Should We Then Live? The Rise and Decline of Western Thought and Culture* (Westchester, IL: Crossway, 1976), 223.

21. For the beginning of the pro-life judicial strategy, see Williams, *Defenders of the Unborn*, 245–46; and Mary Ziegler, *After Roe: The Lost History of the Abortion Debate* (Cambridge, MA: Harvard University Press, 2015).

22. For evidence of this, see David N. O'Steen, "A National Referendum on Abortion," National Right to Life Committee, www.nrlpac.org. O'Steen, executive director of the Na-

tional Right to Life PAC, declared that "the right to life side won" with Donald Trump's election in 2016.

23. For this view, see Adam Liptak, "Alabama Aims Squarely at *Roe*, but the Supreme Court May Prefer Glancing Blows," *New York Times*, May 15, 2019.

24. Rachel K. Jones, Elizabeth Witwer, and Jenna Jerman, "Abortion Incidence and Service Availability in the United States, 2017," Guttmacher Institute Report, September 2019, https://www.guttmacher.org/report/abortion-incidence-service-availability-us-2017; CDC, Abortion Surveillance 1975 (April 1977), 7.

25. Rebecca Harrington and Skye Gould, "The Number of Abortion Clinics in the US Has Plunged in the Last Decade—Here's How Many Are in Each State," *Business Insider*, February 10, 2017.

26. Moira Gaul and Mai W. Bean, "A Half Century of Hope, A Legacy of Life and Love: Pregnancy Center Service Report, Third Edition," Charlotte Lozier Institute, September 5, 2018, lozierinstitute.org/a-half-century-of-hope-a-legacy-of-life-and-love.

27. Richard Glasgow, "Pro-Abortionists Fret over Possible Medicaid Switch," *National Right to Life News*, June 24, 1982, 12; Guttmacher Institute, "Medicaid Funding of Abortion," February 2018, www.guttmacher.org/evidence-you-can-use/medicaid-funding -abortion.

28. Maggie Astor, "What Is the Hyde Amendment? A Look at Its Impact as Biden Reverses His Stance," *New York Times*, June 7, 2019.

29. Kate Bahn and Jamila Taylor, "The Hyde Amendment Punishes Poor Women—and It's Bad for the Economy," *Nation*, September 30, 2016.

30. "Induced Abortion in the United States," Guttmacher Institute, January 2018, https://www.guttmacher.org/fact-sheet/induced-abortion-united-states; Jenna Jerman, Rachel K. Jones, and Tsuyoshi Onda, "Characteristics of U.S. Abortion Patients in 2014 and Changes Since 2008," Guttmacher Institute Report, May 2016, www.guttmacher.org /report/characteristics-us-abortion-patients-2014.

31. Sophia Chae et al., "Reasons Why Women Have Induced Abortions: A Synthesis of Findings from 14 Countries," *Contraception* 96 (2017): 233–41.

32. "Testimonies: I Remember Everything," Silent No More Awareness, www.silentno moreawareness.org/testimonies/testimony.aspx?ID=3994.

33. Frederica Mathewes-Green, "Seeking Abortion's Middle Ground," *Washington Post*, July 28, 1996.

34. Open Data Network, Percent Uninsured in Mississippi, www.opendatanetwork .com.

35. Center for American Progress, Talk Poverty: Poverty Data for Mississippi, 2018, https://talkpoverty.org/state-year-report/mississippi-2018-report.

36. Gaby Galvin, "Abortions Down 24 Percent in U.S.," *US News & World Report*, November 21, 2018, www.usnews.com/news/healthiest-communities/articles/2018-11-21 /abortions-down-24-percent-over-a-decade-in-us.

37. Joyce A. Martin et al., "Births: Final Data for 2017," *National Vital Statistics Reports*, November 7, 2018, https://www.cdc.gov/nchs/data/nvsr/nvsr67/nvsr67_08-508.pdf.

38. William Julius Wilson, *The Declining Significance of Race* (Chicago: University of Chicago Press, 1978). See also William Julius Wilson, *When Work Disappears: The World of the New Urban Poor* (New York: Alfred A. Knopf, 1996).

39. W. Bradford Wilcox, "The Marriage Divide: How and Why Working-Class Families Are More Fragile Today," Institute for Family Studies, September 25, 2017, https://ifstudies.org/blog/the-marriage-divide-how-and-why-working-class-families-are-more-fragile-today.

40. Corinne H. Rocca and Cynthia C. Harper, "Do Racial and Ethnic Differences in Contraceptive Attitudes and Knowledge Explain Disparities in Method Use?," *Perspectives on Sexual and Reproductive Health* 44.3 (September 2012): 150–58; Christine Dehlendorf and Kelsey Holt, "The Dangerous Rise of the IUD as Poverty Cure," *New York Times*, January 2, 2019. For a study of why poor women view single motherhood in a more positive light than more economically affluent women do, see Kathryn Edin and Maria Kefalas, *Promises I Can Keep: Why Poor Women Put Motherhood before Marriage* (Berkeley: University of California Press, 2005).

41. For evidence of this, see Matthew Connelly, *Fatal Misconception: The Struggle to Control World Population* (Cambridge, MA: Harvard University Press, 2008).

42. Amanda J. Stevenson et al., "Effect of Removal of Planned Parenthood from the Texas Women's Health Program," *New England Journal of Medicine* 374 (2016): 853.

43. See, for instance, Edin and Kefalis, *Promises I Can Keep*.

44. US Bureau of the Census, "Estimated Median Age at First Marriage, by Sex: 1890 to Present" (2004), www.census.gov/population/socdemo/hh-fam/tabMS-2.pdf; US Bureau of the Census, "Median Age at First Marriage: 1890 to Present," www.census.gov/content/dam/Census/library/visualizations/time-series/demo/families-and-households/ms-2.pdf; Derek Thompson, "How America's Marriage Crisis Makes Income Inequality So Much Worse," *Atlantic*, October 1, 2013; Kim Parker and Renee Stepler, "As U.S. Marriage Rate Hovers at 50%, Education Gap in Marital Status Widens," Pew Research Center, September 14, 2017, https://www.pewresearch.org/fact-tank/2017/09/14/as-u-s-marriage-rate-hovers-at-50-education-gap-in-marital-status-widens.

45. Denise Grady, "Medical Nuances Drove 'No' Vote in Mississippi," *New York Times*, November 14, 2011.

46. Jilian Mincer, "Exclusive: Abortion by Prescription Now Rivals Surgery for U.S. Women," Reuters, October 31, 2016, https://www.reuters.com/article/us-usa-health care-abortion-exclusive/exclusive-abortion-by-prescription-now-rivals-surgery-for-u-s -women-idUSKBN12V0CC; Michelle Oberman, *Her Body, Our Laws: On the Front Lines of the Abortion War, from El Salvador to Oklahoma* (Boston: Beacon, 2018).

47. "Abortion Rates by Race and Ethnicity," Guttmacher Institute, October 19, 2017, guttmacher.org/infographic/2017/abortion-rates-race-and-ethnicity.

Chapter 4

1. "FRC Hosts Leading Pro-Family Voices in Nationwide Broadcast to Protect Marriage," PR Newswire, May 24, 2004; David Kelly, "In Colorado, a Wellspring of Conservative Christianity," *Los Angeles Times*, July 6, 2004; Esther Kaplan, "Onward Christian Soldiers," *Nation*, July 5, 2004; AP, "Church Coalition Resists Marriage Law," *[Salt Lake City] Deseret News*, June 6, 2004.

2. Sunnivie Brydum, "Ted Haggard Says Same-Sex Marriage Should Be Legal in States," *Advocate*, October 19, 2012.

3. Janet E. Rosenbaum and Byron Weathersbee, "True Love Waits: Do Southern Bap-

tists? Premarital Sexual Behavior among Newly Married Southern Baptist Sunday School Students," *Journal of Religion and Health* 52 (2013): 263–75; NAE, "Sexual Activity," from Grey Matter Research, "Sex & Unexpected Pregnancies: What Evangelical Millennials Think and Practice," May 2012, http://nae.net/wp-content/uploads/2015/05/Data-Sheet-1 _Sexual-Activity.pdf.

4. "How Common Is Pastoral Indiscretion?," *Leadership Journal*, Winter 1988.

5. Aaron Randle, "Who Watches the Most Porn? Not Kansas Anymore," *Kansas City Star*, January 31, 2018.

6. The theology in this section is taken primarily from Timothy Keller with Kathy Keller, *The Meaning of Marriage: Facing the Complexities of Commitment with the Wisdom of God* (New York: Dutton, 2011).

7. Robert Hill, "The Home, the Key to the Situation," *Moody Monthly*, November 1928, 104.

8. Daniel K. Williams, *God's Own Party: The Making of the Christian Right* (New York: Oxford University Press, 2010), 24.

9. "Sex O'Clock in America," *Current Opinion*, July 1913, 113.

10. Gaines M. Foster, *Moral Reconstruction: Christian Lobbyists and the Federal Legislation of Morality, 1865–1920* (Chapel Hill: University of North Carolina Press, 2002), 47–71.

11. *Reynolds v. United States*, 98 US 145 (1879).

12. Robert L. Griswold, *Family and Divorce in California, 1850–1890: Victorian Illusions and Everyday Realities* (Albany: State University of New York Press, 1982), 18–19; Elaine Tyler May, *Great Expectations: Marriage and Divorce in Post-Victorian America* (Chicago: University of Chicago Press, 1980), 26–48; United States Bureau of the Census, *Marriage and Divorce, 1867–1906, Part I: Summary, Laws, Foreign Statistics* (Washington, DC: Government Printing Office, 1909), 22.

13. Beth L. Bailey, *From Front Porch to Back Seat: Courtship in Twentieth-Century America* (Baltimore: Johns Hopkins University Press, 1988), 77–96; William E. Leuchtenberg, *The Perils of Prosperity, 1914–32*, 2nd ed. (Chicago: University of Chicago Press, 1993), 171; William H. Chafe, *The Paradox of Change: American Women in the 20th Century* (New York: Oxford University Press, 1991), 105.

14. Gary Dean Best, *The Dollar Decade: Mammon and the Machine in 1920s America* (Westport, CT: Praeger, 2003), 47–48.

15. May, *Great Expectations*; US Department of Health, Education, and Welfare, "100 Years of Marriage and Divorce Statistics, United States, 1867–1967" (Rockville, MD: National Center for Health Statistics, December 1973), https://stacks.cdc.gov/view/cdc/12831.

16. Beth Bailey, *Sex in the Heartland* (Cambridge, MA: Harvard University Press, 1999), 68–69. For an analysis of the discrepancy between rapidly liberalizing social norms and more conservative laws in the 1950s, see Alan Petigny, *The Permissive Society: America, 1941–1965* (New York: Cambridge University Press, 2009), especially 100–133.

17. Robert O. Self, *All in the Family: The Realignment of American Democracy since the 1960s* (New York: Hill and Wang, 2012), 18; James T. Patterson, *America's Struggle against Poverty in the Twentieth Century*, rev. ed. (Cambridge, MA: Harvard University Press, 2000), 66–67.

18. "U.S. Court Upsets Ban on 'Playboy,'" *New York Times*, October 31, 1958.

19. The tension between permissive personal sexual mores and more conservative public norms in the late 1940s and 1950s is a central theme of Petigny's *Permissive Society*.

20. Carrie Pitzulo, *Bachelors and Bunnies: The Sexual Politics of Playboy* (Chicago: University of Chicago Press, 2011); Nicolaus Mills, "Gloria Steinem's 'A Bunny's Tale'—50 Years Later," Guardian, May 26, 2013; Ruth Rosen, *The World Split Open: How the Modern Women's Movement Changed America* (New York: Penguin, 2000), 94–140; Betty Friedan, *The Feminine Mystique* (repr., New York: W. W. Norton, 1997), 166–94.

21. Donald T. Critchlow, *Phyllis Schlafly and Grassroots Conservatism: A Woman's Crusade* (Princeton: Princeton University Press, 2005), 212–32.

22. Bailey, *Sex in the Heartland*, 119; George H. Gallup, *The Gallup Poll: Public Opinion, 1972–1977* (Wilmington, DE: Scholarly Resources, 1978), 1:492.

23. *Griswold v. Connecticut*, 381 US 479 (1965); *Eisenstadt v. Baird*, 405 US 438 (1972); George H. Gallup Jr., "Current Views on Premarital, Extramarital Sex," Gallup, June 24, 2003, https://news.gallup.com/poll/8704/current-views-premarital-extramarital-sex.aspx. For changes in university campus regulations, see Bailey, *Sex in the Heartland*. For changes in the views of mainline Protestant ministers and denominations, see R. Marie Griffith, *Moral Combat: How Sex Divided American Christians and Fractured American Politics* (New York: Basic Books, 2017).

24. Jason DeParle, "Beyond the Legal Right," *Washington Monthly*, April 1989. For a liberal Protestant evaluation of changing sexual standards in the mid-1960s, see Harvey Cox, *The Secular City*, rev. ed. (Princeton: Princeton University Press, 2013), 227–56.

25. William Serrin, "Sex Is a Growing Multibillion Business," *New York Times*, February 9, 1981; Diana E. H. Russell, *Dangerous Relationships: Pornography, Misogyny, and Rape* (Thousand Oaks, CA: Sage, 1998), 100; Judith A. Reisman, "Child Pornography in Erotic Magazines, Social Awareness, and Self-Censorship," in *Media, Children, and the Family: Social Scientific, Psychodynamic, and Clinical Perspectives*, ed. Dolf Zillman, Jennings Bryant, and Aletha C. Huston (repr., New York: Routledge, 2009), chapter 20. For a critical analysis of the sexual revolution's dehumanization of people, see Mary Eberstadt, *Adam and Eve after the Pill: Paradoxes of the Sexual Revolution* (San Francisco: Ignatius, 2012).

26. For a concise overview of the sexualized culture of the 1970s, see James T. Patterson, *Restless Giant: The United States from Watergate to Bush v. Gore* (New York: Oxford University Press, 2005), 45–51.

27. Thomas Borstelmann, *The 1970s: A New Global History from Civil Rights to Economic Inequality* (Princeton: Princeton University Press, 2012), 89; *Vital Statistics of the United States, 1965*, vol. 3: *Marriage and Divorce*, Table 2-1; *Vital Statistics of the United States, 1969*, vol. 3: *Marriage and Divorce*, Table 2-2. For the argument that liberalized social attitudes toward divorce preceded divorce law liberalization, see J. Herbie DiFonzo, *Beneath the Fault Line: The Popular and Legal Culture of Divorce in Twentieth-Century America* (Charlottesville: University Press of Virginia, 1997).

28. W. Bradford Wilcox, "The Evolution of Divorce," *National Affairs*, Fall 2009.

29. "Advance Report of Final Divorce Statistics, 1988," *Monthly Vital Statistics Report* 39.12 (May 21, 1991): 15, https://www.cdc.gov/nchs/data/mvsr/supp/mv39_12s2.pdf. For changes in American attitudes between the 1950s and the 1970s, see Kristin Celello, *Making Marriage Work: A History of Marriage and Divorce in the Twentieth-Century United States* (Chapel Hill: University of North Carolina Press, 2009), 72–132.

30. Gallup, "Gay and Lesbian Rights," https://news.gallup.com/poll/1651/gay-lesbian -rights.aspx.

31. Margot Canaday, *The Straight State: Sexuality and Citizenship in Twentieth-Century America* (Princeton: Princeton University Press, 2009).

32. ACLU, "Getting Rid of Sodomy Laws: History and Strategy That Led to the Lawrence Decision," www.aclu.org/getting-rid-sodomy-laws-history-and-strategy-led-lawrence -decision; Dudley Clendinen and Adam Nagourney, *Out for Good: The Struggle to Build a Gay Rights Movement in America* (New York: Simon & Schuster, 1999).

33. Gallup, "Gay and Lesbian Rights."

34. For a history of the legal battle over same-sex marriage, see Michael J. Klarman, *From the Closet to the Altar: Courts, Backlash, and the Struggle for Same-Sex Marriage* (New York: Oxford University Press, 2013).

35. For this argument, see Sherif Girgis et al., *What Is Marriage? Man and Woman: A Defense* (New York: Encounter Books, 2012).

36. "When Charles Stanley's Marriage Ended, Prayer Was His Lifeline," *Christianity Today* podcast, September 28, 2016, https://www.christianitytoday.com/ct/2016/september -web-only/charles-stanley.html.

37. Ed Anderson, "Covenant Marriages Get an 'I Don't' from Louisiana Couples," *New Orleans Times-Picayune*, August 10, 2009.

38. David J. Ayers, "Sex and the Single Evangelical," Institute for Family Studies, August 14, 2019, https://ifstudies.org/blog/sex-and-the-single-evangelical.

39. The most popular titles in this genre include Marabel Morgan, *The Total Woman* (Old Tappan, NJ: Fleming H. Revell, 1973); and Tim and Beverly LaHaye, *The Act of Marriage: The Beauty of Sexual Love* (Grand Rapids: Zondervan, 1976).

40. Sara McLanahan, "Life without Father: What Happens to the Children?," *Contexts*, Spring 2002, 37; "Marriage and Men's Health," *Harvard Health*, June 5, 2019, https://www .health.harvard.edu/mens-health/marriage-and-mens-health.

41. Republican Party Platform of 2016, https://www.presidency.ucsb.edu/documents /2016-republican-party-platform.

42. Ashley Rockman, "Newt Gingrich: Marriages, Divorces, Affairs Timeline," *Huff-Post*, May 11, 2011, https://www.huffpost.com/entry/newts-women-newt-gingrich_n _860341; "Wheaton College Takes 'Hastert' out of Center's Name in Wake of Charges," *Chicago Tribune*, May 31, 2015; "Dennis Hastert, Ex–House Speaker Who Admitted Sex Abuse, Leaves Prison," *New York Times*, July 18, 2017.

43. Alison Aughinbaugh, Omar Robles, and Hugette Sun, "Marriage and Divorce: Patterns by Gender, Race, and Educational Attainment," *Monthly Labor Review*, US Bureau of Labor Statistics, October 2013, https://doi.org/10.21916/mlr.2013.32.

44. Andrew L. Yarrow, "Falling Marriage Rates Reveal Economic Fault Lines," *New York Times*, February 6, 2015; Belinda Luscombe, "The Divorce Rate Is Dropping. That May Not Actually Be Good News," *Time*, November 26, 2018; David Leonhart, "Red vs. Blue America on Marriage," *New York Times*, June 12, 2015, https://www.nytimes.com/2015/06/13/upshot /red-vs-blue-america-on-marriage.html.

45. W. Bradford Wilcox, "The Marriage Divide: How and Why Working-Class Families Are More Fragile Today," Institute for Family Studies, September 25, 2017, https://

ifstudies.org/blog/the-marriage-divide-how-and-why-working-class-families-are-more
-fragile-today.

46. Pew Research Center, "Parenting in America: The American Family Today," December 17, 2015, https://www.pewsocialtrends.org/2015/12/17/1-the-american-family-today.

47. Baylor University, press release, "Evangelicals Have Higher-than-Average Divorce Rates, according to a Report Compiled by Baylor for the Council on Contemporary Families," February 5, 2014, https://www.baylor.edu/mediacommunications/news.php?action =story&story=137892.

48. Kim Parker and Renee Stepler, "As U.S. Marriage Rate Hovers at 50%, Education Gap in Marital Status Widens," Pew Research Center, September 14, 2017, https://www .pewresearch.org/fact-tank/2017/09/14/as-u-s-marriage-rate-hovers-at-50-education-gap -in-marital-status-widens.

49. Lindsey Cook, "For Richer, Not Poorer: Marriage and the Growing Class Divide," *US News & World Report*, October 26, 2015, https://www.usnews.com/news/blogs/data-mine /2015/10/26/marriage-and-the-growing-class-divide.

50. For a discussion of these ideas, see Thomas B. Edsall, "Liberals Do Not Want to Destroy the Family," *New York Times*, November 27, 2019.

51. Bruce Western, "Incarceration, Marriage, and Family Life," September 2004, https:// www.russellsage.org/sites/all/files/u4/Western_Incarceration,%20Marriage,%20%26%20 Family%20Life_0.pdf; Dara Lind, "Every Year of a Prison Term Makes a Couple 32 Percent More Likely to Divorce," *Vox*, May 29, 2014, https://www.vox.com/2014/5/29/5756646/every -year-of-a-prison-term-makes-a-couple-32-percent-more-likely-to.

52. Mark DeWolf, "12 Stats about Working Women," US Department of Labor Blog, March 1, 2017, https://blog.dol.gov/2017/03/01/12-stats-about-working-women; Democratic Party platform of 2016, https://www.presidency.ucsb.edu/documents/2016-democratic -party-platform.

53. Julia Jacobs, "U.S. Says It Could Take 2 Years to Identify up to Thousands of Separated Immigrant Families," *New York Times*, April 6, 2019; "Fact Sheet: U.S. Citizen Children Impacted by Immigration Enforcement," American Immigration Council, May 23, 2018, https://www.americanimmigrationcouncil.org/research/us-citizen-children-impacted -immigration-enforcement; Madeline Buiano, "ICE Data: Tens of Thousands of Deported Parents Have U.S. Citizen Kids," Center for Public Integrity, October 12, 2018, https:// publicintegrity.org/immigration/ice-data-tens-of-thousands-of-deported-parents-have -u-s-citizen-kids.

54. Griffith, *Moral Combat*, 241–72.

55. Bob Smietana, "The #MeToo Movement Has Educated Pastors. And Left Them with More Questions," *Christianity Today*, September 13, 2018, https://www.christianitytoday .com/news/2018/september/metoo-domestic-violence-sexual-abuse-pastors-lifeway-2018 .html.

56. John Paul II, "Message of John Paul II on the Value and Content of Freedom of Conscience and of Religion," November 14, 1980, http://www.vatican.va/content/john-paul -ii/en/speeches/1980/november/documents/hf_jp_ii_spe_19801114_atto-helsinki.html.

57. *Bob Jones University v. United States*, 461 US 574 (1983).

58. Kelsey Dallas, "During LGBTQ Rights Town Hall, Top Democrats Call for Limits on

Religious Freedom," *[Salt Lake City] Deseret News*, October 10, 2019, https://www.deseret
.com/2019/10/10/20907180/religious-freedom-presidential-candidates-lgbt-rights.

59. Liam Adams, "Second Expelled Student Sues Fuller for LGBT Discrimination,"
Christianity Today, January 7, 2020, https://www.christianitytoday.com/news/2020
/january/fuller-lawsuit-lgbt-brittsan-maxon-becket.html.

60. Sara Dubow, "'A Constitutional Right Rendered Utterly Meaningless': Religious Exemptions and Reproductive Politics, 1973-2014," *Journal of Policy History* 27 (2015): 1-35.

61. For a conservative defense of religious liberty, see Robert P. George, *Conscience and
Its Enemies: Confronting the Dogmas of Liberal Secularism* (Wilmington, DE: ISI Books, 2013),
115-25.

62. John Paul II, "Message of John Paul II on the Value and Content of Freedom of Conscience and of Religion."

63. *Reynolds v. United States*, 98 US 145 (1879); *Employment Division v. Smith*, 494 US 872
(1990); *Bob Jones University v. United States*, 461 US 574 (1983).

64. *Wisconsin v. Yoder*, 406 US 205 (1972); *West Virginia State Board of Education v. Bar-
nette*, 319 US 624 (1943).

65. Brad Polumbo, "New Bill Strikes the Perfect Balance between Gay Rights and Religious Liberty," *Washington Examiner*, December 9, 2019, https://www.washingtonexaminer
.com/opinion/utah-republican-chris-stewarts-fairness-for-all-act-perfectly-balances-lgbt
-rights-and-religious-liberty.

Chapter 5

1. "Constitution Paid $500 to Capturer of Sam Hose," *Atlanta Constitution*, June 5, 1904;
Daniel Carey, "Capture of Sam Hose Seems to Be Matter of Only a Few Hours," *Atlanta
Constitution*, April 15, 1899.

2. "Negro Tortured and Burned to Death at Stake," *San Francisco Call*, April 24, 1899;
"Burned Alive: Negro Sam Hose Dies at the Stake," *Los Angeles Times*, April 24, 1899.

3. "Strickland Caught," *Louisville Courier-Journal*, April 24, 1899.

4. "Horrible Doom: Negro Murderer and Ravisher Burned at the Stake in Georgia,"
Buffalo Courier, April 24, 1899.

5. Thomas S. Kidd, *Who Is an Evangelical?* (New Haven: Yale University Press, 2019),
65.

6. Ida B. Wells, *Southern Horrors: Lynch Law in All Its Phases* (1892), in *Southern Horrors
and Other Writings: The Anti-Lynching Campaign of Ida B. Wells, 1892-1900*, ed. Jacqueline
Jones Royster (Boston: Bedford St. Martin's, 1997), 59; "Lynching of Sam Hose," *Los Angeles
Times*, June 5, 1899.

7. Sheryl Gay Stolberg, "Six Officers Suspended in Baltimore after a Death," *New York
Times*, April 21, 2015; Sheryl Gay Stolberg, "Suspects in Freddie Gray Case: A Police Micro-
cosm," *New York Times*, May 20, 2015; Richard Perez-Pena, "Six Baltimore Officers Indicted
in Death of Freddie Gray," *New York Times*, May 21, 2015.

8. Kevin Rector, "Freddie Gray Case: DOJ Won't Charge Baltimore Officers," *Baltimore
Sun*, September 13, 2017; Campbell Robertson, "A Quiet Exodus: Why Black Worshipers Are
Leaving Evangelical Churches," *New York Times*, March 9, 2018; Morgan Lee, "Where John
Piper and Other Evangelicals Stand on Black Lives Matter," *Christianity Today*, May 13, 2016,
https://www.christianitytoday.com/news/2016/may/where-john-piper-evangelicals-stand

-black-lives-matter-blm.html; Jemar Tisby, "How Ferguson Widened an Enormous Rift between Black Christians and White Evangelicals," *Washington Post*, August 9, 2019.

9. Todd Richmond, "Who Was George Floyd? Unemployed Due to Coronavirus, He'd Moved to Minneapolis for a Fresh Start," *Chicago Tribune*, May 28, 2020.

10. Richmond, "Who Was George Floyd?"

11. E. M. Beck and Stewart E. Tolnay, "Lynching," *New Georgia Encyclopedia*, https://www.georgiaencyclopedia.org/articles/history-archaeology/lynching; UMKC School of Law faculty project, "Lynchings: By Year and Race," http://law2.umkc.edu/faculty/projects/ftrials/shipp/lynchingyear.html; Charles Seguin and David Rigby, "National Crimes: A New National Data Set of Lynchings in the United States, 1883 to 1941," *Socius* 5 (2019): 1–9; John Sullivan et al., "Four Years in a Row, Police Nationwide Fatally Shoot Nearly 1,000 People," *Washington Post*, February 12, 2019.

12. Darren E. Grem, "Sam Jones, Sam Hose, and the Theology of Racial Violence," *Georgia Historical Quarterly* 90 (2006): 42.

13. Grem, "Sam Jones, Sam Hose, and the Theology of Racial Violence," 42.

14. Michael Anft, "Freddie Gray: The Running Man," *CityLab*, November 10, 2015, https://www.citylab.com/equity/2015/11/freddie-gray-the-running-man/414951.

15. Tracy Jan, "This Is How Economic Pain Is Distributed in America," *Washington Post*, May 9, 2020.

16. John Piper, *Bloodlines: Race, Cross, and the Christian* (Wheaton, IL: Crossway, 2011); Abi Christian, "We Are Agents," Intervarsity Christian Fellowship blog, February 18, 2011, https://intervarsity.org/blog/we-are-agents; Pat Schatzline, "How Long Before We Become a Revelation 7:9 Country?," *Charisma News*, July 12, 2016.

17. National Center for Education Statistics, "Indicator 4: Children Living in Poverty," February 2019, https://nces.ed.gov/programs/raceindicators/indicator_RAD.asp; John Gramlich, "The Gap between the Number of Blacks and Whites in Prison Is Shrinking," Pew Research Center, April 30, 2019, https://www.pewresearch.org/fact-tank/2019/04/30/shrinking-gap-between-number-of-blacks-and-whites-in-prison; Barbara Ferrer and John M. Connolly, "Racial Inequities in Drug Arrests: Treatment in Lieu of and after Incarceration," *American Journal of Public Health* 108 (August 2018): 968–69, https://www.ncbi.nlm.nih.gov/pmc/articles/PMC6050822; Kriston McIntosh et al., "Examining the Black-White Wealth Gap," Brookings, February 27, 2020, https://www.brookings.edu/blog/up-front/2020/02/27/examining-the-black-white-wealth-gap/; Elizabeth Arias, "Changes in Life Expectancy by Race and Hispanic Origin in the United States, 2013–2014," NCHS Data Brief 244, April 2016, https://www.cdc.gov/nchs/products/databriefs/db244.htm.

18. Alex Vandermaas-Peeler et al., "Partisan Polarization Dominates Trump Era: Findings from the 2018 American Values Survey," PRRI, [October 2018], https://www.prri.org/research/partisan-polarization-dominates-trump-era-findings-from-the-2018-american-values-survey.

19. Tara Isabella Burton, "Study: When It Comes to Detecting Racial Inequality, White Christians Have a Blind Spot," *Vox*, June 23, 2017, https://www.vox.com/identities/2017/6/23/15855272/prri-study-white-christians-discrimination-blind-spot; "Who Sees Discrimination? New Survey Shows Republicans and Democrats Perceive Two Different Realities," PRRI, June 21, 2017, https://www.prri.org/press-release/sees-discrimination-new-survey-shows-republicans-democrats-perceive-two-different-realities.

20. Ibram X. Kendi, *How to Be an Antiracist* (New York: One World, 2019).

21. Piper, *Bloodlines*.

22. Emma Green, "Southern Baptists and the Sin of Racism," *Atlantic*, April 7, 2015; Russell Moore and Andrew T. Walker, *The Gospel and Racial Reconciliation* (Nashville: Broadman & Holman, 2016).

23. For more on this, see Jemar Tisby, *The Color of Compromise: The Truth about the American Church's Complicity in Racism* (Grand Rapids: Zondervan, 2019).

24. Mark Cartwright, "Slavery in the Roman Empire," *Ancient History Encyclopedia*, November 1, 2013, https://www.ancient.eu/article/629/slavery-in-the-roman-world.

25. For the connection between the development of an American capitalist economy and the expansion of slavery, see Edward Baptist, *The Half Has Never Been Told: Slavery and the Making of American Capitalism* (New York: Basic Books, 2014). For the slave trade, see Marcus Rediker, *The Slave Ship: A Human History* (New York: Viking, 2007); and Hugh Thomas, *The Slave Trade: The Story of the Atlantic Slave Trade, 1440-1870* (New York: Simon & Schuster, 1997).

26. There are numerous books on slavery, but for a succinct, one-volume treatment of a complex and painful history, see Peter Kolchin, *American Slavery, 1619-1877*, 2nd ed. (New York: Hill and Wang, 2003).

27. Larry Gragg, "West Indies," in *The Historical Encyclopedia of World Slavery*, ed. Junius P. Rodriguez (Santa Barbara, CA: ABC-Clio, 1997), 2:692.

28. Dorothy Sterling, ed., *We Are Your Sisters: Black Women in the Nineteenth Century* (New York: W. W. Norton, 1984), 27. For a firsthand account of an enslaved black woman who experienced the frequent danger of sexual exploitation, see Harriet Jacobs, *Incidents in the Life of a Slave Girl* (numerous editions available).

29. Virginia Slave Laws, December 1662, https://www.swarthmore.edu/SocSci/bdorsey1/41docs/24-sla.html. For the development of American slavery and the racial attitudes to justify it, see Winthrop D. Jordan, *White over Black: American Attitudes toward the Negro, 1550-1812* (Chapel Hill: University of North Carolina Press, 1968).

30. Thomas Jefferson, *Notes on the State of Virginia* (1785), ed. Frank C. Shuffelton (New York: Penguin, 1999), 145–47; George M. Fredrickson, *Racism: A Short History* (Princeton: Princeton University Press, 2002).

31. Kevin Bales, "Slavery in Its Contemporary Manifestations," in *The Legal Understanding of Slavery: From the Historical to the Contemporary*, ed. Jean Allain (New York: Oxford University Press, 2012), 301; Heather Cox Richardson, *To Make Men Free: A History of the Republican Party* (New York: Basic Books, 2014), 6; Walter Johnson, *River of Dark Dreams: Slavery and Empire in the Cotton Kingdom* (Cambridge, MA: Harvard University Press, 2013), 5.

32. For the South's economy after the Civil War, see Gavin Wright, *Old South, New South: Revolutions in the Southern Economy since the Civil War* (New York: Basic Books, 1986).

33. Thomas N. Maloney, "African Americans in the Twentieth Century," EH.net, eh.net/encyclopedia/african-americans-in-the-twentieth-century; Stephen G. N. Tuck, *Beyond Atlanta: The Struggle for Racial Equality in Georgia, 1940-1980* (Athens: University of Georgia Press, 2001), 15. For overviews of racial segregation and the exploitation of black labor in the late nineteenth and early twentieth centuries, see Leon F. Litwack, *Trouble in*

Mind: Black Southerners in the Age of Jim Crow (New York: Alfred A. Knopf, 1998); Jacqueline Jones, *Labor of Love, Labor of Sorrow: Black Women, Work, and the Family, from Slavery to the Present* (New York: Basic Books, 1985).

34. This was Fannie Lou Hamer's experience in 1962. Fannie Lou Hamer, Testimony before the Credentials Committee, Democratic National Convention, August 22, 1964, https://www.americanrhetoric.com/speeches/fannielouhamercredentialscommittee.htm.

35. Richard Rothstein, *The Color of Law: A Forgotten History of How Our Government Segregated America* (New York: Liveright, 2017), 17–76; US Census Bureau, *Statistical Abstract of the United States: 1999*, 169, https://www2.census.gov/library/publications/1999/compendia/statab/119ed/tables/sec04.pdf#; Bureau of Labor Statistics, "African American History Month," February 2009, https://www.bls.gov/spotlight/2009/african_american_history/pdf/african_american_spotlight.pdf.

36. US Census Bureau, "Historical Poverty Tables: People and Families—1959 to 2018," https://www.census.gov/data/tables/time-series/demo/income-poverty/historical-poverty-people.html.

37. Jodi Kantor, "Nation's Many Faces in Extended First Family," *New York Times*, January 21, 2009.

38. US Census Bureau, "Historical Poverty Tables." For an analysis of these trends in Detroit, see Thomas J. Sugrue, *The Origins of the Urban Crisis: Race and Inequality in Postwar Detroit*, 2nd ed. (Princeton: Princeton University Press, 2005).

39. Bureau of Labor Statistics, "Rising Educational Attainment among Blacks or African Americans in the Labor Force, 1992 to 2018," *TED: The Economics Daily*, February 13, 2019, https://www.bls.gov/opub/ted/2019/rising-educational-attainment-among-blacks-or-african-americans-in-the-labor-force-1992-to-2018.htm; Bureau of Labor Statistics, "Unemployment Rate 2.1 Percent for College Grads, 4.3 Percent for High School Grads in April 2018," *TED: The Economics Daily*, May 10, 2018, https://www.bls.gov/opub/ted/2018/unemployment-rate-2-1-percent-for-college-grads-4-3-percent-for-high-school-grads-in-april-2018.htm?view_full.

40. Troy Duster, "Social Issues Lurking in the Over-Representation of Young African American Men in the Expanding DNA Databases," in *Against the Wall: Poor, Young, Black, and Male*, ed. Elijah Anderson (Philadelphia: University of Pennsylvania Press, 2008), 181; Justice Policy Institute, "The Punishing Decade: Prison and Jail Estimates at the Millennium," May 2000, http://www.justicepolicy.org/images/upload/00-05_rep_punishing decade_ac.pdf; Leonard M. Lopoo and Bruce Western, "Incarceration and the Formation and Stability of Marital Unions," *Journal of Marriage and Family* 67 (2005): 722; Thomas P. Bonczar, "Prevalence of Imprisonment in the U.S. Population, 1974–2001," Bureau of Justice Statistics Special Report, August 2003, https://www.bjs.gov/content/pub/pdf/piusp01.pdf; Patrick A. Langan, "The Racial Disparity in U.S. Drug Arrests," Bureau of Justice Statistics, US Department of Justice, October 1, 1995, https://www.bjs.gov/content/pub/pdf/rdusda.pdf; Lucius Couloute and Daniel Kopf, "Out of Prison & Out of Work: Unemployment among Formerly Incarcerated People," Prison Policy Initiative, July 2018, prisonpolicy.org/reports/outofwork.html.

41. Bruce Western, "Incarceration, Marriage, and Family Life," September 2004, https://pdfs.semanticscholar.org/b28f/fa8e2351f69004a82e44923c94c0b563ded9.pdf; National Resource Center on Children & Families of the Incarcerated (Rutgers University), "Children

and Families of the Incarcerated Fact Sheet" (2014), https://nrccfi.camden.rutgers.edu/files/nrccfi-fact-sheet-2014.pdf.

42. National Conference of State Legislatures, "Felon Voting Rights," ncsl.org/research/elections-and-campaigns/felon-voting-rights.aspx; Michelle Alexander, *The New Jim Crow: Mass Incarceration in the Age of Colorblindness* (New York: New Press, 2010).

43. For a case study of this phenomenon in Washington, DC, see James Foreman Jr., *Locking Up Our Own: Crime and Punishment in Black America* (New York: Farrar, Straus and Giroux, 2017). For a historical study of the policy changes that led to mass incarceration and increased police targeting of low-income African Americans, see Julilly Kohler-Hausmann, *Getting Tough: Welfare and Imprisonment in 1970s America* (Princeton: Princeton University Press, 2017).

44. Troy McMullen, "The 'Heartbreaking' Decrease in Black Home Ownership," *Washington Post*, February 28, 2019; Lisa J. Dettling et al., "Recent Trends in Wealth-Holding by Race and Ethnicity: Evidence from the Survey of Consumer Finances," FEDS Notes (Board of Governors of the Federal Reserve System), September 27, 2017, https://www.federalreserve.gov/econres/notes/feds-notes/recent-trends-in-wealth-holding-by-race-and-ethnicity-evidence-from-the-survey-of-consumer-finances-20170927.htm; "The Colour of Wealth: The Black-White Wealth Gap Has Been Constant for Half a Century," *Economist*, April 6, 2019, 35–36; "Median Wealth of Black Americans 'Will Fall to Zero by 2053,' Warns New Report," *Guardian*, September 13, 2017.

45. Jackie Wattles, "Georgia Governor Candidate Stacey Abrams Is $200,000 in Debt. She's Not Alone," CNN Money, April 25, 2018, money.cnn.com/2018/04/25/pf/Stacey-abrams-debt/index.html; Greg Bluestein, "Georgia 2018: Abrams Owes More Than $50K to IRS," *Atlanta Journal Constitution*, March 14, 2018; Greg Bluestein, "Abrams Settles IRS Debt as She Preps for Another White House Run," *Atlanta Journal Constitution*, May 16, 2019.

46. Calvin Schermerhorn, "Why the Racial Wealth Gap Persists, More Than 150 Years after Emancipation," *Washington Post*, June 19, 2019; Antonio Moore, "#BlackWealthMatters: The 5 Largest U.S. Landowners Own More Land Than All of Black America Combined," *HuffPost*, October 28, 2015, https://www.huffpost.com; Michelle Singletary, "Black Homeownership Is as Low as It Was When Housing Discrimination Was Legal," *Washington Post*, April 5, 2018.

47. "African American Students in Higher Education," Postsecondary National Policy Institute, January 20, 2020, https://pnpi.org/african-american-students; "Changes in Pell Grant Participation and Median Income of Recipients," National Center for Education Statistics, September 2016, https://nces.ed.gov/datapoints/2016407.asp; Ben Casselman, "Race Gap Narrows in College Enrollment, but Not in Graduation," *FiveThirtyEight*, April 30, 2014, https://fivethirtyeight.com/features/race-gap-narrows-in-college-enrollment-but-not-in-graduation.

48. United States Census Bureau, "Historical Income Tables: Households," https://www.census.gov/data/tables/time-series/demo/income-poverty/historical-income-households.html; "On Views of Race and Inequality, Blacks and Whites Are Worlds Apart," Pew Research Center, June 27, 2016, https://www.pewsocialtrends.org/2016/06/27/on-views-of-race-and-inequality-blacks-and-whites-are-worlds-apart; Annie E. Casey Foundation Kids Count Data Center, "Children in Poverty by Race and Ethnicity in the United States," https://datacenter.kidscount.org.

49. "The Numbers You Need to Know about the Retirement Crisis," PBS.org, June 13, 2018, https://www.pbs.org/newshour/economy/making-sense/the-numbers-you-need-to -know-about-the-retirement-crisis.

50. James T. Patterson, *Restless Giant: The United States from Watergate to Bush v. Gore* (New York: Oxford University Press, 2005), 167–77; Terry H. Anderson, *The Pursuit of Fairness: A History of Affirmative Action* (New York: Oxford University Press, 2004), 161–216; Jeremy D. Mayer, *Running on Race: Racial Politics in Presidential Campaigns, 1960–2000* (New York: Random House, 2002), 173–200; Harvard Sitkoff, *The Struggle for Black Equality, 1954–1992*, 2nd ed. (New York: Hill and Wang, 1993), 210–35; Roper Center, "How Groups Voted in 1984," https://ropercenter.cornell.edu/how-groups-voted-1984. For a detailed, comprehensive analysis of the negative effect of Reagan's policies on the poor, see Frank Stricker, *Why America Lost the War on Poverty—and How to Win It* (Chapel Hill: University of North Carolina Press, 2007), 183–206.

51. Philip Goff et al., "The Bible in American Life Today," in *The Bible in American Life*, ed. Philip Goff et al. (New York: Oxford University Press, 2017), 16.

52. Jim Tankersley and Ben Casselman, "Black Democrats Say It's the Economy, Still," *New York Times*, June 6, 2019; Peggy Bailey et al., "African American Uninsured Rate Dropped by More Than a Third under Affordable Care Act," Center on Budget and Policy Priorities, June 1, 2017, https://www.cbpp.org/research/health/african-american-uninsured -rate-dropped-by-more-than-a-third-under-affordable-care.

53. Leslie Davis and Hannah Hartig, "Two-Thirds of Americans Favor Raising Federal Minimum Wage to $15 an Hour," Pew Research Center, July 30, 2019, https://www .pewresearch.org/fact-tank/2019/07/30/two-thirds-of-americans-favor-raising-federal -minimum-wage-to-15-an-hour.

54. Claire Zillman, "Who Makes Less Than $15 per Hour? An Explainer in 3 Charts," *Fortune*, April 13, 2015.

55. "Parenting in America: The American Family Today," Pew Research Center, December 17, 2015, https://www.pewsocialtrends.org/2015/12/17/1-the-american-family-today; Eric Garcia, "Who Are the Minimum-Wage Workers of America?," *Atlantic*, April 28, 2015.

56. Ta-Nehisi Coates, "The Case for Reparations," *Atlantic*, June 2014.

57. Robert Rector, "Marriage: America's Greatest Weapon against Child Poverty," Heritage Foundation, September 16, 2010, https://www.heritage.org/poverty-and-inequality /report/marriage-americas-greatest-weapon-against-child-poverty-0. This argument was first publicized in Daniel Patrick Moynihan's "The Negro Family: The Case for National Action" (1965). For a historical study of the controversy surrounding the Moynihan Report and decades of ensuing debate about the black family, see James T. Patterson, *Freedom Is Not Enough: The Moynihan Report and America's Struggle over Black Family Life from LBJ to Obama* (New York: Basic Books, 2010).

58. For example, see Roger Clegg, "Latest Statistics on Out-of-Wedlock Births," *National Review*, October 11, 2013: "Here's a modest proposal: Why don't the NAACP and similar organizations take all the money they use to challenge and complain about the standards that their groups (in the aggregate) don't meet when it comes to university admissions, selective high-school admissions, school discipline, mortgage loans, police and firefighter tests, felon-disenfranchisement laws, employment policies that look at criminal records,

etc., etc., and use that money to figure out ways to bring down the illegitimacy rates that drive all these other disparities?"

59. Elizabeth Wildsmith et al., "Dramatic Increase in the Proportion of Births Outside of Marriage in the United States from 1990 to 2016," Child Trends, August 8, 2018, childtrends.org/publications/dramatic-increase-in-percentage-of-births-outside-marriage-among-whites-hispanics-and-women-with-higher-education-levels.

60. William Julius Wilson, *More Than Just Race: Being Black and Poor in the Inner City* (New York: W. W. Norton, 2009).

61. For an analysis of the racial appeals of white working-class conservatism, see Thomas Byrne Edsall with Mary D. Edsall, *Chain Reaction: The Impact of Race, Rights, and Taxes on American Politics* (New York: W. W. Norton, 1991).

62. Paul Ganster and David E. Lorey, *The U.S.-Mexican Border into the Twenty-First Century*, 2nd ed. (Lanham, MD: Rowman & Littlefield, 2008), 68; Philip Martin, "The Bracero Program: Was It a Failure?," History News Network, July 3, 2006, historynewsnetwork.org/article/27336.

63. Douglas S. Massey, "America's Immigration Policy Fiasco," *Daedalus*, Summer 2013.

64. Massey, "America's Immigration Policy Fiasco"; US Customs and Border Patrol Protection, "United States Border Patrol: Border Patrol Agent Nationwide Staffing by Fiscal Year," March 2019, cbp.gov/sites/default/files/assets/documents/2019-Mar/Staffing%20FY 1992-FY2018.pdf.

65. Mary Jo Dudley, "These U.S. Industries Can't Work without Illegal Immigrants," CBS News, January 10, 2019, https://www.cbsnews.com/news/illegal-immigrants-us-jobs-economy-farm-workers-taxes.

66. Gramlich, "Gap between the Number of Blacks and Whites in Prison Is Shrinking"; Federal Bureau of Prisons, "Inmate Ethnicity," November 30, 2019, bop.gov/about/statistics/statistics_inmate_ethnicity.jsp.

67. Peter Waldman and Kartikay Mehrotra, "America's Worst Graveyard Shift Is Grinding Up Workers," *Bloomberg Businessweek*, December 29, 2017, https://www.bloomberg.com/news/features/2017-12-29/america-s-worst-graveyard-shift-is-grinding-up-workers. See also Helen B. Marrow, *New Destination Dreaming: Immigration, Race, and Legal Status in the Rural American South* (Stanford, CA: Stanford University Press, 2011); and Angela Stuesse, *Scratching Out a Living: Latinos, Race, and Work in the Deep South* (Berkeley: University of California Press, 2016).

68. Vanessa Williams, "Black Women—Hillary Clinton's Most Reliable Voting Bloc—Look Beyond Defeat," *Washington Post*, November 12, 2016. Another survey found that the percentage of black women voters who supported Clinton may have been as high as 98. Pew Research Center, "An Examination of the 2016 Electorate, Based on Validated Voters," August 9, 2018, https://www.people-press.org/2018/08/09/an-examination-of-the-2016-electorate-based-on-validated-voters.

69. Pew Research Center, "A Religious Portrait of African-Americans," January 30, 2009, https://www.pewforum.org/2009/01/30/a-religious-portrait-of-african-americans; Theola Labbé-DeBose, "Black Women Are among Country's Most Religious Groups," *Washington Post*, July 6, 2012.

70. Pew Research Center, "Religious Portrait of African-Americans."

71. Pew Research Center, "Examination of the 2016 Electorate."

72. This is the message of Tisby's *Color of Compromise*.

Chapter 6

1. *Sojourners*, "A List of Some of the More Than #2000Verses in Scripture on Poverty and Justice," https://sojo.net/list-some-more-2000verses-scripture-poverty-and-justice.

2. For this argument, see Marvin Olasky, *The Tragedy of American Compassion* (Wheaton, IL: Crossway, 1992); and Marvin Olasky, *Compassionate Conservatism: What It Is, What It Does, and How It Can Transform America* (New York: Free Press, 2000).

3. Richard White, *The Republic for Which It Stands: The United States during Reconstruction and the Gilded Age, 1865–1896* (New York: Oxford University Press, 2017), 120, 227–30. For the plight of African Americans in the late nineteenth-century South, see Leon F. Litwack, *Trouble in Mind: Black Southerners in the Age of Jim Crow* (New York: Vintage Books, 1998).

4. White, *Republic for Which It Stands*, 782–89, 802–3; Ernest Freeberg, *Democracy's Prisoner: Eugene V. Debs, the Great War, and the Right to Dissent* (Cambridge, MA: Harvard University Press, 2008), 12–14.

5. Tom Metcalf, "Rockefeller Was Almost Three Times Richer Than Bezos," *Bloomberg*, May 21, 2019, https://www.bloomberg.com/news/articles/2019-05-21/john-d-rockefeller-was-almost-three-times-richer-than-bezos.

6. Newport Mansions (Preservation Society of Newport County), "The Breakers," https://www.newportmansions.org/explore/the-breakers; Newport Mansions (Preservation Society of Newport County), "Marble House," https://www.newportmansions.org/explore/marble-house; Biltmore, "Estate History," https://www.biltmore.com/our-story/estate-history; Denise Kiernan, *The Last Castle: The Epic Story of Love, Loss, and American Royalty in the Nation's Largest Home* (New York: Atria, 2017), 63; White, *Republic for Which It Stands*, 511–17, 838–43; Freeberg, *Democracy's Prisoner*, 22.

7. W. Elliot Brownlee, *Federal Taxation in America: A Short History* (New York: Woodrow Wilson Center Press and Cambridge University Press, 1996), 46. For Progressivism, see Michael McGerr, *A Fierce Discontent: The Rise and Fall of the Progressive Movement in America, 1870–1920* (New York: Oxford University Press, 2003).

8. Emmanuel Saez and Gabriel Zucman, "Wealth Inequality in the United States since 1913: Evidence from Capitalized Income Tax Data," National Bureau of Economic Research working paper, October 2014, www.nber.org/papers/w20625.pdf.

9. Jeremy Atack and Peter Passell, *A New Economic View of American History: From Colonial Times to 1940*, 2nd ed. (New York: W. W. Norton, 1994), 575–80, 585.

10. Tax-Brackets.org, "Federal Income Tax Brackets (Tax Year 1943)," tax-brackets.org/federaltaxtable/1944.

11. For a detailed discussion of the economics of this era, see Paul Krugman, *The Conscience of a Liberal*, 2nd ed. (New York: W. W. Norton, 2009), 37–100.

12. William M. McClenahan Jr. and William H. Becker, *Eisenhower and the Cold War Economy* (Baltimore: Johns Hopkins University Press, 2011), 33–37; Joseph A. Califano, "Balancing the Budget, L.B.J. Style," *New York Times*, December 31, 1995.

13. Robert Bauman, *Fighting to Preserve a Nation's Soul: America's Ecumenical War on Poverty* (Athens: University of Georgia Press, 2019), 1–66; James T. Patterson, *Grand Ex-*

pectations: The United States, 1945–1974 (New York: Oxford University Press, 1996), 311–23, 450–52.

14. Thomas Byrne Edsall with Mary D. Edsall, *Chain Reaction: The Impact of Race, Rights, and Taxes on American Politics*, 2nd ed. (New York: W. W. Norton, 1992), 99–136; Daniel T. Rodgers, *Age of Fracture* (Cambridge, MA: Harvard University Press, 2011), 41–76; Thomas Borstelmann, *The 1970s: A New Global History from Civil Rights to Economic Inequality* (Princeton: Princeton University Press, 2012), 122–74.

15. James T. Patterson, *America's Struggle against Poverty in the Twentieth Century* (Cambridge, MA: Harvard University Press, 2000), 174.

16. W. Elliot Brownlee and C. Eugene Steuerle, "Taxation," in *The Reagan Presidency: Pragmatic Conservatism and Its Legacies*, ed. W. Elliot Brownlee and Hugh Davis Graham (Lawrence: University Press of Kansas, 2003), 172–73.

17. Thomas Karier, *Great Experiments in American Economic Policy: From Kennedy to Reagan* (Westport, CT: Praeger, 1997), 77–78; White House Office of Management and Budget, "Historical Tables: Summary of Receipts, Outlays, and Surpluses or Deficits, 1789–2025," https://www.whitehouse.gov/omb/historical-tables; Sylvia Nasar, "The 1980s: A Very Good Time for the Rich," *New York Times*, March 5, 1992; Lawrence Mishel and Alyssa Davis, "Top CEOs Make 300 Times More Than Typical Workers," Economic Policy Institute, June 21, 2015, https://www.epi.org/publication/top-ceos-make-300-times-more-than-workers-pay -growth-surpasses-market-gains-and-the-rest-of-the-0-1-percent.

18. Spencer Rich, "Rich Got Richer, Poor Got Poorer, Study Says," *Washington Post*, July 24, 1991.

19. Zack Friedman, "Student Loan Debt Statistics in 2019: A $1.5 Trillion Crisis," *Forbes*, February 25, 2019, www.forbes.com/sites/zackfriedman/2019/02/25/student-loan-debt -statistics-2019/#7e77f08133fb; "A Growing Number of Americans Have More Credit-Card Debt Than Savings," *MarketWatch*, February 13, 2019, www.marketwatch.com/story/a -growing-number-of-americans-have-more-credit-card-debt-than-savings-2019-02-13.

20. Kevin Kelleher, "Gilded Age 2.0: U.S. Income Inequality Increases to Pre-Great Depression Levels," *Fortune*, February 13, 2019, https://fortune.com/2019/02/13/us-income -inequality-bad-great-depression.

21. "Home Prices Are Rising Faster Than Wages in 80% of U.S. Markets," *Housingwire*, January 10, 2019, www.housingwire.com/articles/47878-home-prices-are-rising-faster -than-wages-in-80-of-us-markets; US Census, "Median and Average Sales Prices of New Homes Sold in United States," https://www.census.gov/const/uspricemon.pdf; "Behind the Ever-Expanding American Dream House," NPR, July 4, 2006, https://www.npr.org /templates/story/story.php?storyId=5525283; Jamiles Larty, "Nowhere for People to Go: Who Will Survive the Gentrification of Atlanta?," *Guardian Atlanta*, October 23, 2018, www.theguardian.com/cities/2018/oct/23/nowhere-for-people-to-go-who-will-survive -the-gentrification-of-atlanta; Brentin Mock, "Where Gentrification Is an Emergency, and Where It's Not," *CityLab*, April 5, 2019, www.citylab.com/equity/2019/04/where -gentrification-happens-neighborhood-crisis-research/586537; National Alliance to End Homelessness, "The State of Homelessness in America," https://endhomelessness.org.

22. National Center for Education Statistics, "Tuition Costs of Colleges and Universities," https://nces.ed.gov/fastfacts/display.asp?id=76; US Bureau of Labor Statistics, "College Enrollment and Work Activity of Recent High School and College Graduates Summary,"

April 25, 2019, https://www.bls.gov/news.release/hsgec.nro.htm; Abigail Hess, "This Is the Age Most Americans Pay Off Their Student Loans," CNBC, July 3, 2017, https://www.cnbc.com/2017/07/03/this-is-the-age-most-americans-pay-off-their-student-loans.html; Abigail Hess, "Here's How Much the Average Student Loan Borrower Owes When They Graduate," CNBC, February 15, 2018, https://www.cnbc.com/2018/02/15/heres-how-much-the-average-student-loan-borrower-owes-when-they-graduate.html; Elissa Nadworny, "College Completion Rates Are Up, but the Numbers Will Still Surprise You," NPR, March 13, 2019, https://www.npr.org/2019/03/13/681621047/college-completion-rates-are-up-but-the-numbers-will-still-surprise-you; William Gale et al., "Student Loans Rising: An Overview of Causes, Consequences, and Policy Options," Brookings, May 2014, https://www.brookings.edu/wp-content/uploads/2016/06/student_loans_rising_gale_harris_09052014.pdf; Federal Reserve Bank of St. Louis, "Student Loans Owned and Securitized, Outstanding," February 7, 2020, https://fred.stlouisfed.org/series/SLOAS.

23. "'I Live on the Street Now': How Americans Fall into Medical Bankruptcy," *Guardian*, November 14, 2019, https://www.theguardian.com/us-news/2019/nov/14/health-insurance-medical-bankruptcy-debt.

24. Center on Budget and Policy Priorities, "A Quick Guide to SNAP Eligibility and Benefits," November 1, 2019, https://www.cbpp.org/research/food-assistance/a-quick-guide-to-snap-eligibility-and-benefits; Margaret H. Davis and Sally T. Burner, "Three Decades of Medicare: What the Numbers Tell Us," *DataWatch*, 1995, https://www.healthaffairs.org/doi/pdf/10.1377/hlthaff.14.4.231; Vivian Yee, "Cuomo to Continue Shrinking State's Share of CUNY's Costs," *New York Times*, January 14, 2016.

25. Kate Santich, "As Rentals Go Upscale, Central Florida's Low-Income Residents Find Their Housing Vouchers Aren't Welcome," *Orlando Sentinel*, August 25, 2018; Lizabeth Cohen, "Only Washington Can Solve the Nation's Housing Crisis," *New York Times*, July 10, 2019.

26. Daniel Friedman, "The Rise of Income Segregation in Post-Recession America," *Harvard Political Review*, August 9, 2017, https://harvardpolitics.com/united-states/the-rise-of-income-segregation-in-post-recession-america; Stanford Center on Poverty and Inequality, "Income Segregation in the United States' Largest Metropolitan Areas," https://inequality.stanford.edu/income-segregation-maps; Richard Florida, "The U.S. Cities with the Highest Levels of Income Segregation," *CityLab*, March 18, 2014, www.citylab.com/life/2014/03/us-cities-highest-levels-income-segregation/8632; Claire Cain Miller and Quoctrung Bui, "Equality in Marriage Grows, and So Does Class Divide," *New York Times*, February 27, 2016.

27. Income figures for the quintiles listed here come from Tax Policy Center, "Household Income Quintiles, 1967 to 2015," www.taxpolicycenter.org/statistics/household-income-quintiles; and US Census Bureau, "Historical Income Tables: Households," https://www.census.gov/data/tables/time-series/demo/income-poverty/historical-income-households.html. The figures given are for 2018.

28. US Census Bureau, "Selected Characteristics of Households by Total Money Income, 2018," census.gov/data/tables/time-series/demo/income-poverty/cps-hinc/hinc-01.html; Jay Shambaugh et al., "Who Is Poor in the United States? A Hamilton Project Annual Report," Brookings, October 12, 2017, https://www.brookings.edu/research/who-is-poor-in-the-united-states-a-hamilton-project-annual-report; Gretchen Livingston, "The Changing

Profile of Unmarried Parents," Pew Research Center, April 25, 2018, pewsocialtrends.org
/2018/04/25/the-changing-profile-of-unmarried-parents; United States Department of Agriculture Economic Research Service, "Food Security in the U.S.," ers.usda.gov/topics/food
-nutrition-assistance/food-security-in-the-us/key-statistics-graphics.aspx; CDC, "Infant
Mortality Rates by State, 2017," www.cdc.gov/nchs/pressroom/sosmap/infant_mortality
_rates/infant_mortality.htm; Katelin P. Isaacs and Sharmila Choudhury, "The Growing
Gap in Life Expectancy by Income: Recent Evidence and Implications for the Social Security Retirement Age," Congressional Research Service, May 12, 2017, https://fas.org/sgp
/crs/misc/R44846.pdf; Debt.org, "Economic Demographics of Democrats," https://www
.debt.org/faqs/americans-in-debt/economic-demographics-democrats; Statista, "Exit Polls
of the 2016 Presidential Elections in the United States on November 9, 2016, Percentage
of Votes by Income," statista.com/statistics/631244/voter-turnout-of-the-exit-polls-of-the
-2016-elections-by-income.

29. "Some Colleges Have More Students from the Top 1 Percent than the Bottom 60,"
New York Times, January 18, 2017.

30. Christian E. Weller, "Credit Card Debt Burdens American Families," Center for
American Progress, n.d. [c. 2006], https://cdn.americanprogress.org/wp-content/uploads
/kf/CREDITCARDDEBTREPORT_PDF.PDF; Urban Institute, "Debt in America," July
2014, https://www.urban.org/sites/default/files/alfresco/publication-pdfs/413190-Debt-in
-America.PDF; Statistical Atlas, "Household Income in Alabama," https://statisticalatlas
.com/state/Alabama/Household-Income; Steven Greenhouse, "Union Membership in U.S.
Fell to a 70-Year Low Last Year," *New York Times*, January 22, 2011; Social Security Administration, "Monthly Statistical Snapshot, January 2020," https://www.ssa.gov/policy/docs
/quickfacts/stat_snapshot/2020-01.pdf; US Bureau of Labor Statistics, "Labor Force Participation Rate for Workers Age 75 and Older Projected to Be over 10 Percent by 2026," May 29,
2019, https://www.bls.gov/opub/ted/2019/labor-force-participation-rate-for-workers-age-75
-and-older-projected-to-be-over-10-percent-by-2026.htm.

31. Federal Reserve Bank of St. Louis, Economic Research, "Real Median Household Income in the United States," September 10, 2019, https://fred.stlouisfed.org/series/MEHOIN
USA672N; National Center for Education Statistics, "Postsecondary Attainment: Differences by Socioeconomic Status," May 2015, https://nces.ed.gov/programs/coe/indicator_tva
.asp; Annie Nova, "Another Challenge in Retirement? Student Loans," CNBC, November
14, 2018, https://www.cnbc.com/2018/11/14/more-older-people-are-bringing-student-debt
-into-their-retirement.html; Leo Sun, "A Foolish Take: Here's How Much Debt the Average
U.S. Household Owes," *USA Today* / Motley Fool, November 18, 2017, https://www.usatoday
.com/story/money/personalfinance/2017/11/18/a-foolish-take-heres-how-much-debt-the
-average-us-household-owes/107651700.

32. Amy Traub, "In the Red: Older Americans and Credit Card Debt," AARP Public
Policy Institute, 2013, https://www.aarp.org/content/dam/aarp/research/public_policy
_institute/security/2013/older-americans-and-credit-card-debt-AARP-ppi-sec.pdf.

33. Mark J. Perry, "Explaining US Income by Household Demographics," AEI, September 11, 2019, https://www.aei.org/carpe-diem/explaining-us-income-inequality-by
-household-demographics-2018-update.

34. Claire Cain Miller, "Americans Are Having Fewer Babies: They Told Us Why," *New
York Times*, July 5, 2018.

35. Caroline Ratcliffe and Signe-Mary McKernan, "Forever in Your Debt: Who Has College Loan Debt, and Who's Worried?," Urban Institute, June 2013, https://www.urban.org/sites/default/files/publication/23736/412849-Forever-in-Your-Debt-Who-Has-Student-Loan-Debt-and-Who-s-Worried-.PDF; Neil Irwin, "How Democrats Would Tax High-Income Professionals (Not Just the Mega-Rich)," *New York Times*, November 19, 2019; Gale et al., "Student Loans Rising."

36. Julissa Trevino, "What Is the Average Law School Debt?," *Nitro*, May 19, 2019, https://www.nitrocollege.com/blog/average-law-school-debt.

37. "Some Colleges Have More Students from the Top 1 Percent Than the Bottom 60."

38. Russell Sage Foundation, "Chartbook of Social Inequality: Real Household Income at Selected Percentiles, 1967–2012 (Reported in 2012 Dollars)," https://www.russellsage.org/sites/all/files/chartbook/Income%20and%20Earnings.pdf.

39. Howard R. Gold, "Never Mind the 1 Percent; Let's Talk about the 0.01 Percent," *Chicago Booth Review*, Winter 2017; Samuel Stebbins, "Want to Be in the Top 1 Percent? Here's What You Have to Earn in Your State," *USA Today*, September 25, 2018.

40. Gold, "Never Mind the 1 Percent"; "Some Colleges Have More Students from the Top 1 Percent than the Bottom 60."

41. Gold, "Never Mind the 1 Percent."

42. Luisa Kroll and Kerry A. Dolan, "The Forbes 400: The Definitive Ranking of the Wealthiest Americans," *Forbes*, October 2, 2019, https://www.forbes.com/forbes-400/#42bb9c6b7e2f; Noah Kirsch, "Members of the Forbes 400 Hold More Wealth Than All U.S. Black Families Combined," *Forbes*, January 14, 2019, https://www.forbes.com/sites/noah kirsch/2019/01/14/members-of-forbes-400-hold-more-wealth-than-all-us-black-families -combined-study-finds/#2b71ead96771.

43. Greg Leiserson et al., "The Distribution of Wealth in the United States and Its Implications for a Net Worth Tax," Washington Center for Equitable Growth, March 21, 2019, https://equitablegrowth.org/the-distribution-of-wealth-in-the-united-states-and -implications-for-a-net-worth-tax; Noah Kirsch, "The 3 Richest Americans Hold More Wealth Than Bottom 50% of the Country, Study Finds," *Forbes*, November 9, 2017, https:// www.forbes.com/sites/noahkirsch/2017/11/09/the-3-richest-americans-hold-more-wealth -than-bottom-50-of-country-study-finds/#15a96fcf3cf8.

44. White House OMB, "Summary of Receipts, Outlays, and Surpluses or Deficits."

45. Drew DeSilver, "5 Facts about the National Debt," Pew Research Center, July 24, 2019, https://www.pewresearch.org/fact-tank/2019/07/24/facts-about-the-national-debt; Nelson D. Schwartz, "As Debt Rises, the Government Will Soon Spend More on Interest Than on the Military," *New York Times*, September 25, 2018; Heather Long and Jeff Stein, "The U.S. Deficit Hit $984 Billion in 2019, Soaring during Trump Era," *Washington Post*, October 25, 2019.

46. DeSilver, "5 Facts about the National Debt."

47. Leiserson et al., "Distribution of Wealth in the United States"; Rocky Mengle and Kevin McCormally, "Where You Rank as a Taxpayer," *Kiplinger*, January 31, 2019; Beverly Bird, "How Do U.S. Taxes Compare to Other Countries?," *The Balance*, November 20, 2019, https://www.thebalance.com/how-us-taxes-compare-with-other-countries-4165500.

48. Kimberly Amadeo, "Trump's Tax Plan and How It Affects You," *The Balance*, June 25, 2019, https://www.thebalance.com/trump-s-tax-plan-how-it-affects-you-4113968.

49. Tyler Fisher, "How Past Income Tax Cuts on the Wealthy Affected the Economy," *Politico*, September 27, 2017, https://www.politico.com/interactives/2017/gop-tax-rate-cut-wealthy.

50. Robert Bellafiore, "Summary of the Latest Federal Income Tax Data, 2018 Update," *Tax Foundation*, November 13, 2018, https://taxfoundation.org/summary-latest-federal-income-tax-data-2018-update.

51. Kathy Wyer, "Survey: More Freshmen Than Ever Say They Go to College to Get Better Jobs, Make More Money," UCLA Press Release, January 23, 2013, newsroom.ucla.edu/releases/heri-freshman-survey-242619.

52. US Bureau of Labor Statistics, "High School Graduates Who Work Full Time Had Median Weekly Earnings of $718 in Second Quarter," *TED: The Economics Daily*, July 21, 2017, https://www.bls.gov/opub/ted/2017/high-school-graduates-who-work-full-time-had-median-weekly-earnings-of-718-in-second-quarter.htm.

53. Claudia Goldin and Lawrence F. Katz, "The Shaping of Higher Education: The Formative Years in the United States, 1890 to 1940," *Journal of Economic Perspectives* 13 (1999): 41.

54. Thomas D. Snyder, "Education Characteristics of the Population," in *120 Years of American Education: A Statistical Portrait*, ed. Thomas D. Snyder (Washington, DC: National Center for Education Statistics, 1993), 10.

55. National Center of Education Statistics, *Digest of Education Statistics*, Table 320: Average Undergraduate Tuition and Fees, 1964–2007, http://nces.ed.gov/programs/digest/d07/tables/dt07_320.asp; College Board, "2018–19 Tuition and Fees at Public Four-Year Institutions by State and Five-Year Percentage Change in In-State Tuition and Fees," *Trends in Higher Education*, https://trends.college-board.org/college-pricing/figures-tables/2018-19-state-tuition-and-fees-public-four-year-institutions-state-and-five-year-percentage.

56. This is calculated based on a federal minimum wage of $1.25 an hour for 1965 and $7.25 an hour for 2019.

57. "Some Colleges Have More Students from the Top 1 Percent Than the Bottom 60."

58. "Economic Diversity and Student Outcomes at the University of West Georgia," *New York Times* interactive feature, www.nytimes.com/interactive/projects/college-mobility/university-of-west-georgia.

59. "Economic Diversity and Student Outcomes at the University of West Georgia." According to the *New York Times*'s interactive feature, "Economic Diversity and Student Outcomes at America's Colleges and Universities," only 1.5 percent of students at the University of West Georgia, 1.2 percent of students at Idaho State University, 1.1 percent of students at Indiana State University, and fewer than 1 percent of students at Emporia State University move from the lowest income quintile to the highest quintile (https://www.nytimes.com/interactive/projects/college-mobility). All of these regional universities attract a predominantly lower-income or middle-income student population, with no more than 25 percent of their student body coming from the highest income quintile.

60. Jennifer Lee, "Georgia's Education Cuts a Growing Burden for Low-Income Students," Georgia Budget and Policy Institute, September 27, 2017, https://gbpi.org/2017/georgias-education-cuts-a-growing-burden-for-low-income-students.

61. Claire Suggs, "Troubling Gaps in HOPE Point to Need-Based Solutions," Georgia Budget and Policy Institute, September 8, 2016, https://gbpi.org/2016/gaps-in-hope-point-to-need-based-aid; Olivia Adams, "The Meaning of HOPE: Scholarship Misses Lower-

Income Students," *Red & Black* (UGA), February 8, 2018, https://www.redandblack.com
/athensnews/the-meaning-of-hope-scholarship-misses-lower-income-students/article_71
a8ef2c-0c74-11e8-b214-03829e6189b1.html; Lucas Daprile, "SC's Poor Play the Lottery, but
the Wealthier Win the Scholarships," *The [Columbia, SC] State*, October 12, 2018, www
.thestate.com/news/lottery/article219049710.html.

62. Adam Harris, "The College-Affordability Crisis Is Uniting the 2020 Democratic
Candidates," *Atlantic*, February 26, 2019; Benjamin Wermund, "The Red State That Loves
Free College," *Politico*, January 16, 2019, https://www.politico.com/agenda/story/2019/01/16
/tennessee-free-college-000867.

63. Kaiser Family Foundation, "Coverage at Work: The Share of Nonelderly Americans
with Employer-Based Insurance Rose Modestly in Recent Years, but Has Declined Markedly
over the Long Term," February 1, 2019, https://www.kff.org/health-reform/press-release
/coverage-at-work-the-share-of-nonelderly-americans-with-employer-based-insurance
-rose-modestly-in-recent-years-but-has-declined-markedly-over-the-long-term; Jennifer
Tolbert et al., "Key Facts about the Uninsured Population," Henry J. Kaiser Family Foundation, December 13, 2019, https://www.kff.org/uninsured/issue-brief/key-facts-about-the
-uninsured-population.

64. Chris Riotta, "GOP Aims to Kill Obamacare Yet Again after Failing 70 Times," *News-
week*, July 29, 2017, https://www.newsweek.com/gop-health-care-bill-repeal-and-replace
-70-failed-attempts-643832; Haeyoun Park et al., "The Three Plans to Repeal Obamacare
That Failed in the Senate This Week," *New York Times*, July 25, 2017; Haeyoun Park and
Margot Sanger-Katz, "How Senate Republicans Plan to Dismantle Obamacare," *New York
Times*, June 22, 2017; Timothy Jost, "Examining the House Republican ACA Repeal and
Replace Legislation," *Health Affairs*, March 7, 2017, https://www.healthaffairs.org/do/10.1377
/hblog20170307.059064/full.

65. Aaron C. Catlin and Cathy A. Cowan, "History of Health Spending in the United
States, 1960–2013," US Centers for Medicare and Medicaid Services, November 19, 2015,
https://www.cms.gov/Research-Statistics-Data-and-Systems/Statistics-Trends-and-Reports
/NationalHealthExpendData/Downloads/HistoricalNHEPaper.pdf; Rabah Kamal et al.,
"How Has U.S. Spending on Healthcare Changed over Time?," Peterson-KFF Health System
Tracker, December 20, 2019, https://www.healthsystemtracker.org/chart-collection/u-s
-spending-healthcare-changed-time/#item-start; Kimberly Amadeo, "The Rising Costs
of Health Care Spending by Year and Its Causes," *The Balance*, February 22, 2020, https://
www.thebalance.com/causes-of-rising-healthcare-costs-4064878.

66. Helaine Olen, "Even the Insured Can't Afford Their Medical Bills," *Atlantic*, June
18, 2017; "Premiums for Employer-Sponsored Family Health Coverage Rise 5% to Average
$19,616," Kaiser Family Foundation, October 3, 2018, https://www.kff.org/health-costs
/press-release/employer-sponsored-family-coverage-premiums-rise-5-percent-in-2018.

67. "Status of State Medicaid Expansion Decisions: Interactive Map," Kaiser Family
Foundation, February 19, 2020, https://www.kff.org/medicaid/issue-brief/status-of-state
-medicaid-expansion-decisions-interactive-map.

68. Tanza Loudenback, "The Average Cost of Healthcare in 21 Different Countries,"
Business Insider, March 7, 2019.

69. Lydia Saad, "More Americans Delaying Medical Treatment Due to Cost," Gallup,

December 9, 2019, https://news.gallup.com/poll/269138/americans-delaying-medical
-treatment-due-cost.aspx; "'I Live on the Street Now.'"

70. Bradley Sawyer and Gary Claxton, "How Do Health Expenditures Vary across the Population," Peterson-KFF Health System Tracker, January 16, 2019, https://www.health systemtracker.org/chart-collection/health-expenditures-vary-across-population.

71. Drew DeSilver, "For Most U.S. Workers, Real Wages Have Barely Budged in Decades," Pew Research Center, August 7, 2018, https://www.pewresearch.org/fact-tank/2018/08/07 /for-most-us-workers-real-wages-have-barely-budged-for-decades; Tax Foundation, "Social Security and Medicare Tax Rates, Calendar Years 1937–2009," https://files.taxfoundation .org/legacy/docs/soc_security_rates_1937-2009-20090504.pdf.

72. Stephen J. Rose, "Manufacturing Employment: Fact and Fiction," Urban Institute, April 2018, https://www.urban.org/sites/default/files/publication/97776/manufacturing _employment_fact_and_fiction_2.pdf; Drew DeSilver, "10 Facts about American Workers," Pew Research Center, August 29, 2019, https://www.pewresearch.org/fact-tank/2019/08/29 /facts-about-american-workers; Andrew Zaleski, "Man and Machine: The New Collaborative Workplace of the Future," *NBR*, October 31, 2016, http://nbr.com/2016/10/31/man-and -machine-the-new-collaborative-workplace-of-the-future.

73. "Healthcare Employment as a Percent of Total Employment," Kaiser Family Foundation, May 2018, https://www.kff.org/other/state-indicator/health-care-employment-as -total; Susannah Snider, "19 Best Jobs for Community College Graduates," https://money .usnews.com/careers/slideshows/19-best-jobs-for-community-college-graduates; Payscale.com, "Average Radiation Therapist Hourly Pay," www.payscale.com/research/US /Job=Radiation_Therapist/Hourly_Rate.

74. Mishel and Davis, "Top CEOs Make 300 Times More Than Typical Workers"; Kroll and Dolan, "Forbes 400"; Gold, "Never Mind the 1 Percent"; Edward Tenner, "Why Do So Many Ivy League Grads Go to Wall Street?," *Atlantic*, February 17, 2012.

75. Amir El-Sibaie, "2019 Tax Brackets," November 28, 2018, https://taxfoundation.org /2019-tax-brackets.

76. ChildTrends, "Children in Poverty," www.childtrends.org/indicators/children-in -poverty.

77. Bradford Richardson, "Religious People More Likely to Give to Charity, Study Shows," *Washington Times*, October 30, 2017; Paul Sullivan, "How Political Ideology Influences Charitable Giving," *New York Times*, November 3, 2018.

78. For more on this, see Steve Corbett and Brian Fikkert, *When Helping Hurts: How to Alleviate Poverty without Hurting the Poor . . . and Yourself*, 2nd ed. (Chicago: Moody, 2012).

Afterword

1. James T. Kloppenberg, *Toward Democracy: The Struggle for Self-Rule in European and American Thought* (New York: Oxford University Press, 2016).